To MY LOVE JONATHAN

HOPE YOU LIKE THE PRESSY

AND I HOPE IT LETS YOU KNOW YOUR

ALWAYS SPECIAL TO ME,

I LOVE YOU,
KRIS X.

New Testament Metaphors

Illustrations in Word and Phrase

New Testament Metaphors

Illustrations in Word and Phrase

by

Anthony Byatt

The Pentland Press
Edinburgh – Cambridge – Durham – USA

First published in 1995
re-printed in 1996 and 1998 by
The Pentland Press Ltd
1 Hutton Close
South Church
Bishop Auckland
Durham

British Library
Cataloguing-in-Publication Data
A catalogue record for this book
is available from the British Library.

ISBN 1-85821-239-1

Typeset by Carnegie Publishing, 18 Maynard Street, Preston
Printed and bound in Great Britain by Bookcraft (Bath) Ltd.

To my daughters, Gillian and Shirley,
in loving memory of Joyce,
faithful wife and mother.

Contents

Contents

  9. Cutting Straight Lines—Accurate Handling of God's Word.   271
 10. Buying Out Time—Using Well Every Opportunity.   273

    Select Bibliography   278

    Index of Metaphors and Illustrations   285

    Index of Greek Words   290

    Index of Subjects   293

    Index of Bible References   309

Preface

The illustrations and metaphors of the New Testament have often been ignored as a whole subject, although many of them have been dealt with in isolation, even to the extent of having a complete book on just one of them, as you will see from the notes and bibliography. But not since J. S. Howson's *The Metaphors of St. Paul* in 1869, has one book dealt with most of the significant ones found in a single word or a short phrase or sentence. It could provide a subject to rival that of Jesus' parables, about which there are literally hundreds of books.

The word 'metaphor' as used in the title, covers all the various technical figures of speech of which this is the leading type. Similes, analogies etc., are all illustrations within this group, and a mere change of form can alter a simile into a metaphor, or vice versa.

The list of contents has been made as detailed as possible, because the chapter headings are merely broad groupings, and certain illustrations could easily come under alternative headings. Don't forget, also, to use the titles on the right when you want to find a suitable spiritual subject, so that you, in effect, reverse the contents round, and find the illustration from its application.

This book is not intended to cover all metaphors comprehensively. Some of the smaller ones did not lend themselves to making a rounded-out presentation, but I will be glad to hear from anyone with suggestions for a possible later revision. In the meanwhile, I hope you enjoy this lively subject as much as I have done in putting it together. If it encourages people to make a closer study of God's Word, so that they see why it is *the* book of treasure without compare, then I shall be well satisfied.

I would like to thank my wife Sue for her help in reading the proofs.
Tony Byatt
Malvern, Worcs.

Abbreviations Used to Identify
Bible Translations

All Translations are published in London unless stated.

ABUV. *American Bible Union Version*, N. Y. 1856–1884.

Adams. *The N.T. in Everyday English*, by Jay E. Adams, 1979, Grand Rapids, Michigan.

Amplified. *Amplified Bible*, Expanded Ed. 1987, Grand Rapids, Michigan.

Anderson. *A New Accurate Translation of the Greek N. T.* by J. G. Anderson, 1984, Naples, FL.

ASV. *American Standard Version*, 1929rp, N. Y.

AV. *Authorised Version, King James' Version.* 1611. (recent editions).

Barclay. *The N.T. A New Translation*, by William Barclay, 1968/1969.

Beck. *The Holy Bible in the Language of Today*, by W. F. Beck, 1976, Nashville, TN.

Berkeley. *The Berkeley Version in Modern English*, Ed. by G. Verkuhl, 1960, 4th ed.

Blackwelder. *Letters from Paul, An Exegetical Translation*, by B. W. Blackwelder, 1971, Anderson, Ind.

Bruce. *An Expanded Paraphrase of the Epistles of Paul*, by F. F. Bruce, 1981rp, Exeter, Devon.

Cassirer. *God's New Covenant, A N.T. Translation*, by H.W. Cassirer 1989, Grand Rapids, Michigan.

Concordant. *Concordant Literal N. T.* 1983rp, 6th ed. Canyon Country, CA.

Conybeare. *The Epistles of Paul*, Trans. by W. J. Conybeare, nd. also in *Life & Epistles of St. Paul*, by W. J. Conybeare & J. S. Howson, 1889 New ed.

Darby.	*A New Translation from the Original Texts*, by J. N. Darby, 1920rp.
Douay.	*Douay Version, Translated from the Latin Vulgate*, 1906rp, Glasgow.
Estes.	*The Better Version of the N. T.* by C. Estes, 1978, 3rd ed. Muscle Shoals, AL.
Fenton.	*The Holy Bible in Modern English*, by Ferrar Fenton, 1931, 5th ed. rev.
Goodspeed.	*The Complete Bible, An American Translation*, by E. J. Goodspeed & others, 1939, Chicago.
Hayman.	*The Epistles of the N. T.* by H. Hayman, 1900.
JB.	*The Jerusalem Bible*, 1966.
K. Int.	*The Kingdom Interlinear Translation of the Greek Scriptures*, 1969, Brooklyn, NY.
Kleist & Lilly.	*The N. T. Rendered From the Original Greek*, by J. A. Kleist & J. L. Lilly, 1956, Milwaukee.
Klingensmith.	*The N.T. in Everyday English*, by Don J. Klingensmith, 1981, Fargo, N. Dakota.
Knox.	*The Holy Bible, A Translation from the Latin Vulgate*, by R. A. Knox, 1956, 2nd ed.
Lamsa.	*The Holy Bible from Ancient Eastern Manuscripts*, by G. M. Lamsa, 1957, 4th ed.
Lattimore.	*The N. T. Newly Translated from the Greek*, by R. Lattimore, 1980, 1982.
Living Bible.	*The Living Bible*, Paraphrased by K. N. Taylor, 1974
LXX Thomson.	*The Old Covenant . . . Translated from the Septuagint*, by Charles Thomson, New ed. by S. F. Pells, 1904.
LXX Muses.	*The Septuagint Bible . . .* in the Translation of C. Thomson, Ed. rev. by C. A. Muses, 1954, Indian Hills, CO.
McClellan.	*The N. T . . . A New Translation*, by J. B. McClellan only Vol. 1, The Four Gospels, 1875.
Moffatt.	*A New Translation of the Bible*, by James Moffatt, 1934 rev. ed.
Montgomery,	*The Centenary Translation of the N. T.* by Helen B. Montgomery, 1924, Philadelphia.
Murdock.	*The Syriac N. T. Translated into English*, by James Murdock, 1896, 7th ed. Boston, Mass.
NAB.	*The New American Bible*, 1980, Nashville, TN.
NASB.	*New American Standard Bible*, 1977rp, Nashville.

NBV.	*The New Berkeley Version in Modern English*, 1969, Grand Rapids, Michigan.
NCV.	*The Word, New Century Version N. T.* 1984, Fort Worth, Texas.
NEB.	*New English Bible*, 1970, Oxford/Cambridge.
NIV.	*New International Version*, 1979.
NJB.	*The New Jerusalem Bible*, 1985.
NKJV Int.	*The New King James Version Greek English Interlinear N. T.* 1994, Nashville, TN.
NRSV.	*New Revised Standard Version Holy Bible*, 1989, Oxford.
NWT.	*New World Translation of the Holy Scriptures*, 1984 Rev. ed. Brooklyn, NY.
Phillips.	*The N.T. in Modern English*, by J. B. Phillips, 1960. 1972 Revised ed. cited as 'Rev'.
RAV.	*Revised Authorised Version*, 1982.
REB.	*The Revised English Bible*, 1989, Oxford/Camb.
Rieu, C. H.	*The Acts of the Apostles*, Translated by C. H. Rieu, 1957.
Rieu, E. V.	*The Four Gospels*, A New Translation, by E. V. Rieu, 1952.
Robertson.	*A Translation of Luke's Gospel*, by A. T. Robertson, 1923, N. Y.
Rotherham, or Roth.	*The Emphasized Bible*, A New Translation, by J. B. Rotherham, 1897, Cincinnati, Ohio.
RSV.	*Revised Standard Version*, 1952, N. Y.
Rutherford.	*Five Pauline Epistles*, by W. G. Rutherford, 1984 new ed. Malvern, Worcs.
RV.	*Revised Version (English)*, 1898rp, Cambridge.
Sadler.	*The Gospel of Paul the Apostle*, trans. by Ralph Sadler, 1892. An excellent scarce work.
Schonfield.	*The Authentic N. T.* by H. J. Schonfield, 1955. Revised as *The Original N. T.*, 1985.
Smith.	*Letters of St. Paul*, Trans. by David Smith, 1942, also in *Life and Letters*, (see Bibliog)
Stern.	*Jewish N. T.* by D. H. Stern, 1989, Jerusalem.
Tanakh.	*The Holy Scriptures*, by Jewish Pub. Society, (Hebrew O. T. only) 1988, Philadelphia.
TCNT.	*The Twentieth Century N. T.* A Translation into Modern English, 1904 rev. ed.

TEV.	*Today's English Version, Good News Bible*, 1976, Glasgow.
TNT.	*The Translator's N. T.* 1973.
Tomanek.	*The N. T. of Our Lord* . . . Trans. by J. L. Tomanek, 1958, Pocatello, Idaho.
Wade.	*The Documents of the N. T.* Trans. by G. W. Wade, 1934.
Wand.	*The N. T. Letters Prefaced and Paraphrased*, by J. W. C. Wand, 1946.
Ward.	*Hidden Meaning in the N. T. by R. A. Ward*, 1969, incl. a new trans. of Ephesians.
Way.	*Letters of St. Paul and Hebrews*, Trans. by A. S. Way, 1926, 6th ed.
Weymouth.	*The N. T. in Modern Speech*, by R. F. Weymouth, cited as 3rd ed. 1909, or 5th ed. 1929.
Williams, C. B.	*The N. T. in the Language of the People*, by Charles B. Williams, 1986rp. Nashville.
Williams, C. K.	The N. T. *A New Translation in Plain English*, by C. Kingsley Williams, 1952.
Wuest.	*The N. T. An Expanded Translation*, by Kenneth S. Wuest, 1961, Grand Rapids, Michigan.
Young.	*Literal Translation of the Bible*, by R. Young, 1903, Rev. ed. Edinburgh.

General Abbreviations

States in the U.S.A. are shown by their zip code abbreviations.

AmBenRev.	American Benedictine Review, Richardton, ND.
AndNewRev.	Andover Newton Review, Newton Centre, MA.
Ant.	Antiquities of Josephus.
AsiaJournTheol.	Asia Journal of Theology, Singapore.
BA	Biblical Archaeologist, Atlanta, GA.
B.C.E.	Before the Common Era.
BibArchRev.	Biblical Archaeology Review, Washington, DC.
Bible Today.	Bible Today, Collegeville, MN.
Biblica.	Biblica, Rome, Italy.
BiblSac.	Bibliotheca Sacra, Dallas, TX.
BibOr.	Bibliotheca Orientalis, Leiden, Netherlands.
BibTheolBull.	Biblical Theology Bulletin, Jamaica, NY.
BT.	Bible Translator, London.
CBQ.	Catholic Biblical Quarterly, Washington, DC.
C.E.	Common Era.
CGT.	Cambridge Greek Testament series, Cambridge.
comm or Comm.	commentary on a Bible book.
cp.	compare with.
CTM.	Concordia Theological Monthly, St. Louis, MO.
EcumRev.	Ecumenical Review, Geneva, Switzerland.
ed.	edition.
Ed.	Editor, General.
Ep.	Epistle.
Ephemirides Theol.	Ephemirides Theologicae Lovanienses, Louvain.
ET.	Expository Times, Edinburgh, Scotland.
EvangQuart.	Evangelical Quarterly, Exeter.
EvangTheol.	Evangelische Theologie, Munich, Germany.
Expositor.	Expositor, The, London.
Forum.	Forum, Sonoma, CA.

ftn.	footnote.
GraceTheolJourn.	Grace Theological Journal, Winona Lake, IN.
GSM.	Greek Student's Monthly, Kingston, Surrey. (see Bibliography under Marshall, A. Ed).
HeythropJnl.	Heythrop Journal, London.
Historia.	Historia, Stuttgart, Germany.
HMSO.	Her Majesty's Stationery Office, London.
Hodder.	Hodder and Stoughton, London.
HTR.	Harvard Theological Review, Cambridge, MA.
ICC.	International Critical Commentary series.
Interpretation.	Interpretation, Richmond, VA.
JBL.	Journal of Biblical Literature, Atlanta, GA.
Jnl or Journ.	Journal.
JnlEvangTheolSoc.	Journal of the Evangelical Theological Society, Lynchburg, VA.
JTS.	Journal of Theological Studies, Oxford.
JournRomStud.	Journal of Roman Studies, London.
JournStudNT.	Journal for the Study of the N. T. Sheffield.
LXX.	Greek Septuagint Version of O. T.
NatGeogM.	National Geographic Magazine, Washington, DC.
n. d.	not dated.
NeoTest.	Neotestamentica, Pretoria, S. Africa.
NIDNTT.	New International Dictionary of N. T. Theology. (see Bibliography under Brown, C. Ed).
NovTest.	Novum Testamentum, Leiden, Netherlands.
N. T.	New Testament.
NTStud.	New Testament Studies, Cambridge.
O. T.	Old Testament.
RechTheol AncMed.	Recherches de Theologie Ancienne et Medievale Louvain, Belgium.
RestorQuart.	Restoration Quarterly, Abilene, TX.
RevBib.	Revue Biblique, Jerusalem, Israel.
rp.	reprint.
RTS.	Religious Tract Society, London.
SCM.	Student Christian Movement, London.
SPCK.	Society for Promotion of Christian Knowledge.
Studium.	Studium, Madrid, Spain.
StudTheol, or ST.	Studia Theologica, Copenhagen, Denmark.
TDNT.	Theological Dictionary of the N. T, (see Bibliography under Kittel, G. Ed).
TynBull.	Tyndale Bulletin, Cambridge.

UBS.	United Bible Societies, London & New York.
U. P.	University Press.
USR.	Union Seminary Review, Richmond, VA.
VT.	Vetus Testamentum, Leiden, Netherlands.
War.	The Jewish War, by Josephus.
ZeitNTWiss.	Zeitschrift fur die Neutestamentliche Wissenschaft, Berlin, Germany.

Introduction

It has been said that a picture is worth a thousand words. A good picture conveys colour, life, feeling and background, qualities difficult to describe adequately. Because the mind builds pictures, a good teacher knows the value of illustrations. They help to paint that picture in such a vivid way that it can be recalled to mind easily, bringing with it much of the background and detail that might otherwise escape for ever.

When we think of illustrations in the Bible, we naturally recall the parables of Jesus Christ. A little story is told that paints a picture, and it reveals a moral or teaches a truth. It is something 'thrown alongside' by way of explanation, for comparison.[1] Often such an illustration saves us having to think too much about the matter; the meaning is obvious. But some illustrations have more depth to them than that, and this is true of many of Jesus' parables. They are designed to stimulate our thinking, to teach much more than is immediately obvious to the mind. They require us to ponder their meaning, and perhaps this explains why there have been so many books about the parables Jesus related.[2]

My purpose is not to add to this literature on the parables, which is already more than adequate. Instead, we will look at illustrations scattered everywhere throughout the pages of the Gospels, Acts and Epistles, illustrations that spring from a simple phrase or a single word. These have often lain neglected while the parables have stolen the limelight. Perhaps this is because they often lie beneath the surface, some of them implicit only in the original Greek and lost to sight in our English translations.

They also require consciously thinking about, like Paul's metaphors, for us to see their value. Indeed, without knowing their background in the life and times of the early Christians those words might slip past unnoticed. Yet each is a little gem, illuminating for us a hidden corner, a shadowy niche containing a spiritual treasure that brings forward all that life and expression and colour found in a fine painting.[3]

The simple example has been given of the phrase, 'the ground is thirsty'. How much more that strikes us with its vibrant feeling than if we had said, 'the ground needs rain.'[4]

Jesus frequently used illustrations or figurative language that centre around the natural world of flora and fauna. There are twenty-four illustrations in the Sermon on the Mount alone, some given as pairs to point up contrasts. Because he had been trained as a carpenter, illustrations connected with that trade also feature, the splinter and the beam, the wooden parts of a trap or stumbling block, the plough and the yoke. Paul chose metaphors drawn from human life, at work and play. Some have a military or nautical flavour, others are legal and educational, but the lighter side – the games and the theatre, was not neglected. As a tent-maker there are natural allusions to the body as a tent, to rents and schisms, to cutting the word of truth as one would cut tent cloth or canvas. Paul's metaphors are sometimes outrageous, with multiple meanings, seemingly inconsistent and mixed up, yet expressed with literary power, evocative appeal and striking impression, like that quite different man of letters, Shakespeare. So, for example, Paul intertwines marriage and baptism to make his point in Romans 7: 1–6.[5]

These illustrations help us in another way. They allow us a better glimpse of the ancient world that was so familiar to the first Christians. In this twentieth century it is often difficult to imagine life in those times, and it is more difficult still if we have never travelled in Bible lands. That is a world apart to begin with, so we are twice removed if we know nothing of either of these backgrounds, the lands and the times. But as we dip into these illustrations from life we build a picture with a background, we gain a vantage point that illuminates those times and throws into sharper relief the people who spoke those words.

One of the best means afforded us to do this is the great mass of papyrus documents discovered early this century in Egypt. Letters, receipts, and all manner of other papyri written in the koine Greek of the day show how words were used, and what they meant in their common, everyday use. We get a fuller, clearer viewpoint as we compare this usage with the way they appear in the gospels and epistles, and our understanding is enriched by this deeper appreciation.[6] This was not a language to be labelled exclusively as 'Biblical Greek', something detached from everyday life, to be associated perhaps with anchorites such as those living in the isolation of the desert community of Qumran.

However, even these enlightening discoveries can be taken to extremes. Some have spoken of 'Hellenizing' the New Testament, giving it solely a later Greek basis. So in recent years there has been an attempt to balance the background more accurately. We must not forget its relation to Hebrew thought, and its most important link with the Greek used in the Septuagint Version of the Hebrew Scriptures. Many of the illustrations we will discuss tie in with those earlier Bible books, with early Judaism and rabbinic thought, and the equivalent Septuagintal expressions.[7]

Care must be taken not to stretch too far these illustrative words and phrases, as some scholars have done. John Howson gave a simple guideline, 'It is of great importance in the interpretation of Scripture, not to press a metaphor beyond the point which it was intended to elucidate.'[8] Yet he was himself charged with doing just that by William M. Ramsay in his references to 'building' and 'edifying', words occurring quite frequently in Paul's vocabulary. Was he drawing an architectural illustration, or had the words become divested of any such idea in Paul's mind? [9]

Often the context helps us to answer that question, and so to widen out the development of the illustration. We need to pay great attention to the immediate context, noting carefully all the little clues of natural expression which are provided. But in addition, parallel usage of the same word or phrase can give much assistance within the wider context of the whole Bible. As Richard Trench once put it, a single word can be like 'a little grain of pure gold capable of being beaten out into a broad extent of gold-leaf.' [10]

The setting and background are equally important to understanding correctly the metaphor, coupled with our own experience in life as it touched that subject. Dorothy L. Sayers illustrates this with the word 'Father' as a metaphor to help in our understanding of God. 'Our common sense assures us that the metaphor is intended to be drawn from the best kind of father acting within a certain limited sphere of activity', rather than that of a cruel or careless father. Misunderstanding a metaphor is usually due to a failure properly to evaluate all the surrounding features implicit in the setting, background and context of the word-picture.[11]

It must also not be forgotten that when we look at words, they must be assigned their proper semantic values in that setting. The writer thought about ideas, and set them down in sentences, so the word itself is not a whole concept, unless it has been singled out deliberately to carry the main stream of thought. But he may well have placed the entire concept within the framework of his illustration or metaphor, and as we examine carefully the parallels and comparisons (or even contrasts), we may see much that is implicit, although it is not directly expressed.[12]

This is why it has been said that a metaphor shatters the normal view in order to widen our horizon, to break out of the familiar mould with a leap into a new dimension, freeing the imagination to engage more easily with new ideas.[13] Sunken treasure is brought to the surface, and then we can see new applications of the underlying principle behind the illustration.

Our quest is not merely a word study. The words or phrases are really themes that develop in different ways, and I have often found in writing this book that they almost develop themselves, with one idea promoting the next, as allusions and associations come readily to mind. It is as if a treasure has been broken up, and only by re-assembling its constituent parts can we come once again to enjoy all its facets.[14]

When Jesus asked the disciples if they had got the sense of several of his illustrations, they said they had, and he continued, 'every Scribe well trained in the Kingdom of the Heavens is like a householder who brings out of his storehouse new things and old.' (Matt. 13: 52 Weymouth.) Does our spiritual grasp of God's Word reveal that we are 'well-trained', so that we can show just what a storehouse of fine things it contains? Some of them may be very 'old' treasures we discovered many years ago that gave us great joy, and about which we never tire of telling in talks and discussions. Others may have been added only recently, and these 'new' treasures show we have not stood still. We have continued to search for further gems to add to the spiritual riches we already rejoice over, and so we truly store up treasure in heaven, and we always have spiritual gifts to impart to our hearers. (Matt. 6:20, 21, Rom. 1:11.)

Bible Translations Used

It will be quickly noticed that many different Bible translations are used in this book. Some readers may find this confusing if they have read only the Authorised King James' Version, or a single modern translation. Why so many different translations?

New translations continue to appear for several reasons: (1), better Hebrew and Greek texts become available as more and more ancient manuscripts are discovered; (2), greater understanding of the original languages as they are more expertly studied, and as other documents (such as the papyri already referred to) are found which illuminate them; (3), progress in the receptor language – in this case the changing nature of our own English language.

But due to the very size of the Bible, no translation is able to excel in all parts, and it is interesting to note how many of the most recent ones have lost accuracy in their endeavours to make their translation dynamic and readable. So an excellent rendering in one place may contrast with a poor rendering in another, and whether this is at the more literal end of the spectrum, or has a tendency to be free or even a paraphrase, again affects the quality of the result.

Because we are looking very closely at particular words or phrases, the degree of difference from one translation to another tends to be accentuated. If we simply wanted the general idea of the passage, variations in a word or two would not be important, but they do become so when the spotlight is focussed precisely on one word or phrase. Sometimes that point has altogether escaped the notice of a host of scholars, and one has to search for the translation that has brought it to light. I have then tried to stay with that translation for the rest of the discussion of that phrase, but even this has not always been possible.[15]

Here there is need to highlight a most specific problem associated with metaphors. The Bible translator has to decide if a metaphor should be carried over in his translation, or whether it is already dead, and should be buried. C. H. Dodd commented on this difficulty, and felt that it is 'sometimes a matter of some delicacy'. However, even if the metaphor is really dead, there may still be some valuable ideas cocooned in the illustration which will convey a fuller picture and paint a more vivid background in the minds of the readers. But quite often translators will not agree on whether a metaphor is dead or not, and we will discuss many examples where one translation brings it to life, while another completely ignores it. Again it was Dodd who said that if an author was 'clearly aiming at picturesque writing . . . we should do him less than justice if we eliminated details that help to evoke a picture.'[16]

So the *New English Bible* (in which Dodd took a prominent part), is one of the translations found conveying such a picture when others do not. What has to be watched is whether a literal translation of an apparently dead metaphor leads to a semantic distortion of the text, which brings us back once again to context. When we look at the whole idea conveyed within that context we can usually detect if it rings true.

The abbreviations following the table of contents list all the Bible translations used, and it is hoped that no prejudice has been shown in favour of any particular one, although those which more often retain the metaphor or illustration without transference are naturally used most frequently. Those using archaic pronouns have not usually been included.

These illustrations not only speak to us today in a very clear and illuminating manner, but they open up a host of further applications, whereby we may be able to assist fellow Christians and those not so convinced, as we talk with them about the great truths proclaimed. I have not unduly sought such applications, so sometimes they are made, and sometimes not. So long as you remain faithful to the central idea in each illustration, I hope that this book will stimulate your own thoughts and applications, and expand your horizons as you discover much of the grand treasure in God's Word.

Notes and References: (see Bibliography for short titles)

1. Skeat, W. W. *Etymological Diction-ary*, 427.
2. Oesterley, W. O. E. *Parables*, 14.
3. Feldman, A. *Parables*, VIII, 244. All forms of speech which contain a comparison can be included.

'Biblical comparisons are bolder and more majestic in conception, and indicate a fresher and more vigorous imagination.' Hoskyns, E. C. in *Cambridge Sermons*, 1938, SPCK, 70 observes,'Can we rescue a word, and discover a universe? Can we study a language, and awake to the Truth? Can we bury ourselves in a lexicon, and arise in the presence of God?' He goes on to show how words can lose their nobility, and instances the words 'church' and 'ecclesiastic,' behind which are the noble Greek words *kuriakon* and *ecclesia*, with much more vigorous meanings.

4. Bullinger, E. W. *Enjoy the Bible*, 391.
5. Guillemard, W. H. *Hebraisms*, Pt II, 58; Howson, J. S. *Metaphors*, 87, 118; Tenney, M. C. *Galatians*, 139; Deissmann, G. A. *St. Paul*, 73f; Park, D. M. *Paul's Metaphors*, 37–40; Marshall, A. Ed. *GSM*. Nov, 1933, 412/3.
6. Moulton & Milligan, *Vocabulary*, Intro. XVII; Carson, D. A. *Fallacies* 64.
7. Moulton, J. H. *Grammar*, Vol. IV, 89; Barr, J. *Biblical Words for Time*, 1962, SCM, 15–17; On the other hand, Ayers, D, M, *English Words*, 136/7, points out that Greek had an important influence on Latin, and many words entering the English language from Latin, also bring in the Greek words behind them.
8. Howson, J. S, *Metaphors*, 70; Lyall, F, *Legal Metaphors*, 186-188.
9. Ramsay, W, M, *Luke*, 294–296 re Howson, J, S, *Metaphors* 46, 47f. Lightfoot, J. B. *Notes on Epistles*, 191.
10. Trench, R. C. *Study of Words*, 33. However, note the caution in using Trench urged by M. Silva, in 'The Pauline Style as Lexical Choice,' 201, 206 of *Pauline Studies*, Essays Presented to Prof. F. F. Bruce, 1980, Exeter, Paternoster P.
11. Sayers, D. L. *The Mind of the Maker*, 1941, Methuen, 19, 20. Neil, J. *Strange Figures*, 18–26.
12. Barr, J. *Biblical Words for Time*, 155, 162; Carson, D. A. *Fallacies*, 66, also 27, 28, and the false etymology that produced 'under-rower' in 1 Cor. 4:1, resulting in an entirely misleading illustration.
13. Dillistone, F. W. *Christianity and Symbolism*, 1955, Collins, 28, 160, 273; W. M. Dixon, *The Human Situation*, 1937, Arnold, 65–67; Cotterell and Turner, *Linguistics*, 301.
14. Barr, J. *Semantics*, 234, 263–6, 269–275.
15. Derrett, J. D. M. *Jesus' Audience*, 205, 206.
16. Dodd, C. H. *Problems*, 147, 149; Waard, J de. *Biblical Metaphors*, 109, 112–115; Wonderly, W. L. *Bible Translations for Popular Use*, 1968, UBS. 119–122 on translation into foreign languages; Cotterell, P & Turner, M, *Linguistics*, 300, where it is pointed out that the TEV renders Gen. 49:27, as a simile, and the RSV renders it as a metaphor, so any distinction in the two figures may be merely technical.

Chapter 1

Agriculture, Plants and the Land

1. Cutting Through the Forest—The Pioneer of Life.

To blaze the trail where no one else has been before is the hope and
aim of many an explorer. In certain situations a leader of others may
be first called upon to mark out the way for them, and so Abraham
led his large family out into the unknown when he left Ur, and Moses
led the Israelites out of Egypt to the Promised Land. But the idea
is applied to Jesus Christ more than to any other man of faith.
From the early age of twelve he 'grew physically and developed
spiritually'. (Luke 2:52 Barclay.) Robertson's translation has the interesting note that this was 'to cut forward like a pioneer in the
forest.'[1] He was undoubtedly more advanced at that age than any of
his contemporaries.

The unique manner in which Jesus 'blazed the way' (Barclay),
was as 'the pioneer of life'. (Acts 3:15 Moffatt, Mont.) In opening
up the real life to mankind he was 'one who begins something, a
pioneer' (TNT note). The book of Hebrews calls him 'the pioneer
of their salvation', and he is also 'the pioneer and perfector of our
faith'. (Heb. 2:10 Mont. RSV, Barclay, 12:2 RSV, also Moffatt.
Mont.) In another sense too, his entry into heaven was as one who
'blazed the way for us'. (Heb. 6:20 C. B. Williams.) This is based
on the thought of running, particularly as when a scout runs ahead
of the main force to find the best route, so Jesus was such a 'forerunner'.

The apostle Paul also felt that his role was often that of a pioneer.
He saw his imprisonment as something that would further the
progress, the 'striking ahead' of the good news, and he hoped that
other Christians would be encouraged to follow his example. (Phil.
1:12–14, 25 K.Int.) Paul was always 'up and doing' (2 Cor. 6:9

Rutherford), and his manifest fondness for Timothy must have been partly due to his showing a similar quality, and the fine progress that young man had made under his training and encouragement. So Paul exhorted him to go on 'striking forward' or advancing, since it would mean his salvation, and that of many others who would follow his example. (1 Tim. 4:15.) How valuable indeed is the role of one willing to be a pioneer, the very best form of leadership possible.

2. The Easy Yoke to Bear—A Balanced Sharing.

In today's modern society, the yoke is fast disappearing, though it is still familiar in many countries of the third world. But the term 'acre' continues to be used as a unit of land measure, disguising well its ancient association – the area a yoke or pair of oxen could plough in one day.[2]

The yoke was often just a straight bar of wood placed across the necks of the oxen as they stood together, with two pairs of long pins driven vertically through the bar, which came down on either side of their necks and were kept in place by thongs under the animals' throats.

When the yoke is used as an illustration or metaphor it has reference to persons who share the yoke. So Paul spoke of 'my trusty yokefellow', possibly with reference to Luke, just one of many 'fellow-workers' to whom he referred as having 'shared my contests as I proclaimed the gospel'. (Phil. 4:2, 3 Bruce.) So this was a yoke of service in fulfilling the will of God, an interesting clue as we come to the main text for this illustration.

Jesus invited the crowd he was addressing to 'Come to me and I will give you rest – all of you who work so hard beneath a heavy yoke. Wear my yoke – for it fits perfectly – and let me teach you; for I am gentle and humble, and you shall find rest for your souls; for I give you only light burdens.' (Matt. 11:29, 30 Living Bible; another translation speaks of a yoke that 'does not chafe' – Schonfield.) So Jesus did not mean that Christianity was an 'easy' religion, requiring little of its followers, but rather that the joy and happiness it generated make the task pleasant, delightful and refreshing, just as a smooth well-fitting yoke or collar would hardly be noticed by the animal bearing it.[3]

Jesus Christ stressed the love of God, which replaced the Mosaic Law with all its regulations. But some Judaisers later tried to retain the law code along with circumcision, which caused Peter to ask, 'How is it, then, that you would now call God in question, by putting a yoke on the necks of the disciples, such as we and our fathers have been too weak to bear?' (Acts 15:10 Knox.)

What a contrast between these two yokes! No wonder the yoke of Jesus was one that could fit perfectly – it made allowances for the imperfections of his followers, but the Mosaic law did not, it only showed up their failure as humans to keep a perfect law. (Romans 3:20.)

But Paul added a necessary warning. 'Do not be unequally yoked together with unbelievers. For what fellowship has righteousness with lawlessness? And what communion has light with darkness?' (2 Cor. 6:14 RAV.) Without doubt, Paul had in mind the principles set out in ancient Israel, not to harness or yoke together an ox and a donkey. (Deut. 22:10, Lev. 19:19.) Because of their different size and weight, the two animals would not be able to pull together as a united team. It would even be unkind to both animals, for the one because it was weaker and could not keep up with its stronger partner, for the other, because it had to do most of the work, and struggle with the extra burden pulling it back.

How well the illustration applies today. To be a fellow worker with Christ is the perfect relationship. He knows our weaknesses and frailty, and can balance out exactly our share with him under the Christian yoke. He bears our weaknesses, putting himself in our place, while we strive to measure up to the example he is setting. 'For we have been made partners with Christ, if only we preserve firm the confidence we had at the beginning.' (Heb. 3:14 Barclay.) But it is still a service, ploughing in the world field with him, sowing the seeds of truth. (1 Cor. 3:8, 9.) True Christianity is not an armchair religion, but is devoted to the task of spreading the Word, and it is the results that bring joy and happiness, as more workers unite to share in the harvest. His yoke really brings us rest and peace of mind.

3. Crushed Reed and Smouldering Wick— Help for the Weak.

After healing a man on the sabbath, Jesus was confronted by the Pharisees, who were seeking to stop his work. But Jesus avoided a conflict, even to the point of telling his followers not to publicize his cures. Matthew explains why he took this course by quoting from Isaiah 42:1–4 concluding with the words,

> A crushed reed he will not break off;
> A smouldering wick he will not snuff out;
> Till he triumphantly vindicates justice,
> And nations confide in his name.
>
> Matt. 12:20 Schonfield Original NT.

Why did Matthew think of this quotation here, and what is meant by the illustration of the reed and the wick? The entire theme of Isaiah was foretelling how God's servant would act during his first coming, in humility (of which the reed or rush was an emblem), with gentleness and long-suffering and not at that time in the role of king. That was to await the day when he would triumphantly vindicate justice, and destroy all his enemies. (Ps. 2:8–12, 110: 1–7.) But now he had come 'to seek and to save what was lost'. (Luke 19:10 Schonfield.)

Jesus' treatment of a crushed reed or a smouldering wick would be in harmony with this attitude. Reeds were used for various purposes, such as measuring lines, writing pens or simple musical instruments, cut by shepherds and punctured with holes to entertain a surprisingly responsive flock of sheep. (Matt. 12:20 Wey. 3rd ed. ftn.) If the reed was found to be crushed or bruised, it was thrown away, and a better one chosen. But a person who was weak and poor, like a crushed reed, was not despised by Jesus Christ. He said,' It is not the healthy who need a doctor, it is those who are ill.' (Matt. 9:12 Schonfield.)

A smouldering wick in a small oil lamp, typical of the first century, tells the same story. Perhaps its owner had almost run out of the all essential oil, or the wick needed renewing. Would Jesus come along and snuff it out, or would he not rather try to give fresh light and hope to those who felt their oil of gladness had run dry, yes, even their very life had perhaps reached a dangerously low ebb? There may even be some reason in viewing the two-part illustration as, not just an example of Hebrew parallelism, but a linked reference to the external aspect of life (the reed) and the life burning within (the wick).

Peter comes to mind as an example at the time of Jesus' death. His denial of Christ three times caused him to go out and weep bitterly. He must have been overwhelmed with his own sense of inadequacy and utter desolation at that moment. He truly seemed like a crushed reed and a smouldering wick, about to desert his master for good. Yet Jesus gave him no verbal reprimand, but simply, 'turned and looked at Peter'. (Luke 22:61, 62 Schonfield.) We cannot easily imagine all that was in that look; was it disappointment, reproof or just forgiveness? Perhaps this illustration suggests it was the latter, for Jesus was not trying to extinguish Peter's life and hopes, or tell him he was useless and worthless, that his sin was unforgiveable, and he should follow Judas Iscariot and end it all.[4]

No, for Jesus knew Peter better than he did himself; he saw his inner struggles, his impetuous and shallow boastings, and on past that to one who would prove eventually to be a great carer for his sheep. So during the forty days before his ascension to heaven, he gave Peter his commission, 'Tend my lambs . . . shepherd my sheep . . . tend my sheep'. (John 21: 15–17 Schonfield.) Peter could hardly escape the repetition of those statements – three times – just the same number as Peter's three denials!

4. The Green Tree—The Death of the Innocent.

As Jesus was being taken away to die, the weeping women onlookers brought home to him the tragedy of the long-term situation – for he could foresee what was coming. 'You should weep for yourselves and your children,' he told them, because a time was coming when both parents and children would suffer miserably, and many would cry out for the mountains to fall on them and put an end to it all. (Luke 23:26–30 Knox.)

Then he referred to an illustration which was based on a proverbial saying. 'If it goes so hard with the tree that is still green, what will become of the tree that is already dried up?' (Luke 23:31 Knox, Ezek. 20:47.) Green wood, with fresh sap in it, was not meant to be burnt up, and so it stood for those who were innocent. But dry wood made good fuel because it kindles easily, so it came to represent guilty ones.[5] Jesus was innocent of the crimes charged against him, but what of Judaism and Jerusalem, piling crime upon crime, and now putting to death the one who was the means to bring life to mankind, the Messiah they were rejecting? (Acts 3:15.)

At the instigation of the Jewish religious leaders, the Romans were bringing death upon the Son of God, the vine, a fruit-bearing green tree. Jesus had told his disciples that they were the branches, a vital part of that fruit-bearing vine, if they stayed in union with him. But those against him would be like dried up branches, to be cast off and burned. When the Romans besieged Jerusalem in 70 C. E., the city was destroyed, as Jesus had prophesied and the women and children suffered terribly. (Josephus War, Book 6, ch. 9 (1) 413.) The guilty Jewish nation was devastated, like a dry withered branch, cut off and thrown into the fire because it was not green and fruit-bearing. (John 15:1, 2, 5, 6, Matt. 3:10.)

Peter may have had that illustration in mind when he used its principle, and told Christians not to be puzzled at their trials, for they could rejoice as ones sharing in the sufferings of Christ. Then he concluded, 'The time is ripe for judgment to begin, and to begin with God's own household; and if our turn comes first, what will be its issue for those who refuse credence to God's message? If the just man wins salvation only with difficulty, what will be the plight of the godless, of the sinner?' (1 Pet. 4:17, 18, Knox.)

5. The Fig Tree in Spring—The Composite Sign.

When Jesus was asked about the sign of his coming again, and the end of the world, he gave a long list of happenings that fills an entire chapter in all three synoptic Gospels. (Matthew 24, Mark 13 and Luke 21.)

Then he adds this illustration as he approached Jerusalem, in those days surrounded by numerous walnut and fig trees, and even palms. 'From the fig tree learn now her parable; as soon as ever her branches are full of sap and bursting into leaf, you know that summer is near. So also do you, whenever you see these things happening, know that He is near, at your very door.' (Mark 13: 28, 29, Montgomery.)

The fig tree has caused some problems for readers, especially the one Jesus cursed, for it is unlike many other trees, almost always carrying fruit, for ten months of the year. The autumn figs (kermouses) stay on the tree all winter, and so can often be found in spring. The first ripe figs, especially valued (bakkooroth or dafour), set early in spring (March) before the leaves are out.[6] First the sap rises, softening the stems, and allowing the buds and leaves to break from their sheaths.[7]

But this was just one of many evidences of approaching summer, the period between Passover and fruit harvest. It was a sign, but a composite one, for a clear evidence like this was accompanied by many others. (Song of Solomon 2:11–13.) So Luke adds the phrase, 'and all the trees!' (Luke 21:30.) The sap rising in the fig tree is evidence of a general but secret movement within the branches and stems of most trees and plants, soon followed by a magnificent outburst of greenery from all quarters of the landscape.[8] That is why Jesus could use this to illustrate the nature of the composite sign he had been talking about in these chapters – its reality lay, not just in one or two happenings, but all of them taking place together.

So was the fulfilment seen in 70 C. E., when Jerusalem was besieged and destroyed by the Romans? No, for only some of these events occurred, and not all of them.[9] So that was not the generation to which he primarily referred. (Mark 13:30.) No wonder it needed Christians to 'Keep watch then, for you do not know when the master of the house is coming – in the evening, at midnight, at cockcrow, or in the morning . . . Be awake and on guard'. (Mark 13: 35–37, Montgomery.)

6. Flowers of a Day—The Brevity of Life.

In the land of Israel a heavy shower of rain at certain times of the year produces a wonderful sight. A seemingly barren landscape suddenly becomes bright and colourful as thousands of flowers appear. But the miracle is short-lived, for they are often flowers of only a day, and the heat of the sun withers them and they die.

In his Sermon on the Mount Jesus raised the question, 'Why should you worry about clothing? See how the wild flowers grow. They do not toil or spin, and yet I tell you, even Solomon in all his splendour was never dressed like one of them. But if God so beautifully dresses the wild grass, which is alive today, and is thrown into the furnace tomorrow, will he not much more surely clothe you, you who have so little faith?' (Matt. 6:28–30 Goodspeed.)

Those flowers included beautiful and colourful scarlet anemones, tulips, hyacinths, gladioli, ranunculus, iris and flax, and not just 'lilies', as some translations put it, a term rather misleading in the western world.[10] Their natural purity of colour and form even made Solomon's grand white and purple robes seem artificial and imitation. Note, too, the second term used – wild grass, for the Arab uses the word 'hashish' to describe all flowers and grass mixed together and used as fuel.[11] In a land where so much wood was needed for fuel, it was scarce, and had to be supplemented by grass and flowers. Does such a brief life warrant that God should not bother to produce flowers of beauty, delicacy and loveliness? Not at all, for his arm is never shortened, so will he not also care for his servants?

James refers to the same illustration, but with a different purpose. 'The rich will disappear like the wild flowers. For the sun comes up with its scorching heat, and dries up the grass, and the flowers wither, and all their beauty is gone. That is the way rich men will fade and die in the midst of their pursuits.' (James 1: 10b, 11 Goodspeed.)

Peter also ties in the illustration with still another different objective, as a contrast to the abiding and enduring nature of God and his word:

> All flesh is like grass,
> And all its glory like the flower of the grass.
> The grass withers,
> And the flower fades,
> But the word of the Lord will last forever.
> (1 Peter 1:24, 25 Goodspeed, Isa. 40:6–8.)

The shortness of man's life is also illustrated by James when he says, 'You are just a mist, which appears for a little while, and then disappears.' (James 4: 14 Goodspeed.) Will we boast of what we are going to do in life, or will we humbly say that if it is God's will we will live to fulfil these goals? (James 4:15.) One day with Him is like a thousand years to us, which gives us a proper perspective from which to view our existence. (Ps. 90:4–6, 12.)

Yet the illustration is still one full of hope and optimism, for we have the chance in that 'one day' to leave behind as beautiful and lovely an impression as those colourful and majestic flowers. Their existence is a pleasure to their grand Creator, and so we can be, too. Don't then, be of little faith, but increase it daily in a wondrous God who cares for us and wants us to enjoy our lives and his exquisite handiwork.

7. Tree Growth—Increasing our Faith.

Paul began his second letter to the Thessalonians by complimenting them on the increase of their faith and love. (2 Thess. 1:3.) Interestingly, he distinguished between the type of growth appropriate to each of these qualities. So for faith he said it 'is growing abundantly', using the Greek word 'huperauxanō' that suggests organic growth that is steady and continuous, like a tree.[12]

When Jesus rebuked his disciples for their little faith, he used the illustration of the tiny mustard seed, which could grow to a tree twelve feet in height.[13] It also answered their question, how can we have more faith? By its very nature, faith is something that has to grow gradually, and if it is fed and nurtured it will go on enlarging itself continually. (Matt. 13:31, 32, 17:19, 20, Luke 17: 5, 6.)

So it is not surprising that the tree is used a number of times in the Bible to represent the servants of God. The Psalmist opens his record by talking about the man who studies God's Word, and grows like a tree responding to the stream beside which it is planted. (Ps. 1:1–3.) Jeremiah uses the same illustration when he speaks of the man who puts his trust in God, for 'He shall be like a tree planted by the waterside, that stretches its roots along the stream. When the heat comes it has nothing to fear; its spreading foliage stays green.' (Jer. 17:7, 8, NEB.) The result of such faith and growth is that men of proven faith are described as resembling big trees, sturdy oak-like terebinths. (Isa. 61:3, Ps. 92: 12.)[14]

Paul may well have had in mind some of these Scriptures when he used this metaphor, and he clinches it when he writes to the Ephesians and Colossians to become strong in faith, with 'deep roots and firm foundations'. (Eph. 3:17 NEB.) 'Be rooted in him; be built in him; be consolidated in the faith you were taught.' (Col. 2:6, 7 NEB.) Just as the tree needs time to develop and put down strong roots, so the Christian does not magically find faith, but needs to work to build it up, and then consolidate it. This explains why a 'newly converted man' was not to be an overseer in God's congregation, for the Greek word is 'neophyte', a newly planted tree. (1 Tim. 3:6, cp. Ps. 127:3 LXX.)[15] How well that consolidation of our faith is recommended by Paul in these words, 'whatever be the point that we have already reached, let us persevere in the same course.' (Phil. 3:16 Weymouth.) A tree adds a ring each year it lives; do we add a ring each year to our faith? Then, like the Thessalonians, such faith will be worthy of commendation, and will become an example for others to follow. (Acts 6:7.)[16]

8. The Irrigating Flood—Love that Increases.

Having commended the Thessalonians for the growth of their faith, Paul went on to mention that 'your love for one another is continually increasing' (Greek 'pleonazō'). (2 Thess. 1:3 TCNT.) By contrast to the steady organic growth of faith like a tree, the word used here suggests instead a diffusive, expansive growth, like a flood that irrigates the land, spreading everywhere.[17]

In his first letter to the Thessalonians, Paul uses the same idea when he says, 'may the Lord fill you to overflowing with love for one another and for every one.' (1 Thess. 3:12, TCNT, see also Phil. 1:9.) Lightfoot observed that the second word is stronger than the first, so that when the two are added together we have 'increase you to overflowing'. Love as a quality can flow like a river, carrying everything with it, and bringing benefits to everything it reaches when directed for the irrigation of the land. As Professor Nygren puts it, 'in Christ there is manifested a Divine love which flows over all the dykes.'[18]

Peter uses the same idea, but extends it to other qualities leading up to love as the pinnacle, and then links it with the fruitful result. 'For if these things exist in you and overflow, they will prevent you from being either inactive or unfruitful regarding the accurate knowledge of our Lord Jesus Christ.' (2 Peter 1:5–8 NWT.)

Paul shows how the fruitful result is obtained when he writes to the Romans about the hope that never disappoints us, 'since God's love floods our hearts through the holy spirit which has been given to us.' (Rom. 5:5 Moffatt.) So love needs to fill the heart, to find the right kind of soil there, in a good and well-disposed heart. (Luke 8:15.) From there it will overflow and make many other persons irrigated and fruitful too.

The total effect of all these qualities spearheaded by love is well summed up in this comment, 'God is able to give you an overflowing measure of all good gifts, that all your wants of every kind may be supplied at all times, and you may give of your abundance to every good work.' (2 Cor. 9:8 Conybeare.)

9. The Treasure, and Pearl of Great Value— Recognizing the Kingdom's Value.

Two of Jesus' parables come within the scope of this book, because they are told within a sentence or two. They follow one another in Matthew 13, and their similarity provides some interesting points of comparison and contrast.

The first concerns a man digging in a field. 'The kingdom of heaven is like a treasure hidden in the field, which a man conceals after finding it. Then out of sheer gladness he goes out and sells everything he has and buys that field.' (Matt. 13: 44 New Berkeley Version.)

It was not unusual for people to hide treasure in the ground in Jesus' day, placed in an old amphora or pottery jar. There were few other places that provided any reasonable security. (Josephus War, Bk. 7, ch. 5. (2)114/115, Matt. 25:25.)[19] Of course, this man may have had some knowledge of a hidden treasure in the area, but his desire to own it legitimately, rather than attempting to steal it, suggests he had a right to be digging there, and found it unexpectedly.[20]

But why was he digging in a field he didn't own? He may have been hired to work there, or had certain legal rights over some produce in the field, although the land belonged to someone else. When Abraham bought the field of Ephron it is distinctly stated that it included the cave and all the trees, so that these need not have been part of the agreement as a matter of course. (Gen. 23:17, 18.) By quickly setting about the purchase of the field, this man recognized the value of this treasure to be worth any cost, and all that he possessed.[21]

The second parable refers to a pearl trader. 'Again, the kingdom of heaven is like a merchant looking for beautiful pearls. Having found one pearl of exceptional value he went out and sold all he possessed and bought it.' (Matt. 13:45, 46 New Berkeley Version.)

Notice the similarities. Both are items of great and unusual value. Those translations that speak of 'a pearl of great price' are misleading. (A.V. Moffatt. etc.) [22] The price, though high, may not compare in any way with the true value. It is because the merchant is very skilled when it comes to pearls, that he also recognizes this flawless paragon of exceptional value.[23] Both persons put the acquisition of this treasure first in their lives, being immediately willing to sacrifice all their possessions, the result of a lifetime's work.

But now notice the subtle differences. The treasure was found by chance, in an unexpected place, for otherwise the man would have bought the field first, to remove any possibility of losing it. But the merchant has been searching for just such a pearl for many years. Each time he saw one that was a little unusual, he wondered if this was the big moment, but, no, he had been disappointed until now. Though the record does not specifically say so, he too must have rejoiced greatly like the man who had found the treasure.

Why did Jesus bother to give two similar parables? Undoubtedly the varied settings would appeal to different groups, but it is this factor of difference that suggests itself as the real reason.

We may have searched long and hard for the treasure of God's Kingdom, or we may have found it quite by chance, when we were not even looking for it. In either circumstance, what will we do?

Will we make every sacrifice to acquire this great treasure while we have the opportunity?

Recognizing Its Great Value

The reaction that Jesus was looking for from his listeners was a realization of the exceptional value of the Kingdom. It was not possible to put a valuation on this pearl, this treasure. Men were not in possession of enough knowledge to evaluate what the Kingdom could do, or would mean to mankind.

So the apostle Paul spoke about the 'unfathomable riches of Christ'. (Eph. 3:8 Knox, NAB, NASB.) A. T. Robertson argues that Paul took this thought from the book of Job, where Eliphaz says of God, 'His works are great, past all reckoning, marvels beyond all counting,' and Job almost repeats his words in response to Bildad, where the Greek Septuagint in both verses uses the same word chosen by Paul 'unfathomable' (Greek 'anexichniastos'). (Job 5:9, 9:10, NJB.)[24] It is impossible for man to trace the untraceable. It is 'a wealth the limit of which no man can ever find.' (Eph. 3:8 Barclay.) Writing to the Romans, Paul adds, 'Frankly, I stand amazed at the unfathomable complexity of God's wisdom and God's knowledge.' (Rom. 11:33 Phillips.)

We still know very little about the universe, despite all man's great discoveries, but we behold enough to appreciate its breathtaking grandeur and beauty. That is the sort of recognition that Jesus was looking for, understanding the value of God's Kingdom as a spiritual treasure beyond compare, worth all the sacrifice of other possessions.[25] It entirely altered the value concepts of those who suddenly realized that God's Kingdom was mankind's only hope. With Jesus' appearance as the king-designate of that Kingdom its treasure was discovered to mankind for the first time, if they could but recognize it. (Matt. 4:17.) That recognition brings with it great joy to the finder.

10. The Wind that Blows Where it Pleases—
The Power of the Spirit.

In that memorable chat with Jesus, the Pharisee Nicodemus confesses that he doesn't understand how anyone could be born again a second time. Jesus used an interesting illustration in answering him. 'The wind blows where it pleases, and you hear the sound of it, but you do not know where it comes from or where it goes. That is just the way it is with everyone who is born of the Spirit.' (John 3:8 C. B. Williams.)

Just what did Jesus mean by his play on the word 'wind', which is the same Greek word for 'spirit' ('pneuma')? The clue is in the final part as it affects those born again from above. Such faithful servants of God are often referred to as 'trees of righteousness', producing a fine fruitage. (Isa 61:3, Ps. 1:3, 92:12, Jer. 17:7, 8. Matt. 7:15–20, John 15:8, Gal. 5:22, 23, Phil. 1:11, Col. 1:10.) This other illustration can help us here, for how is a tree affected by the wind? First we hear the sound as it rustles the leaves, and then we see movement, and if the wind is strong, the branches bend before it. Where trees are in exposed places the prevailing wind permanently bends the branches, and we speak of a wind-swept landscape. In that case we know the usual direction of the wind, but in most situations the wind continually changes, and because we do not see it, we have difficulty in saying where the wind comes from and where it goes to ultimately. All we do observe is how the tree is affected.[26] So Nicodemus could be sure of the fact of spiritual rebirth, though he could not expect to understand fully the mystery of how it happened, or where he would be led.

This helps us to see the application to the spirit-anointed servants of God, those born again. Like the tree, they are filled with the power of the spirit, and are moved by it. They show the fruitage of the spirit in daily walking the Christian way, and at all times they bend and respond readily to the spirit's direction. (cp. Acts 2:2–4.) But an ordinary observer may not appreciate what moves that person.

Unhappily today, there are many who claim to be 'born again', but who show little evidence in their lives that they are really directed by God, and they have not even begun to develop the nine fruits of the spirit, and nor do they seek God's Kingdom first. (Matt. 6:33.)

Jesus himself was the prime example of one obediently responding to the will of God, doing what He wanted right from the time he was baptized, and begotten by God through the holy spirit. (John 5:19, 30, Matt. 3:16, 17.) Yet many Jews said they did not know where Jesus came from, and it took a man whose eyesight was restored by Jesus to tell them he came from God. (John 9:28–33.) So too, the holy spirit is really from God, who himself moves in a way man cannot discern. (Job 9:11.)

But a spirit-anointed Christian still has to watch how he walks, as Paul reminded the Ephesians in his day. So he urged them to keep the spirit 'up to the top', for the pressures of the worldly system cause even Christians to be 'leaky vessels'. (Eph. 5:18 Ward. p.144 cp. 2 Cor. 4:7.)[27]

11. New Wine Into New Skins—New Personalities.

This is one of the better-known illustrations of Jesus, but its value is lost unless we think in terms of the wineskins used in the first century, and still in use in some places today.

How is the wineskin made? Often a goatskin is used, and as soon as the animal has been killed the skin is separated from the flesh by blowing between the two with the lips. The head and feet are cut off, and the body drawn out of the skin through the neck opening. The skin is then tanned and the four feet are sewn up, so that the neck opening is used for filling and emptying the wine.[28]

What was Jesus' argument? He said, 'Neither do they put new wine into old wineskins; if they do, the wineskins will burst, the wine will run out and the wineskins will be ruined. Rather, they put new wine into fresh wineskins, and both are preserved.'(Matt. 9:17 Adams.) New wine exerts a power, it is active, for as it ferments it generates carbon dioxide gas which makes wineskins expand. But if they are old, dry and stiff, with likely weak places due to chafing and carrying, they will not expand, and will burst.

Jesus brought a new teaching, and although the old Law covenant was designed to take the Israelites and Jews up to the Messiah, the challenge was still there, would they be willing to change and accept the new ideas, or would they inflexibly reject them, so that, as it were, the new wine would spill out on the ground and be wasted?

There is a very individual and personal aspect about this illustration. To accept the new wine they would need to become new personalities, new wineskins, as Paul later explained. 'For if a man is in Christ he becomes a new person altogether – the past is finished and gone, everything has become fresh and new.' (2 Cor. 5:17 Phillips.) That meant being willing to expand one's viewpoint, to change, allowing the power of the spirit in Christianity to work away within one and then adapting to its needs. Ancient Judaism had become very set in its outlook and traditions. Jesus did not try to reshape Judaism, but introduced a new power, the spirit of true Christianity, and except for a small minority, Judaism proved that it could not contain or accept that power.[29]

The record in Luke adds another verse. 'And nobody, when he has drunk old wine, wants the new. He says, "The old is better!"' (Luke 5:39 Adams.) This was in answer to the Pharisees' accusation in verse 33 that John's disciples often did the same thing as their disciples. How kind and considerate was that comment. Naturally, the old wine tastes best, and the palate has to be gradually attuned to the new. But if the old wine is running out, then the new wine will have to be used, and it may well prove to be the better vintage in the end when it has matured. So Jesus was patient with John's disciples, gradually taking them over from John and instructing them with the new teachings. Nor did the spirit reveal all the new truths at once, but left many of them for Paul and the other apostles to bring forth, so that by the time the canon of Scripture was complete, they had all that was necessary for salvation.[30]

12. Fine Fruitage—Desirable Christian Qualities.

In his famous Sermon on the Mount, Jesus gave a warning about false prophets, then quickly went into an illustration based on the principle, 'By their fruits you will know them' For 'are grapes gathered from thorns, or figs from thistles?' (Matt. 7:15, 16, C. K. Williams.)

Notice the way desirable fruits were contrasted with undesirable prickly weeds – designed to bring speedy agreement from his audience as they tried to imagine such combinations.

Then Jesus developed the metaphor. Good trees produce fine fruit, but the fruit from rotten trees is worthless. No reasonable person would expect the opposite result, for cause and effect must be related. So the rotten tree can only be cut down and its wood used to feed the fire. So it would be with men that were either true or false. (Matt. 7: 17–20, 3:8–10, Jude 12.)[31]

Paul added to the illustration, talking of Christians as ones who are 'filled with the fruits of righteousness that come through Jesus Christ,' 'pleasing him in everything, bearing fruit in every kind of good work.' (Phil. 1:11, Col. 1:10, C. K. Williams.) We today still hope that our own hard work and that of our friends will 'bear fruit'.[32]

But Paul carried the illustration much further than a merely picturesque idiom. Writing to the Galatians he contrasted the works of the flesh (not fruitage), with the fruitage of the spirit, and then named nine important qualities for Christians to develop. 'But the fruit of the Spirit is love, joy, peace, patience, kindness, goodness, honesty, gentleness, self-mastery: against such things there is no law.' (Gal. 5:22, 23 C. K. Williams.)

The vital point to note is that the Greek word for 'fruit' ('karpos') is singular, so that Paul thought of the spirit of God as if it were a tree. All these different, though related qualities would be found growing on just one tree.[33] Could we picture a single tree carrying nine different fruits? It happens that the Prunus genus of fruit trees includes, quite by coincidence, nine different types: plums, apricots, cherries, peaches, nectarines, damsons, greengages, sloes and almonds. Each fruit grows on its own tree, but could we imagine all nine fruits growing on one single tree? What an appealing and desirable tree that would be indeed! It is not to be found among literal trees, but here Paul tells us it is possible with spiritual trees.

The Christian has to become like that, showing by his Christian qualities that he has God's Spirit, growing as it were, like a single tree within him, and sharing that fruitage with all those with whom he comes in contact. What a fine example that will be, and how it helps others to recognize the *true* Christian.

Yes, that is the test. There are many who *say* they are Christians, but their attitude and manner shows it to be a false and hollow claim. They easily lose self-control or mastery when confronted with a problem, they show little joy or pleasure in wanting to talk about the faith, and often have a smug and self-satisfied outlook, rather than a mild or gentle one.

There is no end to the development of the spirit's fruitage; 'against such things there is no law'. No law that says – this is enough. So a true Christian congregation would be like an orchard of fine trees, carrying such a plentiful crop of luscious fruit that it brings great joy and pleasure to our heavenly Father as he contemplates it.

We think of the trees described in Ezekiel and Revelation that bear their crops each month, or continuously, spiritually speaking. Just as those crops were for the curing of the nations, and so were trees of life, so Christian fruitage has as its end to save others as well as ourselves, and that goes to increase the joy, the peace of mind, the love, the faith that is the precious possession of those who allow God's spirit to rule their lives, rather than the selfish spirit of those who practice the works of the flesh. (Rev. 22:2, Ezek. 47:12, 1 Tim. 4:16.)

13. Salt of the Earth—
Seasoning One Another in Peace.

Salt is used in a number of Scriptural illustrations, for it was a well known commodity in Bible times, just as it is today. Its qualities are varied and valuable, for it preserves and purifies, and is important for seasoning food.[34] So it carried a vivid meaning to those who were using it every day.

The fishermen disciples of Jesus knew that fish they had caught were soon spoilt unless they were quickly salted.[35] It became, then, a symbol of endurance and true value, especially as salt is virtually indestructible. When a covenant was made between peoples, and was intended to last indefinitely, it was called a 'covenant of salt'. It was by such a covenant of salt that God gave the kingdom to David and his offspring, making its endurance through Jesus Christ, David's ultimate son, an absolute certainty, as strong as an oath. (2 Chron. 13:5, Ps. 89:27–29.) [36]

But there was another angle to this aspect of the illustration, for too much salt led to sterility, and such a land became an uninhabited wilderness. (Jer. 17:6.) When Shechem was captured and destroyed, it was said to have been 'sowed with salt' as a symbol of its irretrievable ruin. (Judges 9:45.)[37]

The second aspect of the use of salt is in its ability to purify. Elisha invited God to heal the waters of Jericho by symbolically throwing in a bowl of salt. (2 Kings 2:19–22.) Salt mixed with sacrifices was thought to purify them in a literal way, and it showed the genuine sincerity of the person making the offering. (Lev. 2:13.)[38]

Its third application is the most important source of illustrations – its value for seasoning food. When the cook uses it, the right quantity is important, enough to enhance the flavour of the food itself. The apostle Paul used this idea when he counselled, 'Let your speech at all times be gracious [pleasant and winsome], seasoned [as it were] with salt.' (Col. 4:6a Amplified.)

Both the seasoning and the preservative aspects come together in Jesus' words, found only in Mark. 'Have the salt of friendship among yourselves, and live in peace with one another.' (Mark 9:50b TEV, cp. v. 33, 34.) In other words, do everything possible to keep a relationship well flavoured and tasty, for this is going to help it to endure.

This is where a problem about salt emerges. It has been well said that salt 'flavours everything, but nothing can flavour salt.' [39] No wonder Jesus raised the question in the first part of the above verse, 'Salt is good, but if it loses its saltness, how can you make it salty again?' (Mark 9:50a TEV.)

It is interesting to note that common salt cannot lose its chemical qualities, but this is not true of impure natural rock salt. It can become a spent force, fit only to be thrown outside and trampled underfoot, as for example, on the steps of the Temple in wet weather.[40] It is not even of use for manure, where, when it has its saltness, it acts to hasten the decomposition process. (Luke 14:34, 35.)[41]

Bringing together all these facets in the illustration helps us to understand the great declaration of Jesus to his disciples, 'You are like salt for all mankind'. (Matt. 5:13a TEV.) What did Jesus' mean?

With the teaching Jesus gave to his disciples, they became filled with understanding about God's Kingdom, and they had a message of hope to give to all men. They were to go to all nations to season and purify by their witness, giving flavour to the lives of those who felt bitter and disillusioned with their lot in life.[42] Their discussionss would be gracious and upbuilding, bringing a sense of peace, and where that already existed, helping to preserve and extend it.

They were to act individually as if they were salt cellars, sprinkling a little salt here, dispensing a little there. Though the flavour of salt is a little sharp, suggesting an energizing activity, they were not to act like pepper pots, stirring up a hotbed of strife, causing violent reactions reminiscent of sneezing and disturbance. They would instead bring healing and harmony wherever they went, yet they must give out, and give of their best, without ever becoming a spent force themselves. Those who become insipid, or have lost their salty flavour, often becoming apostates, were fit for nothing but to be cast outside.[43]

14. The Scandal of Stumbling—Obstacles in our Path.

Our English word 'scandal' conceals a fine illustration which throws light on some of Jesus' statements to his disciples. The Greek word 'skandalon' referred to a snare, a stumbling block, and is linked with the spring of a trap, and the stick upon which the bait is placed, which snapped it shut when it was made to spring up. So our modern word suggests that which springs up quickly and causes offence.[44]

Although John the Baptist had identified Jesus without hesitation as the 'Lamb of God,' yet when he was in prison later he had some doubts, and sent an inquiry to ask Jesus if he was the One to come, or would there be someone else? Jesus recommended his disciples to tell John all they had seen and heard, and that would be testimony enough. Then he added in conclusion, 'And happy is the man who finds no cause for stumbling over me.' (Luke 7:17–23 C. B. Williams, Matt. 11:6.)

Some translations leave one in doubt as to who might be the cause for the offence taken, Jesus, or the individual interacting with him. But Jesus was clearly saying that his auditors found a cause themselves. A. T. Robertson comments on this verse, 'Tripped by trap set for one. The devil had set this trap for John.' (Luke Translation notes p173.) Probably John was brooding in prison, even wondering why Jesus didn't seem to be doing anything to have him set free. So his thoughts were turned in on his own plight, and this is precisely when a person can 'take' offense, or allow himself to be 'put off'.[45]

When Jesus spoke in his home synagogue of Nazareth, many of his listeners were amazed and recognized him as a 'local boy', the carpenter's son, whose family was well known to them. This immediately 'put them off', for they could not believe that he had acquired such wisdom. 'And so they found a cause for stumbling over him.' (Matt. 13:57 C. B. Williams.) The evidence was clearly before them, so the cause of stumbling was within themselves.

At the other end of his period of ministry, the time of Jesus' death also caused his disciples to stumble, trapped by their own fear, and the likely consequences that might befall them because they were involved. So they were scattered as the prophecy of Zechariah had foretold. (Matt. 26:31–35, Zech. 13:7.)

But it is an earlier incident, when Jesus first alerted his disciples to his ultimate fate, that shows us something much more serious is involved than a simple matter of taking offence. When Peter urged Jesus to be kind to himself, for this would not happen, Jesus responded vehemently, 'Get out of my way, you Satan! You are a hindrance to me, for this view of yours is not from God but from men.' (Matt. 16: 23, C. B. Williams.)

He then made it clear that life was at stake. The disciple must disown himself and his present life if he would gain everlasting life from God. So stumbling another person would truly be doing Satan's work, and could bring death upon him, just as surely as an animal caught in a trap would lose its life. (Matt. 16:24–27.) Paul endorsed the serious nature of being a cause for stumbling another, so that he lost faith and fell away. (1 Cor. 8:13, Rom. 16:17, 18.)[46]

It is often our own attitude to a matter that is important. Can we convert a problem into something helpful, so that the old saying becomes true, 'the stepping stones by which we rise are the obstacles in our path.' John very simply puts his finger on a never-failing solution, 'Whoever continues to love his brother is always in the light, and he is no hindrance to others.' (1 John 2:10 C. B. Williams.)

15. Successful Ploughing—
Avoiding Obstacles in our Path.

When Jesus asked certain men to become his followers, they all had reasons why they could not answer the call. When we look at those 'reasons' in the closing verses of Luke chapter nine, they were really excuses, for we cannot imagine that Jesus was not prepared to wait for an hour or so while a man said farewell to his family. (cp. 1 Kings 19:19–21.) It is with this background that we can think about his illustration in the final verse in reply to that last excuse: 'No one who sets his hand to the plough and then keeps looking back is fit for the Kingdom of God.' (Luke 9:62 NEB, also C. B. Williams.)

Most translations fail to bring out the point of the present participle here.[47] It is not a question of looking back just once, but continuing to do so, failing to have a real desire to go forward spiritually without hankering after material things, and so failing to avoid the obstacles in our path.

We may think of ploughing in our own country, and consider that it is quite easy for a skilled ploughman to keep his tractor straight, even if his mind wanders from time to time. But Jesus was talking of ploughing by hand in Palestine, where circumstances were very different. The ploughman held in his right hand a small light plough, and with his ox-goad in his left, spurred on the plodding ox or donkey, turning over one single shallow furrow at a time. But as Leslie Farmer observed for himself, 'The ground is covered with stones, so they must keep the "hand to the plough" and not "look back", in order to navigate the furrow round the stones, lest a jagged flint splits the implement.'[48]

So the context shows that Jesus had such stony obstacles in mind when he gave this illustration. Just as it is hard work to plough even a shallow furrow by hand, watching all the time for those stones, so it is often not easy to be a Christian. There will be problems and difficulties, and unless we are closely watching our path, we may not reach our goal. No wonder Paul added, 'forgetting what is behind me, and reaching out for that which lies ahead, I press toward the goal.' (Phil 3:13, 14 NEB.) Yet for all the difficulty of the way, the ploughman still ploughs in hope, for he knows that by his hard work, he will share in the resulting bountiful harvest. (1 Cor. 9:10.)

16. Tied to a Millstone—
Penalty for Stumbling Another.

The grinding mill was a familiar object around many homes in the ancient Middle East. Early in the morning the women got up to grind the flour for the day. (Prov. 31:15.) Bread was freshly baked each day, for in the country at least it was usually unleavened, and because of the heat would not keep until the next day. Usually two women shared the work, for it was hard. They faced each other across the mill, adroitly alternating the turning of the handle of the upper millstone, while the other one scooped up the flour as it fell from the lower, fixed stone. (Matt. 24:41.)[49]

The hand mill itself was formed of two circular stones, measuring about 18–24 inches in diameter. The lower fixed one was convex at the top (it sloped down from the centre to the outer rim). The upper millstone was concave (its lower side hollowed to fit over the sloping lower one). A hole in the centre allowed the grain to be poured in, while a stick formed a handle in a smaller hole to one side for turning the stone.[50]

The Greeks, Syrians and Romans meted out a severe punishment by drowning in the sea with a millstone tied round the neck to weight down the offender. Originally this was any kind of heavy rock, but because millstones were already perforated with holes, it was easier to tie these on, and so it became a proverbial saying. As far back as the time of Abimelech the millstone was used for a violent purpose, a woman throwing one down on his head to kill him. (Judges 9:50–55, 2 Sam. 11:21.)[51]

To many persons it seems that Jesus was very hard and cruel when he said about young children, 'But whoever stumbles one of these little ones who put faith in me, it is more beneficial for him to have hung around his neck a millstone such as is turned by an ass and to be sunk in the wide open sea.' (Matt. 18:6 NWT, Concordant Version, Weymouth ftn., Darby ftn., Mark 9: 42) Unfortunately, many translations fail to properly render the Greek here ('mulos onikos'), usually simply saying, 'large millstone' or 'upper millstone. ' This could refer to the hand mill already discussed, but Jesus was talking about the much larger type, so heavy that it usually required an ass to turn it.

This upper millstone was four or five feet in diameter, and it was set edge on into the very large, fixed, lower millstone which had a wooden centre post. The upper stone was fitted to a pivot from this centre post, with a long wooden horizontal bar extending from it to beyond the opposite rim, where the ass was fastened. As the animal pulled the bar round slowly, the upper stone rolled round the circular trough, crushing the grain in it. Because it reminded some of a chariot, it was called in Hebrew 'rekeb' (chariot), or by the Arabs 'rekkab' (rider).[52]

Why did Jesus refer to this huge millstone when it would be virtually impossible and unnecessary for one of these to be used to drown someone. His illustration was in fact deliberately exaggerated in a form of hyperbole, designed to show how much he condemned and detested anyone guilty of stumbling his little ones. They deserved the sternest punishment. In a parallel illustration such persons would be gathered by the angels and thrown into a fiery furnace to be destroyed. (Matt. 13:41, 42.)

In the final Revelation to John, a strong angel is pictured lifting up a great (Greek 'megas') millstone and pitching it into the sea and adding, 'Thus with a swift pitch will Babylon the great city be hurled down, and she will never be found again.' (Rev. 18:21 NWT.) The illustration is true to the original punishment, but here it is no individual involved, but a great wicked organization that required indeed a very large millstone in symbol to ensure that it was drowned or destroyed for all time. Its wicked course of action in stumbling earth's inhabitants merited the severest punishment, and further justifies Jesus' use of this vivid illustration to show how he regarded the stumbling of others as something so abhorrent and reprehensible.

17. We Reap What we Sow—
Sowing in the Field of the Spirit.

'Have you ever seen a fig tree with a crop of olives, or seen figs growing on a vine?' (James 3:12 Phillips rev.) Why did the disciple James ask this question? He was using the laws in natural creation to urge the right use of the tongue, that it should not be both blessing and cursing people.

The natural law that plants and animals reproduce according to their kind was stated seven times in the first chapter of Genesis. It was this principle that the apostle Paul stressed when he used it in an interesting illustration – 'A man's harvest in life will depend entirely on what he sows.' (Gal. 6:7 Phillips.)

But seed that is sown must involve the field in which it is broadcast. Although Paul clearly extends his illustration to include this, not all translations really make the reader aware of it. The two fields stand in contrast to one another – the field of spiritual things, and the field of the flesh, of materialism. 'If a man sows in the field of his own lower nature, from that lower nature he will reap a life that is doomed to decay. But if he sows in the field of the Spirit, the harvest will be eternal life.' (Gal. 6:8 Barclay.)

By extension of the principle, what the mind and the heart are fixed upon will determine the results. The natural tendency for humans is to slide down to the level of their now imperfect nature, rather than to lift themselves up to the higher plane of spiritual things, purer thought, holy ways, the qualities displayed by God and Christ.

Yet that goal could be reached by so many. Jesus saw the crowds of ordinary persons who were 'bewildered and dejected, like sheep who had no shepherd. "There is a rich harvest," he said to the disciples, "but there are few workers".' (Matt. 9:36, 37 Barclay, John 4:35, 36.) They were urged to pray for more workers in the field, who could teach these people to sow the right seed in the right field, to reap everlasting life. Their teaching needed to nurture the young plants, always remembering the Bible principle, 'I planted the seed; Apollos watered it; but it was God who made the plant grow. It is not the man who plants the seed, or the man who waters it, who is really important; the really important person is God who makes it grow.' (1 Cor. 3:6, 7 Barclay.)

That sowing of the seed also needed to be plentiful, for there will be problems along the way that will threaten our remaining in the spiritual field. Although talking about money contributions, Paul again states a principle of wider application, 'Poor sowing means a poor harvest, and generous sowing means a generous harvest.' (2 Cor. 9:6 Phillips.) It was the practice of the sower in the first century to scatter the seed broadcast, knowing that some would fall on stony ground, and some would be taken by the birds. (cp. Matt. 13:3–8.) He also sowed his seed in often adverse conditions, for if it was not sown, he knew there would never be a harvest at all.[53]

We will not spend the minimum time sowing spiritual things, perhaps thinking that we could safely do a little sowing in both fields, throwing some seed each way while we sit on the fence between. That is a dangerous situation for a Christian! He is likely finally to follow the line of least resistance, and this is where Paul's further counsel fits so well.

'We must never get tired of doing the fine things, for when the right time comes, we will reap the harvest of it if we never relax our efforts.' (Gal. 6:9 Barclay, 2 Thess. 3:13.) Continuing in the right course year in and year out is in itself a test of true Christianity, for the field of the world's temptation is always beckoning attractively urging us to sow seeds there. Our natural fleshly desires incline us that way, so we have need of such encouragement to remain firm for right and righteousness. As Ronald Ward puts it, we must not 'crumple up'.[54]

To aid us in the fight we are reminded of our great example, Christ Jesus himself, 'Consider him who endured such opposition from sinful men, so that you will not grow weary and lose heart.' (Heb. 12:3 NIV.) While we may feel that Jesus was perfect, and so could better resist the opposition, yet the Christian is helped by the holy spirit, and the power of God. 'He is giving to the tired one power, and to the one without dynamic energy he makes full might abound.' (Isa. 40:29 NWT.)

18. Cleaning the Threshing Floor—
A Time of Judgment.

A threshing floor was a familiar sight in Palestine in the first century, as it has continued to be in certain places into our own century. On a hillside that catches the wind a level area of earth is beaten and rammed hard and smooth. When the grain was harvested it was brought here in sheaves ready for threshing. This process could be carried out by hand with flails, but it was more likely to be done by oxen treading the grain, (to thresh meant to trample), or drawing a kind of sledge with sharp stones or flints fixed into wooden slats. These not only separate the grain, but also cut up the straw and stubble. (Micah 4:12, 13.)[55]

It is at this point that the metaphor used by John the Baptizer applies. He said that Jesus would be mightier than he was, and then prophesied, 'He will baptize you with the Holy Spirit and fire. He has the winnowing shovel in His hand and will clean up his threshing floor. His wheat He'll gather into His barn, but the chaff He'll burn in a fire that can't be put out.' (Matt. 3: 11b, 12. Beck.)

Many translations speak here of a 'winnowing fan'. Leslie Farmer thought it meant a 'sort of Japanese paper affair'. But he discovered that it was 'a pole as long as a broom-handle with five or six flat wooden prongs at the end. Wheat and chaff are thrown into the air by means of this big rake, and the wind blows the chaff away.' The heavier grain falls back to the floor as the evening wind carries the chaff and straw away to the side of the floor. Then the winnowing shovel is used on the smaller remainder, the labourer taking care to stand in a position where the wind will blow the chaff away from him, and not all over him. So gradually the floor is cleaned, and finally the grain can be heaped up ready for final sieving and sifting before being stored away. (cp. Luke 22:31.) Any black darnel grains are also removed, for they can cause sickness and illness.[56]

Some of the chaff would be used for people's home fires, and the better straw for the animals, but the residue would be set alight, and the Greek term here is 'fire so fierce that nothing can quench it before it has done its work'.[57] What did John's illustration foretell?

Simply the division of people at the time of the threshing floor judgment. The separation would permit the good grain to be gathered, and God's holy spirit to be poured out upon them, but the baptism of fire would destroy the wicked, useless chaff and stubble, true to the illustration. (Ps. 1:4, Mal. 4:1.) It thus finds a parallel with the parable of the harvest where the angels collect the weeds at the end, and burn them up. (Matt. 13:30, 39–42.)

19. To Prune, Cut Short—The Wicked Destroyed.

The gardener is very familiar with the idea of pruning his trees and shrubs, and his purpose is twofold. First, the action curtails the bad or unwanted growth, and it also encourages the part remaining to throw out new shoots for the betterment of the tree. The Greek verb 'kolazō' conveys this idea of pruning as in trees, to check, curtail or restrain the growth, to keep in bounds, and so later to punish.[57]

When the apostles were upsetting the religious leaders in Jerusalem with their teaching about Christ, they were called before the Sanhedrin, and warned not to spread their message among the people, not even to speak anymore about the matter. The context makes it clear that the aim was to curtail or restrain the apostles, but they in turn objected, saying they could not agree to this request, and must speak about what they had seen and heard. So the Sanhedrin, 'after further threatening them, dismissed them; finding no means whereby they might check (Greek 'kolazō') them because of the people . . .' (Acts 4:15–21 Sadler.) The general idea of punishment, found in many translations, does not fit the context so well here, although some kind of punishment might have been contemplated, but its purpose would have been to stop or curtail their actions.

Quite a different situation is described by John when he talks about the removal of fear by means of love, 'because fear exercises a restraint'. (1 John 4:18 Tomanek.) Love is something very positive, but fear stops people acting in a positive way, and so it becomes a restraining influence upon them. Again the idea of punishment in the sense usually understood does not fit well here, for Robert Law points out that this word ('kolasis'), 'cannot be translated by "torment" (AV), or any word that expresses merely a painful feeling.' So any punishment involved is either retributive or disciplinary.[58]

The use of this illustrative word comes through best in Jesus' parable of the sheep and the goats. Just what is the everlasting or eternal punishment of the goats? It is not torment, as already noted above, but rather this 'punishment is designed to cut off what is bad or disorderly.'[59] 'And these shall go away into age-lasting cutting-off and the just into agelasting life.' (Matt. 25:46 Tomanek.) Trench also rules out any thought of the word carrying the idea of betterment through punishment, so that perhaps the tree or person might throw out some new shoots, and he cites Josephus where the clear thought was punishment with death – a cutting off. (Ant. Book 15, ch.2. (2) 16.)[60] Peter's use of the word also bears this out (2 Peter 2:9), for he describes the same situation that Paul explains in still plainer terms. (2 Thess. 1:9.)

So Jesus, by using this vivid word, was merely showing that the opposite of life is death, or a being cut-off from life. Using the symbol of the tree of life, first found in Genesis (2:9), and which reappears in the last book Revelation (2:7, 22:2), it is appropriate that the wicked are therefore pruned from that tree, they are cut off from its life.

20. Spring Water—Life-Giving Truth.

Water was a precious commodity in Palestine in ancient times, mainly due to the restriction of the main rainfall to October and March, the 'early' and the 'latter' rains. (James 5:7.) Then it often came in heavy downpours, causing flash floods and filling the wadis with swift torrents that quickly drained away. To conserve as much of this water as possible, wells and cisterns were dug, and their remains can still be seen in many places. (Gen. 26:15–22.)[61]

To such a well Jesus came to rest when he was tired. It was the famous Jacob's well in Samaria, dug by the patriarch to ensure his water supply was not dependent on his Canaanite neighbours amongst whom he lived. (Gen. 33:18–20.) Jesus asked a Samaritan woman if she would give him a drink, and she expressed surprise, for Jews would not normally even talk to Samaritans. Jesus replied that he could give her 'living' water if she had but asked him.

She did not realize that Jesus was using water as an illustration, in symbol. So he explained a little more. With 'living' water she would not be thirsty again. 'The water I give will become a spring of water flowing inside him. It will give him eternal life.' (John 4:14 New Century Version.) Still she didn't fully understand, thinking she would no longer need to come and fetch literal water from the well.

Can we fully grasp Jesus' illustration? What did he mean by 'living water'? Those familiar with the Hebrew Scriptures or the Greek Septuagint Version of it, would immediately link the phrase with Jeremiah's comments. He identified Jehovah God as the source of living water, yet the nation of Israel had deserted God, and tried to hew out their own cisterns, but they soon became broken and then held no water. (Jer. 2:13, 17:13.)

What thirst would be slaked by this 'living water'? Amos had prophesied of a thirst for the words of God. The Jews regarded the written law or Torah as answering metaphorically to water. 'As water is priceless, so is the Torah priceless. As water brings life to the world, so the Torah brings life to the world.'[62] But Jesus also tied in the actions of God's holy spirit, which made that water of God's truth life-giving. (John 7:37–39, 3:5.) So the promised helper he would send after leaving his disciples is described as 'the Spirit of truth'. 'But when the Spirit of truth comes he will lead you into all truth.' (John 16:13 NCV.)

The illustration continues true to the distinction between well or cistern rainwater and the distinctive spring of pure water that represents the 'living water'. Cistern water is collected and stored, and so becomes static, and often stagnant. Spring water is living, always on the move, flowing, fresh and vibrant, a true picture of its life-giving property. For the traveller in ancient Israel to find a spring of water dried up in the hot dry season was 'almost a tragic experience'.[63]

In type this is shown as the stream that issues from beneath the threshold of Ezekiel's visionary Temple, and flows out towards the Dead Sea, getting deeper all the time. When it reaches the Dead Sea it brings life to everything. 'Wherever the river flows, all living creatures teeming in it will live. Fish will be very plentiful, for wherever the water goes it brings health, and life teems wherever the river flows.' (Ezek. 47:1–12 NJB.)

One of the unusual results of this life-giving river are the fruit trees on both banks, bearing 'new fruit every month'. (Ezek. 47:12 NJB.) This same picture is repeated in John's vision (Rev. 22:1, 2), and in other places he speaks of the Lamb guiding God's people to 'springs of water that give life,' and giving 'free water from the spring of the water of life to anyone who is thirsty.' In the final verses of Revelation it is the servants of God under Christ Jesus and the holy spirit who extend the invitation to all earth's inhabitants to 'Come' and 'have the water of life as a free gift'. (Rev. 7: 17, 21:6, 22:17 NCV.)

Notes and References: (see Bibliography for short titles)

1. Robertson, A. T. A *Translation of Luke's Gospel*, 1923, N. Y. Doran, 152; Wordsworth, C. *Greek Testament*, Vol. 1, 183, 'clearing away the obstructions in His way, as a pioneer clearing away timber etc., to make roads.' Ayers, D. M. English Words 217, for alternative Latin origin, but still a trail-blazer; Marshall, A. Ed. *GSM* June 1929, 95.

2. Corswant, W. *Dictionary of Life*, 23, 25, 307; 1 Sam. 14:14.

3. Black, M. *An Aramaic Approach to the Gospels and Acts*, 1967, 3rd ed. Oxford. Clarendon P. 183, 'The prevailing sounds are all soft, smooth and pleasant.' Guillemard, W. H. *Hebraisms*, 24; Abrahams, I. *Studies in Pharisaism*, 2nd series, 4–14, an interesting study on 'The Yoke'. Waugh, R. M. L. *Greek Testament*, 72–74; Maher, M, 'Take my Yoke Upon You,' (Matt. 11:29),' *NTStud*. Vol. 22 (1975), 97–103. Even the yoke of the Law was accepted by Israel willingly because it placed them under 'the direct rule of God,' but it later became burdensome; Bruce, A. B. 'The Easy Yoke,' *Expositor*, 5th Series, Vol. 8 (1898), 102–118.

4. Farrar, F. W. *The Life of Christ*, 1907, Cassell, 578–581. A fine description of Peter's situation.

5. Robertson, A. T. *Word Pictures*, Vol. II, 284; Wordsworth, C. *Greek Testament*, Vol. I, 250; NJB footnote, Luke 23:31; Rihbany, A, M, *Syrian Christ*, 278.

6. Farrar, F. W. op. cit. (4), 487, For a tree in spring to show no old or new figs means it is barren; Geikie, C. *The Holy Land*, 160, 'the earliest figs, it appears, are called 'dafour,' which means 'ripe before the time,' and are ready at Gaza about the end of March, before the leaves are well out.'; Derrett, J. D. M. 'Figtrees in the N. T,' in *The Heythrop Jnl*, Vol. 14 (1973), 249–265. 'the figtree has, normally, a long season, and is a very satisfactory tree generally.' (253).

7. Swete, H. B. *The Gospel according to St. Mark*, Greek Text with Intro. Notes. 1913, 3rd ed. Macmillan.

314; Jeremias, J. *Parables*, 120, the rising sap being especially clear to see; Gower, R, *New Manners and Customs*, 119.

8. McNeile, A. H. *The Gospel according to St. Matthew*, Greek Text, with Intro. Notes, 1928, Macmillan, 354; Carr, A, *St. Matthew*, 1901, (CGT), 272.

9. Some commentators have tried by means of various literary devices, to limit the application of certain verses to the first century, see Smith, D. *The Days of his Flesh*, 8th ed. rev. 1910, Hodder, xxix/xxx; Beasley-Murray, G. R. *Jesus and the Future,* 1954, Macmillan, esp. chapters 4 and 5.

10. Morton, H. V. *Steps of the Master*, 232; Tristram, H. B. *Natural History*, 462–465; Farmer, L, *Holy City*, 254; Rops, D. *Daily Life*, 20, 21; Morgan, G. C. *Parables* 18.

11. Van-Lennep, H. J. *Bible Lands*, Vol. 1, 166; Neil, J. *Strange Figures*, 22; Irwin, M, E, 'Considering the Lilies,' *McMaster Jnl of Theology*, Hamilton, Ont. Vol. 2/2 (1991), 20–28.

12. Lightfoot, J. B. *Notes on Epistles*, 98; Milligan, G. *St. Paul's Epistles to the Thessalonians*, Greek Text, Intro and Notes, 1908, Macmillan, 86.

13. Miller, M. S. & J. L. *Bible Life*, 203.

14. Shewell-Cooper, W. E. *Plants and Fruits of the Bible*, 1962, Darton, Longman & Todd, 121; Marshall, A. Ed. *GSM*, Sept. 1929, 107.

15. Deissmann, G. A. *Bible Studies*, 220; Robertson, A. T. *Word Pictures*, Vol. 4, 573.

16. Guillemard, W. H. *Hebraisms*, 40.

17. Lightfoot, J. B. *Notes on Epistles*, 98; Milligan, G. op. cit. (12), 86; Daddow, W. B. *Buried Pictures*, 43–47.

18. Lightfoot, J. B. *Notes on Epistles*,

48; Nygren, A. *Agapé and Eros*, Part 1, 1932, SPCK, 53.

19. Ollivier, M. J. *The Parables of Our Lord*, 1943, Clonskeagh, Browne & Nolan, 59.

20. McNeile, A. H. *Matthew* op. cit. (8), 203; Rihbany, A, M, *Syrian Christ*, 114–117.

21. Van-Lennep, H. J. *Bible Lands*, 125; Oesterley, W. O. E. *Parables*, 81 on who keeps things found; Danby, H. *The Mishnah*, 348/9, Baba Metzia 2. 1. 'Whatsoever has in it aught unusual must be proclaimed.'; Derrett, J. D. M. 'Law in the N. T: The Treasure in the Field,' *ZeitNTWiss*. Vol. 54 (1963), 31–42, an excellent discussion; Bishop, E. F. F. *Jesus of Palestine*, 129.

22. Sharpe, S. *Critical Notes on the Authorised English Version of the N. T.* 1867, 2nd ed. J. R. Smith, 12, low price compared with great value; Burn, J. H. 'The Pearl of Great Price,' *Expositor*, 2nd Series, Vol. 8 (1884), 468–472.

23. Jeremias, J. *Parables*, 199, 200 with examples of actual pearls of extreme rarity and value; Pliny, *Hist. Nat*, IX 15, qualities of pearls, cited in Ollivier, M. J. op. cit. (19), 65, 66. 'The merchants are not allowed to open the shells before buying them. He is a lucky purchaser whose lot contains pearls without a flaw.' Merchants in Palestine would in any case not have had access to the most sought-after pearl-oysters, such as those from the Indian ocean; Bishop, E. F. F. *Jesus of Palestine*, 130 mentions the Persian Gulf pearl fisheries; Marshall, A. Ed. *GSM* May 1928, 43; Burrows, E, 'Notes on the Pearl in Biblical Literature,' *JTS*, Vol. 42 (1941), 53–64, Hebrew references suggest use of pearls rather than 'corals. '

24. Robertson, A. T. *Word Pictures*

Vol. 4. 531; Ward, R. A. *Royal Sacrament*, 40.

25. Linnemann, E. *Parables of Jesus*, 1966, SPCK, 100, It is so unique that, 'The man who does not seize the opportunity is a fool, who if it rained porridge would still not have a spoon.'

26. Westcott, B. F. *The Gospel according to St. John*, Introduction and Notes, 1894, Murray, 51; On the comparison of the action of the wind with persons directed by the spirit, see B. Buetubela, 'John 3:8, l'Esprit-Saint ou le Vent naturel?' *Revue Africaine de Theologie.* (Kinshasa, Zaire), Vol. 4 (1980) 7/55–64; Morgan, G. C. *Parables*, 238–243. Whilst the spirit is an active force, it exerts or produces power.

27. Ward, R. A. *Hidden Meaning*, 144, 150.

28. Van-Lennep, *Bible Lands*, Vol. 1, 121.

29. Trench, R. C. *Studies in the Gospels*, 1867, Macmillan, 177-180; Dodd, C. H, *The Parables of the Kingdom*, 1936, Nisbet, 117; Jeremias, J. *Parables*, 118; Bruce, F. F. *Hard Sayings*, 40, 41.

30. Trench, R. C. op. cit. (29), 182, 183; Jeremias, J. *Parables*, 104; for an alternative view of verse 39 see Good, R. S. 'Jesus, Protagonist of the Old, in Luke 5: 33–39,' *NovTest.* Vol. 25 (1983), 19–36. Good argues that Jesus sought to repair the old Israel, and that the innovations of the Pharisees were like new wine. But this is to ignore the new Israel of God, which Jesus was founding and getting his disciples to savour.

31. This may seem a harsh judgment to some. But the attitude to trees in Bible lands and times was very different to ours. Fuel was needed continuously, and was primarily wood, so if trees did not produce useful fruits, with few exceptions, they were cut down; Van-Lennep, H. J. *Bible Lands*, Vol. I, 27.

32. Conybeare, W. J. *Epistles*, 109, footnote. The metaphor is used both ways – 'bearing fruit' or 'gathering fruit.'

33. Bengel, J. A. *Gnomon*, Vol. 4, 51 footnote, 'Singular, not plural . . . the fruit of the Spirit constitutes an entire whole;' Howson, J. S. *Metaphors*, 103–108; Waugh, R. M. L. *Greek Testament*, 95.

34. Kittel, G, Ed. *TDNT*, Vol. 1, 228.

35. Smith, D, *The Days of His Flesh*, op. cit. (9), 159.

36. cp. Gadsby, J. *Wanderings*, Vol. 2, 360 on Bedouin use of salt to establish truth.

37. Unger, M. F. *Unger's Bible Dictionary*, 1957, Chicago, Moody, 956; see Amplified Bible ftn. to Judges 9:45 on why Abimelech's aim was thwarted.

38. Gadsby, J. *Wanderings*, Vol. 2, 361.

39. Lagrange, Pere M-J. *The Gospel of Jesus Christ*, 1947, Burns Oates, Pt I, 283.

40. Jeremias, J. *Parables*, 168, 169; Black, M. op. cit. (3) 166, 167; Wilson, C. A. *Gospels*, 71; Kittel, G. *TDNT*, Vol. 4. 837; Hutton, W. R. 'The Salt Sections,' *ET*, Vol. 58 (1946/47), 166-168; Bruce, F. F. *Hard Sayings*, 40, 41; Bishop, E. F. F. *Jesus of Palestine*, 164/5; Savage, H. E. *The Gospel*, 77–79.

41. Abrahams, I. *Studies in Pharisaism*, 2nd series, 183 as proverbial and in the Talmud; Mackay, A. I. *Farming and Gardening in the Bible*, 1970, Old Tappan, NJ. F. H. Revell, 213; Mee, A. J. 'Comment,' 476/7, Morrison, J. H. 'Comment,' 525, *ET.* Vol. 46 (1934/35).

42. Montefiore, C. G. *Synoptic Gospels*, Vol. 2, 45; Oesterley, W. O. E. *Parables*, 212/3; Wood, W, S. 'The Salt

of the Earth,' *JTS*, Vol. 25 (1924/25), 167–172; Nauck, W, 'Salt as a Metaphor in Instructions for Discipleship,' *StudTheol*. Vol. 6 (1952), 165–178.

43. At best, such a person becomes tasteless, fatuous, a fool, since the Greek word used in Matt. 5:13b is mōrainō, linked with the adjective mōros, from which is drawn our English word moron. Guillemard, W. H. *Hebraisms*, 8; Smith, D. *Life and Letters*, 565 ftn; Bruce, F. F. *Hard Sayings*, 38, 39; LaVerdiere, E, 'Salted With Fire,' *Emmanuel* (New York), Vol. 97 (1991), 394–400.

44. Skeat, W. W. *Etymological Dictionary*, 538; Barclay, W, *N. T. Words*, 255–258; Moulton, H. K. *Challenge*, 208; Waugh, R. M. L. *Greek Testament* 51.

45. Knox, R. A. *On Englishing the Bible*, 1949, Burns Oates, 34-40, an excellent discussion of skandalon; Mitton, C. L. 'Stumbling-block Characteristics in Jesus,' *ET*, Vol. 82, (1971), 168–172, Mitton suggests that the Greek word was more colloquial than literary, and that Jesus used it to warn his disciples that some things would be difficult to 'take' or 'stomach. '

46. Turner, N. *Christian Words*, 294–297, another excellent discussion.

47. Nineham, D. Ed. *The New English Bible Reviewed*, 1965, Epworth, 82.

48. Farmer, L. *Holy City*, 36; Jeremias, J. *Parables*, 195, 'At the same time he must continually look between the hind-quarters of the oxen, keeping the furrow in sight. This primitive kind of plough needs dexterity and concentrated attention.' Bruce, F. F. *Hard Sayings*, 164–5. Blair, H. J. 'Putting one's Hand to the Plough,' *ET*, Vol. 79 (1968), 342/3, where comparison is made with Elisha's action in 1 Kings 19:21, of burning a yoke of oxen with his plough, to signify a complete break with the past as he set out to follow Elijah. Jesus also expected his followers to entirely break with the past, even 'burning their boats. ' Rihbany, A. M. *Syrian Christ*, 203–204; Leser, P, 'No Man, Having Put his Hand to the Plow,' in Black, M & Smalley, W. A. Ed. *On Language, Culture and Religion: In Honor of Eugene A Nida*, 1974, Paris, Mouton, 241–258. He distinguishes the lighter ard from the plow, and the former would have been used in ancient Israel, although the ard is not known in the English language; Wright, G. E. 'The Last Thousand Years Before Christ,' *NatGeogM*, Vol. 118 (Dec, 1960), 828/9, showing two pictures of ploughing, with a goad in the left hand, and plough held in the right.

49. Gadsby, J. *Wanderings*, Vol. 1, 254; Rihbany, A. M. *Syrian Christ*, 280–282.

50. Geikie, C. *The Holy Land*, 155; Robinson, E. *Biblical Researches*, Vol. 1, 485.

51. Lightfoot, J. *Horae Hebraicae*, Vol. 3, 177, re proverbial saying. Because of the buoyancy experienced in the Dead Sea it would be even more necessary to use a very heavy weight.

52. Unger, M. F. op. cit. (37), 731.

53. Corswant, *Dictionary of Life*, 25, points out that the parable is speaking of the yield per ear, which may be up to 80 to 100 grains, so that each grain sown may yield more than 500 grains on half-a-dozen stems; North, J. L. 'Sowing and Reaping (Galatians 6:7b): More Examples of a Classical Maxim,' *JTS*, Vol. 43 (1992), 523–527.

54. Ward, R. A. *Hidden Meaning*, 119.

55. Gower, R, *New Manners and Customs*, 97; Rops, D, *Daily Life*, 234.

56. Farmer, L, *Holy City*, 44; Gower R, *New Manners and Customs*, 98–100; Bishop, E. F. F. *Jesus of Palestine*, 51, 52.

57. Vincent, M. R. *Word Studies*, Vol. 1, 232; Robertson, A. T. *Word Pictures*, Vol. 3, 53; Abbott-Smith, G, *Greek Lexicon*, 252; Thayer, J. H. *Greek-English Lexicon*, 352, 353.

58. Law, R, *The Tests of Life*, 1914, 3rd ed. Edin. Clark, 290; Rienecker, F & Rogers, C, *Linguistic Key*, 794;

Marshall, A, Ed. *GSM*, Nov. 1934, 503.

59. Kittel, G. Ed. *TDNT*, Vol. 3, 814.

60. Trench, R. C. *Synonyms*, 24. 25; Robertson, A. T. *Word Pictures*, Vol. 1, 201. 202.

61. Rops, D. *Daily Life*, 16, 17; Geikie, C. *The Holy Land*, 24–26.

62. Montefiore, C. G. & Loewe, H. *A Rabbinic Anthology*, 1938, Macmillan, 164.

63. Morgan, G. C. *Parables*, 251–254; Rihbany, A. M. *Syrian Christ*, 176, 177, re the traveller.

Chapter 2

Animals and Birds

1. Serpents and Doves—Wise and Yet Innocent.

It seemed as though Jesus was mixing his similes and his animals, when he gave his disciples this instruction, 'Remember, I am sending you out to be like sheep among wolves; you must be wary, then, as serpents, and yet innocent as doves.' (Matt. 10:16 Knox.) [1] But in Palestine, that land of sheep, these would all be familiar in the daily life of the shepherd. In his care for the sheep, he came to know and understand alike the way of the wolf and the serpent.

The exact qualities to be developed by the disciples have been confused by poor translation. The serpent was not being recommended for subtlety or deception, but rather for its caution and shrewd alertness. The translation 'harmless' (AV) has rested upon a false derivation, and fails to bring out the quality of gentle innocence or purity that Jesus was recommending. The dove was chosen as a symbol of purity because it habitually paired off for life, and showed great fidelity to its mate. For this reason and because of the numerous pigeon population in the country, it was especially suitable as a sacrifice for the poorer families. (Lev. 5:7.)[2]

The apostle Paul echoes the same ideas when closing his letter to the Romans. 'I want you to be wise with reference to what is good, but untainted with reference to what is evil.' (Rom. 16:19 Blackwelder.) Innocence did not, therefore, mean naivity. It suggested that which was unmixed, unblended, unadulterated, like wine without water, and metal without alloy, and if it was like that then it was pure.[3] He puts it more forcefully in his letter to the Philippians, 'so that you may become blameless and pure, unblemished children of God in the midst of a crooked and perverse people.' (Phil. 2:15 Blackwelder.)

The choice of the word 'children' here was deliberate, for Paul paints the same picture when writing to the Corinthians, 'Brothers, do not be like children in your thinking. Where wickedness is concerned be like infants, but in your thinking be mature.' (1 Cor. 14:20 TNT.) They need have no more knowledge of what is bad than an infant, and they certainly did not need to 'experience' those things in order to be able to avoid them. If they developed mature thought, or the vision that God gives, that would guide them, and all they would need to apply that wisdom was a wary alertness, so that, as sheep, they would not fall a prey to the wolves. That is good advice for Christians today.

2. Muzzling and Gagging— Encouraging Right Teaching.

'You shall not muzzle an ox, when it is treading out the corn. Is it [only] for oxen that God cares?' (1 Cor. 9:9 Amplified.) So the apostle Paul quotes the Mosaic law from Deuteronomy 25:4. Walking round and round on the threshing floor trampling the grain, it was viewed as a kindness from God that the oxen could partake of the fruits of the harvest, and not be prevented from doing so by being fitted with a muzzle as happened in some lands.[4]

Why did Paul use this illustration here, when he was talking about the Christian ministry? He explains in verse 11, 'If we have sown [the seed of] spiritual good among you, [is it too] much if we reap from your material benefits?' (1 Cor. 9:11 Amplified.) Yet Paul says he did not use this right, in case it was misunderstood, and hindered the Corinthians' spiritual progress. (1 Cor. 9:12–18.)

Writing later to Timothy, Paul again quotes this illustration, but in a different context, as the previous verse shows. 'Let the elders who are excellent leaders be considered worthy of double honour, especially those who work diligently at preaching and teaching.' (1 Tim. 5:18 Blackwelder.) Whilst some translations place the emphasis upon the aspect of financial reward or pay, Paul would never be among those pressing for 'double pay'.[5] Bearing his own example in mind, it is far more likely that he was recommending the encouragement of such elders, so that they might feel that it was worth all

their endeavours, and they would redouble their efforts in teaching.
(1 Tim. 4:15, 16, 2 Tim. 4:5, Phil. 3:16.)

Jesus Muzzles his Opponents

The same metaphor is used by Jesus in the opposite way, in silencing
or muzzling those who tried to catch him out in his teaching.[6] He
dealt with the Sadducees' question about the woman who had seven
brothers as husband in turn, and explained to them the resurrection
hope. The result was, 'Now when the Pharisees heard that he had
silenced [muzzled] the Sadducees, they gathered together.' (Matt.
22:34 Amplified.)

There was often much competition between the rabbis and the
religious schools. They tried to outwit each other, and purposely laid
traps to bring a teacher down.[7] So now the Pharisees put their heads
together to see if they could come up with a question that would
confound Jesus, and that would bring a double victory, over both
Jesus and the Sadducees. But they were no more successful with
their question on the greatest commandment, for Jesus immediately
responded with another question for them – a real conundrum. Once
again they were muzzled or silenced. 'And no one was able to answer
Him a word, nor from that day did anyone venture or dare to question
him.' (Matt. 22:35–46 Amplified, Matt. 11:25.)

The successful ministry of the Son of God silenced or muzzled
those who tried to impede it, until the time when that ministry had
fulfilled its purpose. Then the ministry of the followers of Jesus took
over, imperfect men trying to copy their perfect model, and so
needing all the help and encouragement that could be given. Nothing
could or should silence or muzzle that ministry, as Gamaliel so
wisely pointed out to his fellow members of the Sanhedrin, 'if it is
of God, you will not be able to stop or overthrow or destroy them,
you might even be found fighting against God.' (Acts 5: 27–42
Amplified.)

3. A Hen that Would Gather her Chicks— Love for Jerusalem and Its Temple.

In the moving song 'Jerusalem' Topol sings these words about the beloved city, found in Psalm 137 verse 5, 'Jerusalem, if I forget thee, may my right hand its cunning lose.' First taken for Israel by King David, the city has gathered associations and memories through the centuries. After the ark of the covenant rested on Mount Moriah, there arose the majestic Temple of Solomon, to which all Israelites came three times a year to worship and praise their God, Jehovah or Yahweh, who put his name there, and established his throne or presence in Jerusalem.

By the time of Jesus the Temple had been enlarged and rebuilt as 'Herod's Temple' and was again magnificent. To the scattered members of the Jewish diaspora, no matter how far away they were, Jerusalem represented to them a sort of spiritual fatherhood. Converts to Judaism were said to come 'under the wings of the Shekinah' or presence of God.[8] The protection given by God was like the wings of a great bird, and his people took refuge under their shadow. (Deut. 32:9–12, Ruth 2:12, Ps. 17:8, 36:7, 57:1, 61:4, 91:4.)

This imagery was further developed and heightened in Psalm 84, one of the grandest Psalms for extolling the glories of the ancient Temple, and the privilege of serving in it, if only as a humble doorman. 'Even the sparrows and swallows are welcome to come and nest among your altars and there have their young, O Lord of heaven's armies, my King and my God! How happy are those who can live in your Temple, singing your praises.' (Ps. 84: 3, 4, Living Bible.)

It may well have been a combination of these ideas that came to Jesus' mind as he reached the stinging conclusion to an already trenchant discourse against the religious leaders of his day. 'O Jerusalem, Jerusalem, the city that kills the prophets, and stones all those God sends to her! How often I have wanted to gather your children together as a hen gathers her chicks beneath her wings, but you wouldn't let me. And now your house is left to you, desolate.' (Matt. 23: 37, 38 Living Bible.) Of all birds, the mother hen is reputed to show the greatest anxiety and love for her offspring, protecting her chicks under the shelter of her wings at any sign of danger.[9] Jesus showed such a great love for those for whom he had come to die, and yet only a tiny remnant was willing to accept him as the Messiah. The majority failed in their hour of test, shouting for him to be put to death, for they wanted Caesar only as king.

That rejection cost the nation of Israel dear! In 70 C.E., they saw their beautiful Temple laid waste and desolate. Never since has it been rebuilt, but a Moslem mosque now occupies the site. Israel again rules the city, but has made it clear it wants no Theocracy restored.[10]

For his part, Jesus fulfilled his prophecy in more ways than in just forecasting the destruction of Jerusalem. On the night before he died he told his apostles that something new was starting, and they were to be its foundation stones. It was the New Jerusalem, a heavenly, spiritual Jerusalem, that would be more glorious than the literal city had ever been. It would be the light for all the nations of the earth, and it would give lasting security and protection to all those willing to look to it. It needed no Temple, for God could be directly worshipped, and his wings would cover all those who run under them for safety. (Rev. 21: 2–4, 22–26.) His rule through his son Christ Jesus would bring peace to all mankind under his Kingdom, for which he had taught his disciples to pray in the Lord's prayer.

4. Throwing Pearls Before Swine— Lack of Appreciation.

Among the many illustrations used by Jesus in the Sermon on the Mount was this proverb, 'Do not give what is holy to dogs, or toss your pearls before swine. They will trample them under foot, at best, and perhaps even tear you to shreds.' (Matt. 7:6, NAB.)

Some scholars take this as an example of chiasmus, a figure of speech where the parallel is drawn by transposing the two final statements. A few translations actually remove the figure to avoid any misunderstanding, 'Do not give what is holy to dogs – they will only turn and attack you. Do not throw your pearls in front of pigs

– they will only trample them underfoot.' (TEV, see also Schon-field.)[11]

Other translations take the response to be that of the swine entirely. Wild boars were once common in the Jordan Valley, and could rend with their tusks.[12] They would certainly not show any appreciation for pearls, and would trample them underfoot so that they would soon be crushed and lost to sight. But the dog could also behave in a wild manner, and was an animal as much despised as the pig in Jewish eyes. (Prov. 26:11, 11:22.)

Some have thought that both animals were simply used by Jesus to depict the heathen and gentiles, and that the words of God were not to be shared with them, but only with those of natural Israel.[13] The entire attitude of Jesus to people of other nations is against this, even though he primarily did direct his disciples to go first to find the lost sheep of Israel. (Matt. 10:5, 6.) But Jesus was certainly referring to sayings and words of wisdom as things that were holy. 'Pearls' were used as an eastern metaphor for precious sayings, and a poetical group of proverbs was called 'a string of pearls' by the Arabs.[14]

The apostle Paul described the class of persons that fitted Jesus' description. They were foolish, God-dishonouring and only interested in the works of the flesh, and showed the very characteristics of the animals to whom Jesus likened them. (Rom. 1: 18–32.)

But this was not all. Peter extended Jesus' illustration and gave it a further twist when he spoke about those persons who had come to know the truth of the Christian way, and had escaped 'the corrupting forces of the world', but then are 'again caught and conquered by them'. The conclusion is worse than if they had remained where they were; 'what happened to them shows that the proverbs are true; "A dog goes back to what it has vomited" and "A pig that has been washed goes back to roll in the mud".' (2 Pet. 2:20–22 TEV.)

Peter's comment is therefore consistent with Jesus' teaching, with a general application to all persons, and not simply the heathen. The illustration also shows there has to be a genuine and permanent change of personality, becoming truly spiritual men, with a continued appreciation for spiritually precious things. If it is only an external change, then natural animal tendencies can soon again manifest themselves, and a person will be in a worse position than before, despising spiritual things like Esau and glad to be back wallowing in mud and mire.

5. Not Kicking Against the Goad— Wisely Avoiding Obstinacy and Rebellion.

The conversion of Saul or Paul was a striking event, a miraculous appearing of Jesus with an even more striking mission. In those few words spoken to him there was also a striking illustration, one that has puzzled many persons. The visionary said to him, 'Saul, Saul, why are you persecuting me? You only hurt yourself by kicking against the goad.' (Acts 26:14 C. H. Rieu.)

This well-known Greek proverb would be familiar to the educated Saul. It referred to the ox-goad, which for many centuries has been used to goad on the oxen ploughing the furrows. On a stout eight to ten-foot pole is fixed at one end a pointed prick to guide on the animals, and at the other is a sharp chisel-like blade used to clean the ploughshare of earth or entangling roots.[15] No wonder such an instrument became a terrifying weapon in the hands of a powerful man. (Judges 3:31.)

The more an ox kicks back against the goad, the more it hurts itself, and is yet unable to remove the persistent irritation. Better by far to submit in obedience to the prodding goad, and so have it applied only occasionally. To kick back is therefore an act of rebellion against the one guiding or directing.[16]

If we think about its application in the case of Saul or Paul, we come to an interesting conclusion. A force within Saul must have been at work to suggest to him that he was taking a most rebellious course. Perhaps the workings of the holy spirit had pricked to his heart, and had shown him that the Christian way was the right one. But he stubbornly refused to accept this, becoming more infuriated against the Christians, stepping up his persecution of them. But this attitude deep within his heart was known to God and Jesus Christ, and this stirring vision put an end to the rebellion once and for all time. Certainly this would explain why Saul was the chosen vessel, because God knew that his heart was right, however much his course of action had appeared to suggest otherwise.

We may see no further use for this illustration, but when we turn to Ecclesiastes 12:11, we find its modern application. 'The words of the wise are like goads, and those of the masters of the assemblies are like fixed stakes, given by the same shepherd.' (C. D. Ginsburg.) The shepherd uses two different ploys to ensure that his methods are effective. With the goad he urges cattle forward, driving them. Do the words of the wise, particularly those of the wisest of all, Jesus Christ, urge us on to gain greater understanding, and to apply such wise admonition to put on the new personality? Or do we show a rebellious attitude, refusing to change our course of life, kicking against the goad?[17]

The fixing of the stakes or pegs will ensure that a shepherd's tent is secure, and that the sheepfold is properly established to keep the sheep safely within. 'Like pegs driven deep' (Eccl. 12:11 JB), the words of the wise can also establish our faith firmly and deeply, so that it can withstand all attack by the enemies of the flock.[18]

In both these ways wisdom is shown. Our faith must not only be firmly rooted, but it needs to continue to advance, because of our imperfect fleshly tendencies, where 'writing books involves endless hard work, and that much study wearies the body'. (Eccl. 12:12 JB.) We need to be goaded to make a greater effort to take to heart all those words of God that will keep us in the narrow way, that straight, single furrow that every Christian needs to take. (Matt. 7:14.)

6. The Camel and the Needle—
The Rich Person's Problem.

Perhaps no illustration is better known than this one, 'a camel could more easily squeeze through the eye of a needle than a rich man get into the kingdom of God.' (Matt. 19:24 Phillips.) Yet it is also a saying that is much misunderstood, partly because of confusion over what the word 'needle' really meant, and partly because it has not always been considered within the total context of Jesus' comments.

Many commentators have tried to explain away the saying by suggesting that the needle was a tiny gate let into the wall, or into a larger gate, and especially used by foot travellers. When the large city gates were closed at sunset, it was still possible for people to enter through this little gate for a further hour or so. The same situation would prevail throughout the Sabbath day, with journeys limited to a little over half a mile beyond the gates. (Neh. 13:19-22, Acts 1:12.)[19] For a camel to get through such a little gate would indeed be a 'squeeze', but it might just be possible, depending upon the size of the camel.

An alternative idea has been suggested for the 'camel' based on the Aramaic word, which can be translated as 'rope. ' (Matt. 19:24 Lamsa.) This suggests that it was a colloquial maritime expression for a ship's towline, which might with difficulty be passed through the eye of a large oriental needle made of ivory, bone or bronze.[20] On the other hand, the Jewish rabbinical proverb sought to make the feat a greater impossibility by substituting 'elephant' for 'camel'.[21]

That Jesus intended the saying to be taken quite literally is made clear by looking at the parallel in Luke's gospel. 'It is easier for a camel to enter and go through the eye of a surgeon's needle (Greek 'belonē') than for a wealthy person to enter the kingdom of God.' (Luke 18:25 Wuest.) The Greek word here is different from the one used by Matthew and Mark, and was the term regularly found in medical writings for the surgeon's needle used in operations. Doctor Luke would be familiar with it, and so chose it on purpose.[22]

If we look again at the context of Jesus' discussion we can soon see that he was using hyperbole, a figure of speech, which by means of exaggeration could emphasize the strength of what was being stated. Why he wanted to convey the idea of an impossible situation is explained when his disciples expressed their great amazement. 'Jesus looked steadily at them and replied, 'Humanly speaking it is impossible; but with God anything is possible'.' (Matt. 19:26 Phillips.)

Jesus twice used the Greek preposition para in this reply, which means 'beside,' or 'by the side of. ' If a person stood by the side of men and looked at it from their level and viewpoint, it was impossible for a wealthy man to be saved, but if he stood by God's side nothing is impossible.[23] This was exactly what the rich man had to do. He must view his life and his riches from God's standpoint, for then he would use them to benefit others, even to the extent of parting with all of them, so that he could devote himself to being a follower of Jesus, helping him in his preaching and teaching work. With this change of heart it now would be also possible for God to save him.

Perhaps we often have a problem which seems impossible of solution. Do we only view it from the human standpoint? Or have we tried to look at it from a more elevated, spiritual position, the way that God would look at it? Perhaps we will find then that the problem has diminished considerably in size, or may even no longer exist. If it is still there, can we seek through prayer to find the solution that God would suggest? There may be many avenues that we could explore which open up possibilities, where before everything seemed impossible.

7. Swallowing a Camel— Ignoring the More Important Matters.

In his forthright exposure of the hypocrisy of the religious leaders of his day, the scribes and Pharisees, Jesus especially noted their tendency to pay great attention to the small things, but to ignore the more important matters, such as justice, mercy and faithfulness. Then he gave a very vivid illustration, which showed he pulled no punches. 'You are blind guides, you who carefully filter a midge out of your drink and then swallow a camel!' (Matt. 23:24 Barclay.)

It was the practice for Jews to filter their wine in particular, because certain tiny insects actually bred in wine, and would not be easy to see. To be certain of removing them all, a filter or strainer was used. This met the Mosaic ordinance which classified these flying insects as unclean, and not to be eaten. (Lev. 11:20, 23, 41, 42.) But Jesus' juxtaposition was not accidental, for while these insects were the smallest, the camel was the largest unclean animal. (Lev. 11:4.)[24] It was, of course, a further example of hyperbole to speak of swallowing or gulping down a camel.

The rules as to what could and what could not be done on a Sabbath or festival, were often most precisely defined. So the Mishnah states, 'Rabbi Eliezer says "On a festival day they may stretch out a filter [over a vessel's mouth] and, on the Sabbath, pour [wine] through it while it is yet stretched out".' (Shabbath 20: 1a Danby.) But the sages differed on a technicality, saying that on a Festival day wine could be poured through only if the filter had already been stretched out, and on a Sabbath day they could only strain wine through a napkin or Egyptian rush basket, because using a filter was classified as sifting work. (Shabbath 20:1b, 2.)

But consider another example from the Mishnah that involved mercy, a far weightier matter that could parallel the camel in Jesus' illustration. 'If a building fell down upon a man and there is doubt whether he is there or not, or whether he is alive or dead, or whether he is a gentile or an Israelite, they may clear away the ruin from above him.' (Yoma 8:7 Danby.) As Robinson points out, 'were there no doubt that the person beneath the ruins were a Gentile, he must be suffered to remain and perish.'[25] How much this reminds us of the parable of the merciful Samaritan, for the man that had been robbed and beaten was ignored by the passing priest, and by the Levite. (Luke 10: 29–37.)

No wonder Jesus said they were blind guides, so blind they couldn't even see a camel!

8. Shepherds and Sheep—Care of the Flock.

It is natural that the pastoral background of many Bible lands should come through in the illustrations used, and none of these more so than that of the shepherd and his sheep. So it causes no surprise to find them mentioned some 700 times in the Bible (including lambs, rams, flocks, sheepfolds etc.), and in two of Jesus' parables, the dividing of the sheep and the goats, and the one lost sheep.[26]

The scope of our consideration here will be to note the areas covered by different aspects of a shepherd's life, for almost everything that can happen to flocks of sheep can apply to those depicted by them – the persons who comprise the flock of God.[27] Much of this pictorial imagery finds its commencement in the (Old Testament) Hebrew Scriptures, and continues into first century Christianity.

God himself is the original shepherd, and Jesus Christ becomes the good or fine shepherd. (Ps. 95:7, 77:20, Isa. 40:11, Jer. 17:16, 23:3, 4, Ezek. 34: 11–16, 23, Mic. 2:12.) They are assisted by many under-shepherds, the patriarchs, the prophets, and later the apostles and elders of the Christian congregation. Their qualities are those of a loving, caring, literal shepherd, who feeds and waters his flock, finding them adequate pasture, and protecting them from marauders and other dangers. (Ps. 23:1–6.) The false shepherds, by contrast, take advantage of the flock, neglecting them, leaving them exposed to wild animals, while they selfishly feed themselves. (Isa. 56:11, Jer. 23:2, Ezek. 34: 1–10.)

First Century Christianity

In building the illustration, Jesus first identified himself as the good or fine shepherd, and the 'door of the sheep'. (John 10:7, 9, 11, 14.) The doorkeeper (John the Baptizer), who has guarded the sheep through the night, as it were, opens the sheepfold to the proper shepherd, and the sheep (God's people), only respond to his voice, which is an actual trait of natural sheep. (John 10: 2–5.)[28] He is distinguished from false shepherds who try to break into the sheepfold and steal the sheep, most of all by his willingness to lay down his life for the sheep, a sacrifice which earned Jesus the additional designation 'the Lamb of God' as foreseen by John the Baptizer. (John 10: 1, 10–15, 1:29, Rev. 7:17, 14:1, 17:14.)

The final point of this section of John is interesting. 'There are other sheep which belong to me, that are not in this sheepfold. I must bring them too; they will listen to my voice, and they will become one flock with one shepherd.' (John 10:16 TEV.) It has been thought that this showed the call of the gentile fold, but a comparison with the parable of the sheep and the goats reveals that these sheep are shown to be responding in the right manner towards Christ's brothers, who quickly came to consist in the first century of both Jews and gentiles, whereas this parable is set much later, when Christ arrives in his glory at the end time. (Matt. 25: 40, 31, 32, Heb. 2:10, 11.)[29]

At other times Jesus referred to this illustration, often just in a word or a phrase, and obviously it was well enough understood by his listeners for them to immediately link the ideas. So when he felt pity for the wandering crowd, he thought of them as 'like shepherd-less sheep, that are mangled and thrown to the ground.' (Matt. 9: 36

Berkeley.) A full grown sheep that has fallen over (or become 'cast down' as it is called), often has great difficulty in getting up again without assistance, and can die if left for a long time. (Compare Ps. 42:11.)[30]

The death of the shepherd, Jesus Christ, would again be a difficult time for his sheep, for he quoted the prophecy that the sheep would be scattered. (Matt. 26:31.) Peter assured Jesus that he would not be stumbled, but he was, even to denying Jesus three times. (Mark 14:27–31.) So Jesus later told Peter three times to feed and care for his sheep. (John 21: 15–17.)

After Jesus' death, his disciples rallied quickly, strengthened by his resurrection appearances. They continued to use the illustration, urging good attention to their task as under-shepherds, caring for the flock and watching for attacks by those who would act like wolves that would 'not spare the flock'. (Acts 20: 28, 29 TEV.) Peter himself referred to the straying sheep returning to their shepherd, and spoke of Jesus as the 'chief' shepherd. Under-shepherds were again reminded how lovingly and tenderly they were to care for the sheep, always leading them from the front by example, as is the practice even today among Middle Eastern shepherds. (1 Peter 2:25, 5:2–4, Heb. 13:20.)[31]

So this is one of the most frequent and valuable of all Bible illustrations, indelibly planted in most of our minds by that superbly worded twenty-third Psalm.[32] Parallels can be drawn from every event in the life of a shepherd and his sheep, and that is why it surfaces time and again in a word here, and a phrase there.

9. Where Eagles Gather— The Far-Sighted Spiritual Eye.

To the ancient patriarch Job a question about the eagle was addressed. 'Does the eagle soar at your command to make her eyrie in the heights? She spends her nights among the crags with a needle of rock as her fortress, from which she watches for prey, fixing it with her far-ranging eye . . . where anyone has been killed, she is there.' (Job 39: 27–30 NJB.)

The eagle's exceptional eyesight has become proverbial – the 'eagle eye'. From a great distance it can search out its food, so Jesus used this illustration when he talked about his 'parousia', or presence. 'When the Son of Man comes, it will be like the lightning that springs up from the east and flashes across to the west. It is where the body lies that the eagles will gather.' (Matt. 24:27, 28 Knox.)[33]

Quite contrary interpretations have been put forward for this verse. Some scholars have seen in the eagle the standard of the Romans bearing an eagle aloft, and their gathering around Jerusalem in 66 and 70 C. E., for its destruction would argue that the Jewish nation had become the dead carcase upon which the Roman eagles would feast. But many commentators reject this idea as not in context, nor does it fit the second presence, when no Roman eagles are involved.[34]

Since Jesus is talking about the nature of his parousia or second presence, and verse 27 has moved from the subject of avoiding the ideas of false prophets to the positive aspect of seeing or perceiving it as in a lightning flash, the final proverbial expression must be linked to that. The parallel passage in Luke 17:20–37 is likewise governed by the question in verse 20, and that linked to it in verse 36/37. True Christians will be like the eagle, having a fine clear spiritual eye, and so swiftly able to perceive the signs that indicate that event, and enjoying the rich spiritual food that goes along with it, even as Daniel had foretold for the end time. (Dan. 12:3.)[35]

10. The Cost of Sparrows— God's Estimate of the Most Insignificant.

Many types of birds known as passerines are found in Israel. Due to the greater variation in temperature, humidity and elevation the spread of species is wider, and the population very numerous. The sparrow is one of the most common birds, and in the Bible is often taken as typical of the entire passerine family. In most periods sparrows were used for food, and often caught for the market by children, either using simple snares or little cages.[36]

Dating from the third century C. E., a tariff of the Emperor Diocletian lists the maximum prices for many commodities, and sparrows are included. They sold for 16 denarii per decade (10 sparrows), and so were cheaper than thrushes and starlings.[37]

If a person could not afford even 10 sparrows, then a smaller number could be bought, as the gospels indicate. A pair of sparrows cost one Roman assarion, which Weymouth puts at roughly equivalent to one farthing. (Matt. 10:29, 30.)[38] But Jesus' observation of market life is evident if we turn to Luke's account, for when buying double the quantity, an extra one is thrown in free. 'The market price of five sparrows is two farthings, isn't it? Yet not one of them is forgotten in God's sight. Why, the very hairs of your heads are all numbered! Don't be afraid, then; you are worth more than a great many sparrows!' (Luke 12:6, 7 Phillips.)

Does this mean that God actually stops to count the number of hairs on each person's head, or counts up the number of sparrows alive at any one time? Matthew's account helps us when it states, 'Yet not a single sparrow falls to the ground without your father's knowledge.' (Matt. 10:29 Phillips.) On the same basis of God's all-comprehending, all-seeing overview, it would not be possible for the enemy of a Christian to remove even one hair without God being aware of what was happening.[39]

If we doubt that God does indeed care for the most insignificant things on this planet, we need only stop to consider the world of the tiniest creatures, which can be examined under a microscope. However minute these are, their perfection of form and function is enough to cause us to exclaim with the Psalmist, 'How many wonders you have done for us, Yahweh, my God! How many plans you have made for us; you have no equal! I want to proclaim them, again and again, but they are more than I can count.' (Ps. 40:5 JB.) Jesus had that same appreciation for God's creation, and whilst we may well gasp with amazement when we see something spectacular and magnificent in size, never forget that God also cares for the things of least significance. He will think more of us if we are humble, and take the lower, less important place. (Luke 14:10, 11.)

11. The Seed-Collector—An Athenian View of Paul.

There is hardly a word used in the Bible that is more variously translated than this one found in the famous chapter describing Paul's clash with the Athenians. Some of the philosophers who heard him expressed their disdain for him by asking, 'What might this picker-up-of-scraps wish to be saying?' (Acts 17:18 Rotherham.)

This very vivid illustration has so many angles to it that we can well understand the variety of translation. Because the idea originates in the habits of a bird that flies here and there picking up seeds, following the plough or haunting the cornmarkets, the bird itself is named by some translations, 'magpie' (NAB), 'rook' (Concordant), 'cock-sparrow' (Phillips), and even 'parrot' (JB). Ronald Knox explains the misunderstanding of the Latin translators, which led to descriptions based on the thought of saying or telling. (Acts 17:18 Knox ftn 2.) So we have 'word-sower' (Douay), 'word-monger (Murdock's Syriac), and 'thought-sower' (Fenton).

But the methods used by this bird illustrate the methods of the man. He is a beggar who picks up scraps of food round the market, that fell from carts (literally!), or were thrown out into the street. By transference to the world of ideas, he collects useless scraps of information, worthless learning, gathered second-hand, undigested and out of context. 'The point of the slur is that Paul seems to have a miscellaneous collection of fragmentary ideas picked up from here, there, and everywhere, in no system and not rightfully his own.'[40] Goodspeed therefore prefers 'rag-picker,' and we find many other terms ranging from the specific to the vague – 'dabbler' (Knox), 'garbage-picker' (Schonfield), 'ignorant show-off' (TEV), and 'vagabond' (Lattimore). Yes, by extension Paul was himself a noetic beggar or tramp, in their view. Perhaps the best description is given in a footnote to Rieu's translation, 'intellectual beach-comber'.

The Athenian philosophers prided themselves on their well-thought out ideas, and in their arguments with each other the Stoics and Epicureans plumbed great depths in order to win the day. They therefore had no time for itinerate philosophers, and they judged Paul to be in this class.[41] But their love of justice allowed him to have a fair hearing, and although this only confirmed the view of some listeners, others said, 'We should like to hear you again on this subject.' (Acts 17:32 Goodspeed.)

To a worldly person steeped in materialism and modern philosophy, Christian ideas may seem at first sight just idle, useless chatter.

But when it is examined more thoroughly, the Bible's teachings will be seen to be reasonable and logical, and Paul's presentation to the Athenians is a lesson for us if we would have our hearers say, 'we will listen to you again another time.'

Notes and References:

1. Dalman, G. H. *Jesus-Jeshua*, 227, which highlights the slight difference in the Jewish proverb. Israel was to God without guile like the doves, but to the nations of the world as wise as serpents.
2. Tristram, H. B. *Natural History*, 211, 220; Jebb, J, *Sacred Literature* . . . 1831 New ed. Duncan & Cochrane, 340–342, which so well sets out the balance obtained by the combined characteristics of the two animals, the simplicity of the dove correcting the excess caution of the serpent, and the prudence of the serpent correcting any stupidity in the dove.
3. Vincent, M. R. *Word Studies*, Vol. 1, 40.
4. Van-Lennep, H. J. *Bible Lands*, Vol. 1, 80–82; Robinson, E. *Biblical Researches*, Vol. 1, 550.
5. Hanson, A. T. *Studies in Paul's Technique and Theology*, 1974, SPCK, 165/6, where Hanson thinks that the proverbial maxim of the labourer being worthy of his wages supports the idea of actual money or pay. But its use at Luke 10:7 has nothing to do with money, but rather the supplying of such necessities as food and drink. To take the thought to Hanson's conclusion would place Paul in the position of actually asking for an Elder's pay to be doubled; Brewer, D. I, '1 Corinthians 9:9–11: A Literal Interpretation of 'Do Not Muzzle the Ox,'' *NTStud*. Vol. 38 (1992), 554–565.
6. Hanson, A. T. op. cit. (5), 162, where the two Greek words for the specific and the general muzzling are shown to be interchangeable later, and so 'to gag anything or anyone.' Ward, R. A. *Hidden Meaning*, 142.
7. Derrett, J. D. M. *Jesus's Audience*, 138, 143.
8. Montefiore, C. G. *Synoptic Gospels*, Vol. 2, 305; Carr, A, *Matthew*, 1901, (CGT), 263.
9. Wordsworth, C, *Greek Testament*, Vol. 1, 84; Tristram, H. B. *Natural History*, 159; Morgan, G. C. *Parables*, 123, 124. cp. Paul as gentle as a nursing mother caring for her children. (1 Thess. 2:7.)
10. Josephus, *Against Apion*, Book 2, (16) 164–167, where the word 'Theocracy' is first found.
11. Glasson, T. F. 'Chiasmus in St. Matthew 7:6,' *ET*, Vol. 68 (1957), 302; Jebb, J, op. cit. (2), 335, 338–340.
12. Robertson, A. T. *Word Pictures*, Vol. 1, 61; Boggis, R. J. E. *Down the Jordan in a Canoe*, 1939, SPCK, 107.
13. Abrahams, I. *Studies in Pharisaism*, 2nd series, 195/6; Montefiore, C. G. *Synoptic Gospels*, Vol. 2, 117/8; Bishop, E. F. F. *Jesus of Palestine*, 81/2; Savage, H, E. *The Gospel*,

223–225; Lachs, S. T. *Rabbinic Commentary*, 139, who suggests the 'dogs' might have been the Samaritans, and the 'swine' the Romans whose banners carried the picture of a wild boar.

14. Tristram, H. B. *Natural History*, 299; Savage, H. E. *The Gospel* 224.

15. Jackson, F. J. F & Lake, K, *Beginnings*, Vol. 4, 318; Thomson, W. M. *The Land and the Book*, 1913, New ed. rev. by J. Grande, Nelson, 304; Burney, C. F. Ed. *The Book of Judges*, 1920, 2nd ed. Rivingtons, 77.

16. Reyero, S. 'Durum est tibi contra stimulum calcitrare,' Hechos de los Apostoles, 26:14,' *Studium*, Vol. 10 (1970), 367–378.

17. Feldman, A, *Parables*, 31; Ginsburg, C. D. *Coheleth . . . Ecclesiastes . . . Commentary, Historical and Critical*, 1861, Longman, 473, for the quotation.

18. Ginsburg, C. D. op. cit. (17), 474/5.

19. Jackson F. J. F, & Lake, K, *Beginnings*, Vol. 4, 10; Van-Lennep, H. J. *Bible Lands*, Vol. 2, 452.

20. Kobert, R, 'Kamel und Shiffstau: Zu Markus 10:25 (par.) und Koran 7, 40/38,' *Biblica*, Vol. 53 (1972), 229–233; Bruce, F. F. *Hard Sayings*, 180–183; Van-Lennep, H. J. *Bible Lands*, Vol. 2, 452; Rihbany, A. M. *Syrian Christ*, 93, 94.

21. Lightfoot, J, *Horae Hebraicae*, Vol. 2, 264/5; Abrahams, I, *Studies in Pharisaism*, 2nd series, 208.

22. Hobart, W. K. *The Medical Language of St. Luke . . .* 1882, Dublin, Hodges, Figgis, 60, 61.

23. Robertson, A. T. *The Minister*, 55; Morgan, G. C. Parables, 98; Barr, S, 'The Eye of the Needle – Power and Money in the New Community: A Look at Mark 10:17–31,' *AndNewRev*, Vol. 3 (1992), 31–44.

24. Bengel, J. A. *Gnomon*, Vol. 1, 409/410; Robinson, T, *The Evangelists and the Mishna*: or Illustrations of the Four Gospels, drawn from Jewish Traditions, 1859, Nisbet, 132/3; Trench, R. C. *On the A. V. of the N. T. . . .* 1859, 2nd ed. rev. J. W. Parker, 172/3, who tells of a Moorish soldier, 'when he drank, always unfolded the end of his turban and placed it over the mouth of his bota, drinking through the muslin, to strain out the gnats, whose larvae swarm in the water of that country.'

25. Robinson, T. op. cit. (24), 133.

26. Gower, R, *New Manners and Customs*, 132–145.

27. For a detailed description of sheep and shepherding, see Geikie, C, *The Holy Land*, 193–207; Rihbany, A. M. *Syrian Christ*, 209–218.

28. Bishop, E. F. F. *Jesus of Palestine*, 297/8, with twentieth-century examples of calling the sheep, including that of a young orphan boy, and 299 on the doorkeeper; Bottino, A, 'La Metafora della porta (Gv 10:7, 9),' *Rivista Biblica*, Bologna, Italy, Vol. 39 (1991), 207–215.

29. Barrett, C. K. *The Gospel acc. to St. John, Intro. Comm. & Notes on the Greek Text*, 1962, SPCK, 312; Sanders, J. N. & Mastin, B. A. *A Commentary on the Gospel acc. to St. John*, 1968, Black, 252. But it is not a question of from where they are drawn, but where they are placed. They listen to Jesus' voice, are gathered (Bodmer P66 ms. reading), and come into the parallel sheepfold, then both folds make up one flock.

30. Keller, P, *A Shepherd Looks at Psalm 23*, 1970, Grand Rapids, Zondervan, 60–63.

31. Bishop, E. F. F. *Jesus of Palestine*, 101.

32. For a shepherd's first-hand experience with sheep applied to this

Psalm, see P. Keller's excellent work, op. cit. (30).

33. Bishop, E. F. F. *Jesus of Palestine*, 236, which notes that 'there is no Palestinian reason' for turning this into 'vultures' as have many Bible translations; Geikie, C, *The Holy Land*, 726/7, on the power of sight and speedy gathering together of birds of prey.

34. McNeile, A. H. *The Gospel acc. to St. Matthew*, 1928, Macmillan 351; Alford, H, *The Greek Testament*, 1874, 7th ed. Rivingtons, Vol. 1, 242; for partly suggesting the other view, see Bruce, F. F. *Hard Sayings*, 232; Morgan, G. C. *Parables*, 128, applying to this world dead to God.

35. Davidson, F. Ed. *The New Bible Commentary*, 1954, 2nd ed. Inter-Varsity, 800; Carr, A, *St. Matthew*, 1901 (CGT), 271; Marshall, I. H. *The Gospel of Luke*, (New Int. Greek Testament Comm), 1978, Exeter, Paternoster Press, 668/9, who considers along with other scholars that Luke has moved the statement to its present position, and therefore it required a restatement of the question, 'Where?'

36. Tristram, H. B. *Natural History*, 201–204; Van-Lennep, H. J. *Bible Lands*, Vol. 2, 292; Bishop, E. F. F. *Jesus of Palestine*, 102, who also mentions the way children used live sparrows as playthings by tieing string to their claws and pulling them back when they tried to fly off.

37. Deissmann, G. A. *Light*, 273/4; MacDonald, D, 'The Worth of the Assarion,' *Historia*, Vol. 38 (1989), 120–123; Findlay, G. G. 'The Worth of Sparrows,' *Expositor*, 2nd Series, Vol. 7 (1884), 103–116.

38. For likely modern equivalents, 'a penny' (Matt. 10:29 REB, NJB, NRSV), 'twopence,' (Luke 12:6 REB), 'two pennies' (NJB, NRSV).

39. Ward, R. A. *Hidden Meaning* 47.

40. Goodspeed, E. J. *Problems*, 133 for the quotation; Rienecker, F & Rogers, C, *Linguistic Key*, 307; Smith, D, *Life and Letters*, 143 ftn; Marshall, A, *Gleanings*, 14, 15.

41. Carter, C. W & Earle, R, *The Acts of the Apostles, The Evangelical Commentary*, 1959, Grand Rapids, Zondervan, 254–256.

Chapter 3

Buildings and Homes

1. The Title-Deed—A Guaranteed Basis of Assurance.

That grand chapter on faith in the book of Hebrews is set in motion with a remarkable introduction. 'Now faith is a solidly grounded certainty about what we hope for, a conviction about the reality of things we don't see.' (Heb. 11:1 Adams.)

The Greek word for 'solidly grounded certainty' is 'hupostasis', and the papyri recovered from the sands of Egypt reveal a fine illustration which can help our understanding of this verse. The word was used in a technical and legal sense in connection with property and ownership rights. Summarizing its various uses, Moulton and Milligan comment, 'in all cases there is the same central idea of something that *underlies* visible conditions and guarantees a future possession.'[1]

Expressing the illustration in this legal manner, another translation renders the verse, 'Now faith is the title deed of things hoped for; the putting to the proof of things not seen.' (Heb. 11:1 Montgomery, also Wuest.) When we possess by right the title-deed to a property, we know for certain that it belongs to us. We may never have seen it, for it may be in another land thousands of miles away, but the title-deed testifies to its very existence, and gives us assurance or proof of that fact.[2]

True Christian faith is like that title-deed. It is an inbuilt assurance about things we cannot see with our physical eyes. So after listing the exploits of many faithful men, they are described as dying without seeing those hopes realized, for they were still future. Their faith was not blind credulity, for they had put it to the test and it had proved to be 'a ground of hope' in God's promise, for 'he has prepared a city for them'. (Heb. 11:16b Adams, Montgomery.) That

55

'city' was so real to them that it was just as if they held a title-deed to a part of it.

Earlier in the same epistle we are reminded that every house is built by someone, and God is the great builder of all things. Using this illustration, the writer remembers the faithfulness of Moses in God's house and the greater Moses, Jesus Christ. (Heb. 3: 1–6.) Then those first century Christians were shown that they could be sharers with Christ, 'if, indeed, we hold firmly till the end to the assurance ('hupostasis') that we had at the beginning.' (Heb. 3:14 Adams.)

Faith causes that hope in God's promise of the future to be put to the test, it brings a conviction of the true existence of that future as a real fact. 'Substantially the words [of Heb. 11:1] mean that faith gives to things future, which as yet are only hoped for, all the reality of actual present existence.' [3] So the ground on which a hope is built has to be solid, and this is the meaning of 'hupostasis', that which stands under, the sub-strata or basis. It is not simply the foundation itself, which needs to be laid at an early stage, whereas a really solid faith is built gradually, and it goes on getting stronger all through a progressive Christian's life. It is the strength underlying, or core supporting the whole house, like the bed-rock on which the enduring house was built in Jesus' Sermon on the Mount.

So faith undergirds or underpins a Christian. It gives assurance and conviction, assuming the nature of a guarantee, giving substance and reality to our hopes. Peter sums it up very well when he explains how to withstand the Devil's onslaughts, likened to the ferocity of a roaring attacking lion (another illustration), and he could certainly speak from experience. 'Stand immovable against his onset, solid as a rock in your faith, knowing that the same kind of sufferings are being accomplished in your brotherhood which is in the world.' Then he shows the relationship between the foundation and faith as the ground of hope, when he adds how God 'shall himself make you complete, shall establish you firmly, shall strengthen you, shall ground you as on a foundation.' (1 Peter 5:9, 10b Wuest.)

2. Building on a Sure Foundation— Reaching Spiritual Maturity.

Jesus' illustration about the house built on rock and the house built on sand, appears in both the gospels of Matthew and Luke. But there is an important addition in the Lukan version. The one who listens and acts on Christ's words 'resembles a man who built a house; he dug and went down deep, and set the foundation (Greek 'themelios') on a rock. When the flood rose, the river rushed against that house but had no power to shake it, because it was securely built.' (Luke 6:48 New Berkeley Version.)[4]

The apostle Paul applied the illustration to spiritual things too. He urged Timothy to tell those with worldly riches to put their hope in God, 'and to treasure up for themselves a sound foundation for the future, so that they may take hold of the life that is really life.' (1 Tim. 6:19 NBV.) Yes, believing that God exists, and that he can reward his servants with the real life is part of that foundation. (Heb. 11:6.)

Paul described himself as 'a wise master builder', (Greek 'architektōn', from which is drawn our English word 'architect'); because he had laid a foundation on which others could build, and what was that basis? 'For none is able to lay another foundation than the one already laid, which is Jesus Christ.' (1 Cor. 3:10, 11 NBV.) But it would be of no value to lay a sure foundation, and then do nothing further. The foundation was only the first, early stage. With another illustration about a tower, Jesus showed that a builder had to consider how to complete the whole project successfully, for if he only reached part way he would be ridiculed by everyone; '"This man started to build and could not finish it," they would say.' (Luke 14: 28–30 NBV.)

If the house was to be a strong one, spiritually able to resist the testing fire of the final judgment, the materials used needed to be of good quality – gold, silver and precious stones, in contrast to wood, hay and stubble, which burn easily. (1 Cor. 3:12–13.) Christians could be assured that such good spiritual building would bring the reward of everlasting life, 'If indeed, you be steadfast in your faith, with your foundation firmly grounded and immovably fixed, and not suffering yourselves to be shifted away from the hope of the Glad-tidings which you heard.' (Col. 1:23 Conybeare.)[5]

So the message behind the illustration is, (a), have a firm solid foundation but, (b) go on to build a secure house of faith upon it. To falter half way, or allow our progress to be hindered by the many troubles and temptations that a Christian has to face, can be fatal. We might even begin to feel that our foundations are shaky and unreliable. So the admonition is, 'Let us leave behind the elementary teachings of Christ and advance toward maturity. Let us not again be laying the foundation . . . .' (Heb. 6:1 NBV.)

How successful are we in our spiritual building programme? Is our house of faith a solid one, where doubts have been replaced by truths from God's Word, and maturity is reflected in our lives through our obedience to God's principles and Christ's words? As a tree does not stop growing when it reaches maturity, we need to go on building, but we have confidence that we have a sufficient fund of spiritual treasure to complete it, to God's praise and our own salvation.

3. Building an Edifice—To Edify and Build Up.

Continuing the idea of the house and its foundation, we turn to another of Paul's words. It is the Greek word for 'edify', ('oikodomeō'), and it means literally to 'build a house'. Our English words 'edify' and 'edifice', have become separated in most people's minds; the former having a metaphorical use and the latter still associated with a literal building. The illustration of these words in the Bible shows their common link very clearly.[6]

At Acts 9:31, the church or congregation was said to be enjoying a period of peace, 'as it continued to be built up spiritually.' (C. B. Williams.) The footnote explains that the word 'spiritually' has been added because it is implied from the context, but even without it no one would think of a setting up of literal buildings. Rather, it 'strengthened itself.' (Lamsa.)

In most cases the upbuilding is a mutual one involving a number of individuals or a body of persons. 'So let us keep on pursuing the things that make for peace and our mutual upbuilding.' (Rom. 14:19 Williams.) In the next chapter the apostle Paul opens by talking to the whole congregation at Rome, but then brings his counsel down to the individual responsibility within the group. 'Each one of us must practice pleasing his neighbour to help in his immediate up-building ('oikodomē') for his eternal good.' (Rom. 15:1, 2 Williams.) Since we may all work in a slightly different way in our building or edifying work, Paul later added that he would not 'build upon foundations laid by other men.' (Rom. 15:20 Williams.)

Writing to the Corinthians, Paul clarified the nature of his building work. 'Knowledge puffs up, but love builds up.' (1 Cor. 8:1 Williams) He illustrates the danger of a little knowledge by referring to food offered to idols. The fully built up Christian knows that an idol is nothing, and is not bothered about the matter, but a weak Christian, because of his past habits and associations with such food, has a conscience about it, and if he sees a fellow Christian 'partaking of a meal in an idol's temple, will he not be emboldened (lit. "built up" footnote) with his over-scrupulous conscience to eat the food which has been sacrificed to an idol?' (1 Cor. 8:10 Williams.)

He will in his mind build a false structure because of his lack of understanding, and we could then be the cause of our brother falling into sin and a bad conscience. If we love our brothers, we will refrain from doing anything that might throw down what has been built up spiritually with considerable effort. Although in quite a different context, Paul's statement of principle well applies, 'For if I try to build again what I tore down, I really prove myself to be a wrong-doer.' (Gal. 2: 18 Williams.) That would equally be true whether it was something that concerned our own faith, or that of our brothers.

So with the foundation laid within the Christian congregation of faith in God, and in the ransom sacrifice of his Son Jesus Christ, the house of faith can be built upon it. To bring this desired result, the congregation had God's Spirit, and also apostles, prophets, evangelists, and teachers, and the building metaphor is extended here by calling such ones, 'pillars' in the congregation. (Gal. 2:9.) Because the congregation in turn maintains the truth throughout its entire structure spiritually, it is called 'the pillar and foundation of the truth.' (1 Tim. 3:15 Williams.)

Those gifts in men are to be used 'for the immediate equipment of God's people for the work of service, for the ultimate building up of the body of the Christ, until we all attain to unity in faith and to perfect knowledge of the Son of God, namely, to a mature manhood, and to a perfect measure of Christ's moral stature.'(Eph. 4:11–13 Williams.) What a fine way to round out this excellent illustration; no wonder Robinson said, 'the picturesqueness of the metaphor must be preserved.'[7]

4. Cornerstone or Topstone?— The Binding Stone in the Building.

This illustration has involved a controversy that still continues in scholarly circles. Two passages in the Hebrew Scriptures are quoted by Jesus and the apostles, and form the basis of the metaphor. 'This is why the Lord Yahweh says this: See how I lay in Zion a stone of witness, a precious cornerstone (Greek LXX 'kephalē gōnia'), a foundation stone; the believer shall not stumble.' (Isa. 28:16 JB.) The Psalmist adds, 'It was the stone rejected by the builders that proved to be the keystone (Greek LXX 'akro gōnia'), (the head of the corner, Thomson's Septuagint; the capstone, NIV).' (Ps. 118:22 JB.)

The question which affects the application of the metaphor is whether a foundation cornerstone is referred to, or a topstone, one that caps the building, completing it and giving it its final binding strength? [8]

Jesus quoted the Psalmist's words, and then added, 'Anyone who falls on that stone will be dashed to pieces, anyone it falls on will be crushed.' (Luke 20: 17, 18 JB, Matt. 21:42–44.) This might seem to support the idea of a topstone, which could then fall onto and crush someone beneath, but it would not accord with the idea of someone stumbling against a stone in that position.

Peter also quoted from this Psalm, when he was before the Sanhedrin (Acts 4:11), and later in his first epistle where he combined it with the quotation from Isaiah 28:16. Then he added these words, 'a stone to stumble over, a rock to bring men down. They stumble over it because they do not believe in the word.' (1 Pet. 2:6–8 JB.)

Whatever the position of this stone may be, there is no uncertainty about its function, and this is what matters in meditating upon the power of the illustration. It does not refer to a hidden foundation stone, but to one that has an important visible position. If it is low down it could be fifteen feet in length, a straight block of stone running up to an important corner. The stones it meets might be fitted below and above to form the actual corner, bonding it together and giving it strength.[9] Someone running could easily stumble against such a stone in his haste to round the corner.

If it was the capstone it might again occupy a corner stone position, but high up, or it could be the so-called 'pyramidion', the final stone which bonds all the other parts together. Certainly Jesus Christ occupies this position towards the other spiritual temple stones. (Eph. 4:15, 16, 1 Pet. 2:4, 5.)

But Jesus' own words added to his quotation from Psalm 118, could suggest that he meant to refer to BOTH positions, and for the application of the metaphor this would be very appropriate, and give it a much greater power. His ransom sacrifice was indeed a cornerstone without parallel to the spiritual building – the structure could not be erected without it, however much the apostles might be its foundation too. (Eph. 2:20, Rev. 21:14.) Yet Christ is also the one that completes the building, and gives it from the top down its binding strength. He is its strength from top to bottom!

Now consider again Jesus' words. Those who stumble over the ransom provision, who reject him as Messiah and Son of God, are destroyed or dashed to pieces. Those who deny that Christ is the head of his body, or spiritual temple, and who refuse to be drawn into a unified, bonded position with him, will find that they will be crushed when Christ executes final judgment.

So Paul could truly say that the building has 'Christ Jesus himself for its main cornerstone. As every structure is aligned on him, all grow into one holy temple in the Lord, and you too, in him are being built into a house where God lives in the Spirit.' (Eph. 2:20–22, JB.)

5. Roof Cover—The Protection of Love.

When Jesus was talking to a large crowd that entirely filled the house where he stayed in Capernaum, a paralytic was brought for him to heal. His friends were rather determined people, so they climbed on to the flat adobe roof and started to dig their way through. They literally 'unroofed the roof' to get in, so that Jesus was much impressed by their faith, and cured the boy. (Mark 2:4.)

The word for roof is the Greek 'stegē', and its use in other scriptures provides an interesting illustration. The verb 'stegō' means to cover, and is allied to our English words deck and thatch. Dropping the initial 's' we are left with 'tego', from which come 'thek' and finally 'thatch', as well as the Irish *teagh* and Gaelic *tigh* – a house (as in Tighnabruaich).[10]

The principal purpose of a roof is to cover or protect the occupants, to 'keep off something which threatens,' and this idea flavours our illustration here. The word is used in Paul's famous chapter on love, but the variety of translation shows that it is not easy to be sure just what Paul meant here. So of love, the NIV says, 'it always protects' just as a roof does. Barclay states that 'love can stand any kind of treatment,' and if a roof is strong and well made it endures all types of weather. Blackwelder translates, 'It does not unnecessarily expose anyone,' with the footnote, 'Literally, it puts a roof over everything.' (1 Cor. 13:7.)

Yet when we consider the scope of love as Paul was defining it, it is true to say that everything the roof can do, true love also does. It bears all strains and pressures, it protects those under its care, and does not expose their weaknesses and shortcomings. Paul also adds in 1 Cor. 9:12, 'We put up with anything rather than hinder the gospel of Christ.' (NIV.) The roof is built to put up with whatever sort of weather (or in Paul's case opposition and hostility), descends upon it.

The Covering Veil

The proverb states that, 'love covers over all wrongs.' It is a similar theme, but the illustration is different. Here the Greek word is 'kaluptō', and refers to a veil thrown over something to cover it up. Urging Christians to let their love for one another be sincere and earnest, Peter quotes the proverb, 'for, "Love throws a veil over countless sins".' (1 Pet. 4:8 TCNT, Prov. 10:12, see also James 5:20.)[11]

A similar expression by David at Psalm 32:1 is quoted by Paul. 'Blessed are those whose wrongdoings have been forgiven, and over whose sins a veil has been drawn.' (Rom. 4:7 TCNT.) But for this to happen there needs to be a repentent course of action, such as David himself showed to God, and which he stated in Psalm 32:5; 'I acknowledged my sin to you, and did not cover up my iniquity.' (NIV.) Similarly, when Israel showed repentence, God also forgave their iniquity, and covered or concealed their sins, by putting them out of mind. (Ps. 85:2.)

Our two illustrations come together through the theme of love. It is love on God's part that covers or throws a veil over the sins of those who show true heart repentence. Christians will do the same as they reflect that love of God, showing it to their friends and neighbours, recognizing that they also are imperfect, and allowing love to be the roof that weathers the storm. True love will come through; it will protect; it will endure.

6. House Administration—Good Stewardship.

As the family is so important in God's view, the illustration of household administration is a natural one, and is developed best in the book of Hebrews. Jesus and Moses are compared, because 'Moses was faithful in all God's household.' But Jesus is counted worthy of greater honour than Moses, just as the founder of a household is more than the household itself. 'Every household is founded by some-one, but God is the founder of everything.' (Heb. 3:2–4, TNT and note, Wade, Conybeare.)

So whilst God is the one over all, Jesus was credited with founding a household within God's arrangement, one into which he invited other faithful Christians, by means of a personal kingdom covenant. (Matt. 19:27, 28, Eph. 2:19.)[12] A further contrast is then drawn between Moses as a faithful servant in God's household, and Christ as a faithful son, 'ruling over God's household. And we are God's household if only we keep our confidence and pride in the hope that is ours.' (Heb. 3:5, 6 TNT.)

So it is that the apostle Paul as a member of God's household, speaks of holding a 'stewardship' (Greek 'oikonomia'). 'I have become a minister, in discharge of the stewardship which God has entrusted to me for your advantage, to give full expression to God's Message.' (Col. 1:25 Wade, 1 Cor. 9:17, Eph. 3:9.)

This word refers to the direction or administration of a household, but where the context is appropriate it has a wider, more general application. to overall administration.[13] The first chapter of Paul's letter to the Ephesians is an important one in describing God's purpose for mankind, by which those faithful and obedient can be brought back under the rule of his household. Release from sin is made possible by Christ's death, and this paved the way for God to make known 'to us the secret of his will, that gracious purpose which he had set himself to fulfil in Christ when the right time should come: his plan (Greek 'oikonomia') is to gather up the whole universe, everything in heaven and earth, to a unity in Christ.' (Eph. 1:9, 10 TNT.)

That 'plan' or 'new order' (Smith) is 'an arrangement' (Adams) that 'is finally to bring to their conclusion all the events in history.' (Barclay.) Then when all unfaithful servants and stewards have been removed for all time, God's restored household, under the rule of his son Christ Jesus, becomes the perfect and only administration, functioning through the Kingdom with its faithful stewards as kings and priests in the places prepared for them in 'my Father's house'. (John 14:2 TNT.)

7. Finding Room, Stretching Out— Intense Love from a Warm Heart.

On two occasions Jesus urged the people and the Pharisees to 'find room' in their hearts and minds for what he was saying. Speaking of John the Baptizer he said to the crowds, 'this I tell you, if you will make room for it in your minds, that he is that Elias whose coming was prophesied. Listen, you that have ears to hear with.' (Matt. 11:14, 15 Knox.) Pre-conceived ideas and prejudices helped to block out these new truths from their minds, but their hearts were also involved. Jesus told the Pharisees, 'you want to kill me because my words find no room in your hearts.' (John 8:37 Rieu.)

But the good news could not be stopped by the opposition of the

Pharisees and Sadducees. It continued to spread and grow rapidly, and Paul asked for the prayers of the brothers, 'that the word of the Lord may run its course triumphantly with us, as it does with you: and that we may be preserved from malicious interference: the faith does not reach all hearts.' (1 Thess. 3:1, Knox, Acts 19:20.)

This was not a new idea, for David had touched on the key to the matter when he said to God, 'I shall run the very way of your commandments, because you make my heart have the room.' (Ps. 119:32 NWT.) Solomon too was praised for his large or generous heart, given to him with wisdom by God. (1 Kings 4:29.) Yes, when the heart is opened out wide, as with Lydia, there is a true response deep down, and a desire to obey God's commands, in fact, to run to do God's will. (Acts 16:14, 15, Gen. 18:2, 6–8.)

In turn, that brings a feeling of freedom, as if one had come suddenly from a cramped place, out into a large room. 'And he proceeded to bring me out into a roomy place. He was rescuing me because he had found delight in me.' (Ps. 18:19 NWT.) That results in great joy and happiness. (Ps. 118:5.)

No wonder the apostle Paul counselled his brothers, 'We are speaking freely to you, Corinthians; we throw our hearts wide open to you. It is not our fault, it is the fault of your own affections that you feel constraint with us. Pay us back in the same coin, (I am speaking to you as to my children): open your hearts wide too.' (2 Cor 6: 11–13 Knox.) What an appeal! Can we feel the force of that even today? If we would really respond as Christians should, will not reserve and aloofness, the flinty rebuff, the cold shoulder, be replaced by a warm-hearted happy openness which dismisses barriers that keep people apart.

Stretching Ourselves in Love

Here the illustration flows over in another direction, yet one closely related to that above. God's command rings out through Isaiah, 'Make the place of your tent more spacious. And let them stretch out the tent cloths of your grand tabernacle. Do not hold back. Lengthen out your tent cords, and make these tent pins of yours strong.' (Isa. 54:2 NWT.)

Imagine a large Bedouin tent made of black goats' skins with thick hair, the whole extending from twenty feet in length to as much as forty feet. With perhaps nine poles set in rows of three, those in the centre are the highest so that rain runs off to the sides, but the whole tent is long and low (about seven feet in height at most), so that the wind catches it the least. The open side is usually turned to the sun, and hanging curtains divide the interior.[14] Prosperity and an enlarged family can bring about an expanded tent. So, too, in a spiritual sense should a hospitable and generous heart be willing to extend love to others more and more.

If our love is going to respond to the heart's new found width and warmth, it has to be stretched, to fill places it never reached before. Think of a rubber band, called upon to encompass an article seemingly much larger than itself. But its elasticity expands it to be able to accomplish that need, and many articles are brought together into a unity they did not previously possess. I remember once using this illustration in a talk, and although I had a very thick half-inch wide elastic band so all could see it, a friend of mine, Alan Stokes, was very nervous that it would snap when I demonstrated it to the audience. It didn't snap, but it could because elastic perishes. Is our love like that? Will it always fully expand, and never give up or perish?

When Peter said, literally rendered, 'out of heart – one another – love you outstretchedly' (1 Pet. 1:22 K. Int), he used the Greek word 'ektenos', meaning 'stretched out'.[15] Later in his epistle he repeated the illustration, 'keep your Christian love reaching out eagerly'. (1 Pet. 4:8 Anderson.) If we stretch out our arms to their fullest extent we may be surprised to see how far we can reach. Does our love have that elasticity to extend itself beyond our normal capacity? We sometimes say to others who try us, 'you really stretch my patience to the limit'. Can our love be similarly extended, but beyond all previous limits, making room in our hearts first of all so as to supply us with the motive for action, love out of a warm responsive heart.

8. The Open Door—Grasping Opportunities.

The old proverb is still frequently used today, 'when one door shuts, another opens.' The metaphor was one that Paul often used too, and always connected with his desire to spread the message of Christ to more and more cities. 'Persevere in prayer: as you pray, keep spiritually alert, and give thanks at the same time. Pray for us too, that God may open up a door for our message.' (Col. 4:3 Bruce.)

Because a door is a way in, it makes a very appropriate illustration, and the greater the opportunity, the larger the door. When Paul was discussing his travel plans, and the possibility of visiting Corinth again after going to Macedonia (in Greece), he added, 'However, my present plans are to remain in Ephesus until Pentecost, for a great door of opportunity stands wide open for me [here], and there are many persons who would like to shut it.' (1 Cor. 16:9 Blackwelder.)

But Paul seems to have felt the power of this metaphor beyond the simple abstract idea of an opportunity. His mental idea of a door seems to have extended itself to the thought of a door to a whole region. 'When I came to the Troad to preach the gospel of Christ there, and found a door wide open for use by the Lord's overruling, I could not take proper advantage of it.' (2 Cor. 2:12 Bruce.) So he was looking beyond the immediate city of Troas to the whole region of the Troad (the north-western part of Mysia) opening up, and yet he was unable in this instance to grasp that opportunity to the full.[16]

The same idea is found in the Bible's last book, in the letter to the Philadelphian congregation. 'See, I have given you a door flung wide open, which no man can close.' (Rev. 3:8 Phillips.) Sir William M. Ramsay suggests a reason why this is said only to this one of the six congregations. 'After passing Philadelphia the road along this valley ascends to the Phrygian land, and the great Central Plateau . . . Philadelphia, therefore, was the keeper of the gateway to the plateau . . . but it would be wrong to infer that Philadelphia alone among the Seven Cities, had a door before it. Each of the Seven Cities stood at the door of a district . . . all had specially favourable opportunities opened to them by geographical situation, and the convenience of communication. But it lies in the style and plan of the Seven Letters to mention only in one case what was a common characteristic of all the Seven Cities.'[17]

Paul saw the open door in yet another sense, one in which he had a special interest through his zealous ministry. Returning to Syrian Antioch after his first tour, 'they assembled the Church, and brought them tidings of all that God had done in conjunction with them, and

that He had opened to the nations a door of faith.' (Acts 14:27
Sadler.)[18] By grasping that opportunity, many non-Jewish gentiles
were able to exercise faith, and become part of the seed of Abraham
with all its attendant blessings.

We can add an interesting associated thought from Paul's words
to Timothy. 'Those who have discharged their ministry will win a
good standing for themselves, and great liberty of speech in their
witness to the Christian faith.' (1 Tim. 3:13 Bruce.) The Greek words
for 'good standing' refer to a good foothold or standing on the steps
of a stair. (cp. 1 Sam. 5:5 LXX.)[19] Picture such a one with a good
foothold standing before the door of opportunity. When it opens, he
is the one ready and able to seize the opportunity, and is able to
fulfil his ministry by speaking boldly in defense of the faith, just as
Paul did.

9. The Key, the Door and the Knock—Opening Up the Scriptures.

Jesus was not slow in exposing the hypocrisy of the scribes and
Pharisees when he came in contact with them, and he was most
critical about their handling of the Word of God, because the Jews
had been 'entrusted with the divine utterances of God'. (Rom. 3:2
Wuest.)

On one occasion he told them, 'you lock the doors of the Kingdom
of Heaven in men's faces, for you will neither go in yourselves nor
let those enter who are trying to do so.' (Matt. 23:13, 14 Goodspeed.)
In the parallel account he takes the illustration further by stating that
they have 'taken the key to the door of knowledge'. (Luke 11:52
Goodspeed.)

By contrast, Jesus sought to use the key of knowledge himself by
skilfully teaching his disciples the Word of God. After his resurrection, he appeared to two of his disciples on the road to Emmaus,
and caused their hearts to burn because 'he was fully opening up
(Greek, 'dianoigō') the Scriptures to us'. Later in Jerusalem to a
larger group of disciples 'he opened up their minds to fully grasp
the meaning of the Scriptures.' (Luke 24:32, 45 NWT.)[20]

The opening of the door of knowledge is taken further by

illustrating the act of knocking, often done in Jewish circles with reverence and politeness. 'Keep on knocking (Greek 'krouō' – reverently) and the door will be opened to you.' (Matt. 7:7 Amplified, Wuest.) The continuous action denotes perseverance and the desire for the door to be opened, yet it is still a respectful attitude, with consideration for the occupant, as the context of the Luke account shows. (Luke 11:5–10.)[21]

But the situation is reversed when the same illustration is used in the letter to the Laodicean congregation. Here Christ is the one standing at the door and knocking. (Rev. 3:20.) It is in reality the same position found in the final chapter of Luke. The disciples were willing to 'open their minds' to be receptive to the Word of God through Jesus' explanations. Yet it involves more than the mind, as the case of Lydia demonstrates, for she 'opened her heart wide to pay attention to the things being spoken by Paul.' (Acts 16:14 NWT.)[22]

The illustration is therefore a double one. When we search and knock, Christ has the key of all knowledge and wisdom, and can open the door to us. (Col. 2:3, Rev. 3:7.) But it can also be that he knocks at the door when we are not actively searching, or perhaps in some unexpected way. How, then, will we respond? Will we open wide our heart or our door, and so humbly allow Christ into our life to teach us?

10. The Footstool—Activity on the Earth.

The illustration of the footstool is one that finds its origin in the Hebrew Bible. The footstool was an item of furniture often met with in the ancient world. They varied in height from a size familiar to us, down to something not much thicker than a small rug. Some had open sides, and the top might be made of interlaced work.[23]

The grand ivory throne of Solomon is described at 2 Chronicles 9:17–19, with six steps leading up to it and a footstool of gold. But this pales into insignificance beside the description of God's great heavenly throne in Revelation chapter four. Whilst the footstool is sometimes referred to other things, its most usual parallel is with the earth. Stephen quoted from Isaiah 66 when he spoke of the impossibility of building a house for God, because God said, 'Heaven is my throne, and earth my footstool.' (Acts 7:49 RSV.) In his Sermon on the Mount Jesus confirmed this when he told his audience not to swear 'by heaven' because it is the throne of God, 'or by the earth, for it is his footstool.' (Matt. 5:35 RSV.)

The metaphor (or sometimes simile), is then picked up from the Messianic Psalm 110 and quoted in the gospels, in Acts and in Hebrews. (Matt. 22:44, Mk 12:36, Luke 20:43, Acts 2:35, Heb. 1:13.) The last expression is the clearest and most developed. 'But when Christ had offered for all time a single sacrifice for sins, he sat down at the right hand of God, then to wait until his enemies should be made a stool for his feet.' (Heb. 10:12, 13, RSV.)

The early Christians were reminded in their day that although they had the promise of everything being placed under the feet of Christ, 'we do not yet see everything in subjection to him.' (Heb. 2:8 RSV.) Revelation then describes the power and authority of Christ's Kingdom taking over after that long waiting period. Immediately the promise is fulfilled, Satan is 'thrown down to the earth' in defeat, and finally completely crushed under foot. (Rev. 12:7–12 RSV, Rom. 16:20.)

Perhaps the final word goes to the prophet Isaiah, who spoke of a new heavens and a new earth, and described conditions then in a graphic manner. (Isa. 11 & 65.) After again referring to the destruction of those not serving God, he adds the wonderful promise about the footstool, the earth: 'and I will make the place of my feet glorious'. (Isaiah 60:13 RSV.) When men today talk about the earth being made desolate, either by means of nuclear war or ecological disaster, that promise is all the more valuable to Christians. Truly, a beautiful throne calls for a beautiful footstool to grace it in splendour.

11. The Prominent Light—Giving out the Light.

In his Sermon on the Mount, Jesus used many illustrations – in fact they tumbled out one after another. Two different metaphors are combined to give strength to his argument. 'You are the light for the world. A city built on a hill-top cannot be hidden. No one lights a lamp to put it under a tub, they put it on the lamp-stand where it shines for everyone in the house. In the same way your light must shine in people's sight, so that seeing your good works, they may give praise to your Father in heaven.' (Matt. 5:14–16 NJB.)

It was quite likely that the city on a hill-top was within their sight as Jesus spoke. 'One of the most striking objects in the prospect from any of these hills [in Galilee], especially from the traditional Mount of the Beatitudes, is the city of Safed, placed high on a bold spur of the Galilean Anti-Lebanon.'[24] Safed (from a Hebrew root meaning 'observe') is a modern city not mentioned in the Bible, but it was the site of one of the fortresses existing in 66 C. E., when the Jews revolted against the Romans.[25]

Starting in Jerusalem, one of a chain of bonfires was lit here to announce the beginning of a new month, for at an elevation of 2, 750 feet above the Mediterranean Sea, and almost 3, 500 feet above the Sea of Galilee, it was a fine eminence in the Galilee region.[26]

Then Jesus switched abruptly to a typical humble home, such as many of his hearers lived in. A little pottery lamp would be set in a prominent place to give as much light as possible. This would be either on a little ledge inside the house, or in a small aperture serving as a window, to guide a traveller home at night. It would not be placed under a tub or bushel measure, which the NJB footnote explains was 'a small receptacle on legs'. If the family left the house for a short time they might cover the light temporarily, for snuffing it out meant considerable smoke from the flaxen wick.[27] But it would serve no useful purpose like that, and would waste the precious olive oil. Is our light seen by all, or is it hidden and wasted for fear of what others may think if we speak out? Of course, our Christian life would have to harmonize with what we said, or our hearers would not praise God.[28]

The apostle Paul used a similar illustration in writing to the Philippians, but with a different simile. 'In the midst of an evil-disposed and perverse generation, [in which] you are seen shining like stars in a dark world, offering to men the Message of Life.' (Phil. 2:15 TCNT.) What a contrast, multitudes of bright stars shining in a dark sky! It seems to stress the individual light coming from every star, each of which the great Creator knows by name. (Ps. 147:4.) This very personal aspect is comforting to those who may say that what they can do is so small as not to be worthwhile. But that is not true, for it is the multiplicity of light from every seemingly tiny star that so impresses us as we gaze into the majestic heavens.

This illustration is also drawn from the Hebrew Scriptures, for 'Those who are wise will shine as brightly as the expanse of the heavens, and those who have instructed many in uprightness, as bright as stars for all eternity.' (Dan. 12:3. NJB.) They gain ever-lasting life by their obedience to Jesus' illustration, and can save many others who listen to them, and take notice of the shining light of truth from God's Word. (1 Tim. 4:16.)

12. The Tent Dweller—Temporary Residence.

In Bible lands the wanderer and nomad is still to be found, moving his tents from place to place, often in search of fresh pasture for his animals. In the first century, the black tents of the Bedouin Arabs were even more in evidence, so tent life is often mentioned in the Bible, right back to the time of the patriarchs, and especially Abraham. The loss of the tent symbolized the destruction of a person's prosperity, as Jeremiah 10:20 explains, 'My tent is wrecked, the ropes all broken; my children are no more, they are all gone, none left to raise my tent again, to hang up its curtains.' (Moffatt.)

In that great chapter on faith – Hebrews 11, the course of Abraham is commended, because he left his fixed abode in Ur of the Chaldees, and followed God's direction, leading him to a distant promised land, where he and his family were continually on the move, and 'residing in tents'. The contrast is then expressed in terms of Abraham's hope and goal. 'He was waiting for the City with its fixed foundations, whose builder and maker is God.' (Heb. 11:9, 10 Moffatt.) To Abraham, whether men lived in tents or more seemingly permanent homes, it was really only God who could provide the truly fixed foundations.

This supplies the clue to Paul's illustration about the tent. Because man's present life is so short upon the earth, he likens his body to a tent. John Gadsby adds: Paul 'forcibly expresses its uncertain duration, pitched here today, in health and vigour, but removed tomorrow, the place thereof knowing it no more.' (cp. Isa. 38:12.)[29]

So Paul comments, 'I know that if this earthly tent of mine is taken down, I get a home from God, made by no human hands, eternal in the heavens . . . I do sigh within this tent of mine with heavy anxiety – not that I want to be stripped, no, but to be under cover of the other, to have my mortal element absorbed by life.' (2 Cor. 5:1, 4 Moffatt.) Paul knew that it had been God's purpose in the beginning that man should live forever upon the earth, but sin and death had robbed him of that until Christ came to once again open the way to the real life, with the newly revealed destiny for the apostles and many others of a heavenly hope. His present tent seemed so buffeted and frail that it made him sigh with anxiety, and we recall some of those events he underwent for the sake of the good news. (2 Cor. 11: 23–27.)[30]

Peter used the same illustration in his second letter, conscious that his time to exhort his brothers might be short. 'So long as I am in this tent, I deem it proper to stir you up by way of reminder, since I know my tent must be folded up very soon – as indeed our Lord Jesus Christ has shown me.' (2 Peter 1:13, 14 Moffatt.) He was referring to Jesus' statement recorded at John 21:18, 19, and tradition suggests that Peter was put to death by his opposers.[31]

Is this the end of this illustration? Or is it applied in any other way to something quite different? The apostles were well aware of the tabernacle or tent in the wilderness, after Israel came out of Egypt, designed to be set up and taken down for easy transit. Then it was replaced in time by the more permanent Temple of Solomon. But even the temples were merely transitory, for then a further comparison was made. Jesus Christ is high priest 'of the Holy place, a public minister. And of the Real Tent, which the Lord pitched and not man.' (Heb. 8:2 Roth.) The argument is developed and 'the greater and more perfect tent not made by hand' is shown to be in heaven, where the resurrected Christ Jesus is received into the true 'Holy place'. (Heb. 9:11, 12 Roth.) Thus for perhaps the first time, a 'tent' is established permanently in heaven.

Notes and References:

1. Moulton & Milligan, *Vocabulary* 660; Wuest, K. *Word Studies, By-paths*, 18, 19.
2. Moulton, J. H. *Rubbish Heaps*, 28, 29; Waugh, R.M.L. *Greek Testament* 77, 78; *Translator's* N. T. note 528.
3. Nicoll, W. R. *Expositor's Greek Testament*, Vol. 4, 352.
4. Van-Lennep, H. J. *Bible Lands*, 422; Bishop, E. F. *Jesus*, 85, for a modern example of failure to provide a solid foundation.
5. Bengel, J. A. *Gnomon*, Vol. 4, 164, which adds, 'stable (settled), suggests the idea of internal strength, which believers themselves possess; just as a building ought to lean (rest) uprightly and solidly on the foundation first of all, but afterwards to cohere securely, and firmly to stand together, even by its own mass (compact solidity of structure).' Moulton, H. K. *Challenge*, 188/9; Howson, J. S. *Metaphors*, 59, 60, 78–82; cp. Eph. 2:20, 21 on the spiritual temple of heavenly stones built upon the foundation of apostles and early Christian prophets. See also J. Shanor, 'Paul as Master Builder. Construction Terms in 1 Corinthians. ' *NTStud.* Vol. 34 (1988), 461–471.
6. Skeat, W. W. *Etymological Dictionary*, 188; Howson, J. S. *Metaphors*, 47–59; Turner, N. *Christian Words* 428–430; Moulton, H. K. *Challenge*, 134–136.
7. Robinson, J. A. *Ephesians*, 182.
8. Kittel, G. *TDNT*, Vol. 1, 792/3. J. Jeremias contests strongly for the idea of a topstone or final stone; (see also Bishop, E. F. *Jesus*, 224).

He is answered by R. J. McKelvey in 'Christ the Cornerstone,' *NTStud.* Vol. 8 (1962), 352–359, on the basis of Jewish exegesis, that the Grundstein is the determinative corner stone binding the walls to the foundation. See also Robertson, A. T. *Word Pictures*, Vol. 4, 528/9; Selwyn, E. G. *First Peter*, 163; Jackson & Lake, *Beginnings*, Vol. V, 374; Robinson, J. A. *Ephesians* 163/4, and for a detailed summary of all views, concluding that it was a mixed metaphor, Turner, N. *Christian Words*, 86–88.
9. Robinson, J. A. *Ephesians*, 69.
10. Moulton & Milligan, *Vocabulary*, 587; Robertson, A. T. *Word Pictures*, Vol. 4, 178; Skeat, W. W. *Etymological Dictionary*, 158 (deck), 639 (thatch); Thayer, J. H. *Greek-English Lexicon*, 586.
11. Selwyn, E. G. *First Peter*, 217; Robertson, A. T. *Word Pictures*, Vol. 6, 68.
12. Westcott, B. F. *Hebrews*, 75–77; Bruce, F. F. *The Ep. to the Hebrews*, 1965, (New London Commentary), 56–59.
13. Kittel, G. *TDNT*, Vol. V, 153/4; Reumann, J, 'Oikonomia-Terms in Paul in Comparison with Lucan Heilsgeschichte,' *NTStud.* Vol. 13 (1967), 147–167, "Oikonomia" means "administration" more often than "plan of salvation" – if indeed, it ever has that sense in the Pauline corpus.' (166).
14. Conder, C. R. *Tent Work in Palestine*, 1880, Bentley, 339. 340.
15. Ward, R. A. *Hidden Meaning* 139; Klingensmith well translates this, 'Let your love reach out to each

other,' but somehow he lost the heart aspect so important here. Wordsworth, C, *Greek Testament*, Vol. II, on 1 Peter 4: 8, adds, 'intense: stretching itself forward to the end without interruption.' (p64) See also Vine, W. E. *Expository Dictionary*, under 'Stretch. ' To this thought can be added Greek 'epieikes', used in Phil. 4:5 with the meaning, reasonableness, softness, a measure of elasticity, yielding, not insisting on our rights. Robertson, A. T. *Word Pictures* Vol. 4, 459; Barclay, W, *N. T. Words*, 94–96.

16. Ramsay, W. M. in *Hastings' Bible Dictionary*, Vol. IV, 813/4.

17. Ramsay, W. M. *The Letters to the Seven Churches of Asia*, 1909, Hodder, 404–406.

18. Deissmann, G. A. *Light*, 300, and note 2 points out that this was because Paul became a Greek to Greeks, using the popular Hellenistic language, which became the medium for the Christian Scriptures.

19. Robertson, A. T. *Word Pictures*, Vol. 4, 575; Howson, J. S. *Metaphors*, 63–65; Pope, R. M. *Studies*, 27–30.

20. Lightfoot, J. *Horae Hebraicae*, Vol. III, 129; Moulton, H. K. *Challenge*, 180–181.

21. Wuest, K. *Word Studies, Nuggets*, 87; but Trench, R. C. in *Notes on the Parables of our Lord*, 1889, p336 notes that to seek is more than to ask, to knock more than to seek.

22. Thayer, J. H. *Greek-English Lexicon*, 140.

23. Wilkinson, J. G. *The Ancient Egyptians, Their Life & Customs*, 1988rp, Vol. 1, 68.

24. Stanley, A. P. *Sinai and Palestine*, 1887, new ed. Murray 429.

25. *Josephus Wars*, Book 2, ch. 20, 6 (573); Robinson, E. *Biblical Researches*, Vol. 3, 74, 75; Savage, H. E. *The Gospel*, 80/81; Bishop, E. F. *Jesus*, 73 considers the reference too general, as many villages were built on hills. Oesterley, W. O. E. *Parables*, 213, considers it referred to Jerusalem.

26. Zev Vilnay's *Israel Guide*, 1973, Jerusalem, 525–527; Dov Nir's *New Guide to Israel*, 1973, Ward Lock, 297, 304; Stanley, A. P. *Sinai and Palestine*, (op. cit 24), 429; Lachs, S. T. *Rabbinical Commentary*, 83, reads it as 'a fire set on a hill' in reference to the chain of bonfires.

27. Tait, A. *The Charter of Christianity*, 1886, Hodder, 117; Jeremias, J. *Parables*, 120/1, thinks this is best rendered, 'They do not light a lamp in order to put it out again immediately.' He sees in this kindling and extinguishing a similar contrast to the salt (the seasoning cast away). But the context seems to fit best as it stands in NJB, and most other translations.

28. So whether individually, or collectively as a congregation, like the city, Christians need to give out this light. Morgan, G. C. *Parables*, 14.

29. Gadsby, J. *Wanderings*, Vol. 1, 449 footnote; Abrahams, I. *Studies in Pharisaism*, 2nd series, 50; Wuest, K. *Word Studies, Nuggets* 39; Rihbany, A. M. *Syrian Christ*, 171–173, 'home' does not have much meaning to an Arab or Syrian. His way of outdoor life makes him a permanent sojourner; his tent is his shelter and that suffices.

30. Gillman, J. 'Going Home to the Lord.' *Bible Today*, Vol. 20, (1982), 275–281.

31. Cullmann, O. *Peter: Disciple, Apostle, Martyr*, 1953, SCM, 187 and notes.

Chapter 4

Daily Life

1. The Light and the Lamp—
Jesus and John the Baptist.

The message on the lips of John the Baptist seemed a little confusing to some of his listeners at first. Who was he talking about, and just what was John's role to be? They were not to be left in doubt for long. When Jesus came to John to be baptized, it was to start something entirely new, and not a baptism of repentance for sin, since Jesus had no sin to wash away.

As the gospel record states so clearly, 'There was a man named John, who was sent by God. He came to tell people about the Light. Through him all could hear about the Light and believe. John was not the Light, but he came to tell people about the Light. The true Light that gives light to all was coming into the world.' (John 1:6–9, NCV.) Many translations refer to 'that light,' and fail to place the emphasis, through the definite article on 'the light,' on Jesus Christ who was unique in his coming and commission from God. Jesus himself said, 'I am the light of the world.' (John 8:12, 9:5, 3:19, 12:35, 36.)

By contrast, John was just 'a lamp' (Greek 'luchnos'), giving out a little light, and not by any means the light itself. So Jesus paints a graphic illustration when he says to the Jews who had been enquiring from John the Baptist, 'John was like a burning and shining lamp. And you were happy to enjoy his light for a while.' (John 5:35 NCV.) But then Jesus shows how the Father 'has given proof about me himself', and this was through the miracles he accomplished, the truth he explained, and the prophecies he fulfilled. (John 5:36–40.)

J. B. Lightfoot has pointed out that the phrase in John 5:35, 'implies that the light is not inherent, but borrowed,' it is kindled, as in Matthew 5:15 and Luke 12:35.[1] Very few translations reflect this, but it is interesting to note the slight change made in the *New Jerusalem Bible* compared with the earlier *Jerusalem Bible*'s 'alight'. 'John was a lamp *lit* and shining,' but perhaps Knox captures the idea best, 'He [John] after all was the lamp lit to show you the way.'

What a fine illustration! The lamp lit by God to point out the way, but then this lamp pales into insignificance when the real light appears. Just as the street lamps seem to grow dim by comparison when the daylight arrives.

Although this rather special illustration is confined to this happening, and in other places the disciples, for example, are called the 'light of the world',[2] there is one further passage where Peter seems to pick up the simile and use it in another setting.

After discussing Jesus' transfiguration and the word of prophecy, Peter continues, 'It is with good reason that you are paying so much attention to that word: it will go on shining, like a lamp in some darkened room, until the dawn breaks, and the day-star rises in your hearts.' (2 Peter 1:19 Knox.) The lamp of prophecy turned into full light at that transfiguration scene.

The Greek word for 'day-star' is 'phōsphoros', one familiar to us in the English phosphorus.[3] It means to bear or bring light, and as the day-star heralds the dawn, so Jesus Christ does the same at his second coming or presence. The lamp that previously was needed to guide the way, has served its purpose, and can fade away as the fulfilment gives the clear evidence of reality.

2. The Metal Mirror—Partial Understanding.

The metal mirror was well-known in the ancient world, especially Egypt, and could be made from copper, bronze or silver. An idea of how common it was can be obtained from the number that would be needed to make the bronze laver in the tabernacle, for the women contributed their mirrors for this purpose. (Exodus 38:8.)[4]

But if you have ever tried to look at your reflection in a sheet of copper or bronze, you will appreciate how fine our own mirrors are by comparison. Ancient mirrors needed continual polishing, and even then the image was hazy and blurred. This is just the point of the Bible illustration.

James uses the illustration as a simile in a direct way. 'A man who listens to the message, but never acts upon it is like one who looks in a mirror at the face nature gave him. He glances at himself and goes away, and at once forgets what he looked like. But the man who looks closely into the perfect law, the law that makes us free, and who lives in its company, does not forget what he hears, but acts upon it; and that is the man who by acting will find happiness.' (James 1:23–25 NEB.)

The link with the mirror is strengthened by the idea of 'looking closely' into the perfect law, based on love, which covers all that a Christian does. The same Greek word 'parakuptō' is used in 1 Peter 1:12, where Wuest's translation fully brings out its meaning; 'things angels have a passionate desire to stoop way down and look into.' (Also Weymouth ftn.) When we look closely at something we may need to stoop down and peer at it, and this is rather like peering closely into a metal mirror, to try to get as clear a view as possible. Then we will not forget what we see, but endeavour to act upon it.[5]

This takes us very naturally to what the apostle Paul had to say. 'For at present we see in hazy outline by means of a metal mirror, but then it will be face to face. At present I know partially, but then I shall know accurately even as I am accurately known.' (1 Cor. 13:12 NWT.) The understanding of God's purpose possessed by Paul was like the image in a metal mirror, just a partial, hazy one compared with what Paul knew would come in the future, once God's Word was completed, and the fulfilment of prophecy along with all the events of the End time, had illuminated that understanding. As we look back to Paul's day, we can appreciate his remark, and yet we have not fully arrived at that complete understanding for which Paul yearned.

This progressive aspect is evident in Paul's other thought involving the mirror. 'And we, all of us, with faces unveiled, reflecting as mirrors the splendour of the Lord, are being transformed into the same likeness with ever-increasing splendour. This is the work of the Lord who is the Spirit.' (2 Cor. 3:18 TNT.) To improve the reflective qualities of the metal mirror, it could be polished and burnished again and again. So too, for us, to ever-increasingly reflect the splendour of the Lord, requires us to work continually on our reflective qualities.[6]

Then a process takes place which Paul refers to by using the present tense, 'are being transformed'. More and more we conform our minds and hearts to that model or pattern revealed by Christ, which sets us such an example. Paul describes this by using the same word 'transformed' (Greek 'metamorphoō'), at Romans 12: 1, 2. That change is a permanent one from within, not a merely outward transfiguration, such as Satan could put on. (2 Cor. 11:14.)[7]

By contrast, Christ's example is mentioned at Hebrews 1:3a, 'He [Christ] radiates God's glory'. (TNT.) The word here (Greek 'apaugasma'), means to beam forth, like the sun's rays, conveying light and warmth. So Christ perfectly conveys the Father's every quality. This flashing *forth* is a more direct means, because he is the light, than that of reflection or flashing *back*.[8]

The strength of this illustration lies in the nature of the metal mirror of that time. It would be much diminished by merely replacing it with the idea of the modern mirror, which requires little effort to reflect a clear image. May we all keep on working to polish and improve our reflection, so that it is a worthy one, not forgetting, through prayer, to call upon God's holy spirit to assist us.

3. Valued and Useful Vessels— Being Fit for an Honourable Purpose.

Writing to Timothy, the apostle Paul drew upon an interesting illustration to show how Christians could gain and keep God's approval. 'Now in any great house there are not only utensils of gold and silver, but also others of wood or earthenware; the former are valued, the latter held cheap. To be among those which are valued and dedicated, a thing of use to the Master of the house, a man must cleanse himself from all those evil things; then he will be fit for an honourable purpose.' (2 Tim. 2:20, 21, NEB.)

When a person shows by his right course of action that he is really a Christian, he becomes a workman or vessel approved by God, able to handle properly the Word of God, and is then entrusted with the good news, to tell it out fearlessly. (2 Tim. 2:15, 1 Thess. 2:4.) The light of truth within us becomes a treasure, so Paul uses the same metaphor when he says, 'We have a treasure, then, in our keeping, but its shell is of perishable earthenware; it must be God, and not anything in ourselves that gives it its sovereign power.' (2 Cor. 4:7 Knox.)[9]

But a Christian needs to continue in the household of God as a valuable vessel for an honourable purpose. Even a profession of Christianity without actions which demonstrate it, can disqualify us as fit vessels. (Titus 1:16.) An interesting play on words in Romans 1:28 is lost in many Bible translations. W. J. Conybeare catches the thought when he says of those who reject God, 'they thought fit to cast out the acknowledgment of God. God gave them over to an outcast mind to do the things that are unseemly.' (footnote.) So a person becomes a castaway when his faith suffers shipwreck. (See chapter 11, number 7.)

How does Paul's metaphor of the vessels apply here? In the last two quotations (from Titus and Romans), the Greek word 'adokimos' is used, meaning 'disqualified' or 'rejected;' an 'outcast,' and a 'castaway. ' He applies the same word to his own case when he states, 'I discipline my body and bring it under control, lest I preach to others and be thrown out myself.' (1 Cor. 9:27 Klingensmith.)[10]

If a waterpot became cracked and could not hold water, it would no longer be fit for its purpose. It might be thrown out altogether, or relegated to an inferior, less honourable use in a meaner part of the house. Today we sometimes say about an argument that it 'won't hold water' or will not stand the test, and so we throw it out as useless. In the final analysis Paul did not want that to happen to him, to be disapproved, and rejected as one unable to hold the water of truth faithfully.[11] So he fought hard to maintain his faith. How fine an illustration for us today, that we too might maintain our place in God's household as vessels fit for an honourable purpose. True, we may at times seem to be 'leaky vessels', but we can pray for God's spirit to keep on filling us up again.

4. An Undefiled Vessel—Clean Inside and Out.

The meticulous rules that frequently guided the Pharisees came in for scathing criticism from Jesus, especially in the well-known twenty-third chapter of Matthew. One of these matters concerned the ritual cleanness of vessels. Jesus told them, 'You clean the outside of the cup and the dish, while the inside is full of greed and self-indulgence. Can't you see, Pharisee? First wash the inside of the cup, and then you can clean the outside.' (Matt. 23: 25, 26 Phillips.)

The Mishnah sets out the detailed rules recorded later in its tractate entitled 'Kelim – Vessels. ' One of the principal ideas is expressed this way, 'Earthenware vessels and vessels of alum-crystal are alike in what concerns uncleanness; they contract uncleanness and convey uncleanness through their airspace . . .' (Kelim 2. 1.) [12] So the air or atmosphere is somehow altered inside the vessel by being enclosed, and is no longer fresh and clean. Jesus' simple remedy was to clean the inside first, or applying the metaphor, for the Pharisees to clean up their motives and heart condition, removing all wrong ideas of selfishness, pride and greed. Then the outside would automatically follow in accordance with their own ritual ideas. [13]

Jesus' comment in Luke's gospel is a little different. 'Don't you realize that the one who made the outside is the maker of the inside as well? If you would only make the inside clean by giving the contents to those in need, the outside becomes clean as a matter of course.' (Luke 11:40, 41 Phillips.) Nigel Turner suggests that the phrase 'the [things] inside' (Greek 'ésōthen'), should be treated as an adverbial accusative meaning 'inwardly,' and would then render it 'Give alms from the heart (sincerely)'. [14] They should not only be generous in giving, but it should be heartfelt and genuine.

The maker of the earthenware vessel did not choose a lump of clay contaminated in one half which he would then place on the inside. Both outside and inside come from the same clean piece of clay. But was Jesus here seeing beyond the earthenware vessel, as he thought in terms of his metaphor? If so, then was he talking about God as the great Potter of all human creatures, and that it was certainly God's intention that men should give or serve from a clean, pure heart and motive? Inside they should be holy, and free from all spiritual defilement, and then it would be a comparatively easy matter to keep the outside of their bodies clean too.

5. Rinsings and Offscourings—
Outcasts from the World.

It is very difficult for us today to quite appreciate the very low opinion of Christians held by the ancient world. Not only did Christianity challenge the cherished ideas of Jews and Romans alike, but its following for the most part appeared to be ignorant and common men, simply intent on upsetting the establishment. (Acts 4: 13, 1 Cor. 1:26–29.)

The apostle Paul summed up this attitude by the use of two very striking words. After describing the treatment meted out to himself and his fellow disciples, which made them an exhibition to the world, he concluded, 'Until now, we are regarded as the rubbish (Greek 'perikatharma') of the world, the offscouring (Greek 'peripsēma') of society.' (1 Cor. 4:9–13 Blackwelder.)

The word for rubbish referred to the rinsings from say, a dirty water-carrying jar, swilled around before being cast out, and considered as filth and scum to be quickly washed away. But then this was coupled with another equally opprobrious term – offscouring! It might still be necessary, having rinsed out a vessel, to scour or scrape the dirt from its inside, for if left there it could only contaminate and pollute anything clean put into it.[15] That was the viewpoint of many about Christians in the first century, well summed up by the paraphrase, 'everybody thinks himself well rid of us'. (1 Cor. 4:13b Knox.) Schonfield, in his *Original New Testament*, adds the footnote, 'The metaphor is taken from the Athenian custom in the event of some dire calamity of throwing some of the human "scum" of the city into the sea, to "clean off" the guilt of the people.'[16]

Paul could testify to this from his personal experience. When he was rescued from the Jews by some Roman soldiers after a commotion in the Temple, the chiliarch (commandant) allowed Paul to put his case, but he was interrupted part-way through with the cry, 'Down with him! A scoundrel like that is better dead!' (Acts 22:22b NEB.) Reason and scripture were not listened to by these men whose emotions were outraged, and their entrenched positions attacked. Little wonder that history records how many of those early Christians were thrown to the lions, sometimes as scapegoats blamed on some pretext like setting Rome on fire, but more often simply because their contrary course to society generally made them outcasts and vile persons. (1 Peter 4:4.)

Interestingly, both these ideas appear again in a different context in the Hebrew Scriptures. It is the Israelites who express how they feel God views them as they contemplate the loss of their precious city Jerusalem, after its fall to the Babylonians. In their dejection and desolation, and recognition of the nation's disobedience and sin, they feel cut off from their God. 'You have covered Yourself with a cloud that no prayer can pass through. You have made us offscouring and refuse among the nations. All our enemies have gaped at us and railed against us.' (Lam. 3:44–46, Amplified.)

Although the illustration is the same, the situation is very different. The exiled Israelites felt sadness and despair, but the early Christians felt happiness and even pride in the same condition. How could there be such a contrast? The way the nations viewed both groups was no different, for they hated and despised them all. But it was how they stood with God that counted. The Israelites felt God had left them and they were lost. The Christians knew God was with them, and they enjoyed a close relationship with him – that made all the difference. So Paul could well sum up the matter in answer to his own question, 'Who can separate us from Christ's love? . . . As it is written, "For your sake we are put to death all day long; we are considered sheep to be slaughtered." No! In all these things we are more than conquerors through the One [God] who loved us.' (Rom. 8:35–37, Adams.)

6. Leaven that Ferments—Pervasive Power.

To the Hebrews leaven had a particular significance. In the Mosaic Law provision was made for the Passover or 'feast of unleavened bread', which would remind the Israelites of how they left Egypt at a moment's notice, not having time to wait for leavened bread to rise so that they could take supplies with them. (Exodus 12: 31–34.)

When they celebrated the Passover, they had to remove all leaven from their homes, and eat only unleavened bread for seven days. (Exodus 12:14, 15, 18–20.) Leaven came to represent an influence that was bad, partly because it seemed that bad spread gradually through food and through people, rather in the way that leaven gradually permeated the flour until it was all in ferment. But it also became a habit for many housewives on the move continually, to save a piece of dough until the next baking, by which time it had often become dirty and dusty, and could be a carrier of disease, another reminder of something becoming polluted.

When Jesus said to his disciples, 'Be on your guard against the leaven of the Pharisees and Sadducees,' they naively thought he was speaking literally, perhaps because they were sensitive to the fact that they had forgotten to bring some bread with them on the journey, or as we might say, we had forgotten our sandwiches. But that was not his meaning, so he eventually had to speak plainly, and they at last realized he meant, 'they were to be on their guard, not against baker's leaven, but against the teaching of the Pharisees and Sadducees.' (Matt. 16:5–12 NEB.) Because their traditions contradicted God's Word, their teaching had spread such wrong ideas that it caused them to even reject the Messiah, the Son of God.

The apostle Paul twice made the statement, 'A little leaven leavens all the dough.' (1 Cor. 5:6, Gal. 5:9 NEB.) This saying may have had a Rabbinic origin, and this would explain its use by Paul.[17] In the first instance it referred to a bad case of immorality within the congregation at Corinth, and Paul urged action, for condoning the practice would only lead to corruption of the entire congregation, and the loss of God's blessing. 'Purge it out, and then you will be bread of a new baking,' he added. (1 Cor. 5:7 NEB.) They must remove such a man to prevent further contamination by the 'leaven', a wrong moral influence with pervasive power. (1 Cor. 5:1–13.)

The second example was of a stumbling block or hindrance being placed in the way of the Galatians. Judaisers from Jerusalem had tried to discredit Paul, saying that the Galatians should be circumcised and keep the Mosaic Law, and so this only confused and upset them. Paul stressed the need for 'faith active in love' and warned them about listening to this 'leaven' that could so easily spread throughout the new congregations in Asia Minor. (Gal. 5:1–12.) Such persuasion could not come from God, for it hindered their spiritual progress, and kept them from fully appreciating the truth.

7. Babes Still on Milk—Lack of Maturity.

One of the great illustrations of contrast made by the apostle Paul, was that of the baby and the adult. When we consider the depth of understanding and appreciation evident in Paul's writings, we can excuse a sense of frustration and impatience which shows through whenever he deals with this theme.

'Accordingly, brothers, I was not able to speak to you as spiritual men (Greek 'pneumatikos'), but as ordinary human beings, as infants in Christ. I fed you with milk, not with solid food, for you could not yet take it. Indeed, you still cannot.' (1 Cor. 3:1, 2 TNT.) The contrast is between babes or infants (Greek 'nēpios') not able to talk or chew, and adults (Greek 'teleiōs'), arriving at the end, being of age, full grown, mature.[18]

Have you ever spoken to an audience of supposedly spiritual Christians, and found that they were not on your 'wave-length' and seemed completely to lack that deeper spiritual dimension? That is how Paul must have felt on this occasion. He evidently felt a great sense of disappointment at the lack of maturity, the lack of spiritual growth.

In the controversy over the author of the book of Hebrews, it is interesting to compare a passage there which suggests Paul as its author, for it has that same ring or tone about it noted in his letter to the Corinthians.

'By this time you ought to be teachers, but you need someone to teach you again the very first principles of God's revelation; you have come to need milk, not solid food. For anyone who lives on milk has no experience of the message of righteousness; he is an infant. But solid food is for mature men, who have perceptions trained by practice to distinguish between good and bad.' (Heb. 5:12–14 TNT.)

To explain how Christ Jesus was a priest like Melchizedek of old, required experience and understanding of God's Word – of spiritual truths, which by now those Hebrews should be teaching others about. So he urged them, 'let us leave behind the elementary stages of the message of Christ . . . . Now let us go on to advanced teaching. (Heb. 6:1, 2, TNT.)

To remain as 'little children' was to risk being 'blown about by every wind of false teaching.' (Eph. 4:14 TNT, see also chapter 11, number 4.) But young Timothy was a fine example of one who had taken to heart the excellent instruction he had received, and this would continue to help him 'to grow up spiritually yourself'. (1 Tim. 4:6 TNT.)

Peter also uses this simile, but it is found in a more gentle context, and the contrast is missing. He seems content to illustrate merely the first stage of a Christian's growth. 'As new-born babies are eager for their mother's milk, you too should be eager for that pure spiritual milk on which you will thrive and come to salvation.' (1 Pet. 2:2 TNT.)

Paul adds another aspect to the contrast that characterizes his discussions. 'Brothers, do not be like children in your thinking. Where wickedness is concerned be like infants, but in your thinking be mature.' (1 Cor. 14:20 TNT.) They should *not* have experience in things not becoming a Christian. Have we followed Paul's wise counsel, avoiding things of the world which can damage our integrity, but advancing to full maturity in our thinking as truly 'spiritual men'?

8. The Way—The Principles of Christianity.

'The Way' has been called 'the leading Scriptural metaphor', and this is primarily because of the importance of the idea.[19]

The theme is evident in the Old Testament Hebrew Scriptures. The Exodus from Egypt set the Israelites on 'the way' to the promised land, but it proved to be a long, hard one. Then when the nation went into captivity to Babylon, the exiles were searching and looking for 'the way' back again.

But these two physical returns to the land of promise did not really compare with the need to find a spiritual way back to God, when the nation went off course and fell into false worship and idolatry. Then God himself would appeal to them as their teacher and instructor so that 'when you swerve to right or left, you hear a Voice behind you whispering, "This is the way, walk here".' (Isa. 30:21 Moffatt.) It has been summed up in this sentence, 'The Way was ever towards a Divine presence, undertaken by a Divine invitation, and under Divine guidance, with a divinely promised blessing in store.'[20]

That way became ever more finely delineated when Jesus Christ gave clear direction to the nucleus of the early Christian congregation. He first identified his own position and example when he told Thomas, 'I am the way and the truth and the life. No one can come to the Father except through me.' (John 14:6, C. B. Williams.) So prayer is addressed to God through his Son, and he is the trail blazer. (Heb. 12:2, 3.)

After Jesus' death the establishment of the Christian congregation through the guidance of the holy spirit gradually made it clear that this was the channel that God was using to accomplish his purpose. It was variously called the way of salvation or the way of God. (Acts 16:17, 18:25, 26.)

None of these passages so far cited would seem to justify this illustration being called 'a leading metaphor'. But the remaining instances are mainly examples of the word entirely unmodified by dependent genitives, (i.e. 'hē hodos'). This is a distinctive form, able to stand alone, and denotes that the word had assumed a technical or absolute sense as a title or label by which this group had become known, perhaps at first merely in an endeavour to find some manner of description for these unusual people, in the same way in which 'Christian' was used.[21]

It is first in connection with Saul's frenzied persecution that this technical sense emerges, perhaps because there was need of a label in the letters from the high priest to the Damascus synagogues, 'that if he [Saul] found any men or women belonging to The Way he might bring them in chains to Jerusalem.' (Acts 9:2, 22:4, C. B. Williams.)

Some twenty years later, when Paul (now a follower of The Way himself), was in Ephesus having lively discussions in the synagogue, the Jews were 'criticizing The Way before the people', and this was shortly followed by a dispute 'about The Way' which threatened the money-making activites associated with the sale of little images of Diana. (Acts 19:9, 23, C. B. Williams.)

Some time later, back in Jerusalem, Paul was accused of taking Greek friends into the Temple, beyond the demarcation barriers, and this led to a trial before the Jewish council, and then before governor Felix in Caesarea. There Paul testified that 'in accordance with The Way – that they call heresy – I continue to worship the God of my forefathers.' Little wonder that when Felix adjourned the trial it could be said of him that he 'had a fairly clear conception of the principles involved in The Way.' (Acts 24:14, 22, C. B. Williams.)

This statement by Paul suggests that 'The Way' was a term adopted by the Christians themselves, for it is contrasted with 'heresy'. Its central position in this absolute sense certainly justifies its description as a leading metaphor in Scripture.

9. Narrow Path, Broad Way— One to Follow and One to Avoid.

Jesus' colourful Sermon on the Mount is replete with fine illustrations, but perhaps none is so vivid as when he spoke about the two ways. 'Go through the narrow gate. The gate is wide, and the way is broad that leads to destruction, and many are going that way. But the gate is small, and the way is narrow, that leads to life, and only a few are finding it.' (Matt. 7:13, 14 Beck.)

The two ways was a familiar idea to many of Jesus' listeners. Moses had set such a choice before the Israelites when they were about to enter the promised land, and a similar choice was given to them just before Jerusalem fell to the Babylonians. (Deut.30:19, Jer.21:8) But Jesus' illustration painted a graphic picture of what each way was like.

The broad and spacious way is linked to two Greek words; 'plateia' (broad, wide), and 'euruchōros' (broad country or place).[22] Have you ever crossed a wide plain or moor with no signposts to guide you, and no boundaries or fences? You can soon be lost, with no landmarks in sight. It may seem easy to make progress, especially if you don't care where you are going. That is how this world appears to many today – they take no thought as to their goal in life, but they drift aimlessly, living only for today, and not wanting to place any boundaries to their course of action, a course often described as 'free and independent'. Jesus said most people were like that, on a course that meant their destruction. (cp. Rom. 1:28–32.)

The opposite course was not easy, but it did lead to life. A fine description of a 'narrow path' is given by Josephus when he explains how the great rock of Masada, on the shore of the Dead Sea could be climbed. 'The former (path) they call the snake, seeing a resemblance to that reptile in its narrowness and continual windings; for its course is broken in skirting the jutting crags and, returning frequently upon itself and gradually lengthening out again, it makes painful headway. One traversing this route must firmly plant each foot alternately. Destruction faces him; for on either side yawn chasms so terrific as to daunt the hardiest. After following this perilous track for thirty furlongs, one reaches the summit.' (War Book VII, ch. 8, (3), 282–284 Loeb edition.)

A difficult ascent, fraught with danger, and the possibility of losing out by departing from the path. No wonder Paul and Barnabas strengthened the disciples in Asia Minor, 'encouraging them to be loyal to the faith, saying, "We must suffer much to go into God's Kingdom".' (Acts 14:22 Beck.) That path is very much like climbing a mountain, which will take all our strength and endurance. (Micah 4:1, 2.) But notice that Jesus' first command is, 'Go through the narrow gate'. Yes, get started on the road to life by means of dedication to God, despite the way being cramped by persecution and tribulation.[23]

Progress on that road is not going to be in one's own strength alone, but God promises to help us by his holy spirit. If God is on our side because we are loyal to him, nothing can separate us from his love and his narrow path, and we will be victorious in the end. (Romans 8:26–39.)

10. Straight Roads—Directing our Feet Successfully.

The Roman roads of the apostle Paul's day are still with us in many

parts of Europe, and their straight course is almost proverbial. Among
the hardships that Paul listed is included, 'I have been constantly on
the road.' (2 Cor. 11:26 NEB.) Some might take issue with this
rendering, saying that Paul did not use the roads as much as might
be thought. But if one traces his journeys as recorded in Acts, he
did use the roads a great deal, and must have appreciated their value
in his ministry, for all their problems.[24]

With the relatively slow methods of travel in Bible times, keeping
the distance to a minimum by means of a straight road was most
important. But the idea of a strong and solid road is also associated
with the Roman method, as their durability to this day testifies. So
the illustration is an understandable one, although the principles were
appreciated before Roman times; they just brought roads to their
greatest height of achievement. The other aspect coming through in
the metaphor was that of making the road smooth, especially for foot
travellers. Market places were often covered with marble, some roads
in towns were provided with flatter stepping stones across them, and
blocks of lava could provide a sort of crazy paving.[25]

Writing to the Thessalonians, Paul applies the illustration in almost a literal sense. 'May our God and Father, and our Lord Jesus
Christ, prepare us a straight road to you.' (1 Thess. 3:11 Sadler.) He
uses the same Greek word ('kateuthunō') to express his hope that
God may continue to keep their hearts straight so far as their devotion to him is concerned. (2 Thess. 3:5.)

When John the Baptizer was born his work of preparation for the
Messiah was clearly outlined, and included how he would 'direct
and guide our feet in a straight line into [the] way of peace.' (Luke
1:79 Amplified Bible, and Robertson's translation note – 'to make
perfectly straight'.) When John grew up and actually began his
ministry the idea was repeated, and sounds more like the instructions
of a Roman road engineer than a quotation from the prophet Isaiah
(40:3–5). 'Every valley and ravine shall be filled up, and every
mountain and hill shall be levelled down, and the crooked places
shall be made straight, and the rough roads shall be made smooth.'
(Luke 3:5 Amplified.)

Those opposed to God continually tried to twist his words and
ways so as to mislead his servants. Paul exposed Elymas the magi-
cian with some indignant and stinging phrases, including, 'Will you

never stop trying to make the Lord's straight paths crooked?' (Acts 13:10 Goodspeed.)

The illustration has a novel twist to it in the case of Balaam and his ass. (Numbers 22.) An angel blocked the narrow road between two stone walls bordering vineyards, so the ass, alone able to see the angel, tried to turn aside, whilst Balaam beat the animal in an endeavour seemingly to pursue his literally straight course. When it first crushed his foot against one wall, and then lay down, Balaam became infuriated. After the miraculous conversation with the ass, his eyes were able to see the angel for the first time, and then he heard his well-deserved rebuke, which is summarized by Peter in speaking of all those who tried to follow Balaam's course of resisting God and his ways. 'Leaving the straight road, they have gone astray and followed in the steps of Balaam.' (2 Peter 2:15 TCNT.) What may seem to be straight to certain persons, may be deceptive and twisted from God's viewpoint.

The course of a river is here helpful and instructive. It winds and twists with many bends and changes of course, because it follows the line of least resistance. So is the course of a weak and inconsistent person, who allows expediency to change his course when difficult situations arise. Peter was guilty of this when he stopped eating with gentiles because of what others might think of him. (Gal. 2:11–14.)[26]

The course that gains God's blessing is not one of twisting his teachings and ways, but making them as easy as possible for others to understand and follow. Even those who may be spiritually 'lame' can be helped to make progress along His way. If discipline is necessary, and some feel for a time disheartened, help given then can keep the weak ones on course, and they will feel encouraged to persist, with happy results. 'Therefore, "lift again the down-dropped hands, and straighten the weakened knees; make straight paths for your feet," so that the lame limb may not be put out of joint, but rather be cured.' (Heb. 12:12, 13 TCNT, Isa. 35:3, Prov. 4:25–27 LXX.)

11. Walking—Good Relationships.

When Jesus heard that Lazarus had died, he decided to return to Judea, but his disciples tried to dissuade him out of concern for his safety. His reply must have made them wonder exactly what he meant. 'Are there not twelve hours of daylight? If a man goes walking by day he does not stumble because he sees the world bathed in light. But if he goes walking at night he will stumble since there is no light in him.' (John 11:7–10 NAB.)

As they pondered this saying, the disciples would realize that Jesus was using the word 'walking' in a double sense, for he had already said to them, 'I am the light of the world. No follower of mine shall ever walk in darkness; no, he shall possess the light of life.' (John 8:12 NAB.) Jesus was assuring them that his hour had not yet come, the 'twelve hours' of day meant that he still had things to do, and he would be safe, for the hazardous dark night was not yet so close.

But long before this, 'walking' had been used in a metaphorical sense. Enoch and Noah were said to have 'walked with God' and the Psalmist spoke of the one who 'walks blamelessly' while Proverbs said that God is 'the shield of those who walk honestly'. (Gen. 5:24, 6:9, Ps. 15:2, Prov. 2:7 NAB.) When Amos asked the question, 'Do two walk together unless they have agreed?' we can appreciate what it meant to 'walk with God' – to have a close relationship, to be in harmony with him, and to accept his counsel. (Amos 3:3 NAB.) All that God required was 'to do right and to love goodness, and to walk humbly with your God.' (Micah 6:8 NAB.)

The usual word for 'walking' is Greek 'peripateō', to walk about, to go around here and there. Where it stands as a metaphor it refers to one's way of life, conduct and attitude, and many modern translations transfer the metaphor to ideas like this. Jesus is the best example to follow, for 'He who says he abides in Him ought himself also to walk just as He walked.' (1 John 2:6 NKJV.)[27]

The apostle Paul used this illustration in combination with various aspects of 'walking with God' or his qualities and right attributes. We need to 'walk by faith, not by sight' (2 Cor. 5:7), to 'walk worthy of the Lord, to please Him in all things' (Col. 1:10, Eph. 4:1), 'walk without stumbling' (walk with exactness – footnote, Eph. 5:15), to 'walk in love, as Christ also loved us' (Eph. 5:2), to 'walk not after the flesh, but after the Spirit' (Rom. 8:4) and to 'walk in newness of life.' (Rom. 6:4 all Conybeare.)

Writing to the Corinthians, Paul skilfully uses word play, as he does so often, first speaking of walking as a similitude, and then repeating it with a literal meaning. 'I expect to be bold against some among you who reckon us as walking after the flesh. For though we walk in flesh, yet our warfare is not after the flesh.' (2 Cor. 10:2, 3 Sadler.)

John also used the metaphor in the same way, but perhaps because of the apostasy rampant in his old age, he stresses the aspect of truth. 'It has given me great joy to find some of your children walking in the path of truth . . . This love involves our walking according to the commandments.' 'For it has given me great joy to have the brothers bear witness to how truly you walk in the path of truth.' (2 John 4, 6, 3 John 3, 4 NAB.)

In a few places, a different Greek word, 'stoicheō', is used. It is more precise in meaning than 'peripateō', 'to be in step with', 'in rank', 'leading a closely regulated life'.[28] Paul encouraged the Philippians with the words, 'seeing we have pressed forward to this point let us keep our place there in rank.' (Phil. 3:16–18 Sadler.) He also exhorted Christians to 'let our steps be guided ['stoicheō'] by the Spirit.' In that way, we can 'walk orderly' or 'tread in the steps of that Faith which our father Abraham had while yet uncircumcised.' (Gal. 5:25, Rom. 4:12 Conybeare.)

There are many other references to 'walking with God', bringing our life pattern into harmony with the teachings of his word, the Bible, and so coming into that sort of relationship which we enjoy when we walk along in close conversation with a treasured friend.

12. The Antidote—Christ's Ransom.

The Greek word for 'ransom' is 'lutron', found in that well-known verse of Matthew 20:28, where it is said of Jesus that he would 'give his soul a ransom for many'. (Concordant Version.)

The illustration of a 'ransom' is familiar in today's modern world, when hostages are taken and held to ransom. The price demanded may vary tremendously, not because there is any basic difference between one person's life and another, but due to the material possessions they may be thought to have, and the audacity and temerity of the captors. In ancient times, Josephus used the word in reference to all the beautiful and precious ornaments of the Temple, saved by giving as a ransom one very valuable solid bar or rod of gold. (Ant. Book 14, ch. 7, (1) 107f.)

But in the case of Jesus Christ, who is it that instigates or requires the provision of the ransom? Some bizarre ideas have been proposed by a few scholars. The Scriptures are clear though, 'He who spares not his own Son, but gives Him up for us all.' (Rom. 8:32 Concordant.) As Edwin Abbott points out, 'giving' implies simply a gift, to 'give up' implies 'the sacrifice of something precious'.[29]

This brings us to why such a sacrifice was considered fitting and right by Almighty God? The more interesting aspect of our illustration comes to the fore here. The apostle Paul wrote to Timothy, 'A Man, Christ Jesus, Who is giving Himself a correspondent Ransom for all.' (1 Tim. 2:6 Concordant.) The word for 'correspondent ransom' or 'corresponding ransom' (NWT), here is Greek 'antilutron', its only use in the Scriptures, for it is not even found in the Septuagint.[30] Many translations make no distinction in the way they translate this word from the simple Greek 'lutron', 'ransom,' but as Ellicott points out, the preposition 'anti' is not to be viewed as redundant. 'If we are to see any special force in the anti, we may say that it expresses that the 'lutron' is equivalent in value to the thing procured by means of it.'[31] So we then ask, what was lost that needed to be bought back, equivalent in value? It was all that Adam lost for the human race when he sinned, life-rights for himself and his offspring. Jesus' ransom bought back those life rights, and so Paul calls him 'the last Adam'. (1 Cor. 15:45.) That was why he needed to be a perfect man, to balance or be the equivalent of the first Adam, the only other perfect man to have walked the earth. Jesus being a 'corresponding ransom' was a provision by God himself to answer the requirement of his own perfect justice, a life for a life. (Ex. 21:23, Lev. 24:18, Num. 35: 30, 31.)

Now we can appreciate the illustrative nature of this rare word 'antilutron'. William Barclay explains it nicely, 'It is worth noting in the passing that in the Orphic literature it is used to mean an "antidote", and "remedy". Christ's death, we could understand it, is the "antidote" for the poison, and the "remedy" for the disease of sin.'[32]

An antidote is just the right amount to balance or negate the poison against which it is administered; in other words it corresponds. Jesus' transfer to earth as a perfect human was made to match with Adam, and by Jesus thus voluntarily laying down his life, and his heavenly Father permitting that life to be 'given up', Jesus became a 'corresponding ransom'.

What an excellent illustration to help us to appreciate all that is involved in this most important of all ransoms. Matthew 20:28 now takes on still greater meaning. If those perfect life-rights have been bought back, they can be applied to any number of persons, many millions even, without limitation, depending only on how many seek to avail themselves of that provision by their faith and Christian course. (Rev. 22:17.)

13. Food and Refuse—
Finding the Truly Precious Things.

After a famous occasion in the gospels, Jesus gave his disciples a lesson in how to view priorities in life. After feeding the 5,000 Jesus said to his disciples, 'Pick up the pieces that are left, that nothing be wasted.' (John 6:12 C. B. Williams.) The twelve large baskets of scraps exceeded by far what they had started with, five loaves and two fish – a miracle indeed! Still nothing material left over was to be wasted. No refuse was left to disfigure that lovely countryside.

When crowds came searching for him next day, Jesus suggested it was because they had been fed so well. Then he told them how to compare material and spiritual things, 'Stop toiling for the food that perishes, but toil for the food that lasts for eternal life, which the Son of Man will give you, for God the Father has given him authority to do so.' (John 6:27 C. B. Williams.) When they asked what they must do, he said, 'The work that God demands of you is this, to believe in the messenger whom he has sent.' (John 6:29 C. B. Williams.)

They asked what work or sign Jesus was going to do, for didn't
the Israelites eat manna, bread from heaven? But he implies that the
manna only came from the skies, it was not the real bread from his
Father in heaven. When they asked for this, he made the metaphor
clear. 'I am the bread that gives life. Whoever comes to me will
never get hungry, and whoever believes in me will never get thirsty.'
(Verse 35.)

The Jews failed to fully perceive the illustration, and confused
Jesus' literal human birth with his true origin. So he enlarged the
metaphor to make it still clearer. 'I am the bread that gives life.
Your forefathers in the desert ate the manna, and yet they died. But
here is the bread that comes down out of heaven so that anyone may
eat it and never die. I am this living bread that has come down out
of heaven. If anyone eats this bread, he will live forever, and the
bread that I will give for the life of the world is my own flesh.'
(John 6:48–51 C. B. Williams.)

But this was misunderstood once again. Instead of realizing that
he talked of his sacrificial death, they interpreted it as some sort of
cannibalism. 'As a result of this many of His disciples turned their
backs on Him and stopped accompanying Him.' (Verse 66) But the
twelve saw there was nowhere else to go and their spokesman Peter
said, 'To whom can we go, Lord? You have the message that gives
eternal life, and we have come to believe, yes more, we know by
experience, that you are the Holy One of God.' (John 6:68, 69 C.
B. Williams.)

When Paul wrote to the Philippians he showed he well appreciated
all that Christ had done, and that he had carefully compared material
and spiritual things, and identified that which was truly precious and
of lasting worth. He summed it up in a classic passage, 'Yes, indeed,
I certainly do count everything as loss compared with the priceless
privilege of knowing Christ Jesus my Lord. For His sake I have lost
everything, and value it all as mere refuse, in order to gain Christ
and be actually in union with Him.' (Phil. 3: 8, 9a C. B. Williams.)

The word 'refuse' (Greek 'skubalon'), refers to food thrown away
from the table, the leftovers of a feast, and both Jews and Romans
placed much store on feasting and revelling. Perhaps there is a link
with verse 2, where Paul refers to the Judaizers that often troubled
him, 'Look out for those dogs, those mischief-makers, those self-

mutilators!' They thought of themselves as much in God's favour, as if seated at his banquet, where only the leftovers were thrown to the dogs, the gentiles with whom Paul associated. So Paul inverts the picture, literally 'turns the tables'; what the Judaizers eat and value has been thrown from the table, and they are the dogs eating the refuse from the feast.[33]

All that Paul had previously lived for he now valued as nothing – his prestigious parentage, his high station in Pharisaism, his adherence to Mosaic Law and 'outward privileges' and all the material benefits that flowed from such a position – those he now counted altogether as refuse. His course right to the end showed that he remained faithful to that valuation. (Phil. 3:3–7.)

Today the 'refuse' of this system is far greater. Materialism grips the world, and men give their all for position, prestige and wealth. The Christian has to fully appreciate spiritual things in order to keep thinking as Jesus and Paul did. John summed it up so well, 'because everything that is in the world, the things that our lower nature and eyes are longing for, and the proud pretentions of life, do not come from the Father, but from the world; and the world is passing away and with it the evil longing it incites, but whoever perseveres in doing God's will lives on forever.' (1 John 2:16, 17 C. B. Williams.)

14. Destroying Rubbish by Burning—Gehenna.

One day in early September 1973, I walked with my friend Fred Stead into a secluded valley just south of old Jerusalem. It is called the Valley of Hinnom (Ge-hinnom), and runs off the main Kidron Valley. We had left behind the noise and bustle of the narrow streets of the city, and the peaceful, tranquil calm of this little ravine on a lovely summer's day was a marked contrast. Yet its history is a still greater contrast.

The south side of the valley is quite natural in its steep contours, but the side nearest to the old walls slopes more gradually, for it hides the city's ancient rubbish dump. To meet the Jewish requirement of purity, the streets of ancient Jerusalem were swept every day, and all other rubbish was disposed of. The Dung Gate (or Gate of the Ash-Heaps), gave access from the old city onto the Valley of

Hinnom at its deepest eastern end. Professor Jeremias adds, 'the Valley of Hinnom was a place of abomination from ancient times, since it was connected with the worship of Moloch (2 Kings 23:10, Jer. 2:23 and elsewhere), ... It was still in modern times the place for rubbish, carrion and all kinds of refuse.'[34]

Fires were kept burning continually to destroy dead bodies of criminals and animal carcases, hence the ash-heaps. No living persons were consigned there, and King Josiah made it a place of defilement to prevent the idolatrous practice of human sacrifice and torture in the fire of Molech.[35]

What did Jesus mean when he suggested tearing out a right eye, or losing a right hand, rather than being consigned to Gehenna? (Matt. 5:29, 30, Mark 9:43–47.) Since all mankind has sinned and made mistakes, a literal application might suggest that only left-handed and left-eyed persons would survive into God's Kingdom! So clearly the illustration was designed to show that anything as precious as a right eye or a right hand was better dispensed with if it was likely to stumble us.

It is important to remember the exact use of the Valley of Hinnom to apply the illustration or symbol correctly, a point where many scholars have gone astray. If God would not countenance any torment of humans in Israel's day in that valley, then he would not change that principle at any future time. (2 Chron. 33:6.) Gehenna had become a symbol of complete destruction. What was not eaten by dogs or maggots, was destroyed by fire. (Mark 9: 48, 49.)[36]

So for humans it would not be a place of torture, for God had already decreed against that because he is a God of love, but rather the illustration only fitted the symbol by representing complete destruction of the wicked, and there was never any question of torment in a hell of fire, since Jesus specifically named 'both soul and body to destroy in gehenna'. (Matt. 10:28, Roth, cp. Phillips, and Matt. 13:40, Luke 17:29, 30, Isa. 66: 24.)

15. Sounding Out—Spreading the Good News.

The apostle Paul opened his famous chapter on love by saying that even if he could speak every language used by men and angels, but did not have love, 'I am no better than echoing bronze, or the clash of cymbals.' (1 Cor. 13:1 Knox.)

We are all well aware of the harsh sound of a clash of cymbals used on its own, but what is the 'echoing bronze'? (Greek 'chalkos ēcheō') This has often been rendered by a noisy or clanging gong, although scholars have never satisfactorily referred it to a known musical instrument. But a recent suggestion would identify these as bronze acoustic vases, 'sounders' or echoers, used to amplify sound in the stone amphitheatres so often found in the Greek and Roman world. Ronald Knox's rather literal translation therefore captures the idea that Paul would just be like an empty echo from a lifeless piece of metal.[37]

A similar word is found in Paul's first letter to the Thessalonians, but with a vital difference. Paul commends them for the way they have made known the good news, both by word of mouth and example. 'You have become a sort of sounding-board from which the Word of the Lord has rung out.' (1 Thess. 1:8 Phillips.) Is 'sounding-board' a justifiable translation for the Greek 'exēcheō'? The preposition 'ex' or 'ek' adds the idea of sound spreading out, being distributed abroad, so the word means 'to resound, be caused to sound forth or ring out'.[38]

The purpose of a sounding-board is to reinforce the tones of a musical instrument by sympathetic vibration, so that the sound is carried to a greater distance, and is richer and more resonant. This was just what the Thessalonians were doing, and so the illustration is well brought out by Phillips' rendering.

If the Thessalonians successfully sounded out the message, the responsibility then passed to those who heard it. Would they be like the Israelites, of whom sadly it was said, 'Yet the message proclaimed to them did them no good, because they only heard and did not believe as well.' (Heb. 4:2b Phillips.) Another little illustration emerges here, for the Amplified Bible renders the last part, 'it was not mixed with faith'.[39] There has to be a response from the hearer. He has to recognize the theme, like a musical tune, then show appreciation and a liking for it, resulting in enjoyable listening. Spiritually speaking, that response is mixed with an appreciation resulting in faith, bringing great joy to the receptive hearer of the good news. When we hear good news, we cannot help but tell or sound it out.

Notes and References:

1. Lightfoot, J. B. *On a Fresh Revision of the English N. T.* 1872, 2nd ed. Macmillan, 118.
2. Abrahams, I. *Studies in Pharisaism*, 2nd series, 15.
3. Trench, R. C. *Synonyms*, 160; Skeat, W. W. *Etymological Dictionary*, 448.
4. Corswant, W. *Dictionary of Life* 185; Gadsby, J. *Wanderings*, Vol. 2, 324/5.
5. Nicolson, W. M. *Classical Revision of the Greek N. T.* 1878, Williams & Norgate, 66; Guillemard, W. H. *Hebraisms*, 108; Marshall, A. Ed. *GSM* Dec. 1927, 23; Neirynck, F. 'Parakupsas Blepei,' *Ephemirides Theol. Lovanienses*, Vol. 53 (1977), 113–152, rejects the idea of 'stoop or bend down,' but accepts the idea of 'peering in' as at a window.
6. Robertson, A. T. *Word Pictures*, Vol. 4, 179, Corinth was famous for its mirrors, 223; Neuburger, A. *Technical Arts*, 59, speaks of the solid cast highly polished Greek and Roman mirrors, Marshall, A, Ed. *GSM* Jan. 1928, 27 'beholding, reflecting, and changing go on simultaneously.' Feuillet, A, 'The Christ-Image of God According to St. Paul,' *Bible Today*, Vol. 1, (1965), 1409–14, would render 2 Cor. 3:18, 'contemplate in a mirror.' Lambrecht, J. 'Transformation in 2 Cor. 3:18,' *Biblica*, Vol. 64, (1983), 243–254.
7. Trench, R. C. *Synonyms*, 254/5; Marshall, A. Ed. *GSM*, July, 1932, 293.
8. Moulton, J. H. *Grammar* Vol. 2, 298; Westcott, B. F. *Hebrews*, 10, 11.
9. Gadsby, J. *Wanderings*, Vol. 2, 37, showing it was the usual practice to bury earthen vessels in a secret place if they contained deeds or anything precious. By contrast, a Christian shares his spiritual treasure with others.
10. Robertson, A. T. *Word Pictures*, Vol. 4, 150; Smith, D. *Life & Letters* 276, 165 note; Deissmann, G. A. *Bible Studies*, 259–262 on 'dokimios'; Wuest, K. S. *Word Studies* Vol. 3, *Golden Nuggets*, 113–115; Simpson, E. K. *Words Worth Weighing*, 17, 18, does not like 'castaway,' and prefers the idea of 'counterfeit,' rendering the final phrase, 'I myself should prove base metal.' Willis, R. B. ' 'Adokimos'-'Castaway'-'Rejected'.' *USR*, Vol. 32 (1920/21), 315–325.
11. Deissmann, G. A. *Light*, 51, on the estimation of ancient potsherds, cp. Isaiah 45:9; Wilson, C. A. *Letters*, 36; Duff, P. B. 'Apostolic Suffering and the Language of Processions in 2 Cor. 4:7–10', *BibTheolBull*. Vol. 21, (1991), 158–165.
12. Danby, H. *The Mishnah*, 606; Schurer, E. *A History of the Jewish People in the Time of Jesus Christ*, 1885, Edin. Clark, 2nd Div. Vol. 2. 107/8.
13. Neusner, J. 'First Cleanse the Inside. The "Halakhic" Background of a Controversy-Saying.' *NTStud*. Vol. 22 (1976), 486–495; Maccoby, H, 'The Washing of Cups,' *JournStudNT*, Vol. 14, (1982), 3–15, rejects Neusner's arguments, and correctly emphasizes Jesus' metaphorical application.

14. Turner, N. *Grammatical Insights*, 57.
15. Wilson, C. A. *Letters*, 37; Moulton & Milligan, *Vocabulary*, 506, 510.
16. Smith, D. *Life & Letters*, 254, 'the scapegoat of all'; Sadler's translation in the footnote also widens it out to refer to 'anything wiped off,' e.g. 'the sweepings of the streets.'
17. Abrahams, I. *Studies in Pharisaism*, series 1, 51–53; Neil, J. *Strange Figures*, 26–28, as to how it spreads, and is therefore an appropriate figure.
18. Thayer, J. H. *Greek-English Lexicon*, 425, untaught, unskilled; Robertson, A. T. *Word Pictures*, Vol. 4, 538, those who have 'never cut their eye-teeth,' and are not able to speak or talk. Vol. 5, 371; Arndt & Gingrich, *Greek-English Lexicon*, 809, 537. The Teleioi are the same as the pneumatikoi, spiritual men, see Lightfoot, J. B. *Philippians*, 153, cp. Phil 3 15; Moulton & Milligan, *Vocabulary*, 629. Lightfoot, J. B. *Colossians*, 168/9, on Col. 1: 28, with regard to the metaphor borrowed from the ancient mysteries, where the contrast is made between the 'fully instructed, as opposed to the novices.' See also Furnish, J. '"As Babes in Christ" – some proposals regarding 1 Corinthians 3:1–3.' *JournStudNT*, Vol. 7 (1980), 41–60.
19. Whitefoord, B. 'The Leading Scriptural Metaphor. The Way.' *Expositor*, 1894, 4th series, Vol. 10, 450–457.
20. Op. cit. (19), p. 454.
21. Hort, F. J. A. *The Way, The Truth, The Life*. 1893, Macmillan, Hulsean Lecture for 1871, 28–31; Jackson, F. J. F. & K. Lake, Ed. *Beginnings*, Vol. 5, 391/2. Fitzmyer, J. A. *Essays on the Semitic Background* of the *N. T.* 1971, Chapman, 281–283, compares the similar usage of 'The Way' in an absolute sense by the Essenes, and that this may be based on Isa. 40:3.
22. Earle, R. *Word Meanings*, 8; Arndt & Gingrich, *Greek-English Lexicon*, 666, 326; Thayer, J. H. *Greek-English Lexicon*, 515, 262.
23. Bengel, J. A. *Gnomon*, Vol. 1 205; Mattill, A. J. 'The Way of Tribulation,' *JBL*, Vol. 98 (1979) 531–546.
24. Baly, D, *Geographical Companion to the Bible*, 1963, Lutterworth Press, 130; Bouquet, A. C. *Everyday Life in N. T. Times*, 1953, Batsford, 95–97; Neuburger, A. *Technical Arts* 450–460; Ramsay, W. M. 'Roads & Travel in the N. T. ' in *Hastings' Dictionary of the Bible*, Vol. 5, 383–391; R. M. Pope, *On Roman Roads with St. Paul*, 1939, Epworth.
25. Bouquet, A. C. (op. cit. 24), 97; Neuburger, A. *Technical Arts*, 457–460.
26. Simpson, E. K. *Words Worth Weighing*, 31.
27. Brown, C. Ed. *NIDNTT*, Vol. 3, 943–945; Holloway, J. O. *Peripateō* as a Thematic Marker for Pauline Ethics, 1992, San Francisco, Mellen Research U. P. 8+264pp.
28. Kittel, G. Ed. *TDNT*, Vol. 7, 666–669; Brown, C. Ed. *NIDNTT*, Vol. 2, 451, 452.
29. Abbott, E. A. *Paradosis*, 1904, Black, 14 footnote.
30. William Thomson used the word 'corresponding' in his *N. T. Translated from the Greek* as early as 1816 (Kilmarnock, Crawford, 3 vols). One of the most recent Bibles to cite it is S. Zodhiates, *The Hebrew-Greek Key Study Bible*, 1984, Baker, Grand Rapids, 1665, where the Lexicon states, 'Antilutron – 487 from anti (473) in return, or corresponding, and lutron (3083), a ransom (1 Tim. 2:6).'

31. Nicoll, W. R. Ed. *Expositor's Greek Testament*, Vol. 4. 105; Ellicott, C. J. *A Critical & Grammatical Commentary on the Pastoral Epistles with a Revised Translation*, 1861, 2nd ed. Parker, Son & Bourn, 30; Moulton, J. H. *Grammar*, Vol 1, 105.

32. Barclay, W. *N. T. Words*, 192; Turner, N, *Christian Words*, 105 citing Orphica Lithica, ed. Abel 593.

33. Moulton & Milligan, *Vocabulary*, 579, dung, leavings, gleanings, decayed refuse; Vine, W. E. *Expository Dictionary*, 187; Lightfoot, J. B. *Philippians*, 149.

34. Smith, G. A. *Jerusalem*, 1907, Hodder, Vol. 1, Ch. 7, 170–180; Jeremias, J. *Jerusalem in the Time of Jesus*, 1969, SCM, 17.

35. Warren, C, in *Hastings' Dictionary of the Bible*, Vol. 2. 385–388, following Buxtorf, Lightfoot and Kimchi. *Int. Standard Bible Encyclopedia* Vol. 3, 1393/4.

36. Fields, W. W. '"Everyone Will be Salted with Fire" (Mark 9: 49),' *GraceTheolJnl*, Vol. 6, (1985), 299–304, Hebrew mlh (destroy), was understood as salt in the transition to Greek.

37. Harris, W. '"Sounding Brass" and Hellenistic Technology,' *BibArchRev*, Vol. 8 (1982), 38–41; endorsed by Klein, W. W. 'Noisy Gong or Acoustic Vase? A Note on 1 Corinthians 13:1.' *NTStud*, Vol. 32, (1986), 286–289.

38. Arndt & Gingrich, *Greek-English Lexicon*, 276; Ellingworth, P & E. A. Nida, *A Translator's Handbook on Paul's Letters to the Thessalonians*, 1976, United Bible Societies, 13.

39. The textual problem here is discussed by Westcott, B. F. *Hebrews*, 93/4; Bruce, F. F. (New London) *Commentary on the Ep. to the Hebrews*, 1965, Marshall, Morgan & Scott, 70.

Chapter 5

The Games and Entertainment

1. The Herald—
Proclaiming Peace Through Jesus Christ.

The valley of Olympia in the south-west corner of Greece has become world-famous for its ancient games. Whether the apostle Paul ever went there when he stayed about 70 miles away in Corinth, we do not know. But the Isthmian Games were held near-by every two years. As a Jew, he would probably have avoided them, but as a Christian he would be interested in going there to witness to the throngs of foreign visitors, and he would probably supply many tents to provide shelter for them. It is certainly difficult to imagine that his metaphors of the games could be so vivid and present in mind if he had never actually witnessed the events.[1]

The heralds, or spondophores, were important figures at the games. Six months before the Olympic Games began, these heralds were sent out to all the cities of the land to proclaim the festival, and that began the period of intensive training for most of the athletes. At the games themselves, the heralds announced the beginning of the contest with trumpet blasts, then in turn gave the names of each competitor, his father's name and the city he represented; they also proclaimed the rules. When the judging was completed after each event, a herald announced the winner in strident tones.[2]

Paul uses this aspect of the illustration when writing to the Romans, putting himself in the place of one of these heralds (Greek 'kērux'). Speaking of calling on the name of God in fulfilment of Joel 2: 32, he asks how they are going to put their trust in one about whom they have never heard? Then he continues, 'And how shall they hear without a herald? And how shall they act as heralds unless they receive a commission? As has been written, How seasonable are the feet of those who bring the good message of peace.' (Romans 10:14, 15, Sadler.) When the heralds went through the Grecian cities to proclaim the games they also declared the Olympic truce. From that time on wars in progress had to stop, on pain of heavy fines. In 424 B. C. E., the people of Sparta broke the truce three weeks after the heralds had proclaimed it, by attacking the city of Lepreum. They were fined, and when they refused to pay, they were excluded from the games, a disgrace they never lived down. So truly the heralds did proclaim peace throughout the land.[3]

That peace for Christians came about through the ransom sacrifice of Jesus Christ, and Paul proudly states, 'This is the testimony, too, of which I have been appointed a herald and apostle . . .', 'that gospel of which I have been appointed a herald, apostle and teacher.' (1 Tim. 2:7, 2 Tim. 1:11 Bruce.)

Of course, it would be of no value to serve as herald to proclaim good news to others, and then fail to live up to that in his own life. So that is why Paul added, 'I discipline my body strictly and keep it under, in case I myself should be disqualified after I have acted as herald, proclaiming the rules to others.' (1 Cor. 9:27 Bruce and footnote. Conybeare – after 'having called others to the contest . . .') Yes, Paul firmly believed that a Christian should 'persevere in your work, for if you do you will save both yourself and those who listen to you.' (1 Tim. 4:16 Goodspeed.)

2. Running the Race—Our Life Course.

The races were the most outstanding part of the games, for the Greeks were fleet of foot, and well used to carrying news from place to place by runner. Paul must often have been overtaken on his many travels by such runners, a further reminder to strengthen his use of the illustration. It was natural for him to refer to the race when he wrote to the Corinthians, 'Do you not know that though the runners in the stadium all run only one receives the prize? Run in such a manner that you may win.' (1 Cor. 9:24 TNT.) Each Christian was in the race for life, and he needed to stay the course faithfully to the end. Paul often alluded to this in his own personal case, as when he went up to Jerusalem to discuss with the older men his preaching work, so that he could make sure he was not 'running, or should already have run, in vain'. (Gal. 2:2 Weymouth 3rd ed. Phil. 2:16.)

The key to winning such a race lay in the intense and sustained effort that had to go into it, both in the work of training which could last for as long as ten months, and in the race itself.[4] It would be of no value for such a runner to drop out halfway, or to fail to stay the course to the end, for all his efforts would be wasted. 'But I count my life of no value to myself, if only I may complete the course marked out for me, and the task that was allotted me by the Lord Jesus – which was to declare the Good News of the Love of God.' (Acts 20:24 TCNT.) No wonder Paul put such effort into his missionary tours, his study and writing, and did not spare himself despite the difficulties he encountered. Near the end of his life he could therefore say with some confidence, 'I have run the great race, I have finished the course, I have kept the faith.' (2 Tim. 4:7 REB.)

How does this metaphor help Christians today? After recounting the fine examples of faith from ancient times in the eleventh chapter of Hebrews, we are then admonished, 'With so many witnesses in a great cloud all around us, we too, then, should throw off everything that weighs us down and the sin that clings so closely, and with perseverance keep running in the race which lies ahead of us. Let us keep our eyes fixed on Jesus, who leads us in our faith, and brings it to perfection . . .' (Hebrews 12:1, 2a NJB.)[5]

Yes, Jesus is the front runner who reached the goal, and we can find no better example to focus our eyes upon intently.[6] He certainly threw off every weight, lacking material possessions, and not placing store upon home or relatives. (Matt. 8:20, 12:47–50.) His own purpose was to seek first the Kingdom and God's righteousness, and in his Sermon on the Mount he urged his followers to do likewise. (Matt. 6:31–33.) Times may have changed quite radically from those Roman ones, but the things that weigh us down have not, except that they have become more subtle and deceptive, so that even many who call themselves Christians find their lives full of materialism, pleasures and arm-chair lethargy. They see no race to run in, no need for any spiritual training beyond a Sunday morning sermon, no real effort or challenge in their so-called Christianity.

It is so easy, then, for Christians to sin, or miss the mark (see chapter 9, number 4), which we are bound to do because we are all imperfect. But that is all the more reason for stripping off any clothing that clings too closely to us, and impedes us in the race. How far would a runner get if he tried to race in his long robe, soon tripping over its clinging folds? [7] We have to do everything possible to throw off the results of our imperfections, even though it means a hard and continuous struggle. But that is what the Christian race is all about, becoming a new personality, with Christ as our example and model. Only then could we share Paul's confidence in reaching the goal and winning the race for life. (Ps. 119: 32.)[8]

3. Tripping Over a Stone—The Stone of Stumbling.

How easy when running a race to suddenly trip over a stone and stumble, instantly losing your position among the runners, and perhaps the race. Continuing his metaphor of the race in Romans 9:16, the apostle Paul refers to Israel and its failure to keep the Law covenant perfectly. So why did they not find righteousness? 'Because they didn't pursue it by faith but as though they could do so by works; they tripped over the "stumbling stone". As it is written: "See, I am placing a stone in Zion that people will trip over and a rock that will make them fall, but whoever depends on Him will not be put to shame".' (Rom. 9: 32, 33 Adams.) What shame for an athlete to trip over, and then come in last in the race, or maybe not at all!

The word 'stumbling' carries the thought of cutting or striking against, and is used in Matthew 4:6 when Jesus was tempted, and told that angels would carry him up, and not let his foot strike against a stone. At the Pythian Games on one occasion a chariot struck the turning-post and the resulting collision brought disaster.[9]

Identifying that stumbling stone as the acceptance of the Messiah, Christ Jesus, Paul makes the contrast that while to the Greeks or gentiles it was foolishness to view him as the Christ, to the Jews it was a stumbling block. (1 Cor. 1:22, 23.) Peter also has a similar thought, but adds an interesting reason.

After quoting from Isaiah 28:16, which foretold how the rejected stone would become the headstone of the topmost corner, he said of Christ that he was 'a stone to trip men's feet, a boulder they stumble against. They stumble over God's word, and refuse it belief.' (1 Peter 2:8 Knox.)

After quoting from this same prophecy in Isaiah, Jesus himself told the Jews, that this was why the Kingdom of God would be taken away from them and given to a nation that did produce its fruits. Then he added, 'whoever trips on this Stone will be broken to pieces, and whoever it falls on will be pulverized.' (Matt. 21: 43, 44 Adams.)[10]

Why did Jesus seem to turn the illustration upon its head? Note that their stumbling comes first, so that they not only lose the race but they are utterly broken to pieces, like that chariot that met complete disaster. Because of their failure as a nation, they received the adverse judgment of God, committed to the Son to execute, so that the 'stone' in turn falls upon them and destroys them.[11]

4. The Umpire—Let Christ Jesus Control.

How would you feel if you had run a great race, and felt sure that you had won, only to be disqualified afterwards by the judge? That was another danger that the apostle Paul warned about when he wrote to the Colossians, 'Do not let anyone who delights in false humility and the worship of angels disqualify you for the prize.' (Col. 2:18 NIV.)

The word 'disqualify' here is a rare Greek word drawn from 'brabeus' 'an umpire. ' With the preposition 'kata' added it carries the idea 'to decide against' and so means 'to cheat you of the prize' (Sadler), 'to decide as an umpire against one'.[12] It is used of a contestant who deserves the prize, but is condemned by the umpire and judge, so that another person receives it. This might even be achieved by bribing the umpire, and ancient records show that this increased as the various Grecian games lost the high standards which originally prevailed.[13]

What, then, was the point that Paul was making? The Colossians were running a fine race, but false teachers were doing their best to rob them of the prize at the end. He deliberately widens out its application to include any form of deprivation of that prize. These ones would trip up the runners, or frustrate all their efforts to reach the goal by their fleshly human ideas and frame of mind, trying to turn aside Christians from their course. (Gal. 5:7.)[14]

Continuing his argument, Paul opens the third chapter to the Colossians by referring to Christ seated on the right hand of God. Then he urges them to take a course that reflects that of a true Christian, adding, 'And let the peace of Christ act as umpire in your hearts . . .' (Col. 3:15 Roth.) So wherever there is any conflict concerning the right course to take, we will let the spirit or mind of Christ take control or act as umpire to make a judgment for us ('have the final say' – Adams). We will know that his umpiring will never be swayed by bribes, it will never be defective, depriving us of the right decision.[15]

But Christ is to act as umpire or judge in a greater sense than in our hearts. In his famous address to the Athenians, Paul concluded by explaining how God was now urging men everywhere to repent, 'because he has fixed the day on which he will have the world judged, and justly judged, by a man of his choosing; of this he has given assurance to all by raising him from the dead.' (Acts 17:31 NEB.)

Describing that judgment at the end of the race, Paul adds, 'For we must all be made manifest before the Judgment seat of the Christ, that each one may get his award for the things done through the body, according to the things he has practised, whether it is good or vile.' (2 Cor. 5:10 NWT.) That judgment will be fair and honest, but it will also be searching, so that Ronald Knox used the phrase, 'All of us have a scrutiny to undergo . . .' May we be able to show that nothing has deflected us from the race, no false teachings have been allowed to creep in, but that we have kept a loyal and faithful course, so that Christ as the great umpire will have no cause to disqualify us.

5. The Victor's Crown—Reaching the Goal.

When the apostle Paul spoke about the victor's crown given to the winner of the race, he used a contrast rather than a comparison. 'Their reward is a wreath that withers; ours lasts forever. That is why I run with a purpose . . .' (1 Cor. 9: 25b, 26a TNT.)

For the Olympian Games the winner was awarded a crown of wild olive leaves. For the Isthmian Games it was at first a wreath of parsley, but later it was made of pine leaves, as Corinth and its neighbourhood abounded in groves of pine trees. To Paul, the attendant fame for the winner counted as nothing, so that he could make a direct contrast between the fading, withering leaves of the crown put around the head, and the one that lasts for ever. Peter also added, 'And when the chief shepherd has been made manifest, you will receive the unfadable crown (Greek, 'stephanos') of glory.' (1 Peter 5:4 NWT.) The Greek word here comes from the name of the flower amaranthus, which never withers, and revives when it is moistened with water – a fine symbol of that unfading crown. How happy is someone who endures, for 'he will receive the winner's crown of life.' (James 1:12 Adams, Rev. 2:10.)[16]

The winner's crown was awarded by the judge, and the true judge is righteous and makes no mistakes. (2 Tim. 4:8.) But what influenced that judgment? Paul takes up that angle when he comments, 'No athlete is ever awarded the wreath of victory unless he has kept the rules.' (2 Tim. 2:5 TCNT.) This did not simply refer to those rules that governed the actual contests, and which were strictly enforced, but also the rules of training, exercise and diet over a ten-month period, without which no one could hope to gain the victory, so great was the competition.[17]

For the Christian, the Bible is his set of rules or principles. It provides his spiritual diet and his godly training, and again Paul draws the comparison, 'For bodily training is beneficial for a little; but godly devotion is beneficial for all things, as it holds promise of the life now and that which is to come.' (1 Tim. 4:8 NWT, 1 Cor. 9: 25a.)

The athletic runner was not just judged on speed alone. Although we know very little of the detail due to lack of ancient records, it did involve style and rhythm, and all-round balance of perfect performance. So the Christian too is exhorted to remain balanced, to 'keep his senses' or 'be mentally stripped for action, perfectly self-controlled.' (1 Peter 1:13 NEB.) How sad if, near to the finishing line, he should be robbed of the prize because of failing to hold fast to the faith. (Col. 2:18, 19.)

So Paul's admonition to Timothy was to so run the race that he could get 'a firm hold on the everlasting life'. (1 Tim. 6:12 NWT.)

Here the aorist imperative pinpoints one decisive act of grasping the crown firmly. That is the bold, zealous attitude Christians should display.[18]

6. Team Spirit—Working Together.

Paul showed his concern for the faith of the Philippians when he wrote to them, 'I would like to hear that you are standing firm, united in spirit; that you are one team with one purpose in the struggle for the faith of the Gospel, and that you are facing your opponents quite unafraid.' (Phil. 1:27 TNT.) The word for 'team' incorporates the Greek 'athleō', from which our English 'athletics' is derived, a striving together or, side by side. Later in the same letter he refers to the women who worked along with him and 'shared my struggles'. (Phil. 4:13 TNT.) In that verse he speaks also of the one who could continue to assist these women as a 'trusty yokefellow' (Bruce) or 'true teammate'. (Living Bible.)

The Olympic games were all linked with individual competition, but there were some team events in other places, notably a relay race in Panathenaea, and in the chariot races team rivalry was carried to excess as factions supported the Whites, the Reds, the Greens or the Blues.[19] But Paul always stresses the co-operation, the standing together as one, rather than the rivalry that could even become frenzied and dangerous.

A particularly endearing term cannot fail to be tied in with the idea of working together. It is 'fellow-worker' which Paul uses repeatedly in various letters. In the verse already discussed he speaks of all his fellow-workers, along with the women, who had struggled to work with him in spreading the good news. (Phil. 4:3.) Some of these fellow-workers had risked their lives for Paul, and their faithful support gave him great joy and encouragement. (Rom. 16:3, 2 Cor. 1:24, Col. 4:11, 12.) Titus he could describe as his 'colleague and fellow worker in your interests.' (2 Cor. 8:23 JB.) But finest of all these expressions is when he tells the Corinthians, 'We are God's fellow workers; you are God's harvest field, God's building.' (1 Cor. 3:9 TCNT.) So the idea of organization associated with the word 'work' or Greek 'ergon', comes through in its strongest sense, for 'both planter and waterer, so far from being rivals, are in this case one in aim.' (v8, Way.) 'Whether they plant or water, they work as a team.' (NEB.) The field is the world, and all true Christians wherever they may be, are working with God to spread his good news of the Kingdom.

7. The Boxer—Fighting Effectively.

Like Shakespeare, Paul was fond of making a quick change in his metaphors. So with one breath he is talking about the race, and the next he has changed to the boxer. 'As boxer I hit home, I do not spend my force on air.' (1 Cor. 9:26 Rutherford.) So he didn't want to waste his blows on a non-existent opponent; 'my boxing is no shadow-boxing' (Bruce). In fact, it was his own body that was the adversary with which he was engaged in a never-ending battle. (Rom. 7: 21–25.)

In order to win the battle he said he had to 'pummel my body and lead it as a slave.' (1 Cor. 9:27 NWT.) The word for 'pummel' is Greek 'hupōpiazō', and it refers to the part of the face under the eye, and so to beat one black and blue there, to give a black eye as we would say, though later usage extended this to other parts of the body.[20]

The only other occurrence of the word in the Greek Scriptures is at Luke 18:5, where the widow so continually harasses the judge that for his own peace and quiet he sees she gets justice, 'so that she will not keep coming and pummeling me to a finish' (NWT). Her 'browbeating' has been seen here as an example of hyperbole – an exaggerated view to drive home a point – but to the judge it may not have seemed like that. He may have been so worn down, and felt so bruised mentally, that he literally thought of it as a situation likely to finish him off. Or it may be viewed from the aspect of onlookers, so that she caused him to lose face, and he saw his prestige being destroyed.[21]

So how does this illustration fit the situation Paul is describing, and our own fight today with our imperfections? The widow was persistent, wearing away her opponent until he gave in. Paul had to persevere against his body, continually disciplining it, fighting against its desires and inclinations, its tendency to give in to the flesh if it had the slightest chance. The ancient boxing contest could go on for many hours, for the main tactic was to wear down your opponent; the match which gave victory to Diagonorous of Rhodes lasted for six hours.[22]

How true the proverb, where the Septuagint Version uses the same word ('Blood shot eyes and bruises . . .' LXX Thomson). 'Hurts that bruise cruelly, chastisement felt deep within, are sin's best remedy.' (Prov. 20: 30 Knox.) That Paul won his battle can encourage us today, for although we might never attain to his missionary and literary heights, we are no different with regard to the battle we have with our sinful and imperfect bodies.

8. The Wrestler—A Constant Struggle.

Paul's battle, like our own, was not just with his own human imperfections and failings. 'For our wrestling is not against flesh and blood, but against the principalities, against the powers, against the world-rulers of this darkness, against the spiritual hosts of wickedness in the heavenly places.' (Eph. 6:12 ASV.) The Greek word for 'wrestling' is 'palē', meaning to throw or swing, and it was the object of the ancient wrestling match to throw an opponent to the ground and hold him down. The contestants struggled hard and long to get one another off balance so that they could execute such a throw or swing, as depicted on many vase paintings. Each successful throw counted one point in the match, and the first to get three points was the winner.[23]

But the struggles and wrestling of the Christian differs from those ancient games in one important way. They had to abide by the rules which were rigorously applied by the judges, 'the wrestler does not win the crown unless he wrestles lawfully'. (2 Tim. 2:5 Conybeare.) For example, no point was marked up when an opponent was thrown if the challenger's knee touched the ground, and he was penalized with the judge's whipstick across his back.[24] But the unseen enemy Paul writes about cares nothing for rules or right principles; he is a liar, a deceiver and a murderer. (John 8:44.) How difficult is our struggle against that sort of enemy. No wonder Paul said, 'I weary myself in wrestling . . .' (Col. 1:29 Sadler.) And when he was thrown down, he was comforted by his brothers sharing his setback. 'You did well in making yourselves sharers in the fall I got.' (Phil. 4:14 Sadler, with footnote – Greek 'thlipsis' means in wrestling 'a fall'.)

When we really have to struggle and wrestle with something that seems beyond human power, we may say we suffer 'agony of mind', a thought that is derived from the Greek 'agōnia', and originally meant contest, wrestling, struggle, often bringing great pain. (1 Cor. 9:25.) Paul used that word when he urged Christians, 'Struggle your hardest in the good contest for the faith.' (1 Tim. 6:12 Weymouth 5th ed.) Nor was he alone in such counsel, for Jude adds, 'contend vigorously for the faith.' (Jude 3, Adams.) Jesus told his disciples, 'Strain every nerve to force your way in through the narrow gate.' (Luke 13:24 Weymouth 3rd ed., – 'Exert yourselves vigorously . . .' NWT.) So intense struggle and effort is involved, and yet we need not despair and think it is hopeless, for God has assured us that where human efforts might fail, his spirit can make us strong and will give us the victory, through Jesus Christ, so that we are more than conquerors. (Romans 8: 35–39.)[25]

9. Fighting Beasts in the Arena—
The Need for Trust in God.

A verse that has often puzzled Bible readers is where the apostle Paul pictures himself in the arena at Ephesus, and says, 'And if, to use the popular expression, I have "fought with wild beasts" here in Ephesus, what is the good of an ordeal like that if there is no life after this one.' (1 Cor. 15:32 Phillips.) The phrase 'after the manner of men' (AV), rendered here as 'the popular expression' indicates that he meant this metaphorically rather than literally, for we find no mention of such a literal incident with wild beasts in his very full catalogue of events befalling him in 2 Corinthians 11:23 forward, or in the Acts of the Apostles.[26]

The account at Acts 19: 29–41, shows how the mob became worked up over the threat to the worship of Artemis, inflamed by popular speech to look upon Paul as a danger to both their religion and their business, and so to their very way of life. They rush Paul's friends into the amphitheatre, and Paul would have gone to help them and to try to calm the people, but he was restrained from doing so by both the disciples and officials of the games. That was an ugly and frightening event, and this or another similar situation must have remained vividly in Paul's mind, so that he later said, 'We should like you, our brothers, to know something of the trouble we went through in Asia. At that time we were completely overwhelmed, the burden was more than we could bear, in fact we told ourselves that this was the end.' (2 Cor. 1:8 Phillips.)[27]

Sir W. M. Ramsay suggested that this passage revealed Paul's excellent understanding of both Greek and Roman matters. He coupled a platonic view of the mob as dangerous beasts with the picture of the Roman sport of releasing wild beasts upon hapless offenders in the arena, so conjuring up this illustration which tied in well with the large theatre in Ephesus. That depraved men could become bestial in character was testified to by Paul. (Rom. 1:21–23.)[28]

Having come so close to death on numerous occasions, we could take this reference as a possible indication that this occasion frightened him more than most of the others. In his previous letter he had mentioned the many opposers in Ephesus, and yet the great opportunity for a spiritual harvest out-weighed the danger, and made him want to stay. (1 Cor. 16:8, 9.) So we can fully endorse his further comment, 'It was God who preserved us from such deadly perils, and it is he who still preserves us. We put our full trust in him and he will keep us safe in the future.' (2 Cor. 1:10 Phillips.) Perhaps we can now see more clearly why he really believed that.

10. Throw of the Dice—The Risks of a Christian Life.

Amongst the many deceptions the apostle Paul warned about was that of being 'tricked by the sleight of men, and led astray into the snares of the cunning.' (Eph. 4:14 Conybeare.) The word for 'sleight' in Greek is 'kubeia', in which we will readily recognize our own word 'cube,' referring to the dice. A kubion was a gaming-house. This was a very appropriate metaphor to express the nature of the trickery, for the player frames the cast of his dice in such a way that the numbers turned up will always further his own object.[29] We would be very naive if we were deceived by such trickery, and yet it was necessary to warn Christians of this, for even Jesus himself said, 'the children of this world are considerably more shrewd in dealing with their contemporaries than the children of light.' (Luke 16:8 Phillips.)

In that situation, the dice was thrown against the Christian, placing him at a deliberate disadvantage. But Paul also referred to the throw of the dice, as it were, in life. Speaking of the ministrations of Epaphroditus, he said, 'for it was through the work of the Lord that he came near to death; for he hazarded his very life to supply what was lacking in the help you sent me.' (Phil. 2:30 Montgomery.) Such a person was known as a 'hazarder' (Greek 'paraboleuomai'), one who was so selfless that he risked his life in behalf of others, perhaps to nurse them through plague and fever, or as in an inscription from the second century C. E., discovered near the Black Sea, of a legal advocate who risked his life by taking his clients' cases even up to the emperor himself.[30]

Lightfoot therefore translated this passage in Philippians 'having gambled with his life'. It was a game of chance, but it meant literally 'having thrown self beside' (K. Int). Out of true love for one's neighbour, a Christian is willing to push aside his own desires and wants, so that he echoes Paul's words, 'None of us lives for himself alone . . . if we live it is for the Lord we live, and if we die it is for the Lord we die. Living or dying, then, we belong to the Lord.' (Rom. 14:7, 8 TNT.) It was such an attitude to life with the hope of a resurrection in view, that helped Christians to face up to terrible persecution, even to being thrown to the lions in the Roman arena.

Yet for all that, a Christian will still be careful with his life, for it has been given to him by God, and is precious and holy. He will seek to use it wisely in the service of God and Christ. He will also recognize the truth of the wise writer of old who said, 'I returned to see under the sun that the swift do not have the race, nor the mighty ones the battle . . . because time and unforeseen occurrence befall them all.' (Eccl. 9:11 NWT.) So where he can do so, a Christian will guard against possible happenings of that sort, not hazarding his life needlessly. An actual example is recorded in the Bible when Jacob sent his ten sons to Egypt to buy grain because of the famine. 'But Jacob did not send Benjamin, Joseph's brother, with his other brothers, because he said; "Otherwise a fatal accident may befall him".' (Gen. 42: 4 NWT.) He had already suffered the loss of one beloved son, Joseph, and wanted to avoid the heart-rending loss of his one remaining much-loved son. He didn't want to expose him to a possible accident on a dangerous journey.

Two apparent opposites thus come together. The wise Christian will watch that he is not tricked by false teachers, or the worldly-wise selfish ones of this world, who throw the dice to suit themselves. But he will also use his life wisely, not risking it needlessly, as David felt his three chieftains had done when they fetched water from his favourite well, and he poured it on the ground, because to him it represented their life-blood. (2 Sam. 23: 15–17.) But there are occasions when it is right for a Christian to 'throw the dice' with his life, hazarding it in the service of God for the benefit of others. On such occasions if the dice seems loaded against him and he loses his life, he can be sure that in reality Almighty God still has it playing in his favour, because 'whoever loses his life for My sake will find it.' (Matt. 10:39 Adams.)

11. The Actor—The Hypocrite.

The Greek word for 'actor' is 'hupokritēs', which originally meant 'one who answers. ' In early Greek drama the chorus played the principal part, and the actor only occasionally 'answered' the chorus. By the fifth century B.C.E., the actor had emerged in his own right, but it became a fixed custom to have only three principal actors with speaking parts, although there could be any number of mute extras. So to represent many different characters, the three actors used a variety of linen masks, which covered the entire head, except for the mouth and part of the eyes. The same characters might have different masks to represent changes played as the drama proceeded, perhaps from merry to very sad. Meaning was conveyed by tone of voice and gesture. 'Niceties of facial expression would have been entirely lost in the vast expanse of a Greek theatre. The tragic mask, on which were depicted in bold and striking lines the main traits in the character represented, was really much more effective, and could be seen by the most distant spectator.'[31]

Due to this particular method of acting, the word 'hupokritēs' came to mean, not just 'play-acting', but to 'act under a mask' or 'one who pretends to be what he is not', so coming right down to our modern word 'hypocrite'.[32] This powerful illustration clearly emerges in Jesus' condemnation of the scribes and Pharisees as hypocrites. 'So when you do good to other people, don't hire a trumpeter to go in front of you – like those play-actors ('hupokritēs') in the synagogues and streets who make sure that men admire them.' (Matt. 6:2 Phillips.) Christians were not to pray where people would see them, on a prominent street corner, as an actor might perform on a stage before an audience. (Matt. 6:5.)

Then perhaps in reference to the actor's mask Jesus used a telling word-play. 'Moreover, whenever you are fasting, stop being like the actors on the stage of life, of a sad and gloomy countenance, for they mask their faces in order that they may appear to men as those who are fasting.' (Matt. 6:16 Wuest.) The word-play is brought out by the *Expositor's Greek Testament* 'they disfigure (Greek 'aphanizō') (their faces) that they may figure (Greek 'phanōsis') well before men.' (Vol. 1 p. 123) Jesus also condemned the Pharisees' hypocrisy in the famous twenty-third chapter of Matthew, (esp. v. 13, 15, 23, 25, 27–29).

It has been argued by Jewish apologists that this picture of the Pharisees is quite mistaken and wrong, and that the rabbis spoke against hypocrisy. After looking at the word in its application under various situations, including the pagan religion of Rome, W. H. Bennett observed that the Pharisees 'hypocrisy consisted in the fact that with them holiness of form and ritual had become largely dissociated from holiness of character, justice, mercy and love; their control of minute details broke down in many points, and instead of frankly admitting their incapacity to deal, by means of precise rules, with all the exigencies of life, they strove to hide their failure with the quibbles and evasions of a feeble and dishonest casuistry.'[33]

But many scholars show that the word 'hupokritēs' has a darker and more evil tone. There is no doubt that for at least *some* Pharisees, the original dissembling and dishonest covering up, led to a corruption of character, and to the avarice and a desire to maintain a prominent position that Jesus so forthrightly exposed and condemned. He spoke about them as a class or group, but it is equally clear that there were those like Gamaliel, who was not denied the credit for his honest viewpoint and wise words in Acts 5: 34–40.[34]

The association of hypocrisy with wickedness is clear from Paul's admonition, 'Your love must not be a superficial pretense (Greek 'anhupokritos'). You must hate evil, and you must give your unshakeable loyalty to what is good.' (Rom. 12:9 Barclay.) It may be true that today's world 'wears a mask', but the Christian is not of the world, and stands apart from its ways, promoting always the genuine love that can be clearly seen to reflect the love that God and Christ have shown to mankind. (1 Cor. 13: 1–13.)[35]

12. The Chorus—Abundant Supplies.

The abundance of most natural resources, plants, trees, and animals upon the earth, suggests that God is not one who is sparing or stingy in what he provides. This is borne out in the Scriptures by the interesting and illustrative Greek word 'chorēgeō', with the root meaning 'chorus'.

The background here goes back to the theatre in Athens, where wealthy citizens were liable to perform a public service at their own personal expense. There were various kinds of service, but the one connected with this word was the supply of a chorus or dancing team, in a Greek drama. This involved great expense for the full training and equipment of some fifty persons, and so the word came to mean, 'supply fully and abundantly', especially in its strengthened form with the prefix 'epi' as 'epichorēgeō', 'over and above'. Whilst the idea of 'supply' is found in most translations, they do not all stress the lavish generosity involved.[36]

Paul uses the word on several occasions. Taking the natural resources of abundant seed he used this to urge the Corinthians to show generosity, 'Now he that abundantly supplies ('epichorēgeō') seed to the sower and bread for eating will supply and multiply the seed for you to sow and will increase the products of your righteousness. In everything you are being enriched for every sort of generosity, which produces through us an expression of thanks to God.' (2 Cor. 9:10, 11 NWT.)

Paul was speaking from experience, for, writing to the Philippians he testified, 'For I know that "these things shall fall out to my salvation", through your prayers, and through the supply of all my needs by the Spirit of Jesus Christ. ' (Phil. 1:19 Conybeare, with the footnote 'the supplying of all needs [of the chorus] by the Choregus.')

It is particularly with regard to God's holy spirit that Paul highlights its abundance. He asks the Galatians the question, 'Have you received so many benefits in vain . . . ? Whence, I say, are the gifts of Him who furnishes you with the fulness of the Spirit . . . ?' (Gal. 3:5, Conybeare.) This can only come through faith like that of Abraham, not through carrying out the Mosaic Law. Smith renders the phrase, 'lavishing ('epichorēgeō') the Spirit upon you', which points up its abundance, with no limitation by God.

In all this, Paul reminds us not to forget the place of Jesus Christ as head of his spiritual congregation, 'from whom the whole body by the joints which bind it, draws full supplies ('epichorēgeō') for all its needs, and is knit together, and increases in godly growth.' (Col. 2:19 Conybeare.)

Can we learn any lesson from this illustration of the super-abundance of all that God supplies? It may well be that we have been used to asking in prayer for 'a portion' of God's spirit. Does this suggest that we might be placing a limit on God's bounteous provision? John states quite emphatically 'God does not give the Spirit sparingly.' (John 3:34b Montgomery.) He knows how much we need in a particular situation, and he will not run short of holy spirit, so we can safely leave it to him to decide on the amount. Rather, like the apostles, we will pray to 'be filled with the Spirit'. (Eph. 5: 18b Smith.) Although we do not know the size of 'one portion', the very tenor of this illustration would suggest that it would be limiting. Elisha asked for two portions of the amount of spirit that Elijah had enjoyed, but this was to enjoy a firstborn son's inheritance of a double portion set out in the Law. (Deut. 21:17, 2 Kings 2:9, 10.) The apostolic request to be filled with the spirit would therefore be more appropriate, for God knows exactly how much we need at any one time.

13. Triumphal Procession—Captives and Victors.

After Jerusalem and its Temple fell to the Romans in 70 C. E., a great triumphal procession was celebrated in Rome where not only were the captives paraded, but also the booty from the Temple, its seven-branched candlestick, shewbread table, and other items of furniture. This, the 320th procession of its kind to be held, is depicted in part there on the Arch of Titus.

The Greek word 'thriambos' is the Latin *triumphus*, the name of a festal hymn to the god Bacchus which was used in the spectacle, and so gave its name to the entire glorious victory procession. It is not surprising that this great event should be used by Paul as an illustration. But it appears in two strikingly different settings.[37]

Writing to the Colossians, Paul outlines the benefits of Christ's death. Christians have been 'made alive' by cancelling the Mosaic Law that exposed them as sinners. But his death and resurrection also signalled victory over all those authorities that thought *they* had triumphed. So the tables were turned, and by means of his death, Christ 'discarded the cosmic powers and authorities like a garment; he made a public spectacle of them and led them as captives in his triumphal procession ['thriambeuō'].' (Col. 2:15 NEB.) What a picture of Christ as King of God's triumphant kingdom!

Then in his second letter to the Corinthians, Paul focuses on another part of the procession. 'Now thanks be to God, who always gives us a place of honour in Christ's triumphal procession! He spreads abroad the fragrance of His knowledge through us wherever we go. To God we present the sweet fragrance of Christ alike among those who receive His salvation and those who perish for lack of it. Among the latter it is an odour of death, which leads to death; among the former an odour of life, imparting life.' (2 Cor. 2:14–16 Bruce.)[38]

As the victorious general entered Rome in his chariot at the head of his soldiers, great crowds praised and applauded him. Flowers and garlands were heaped upon him and flung in the way, while the air was filled with the odour of incense from many temple altars in the city. Similarly, many spectators rejoice in Christ's victory; and his followers or soldiers join in with their praises, and it is like the sweet smell of incense. It reminds us of Christ's entry into Jerusalem, when the common people welcomed him and threw palm branches before him. (Matt. 21:7–11, 15–17.) But the Scribes and Pharisees did not share that welcome, and those who oppose Christ, or are his captives, smell nothing sweet or pleasant in his triumphal procession, for to them it means defeat and death, just as many of the prisoners were later executed.

Paul's illustration could well be classified as a military metaphor, but it is placed in this section because of its connection with our next illustration.

So Paul has completely reversed the roles of all those taking part in Almighty God's triumphal procession. He leads it in honour to his King and general Jesus Christ to whom every knee must bow, instead of a pagan general. The captives are not the Jews who were once God's people, but are the enemies of God and Christ, the authorities and powers of this world that often rise up against God. The victors are God's servants who spread everywhere the fragrance of God's Kingdom as they tell out its good news, instead of idolatrous incense to pagan gods.

Paul's clever inversion gives double emphasis to his metaphor. That also seems as triumphant as the very victory he records. May we be able to share in that triumphal procession on the victorious side of God's Kingdom.

14. Posted on a Placard—Openly Exposed.

Modern society is well used to the placard. All types of advertisements litter our cities, our public transport and our reading material. People depicted on those posters or placards are openly exposed, as it were, to the public gaze, which is not always an approving one. That is just how it was with Jesus Christ.

The Greek word 'prographō' literally means, 'to write beforehand' or to be placarded, 'posted up'.[39] The apostle Paul told the Galatians, 'O senseless Galatians, who is it that brought you under evil influence, YOU before whose eyes Jesus Christ was openly portrayed [placarded – Moffatt] impaled.' (Gal. 3:1 NWT.) They had seen the clear evidence of the treatment meted out to Christ at his death, just as if it had been shown on posters everywhere, so that it was in their mind's eye, and yet they had allowed these deceptive evil influences to creep in and subvert their faith. What a vivid illustration to bring home to them what their course of action implied. They could even end up rejecting Jesus' sacrifice, and so expose him to greater public shame, as if impaling him a second time. (Heb. 6:4–6.)

Another word, not in any way related, is yet similar in the resulting situation. It is the Greek 'theatron'.[40] The letter to the Hebrews mentions how they had 'endured a great contest under sufferings, sometimes while you were being exposed as in a theater both to reproach and tribulations, and sometimes while you became sharers with those who were having such an experience.' (Heb. 10: 32b, 33 NWT.) The Greek or Roman amphitheatre is well-known from the many remains extant in various countries, and those at Ephesus and Caesarea are especially popular. By their very nature, with tier upon tier of rising stone seats in a great half circle round an open stage, it would seem that an audience was all around and above, and the actors profoundly exposed to everyone's gaze – and to their insults and much more if the actors did not meet with approval.

Then Paul takes the same idea and illustration, and sets it on a world stage. 'For it seems to me that God has put us the apostles last on exhibition as men appointed to death, because we have become a theatrical spectacle [Greek, 'theatron', – 'a gazing stock' – Conybeare, ASV] to the world, and to angels, and to men.' (1 Cor. 4:9 NWT.) By their very different course of action as Christians from the rest of the pagan Roman world around them, it seemed that all eyes in heaven and on earth were upon them, and they appeared fools for Christ's sake, and might even face death at the hands of their opposers.

Yet the illustration is not without its encouraging side. In the twelfth chapter of Hebrews we are reminded that 'we have so great a cloud of witnesses surrounding us' (lit. 'spread about us' – Westcott) (Heb. 12:1 NWT), that they are like the audience in the amphitheatre, and some of their names and faith have been discussed in the previous eleventh chapter of Hebrews. They help and stimulate us to copy their example, just as the young man in Elisha's day was fortified when his eyes were opened to see the great heavenly host all around him who were with him and for him. (2 Kings 6:15–17.)

May we always remember that favourable audience of witnesses when the worldly audience would rob us of our faith and joy.

Notes and References:

1. Broneer, O. 'The Apostle Paul and the Isthmian Games,' *BA*, Vol. 25 (1962), 2–31, on general background.
2. Poole, L & G. *History of Ancient Olympic Games*, 1965, Vision Press, 2–5, 38; Robertson, A. T. *Word Pictures*, Vol. 4, 150; Howson, J. S. *Metaphors*, 170/1; Marshall, A, Ed. *GSM* Nov/Dec. 1930, 163/4, 167, 'The Good Fight,' gives an excellent summary of many of the words Paul used in connection with the games; for a useful list of N. T. references, see *CGT*, *Philippians*, Ed. H. C. G. Moule, 1906, 103–106, 'St. Paul's Use of Athletic Metaphors.' Pfitzner, V.C. *Agon Motif*, 94, 95.
3. Poole, L & G, op. cit. 39/40.
4. Poole, L & G, op. cit. 42/43; Dodd, C. H.'Some Problems of N. T. Translation,' *BT* Vol. 13, (1962), 148/9, 'agōnizomenos'; Waugh, R. M. L, *Greek Testament*, 85; Howson, J. S. *Metaphors*, 137–153; Derrett, J. D. M. ''Running' in Paul: The Midrashic Potential of Hab. 2:2.' *Biblica*, Vol. 66, (1985) 560–567; Marshall, A, Ed. *GSM*, Dec. 1930, 167, for other suggestive features of the illustration; Moule, H. C. G. *Philippian Studies* n. d. Pickering & Inglis, 184, freely renders Phil. 3:13, 'and towards the things in front stretching out and onward like the eager racer . . . I press on.' Pfitzner, V. C. *Agon Motif*, 86, 87, 99–103, 134–138.
5. C. B. Williams renders the first part of this verse, 'We have so vast a crowd of spectators in the grandstands . . .' Westcott also notes the 'amphitheatre' metaphor. – *The Ep. to the Hebrews, Greek Text with Notes*, 1889, Macmillan, xlviii; Marshall, A, Ed. *GSM* Feb. 1931, 175, 'spectators of our 'course' surrounding us on all sides.' J. D. Robb, 'Hebrews 12:1,' *ET*. Vol. 79, (1968), 254, questions the race aspect, and prefers 'struggle,' but Dodd, C. H. op. cit. (4), refutes this idea.
6. Barclay, W, *N.T.Words*, 54–57.
7. Poole, L & G, op. cit. 1, 2; Turner, N. *Christian Words*, 42/3, 'a wrap which encumbers the runner.'
8. Noack, B, 'Celui que court, Rom. 8:16,' *StudTheol*. Vol. 24, (1970) 113–116, showing that 'running' is quite compatible with Hebrew and Rabbinical thought as found in this Psalm, and the link through Romans 9:15, 16. We must have God behind us in the race.
9. Robertson, A. T. *Word Pictures*, Vol. 4, 386; Smith, D, *Life & Letters*, 429 ftn; Earle, R, *Word Meanings*, 194, likens it to stubbing one's toe and falling.
10. Verse 44 is omitted by some manuscripts. Metzger, B, M, Ed. *A Textual Commentary on the Greek N. T.*, 1975, corrected ed. United Bible Societies, 58, regards it as ancient and retains it in brackets.
11. Deissmann, G. A. *Bible Studies*, 225/6, destroys rather than winnows, evidence for this meaning of the Greek word.
12. Thayer, J. H. *Greek-English Lexicon*, 330.
13. Pittman R. T. *Words and Their*

Ways, 33; Wordsworth, C. *Greek Testament*, Vol. 2. 327; Daddow, W. B. *Buried Pictures*, 117/8; Poole, L & G. op. cit. (2), 111; Waugh, R. M. L. *Greek Testament*, 84; Sadler ftn, 'to give judgment against one as brabeus . . . and so to deprive one of the prize, with collateral action of cheating.' Brown, C. Ed. *NIDNTT*, Vol. 1, 648.

14. Lightfoot, J. B. *Colossians*, 193.

15. It is interesting to note in *Josephus Ant.* 6, 3, (1) 31, based upon 1 Samuel 7: 15, 16, that Greek dikazein and brabenein are closely linked when it is said of Samuel that he 'judged their causes and so continued for long to administer perfect justice.' (Loeb translation) cp. Lightfoot, J. B. *Colossians*, 221 and Daddow, W. B. *Buried Pictures* 119–122, re testing for the true umpire. Pfitzner, V. C. *Agon Motif*, 154–156. Field's evidence is not so strong as Pfitzner would suggest.

16. Trench, R. C. *Synonyms*, 75f; Robertson, A. T. *Word Pictures*, Vol. 4. 149; Poole, L & G, op. cit. (2), 5, 99; Waugh, R. M. L. *Greek Testament*, 84/5; Wuest, K, *Word Studies*, Vol. 3. *Bypaths*, 61–68; Marshall, A Ed. *GSM*, Dec. 1930, 167, 'amarantus flos, symbolum est immortalitatis.' – Clement of Alexandria. Robertson, A. T. *Word Pictures* Vol. 6, 132. Pfitzner, V. C. *Agon Motif*, 104–108, 183–185.

17. Wordsworth, C. *Greek Testament*, Vol. 2, 472, citing Pausanius book 5, 21, that there were six statues of Jupiter at Olympia made from the fines levied on athletes; Wuest, K. op. cit. (16) 53, 54; Marshall, A. Ed. *GSM*, Nov-Dec 1930, 163/4, 167; Howson, J. S. *Metaphors*, 154–158.

18. Poole, L & G, op. cit (2), 29, 30, 48/9; Rienecker, F et al, *Linguistic*

Key, 634; Marshall, A. Ed. *GSM*, Jan. 1931, 171.

19. Cary, M, & Haarhoff, T. J. *Life and Thought in the Greek and Roman World*, 1942, 3rd ed. Methuen, 156/7; Pfitzner, V. C. *Agon Motif*, 114, 115, 119, 120.

20. Pittman, R, T. *Words and Their Ways*, 20; Nicolson, W. M. *Classical Revision of the Greek N. T.* . . . . . 1878, Williams & Norgate, 115; Daddow, W. B. *Buried Pictures*, 78/9; Robertson, A. T. *Word Pictures*, Vol. 4, 149; Wordsworth, C. *Greek Testament*, Vol. 2, 114; Bishop, E. F. F. *Jesus of Palestine*, 199; Simpson, E. K. *Words Worth Weighing*, 14/15. Pfitzner, V. C. *Agon Motif*, 90, 91.

21. Bengel, J. A. *Gnomon*, Vol. 5. 413; Derrett, J. D. M. 'Law in the N. T: The Parable of the Unjust Judge.' *NTStud*. Vol. 18, (1972) 178–191, ' 'my face has been blackened,' means 'I have been disgraced'.' (190); Dodd, C. H. op. cit. (4) 147, where Dodd considers the metaphor to be dead in Luke 18, but where it still vividly illustrates the feelings involved, and so retains a value; Earle, R, *Word Meanings*, 232, where the AV translation of Luke 18:5 'weary' is described as 'very weak.'

22. Poole, L & G, op. cit (2), 70/71; Howson, J. S. *Metaphors*, 159–167.

23. Poole, L & G, op. cit. (2), 59–66; Ward, R. A. *Hidden Meaning*, 151; Robertson, A. T. *Word Pictures*, Vol. 4, 550; Sadler ftn to Eph. 6:12; Daddow, W. B. *Buried Pictures*, 78–81; Levine, E, 'The Wrestling-Belt Legacy in the N. T. ' *NTStud*. Vol. 28 (1982), 560–564, on girding the loins for battle.

24. Poole, L & G, op. cit. (2), 59–62.

25. Skeat, W. W. *Etymological Dictionary*, 11. under 'agony'; Pittman, R.

T. *Words and Their Ways*, 28, cp. Luke 22:44 re agony; Dodd, C. H. op. cit. (4), 149, 'a reminder of the sustained effort . . . demanded.' See also Weymouth 3rd ed. ftn to John 18:36, and the prolonged struggle brought out by the imperfect tense used; Yahuda, J, *Hebrew is Greek*, 559. Pfitzner, V. C. *Agon Motif*, 109–111, 128, 159.

26. See Conybeare ftn to 1 Cor. 15:32, and also Sadler in his Appendix to his translation 60–62. Maltherbe, A. J.'The Beasts of Ephesus', *JBL*, Vol. 87 (1968), 71–80.

27. Alford, H. *Greek Testament*, Vol. 2, 613 (7th ed. 1877), thought that Corinthians was written before the events described in Acts 19, but many recent chronologers consider the three years of the Ephesian ministry to take up parts of 53–55 C. E. and that First Corinthians was written near to the end of that time or very shortly afterwards. See the discussion G. Ogg, *The Chronology of the Life of Paul*, 1968, Epworth Press, 134–139, who thinks 54–57, and the chart at the end of Jewett R. *A Chronology of Paul's Life*, 1979, Philadelphia, Fortress Press, and 134; also Bruce, F. F. *N. T. History*, 1969, Nelson, 312/3.

28. Ramsay, W. M. *St. Paul The Traveller and the Roman Citizen*, 1927, 16th ed. Hodder & Stoughton, 230/1; The Great Theatre was about 495 feet in diameter, and held some 25, 000 spectators, and overlooked the city in a hollow on the slope of Mt. Pion. Unger, M. F. *Archaeology and the N. T.* 1962, Pickering & Inglis, 254/5.

29. Jones, H. S. & McKenzie, R. Ed. Liddell & Scott, *A Greek-English Lexicon*, 1951rp, 9th ed. Vol. 1, 1004; Pittman, R. T. *Words and Their Ways*, 23; Bengel, J. A.

Gnomon, Vol. 4, 93; Robinson, J. A. *Ephesians*, 101/2; Westcott, B. F. *Ep. to the Ephesians, Greek Text with Notes*, 1906, Macmillan, 64, 194; Robertson, A. T. *Word Pictures*, Vol. 4, 538.

30. Waugh, R. M. L. *Living Words*, 30; Deissmann, G. A. *Light*, 88; Ayers, D. M. *English Words*, 212, the game of dice, 'Hazara' is from the Arabic, 'Al-zahr' – 'the die.'

31 Haigh, A. E. *The Attic Theatre*, 1889, Oxford, Clarendon Press 198–222, quotation from 219.

32. Robertson, A. T. *The Minister*, 59; Marshall, A, *Gleanings*, 39; Batey, R. A. 'Jesus and the Theatre,' *NTStud.* Vol. 30, (1984), 563–574; Kittel, G. Ed. *TDNT*, Vol. 8, 565–569.

33. Bennett, W. H. *The Mishna as Illustrating the Gospels*, 1884, Cambridge, Deighton Bell, 46–52, quotation from 47; Montefiore, C. G. *Rabbinic Literature and Gospel Teachings*, 1930, Macmillan, 118f., replying to Abrahams, I. *Studies in Pharisaism*, 2nd series, 30–32; Smith, D. *The Days of His Flesh*, 1910, 8th ed. rev. Hodder & Stoughton, 102.

34. Barclay, W, *N. T. Words*, 140–143; Turner, N, *Christian Words*, 219; Robinson, W. G. *N. T. Treasure*, 26–29; Amory, F. 'Whited Sepulchres: The Semantic History of Hypocrisy to the High Middle Ages,' *RechTheolAncMed*, Vol. 53, (1986), 5–39 showing that in the first century the word had even become associated with apostasy.

35. Wuest, K, *Word Studies*, Vol. 3, *Golden Nuggets . . .* 109; Marshall, A. Ed. *GSM* July 1933, 383 'Hypocrites,' quoting Lukyn Williams, 'It does suggest satisfaction with the mask rather than the reality, interest in the outside of things rather than

what is within. It suggests, in fact, superficialism.'

36. Pittman, R. T. *Words and Their Ways*, 34/5; Smith, D, *Life & Letters*, 203 ftn; Thayer, J. H. *Greek-English Lexicon*, 670; Vincent, M. R. *Word Studies*, Vol. 1, 323; Waugh, R. M. L. *Living Words*, 29; Sadler ftn to 2 Cor. 9:10; Ayers, D. M. *English Words*, 229, in addition, our word 'orchestra' comes from the area where the chorus danced, which is now used by the seated musicians.

37. Smith, D, *Life & Letters*, 561 ftn; Pittman, R. T. *Words and Their Ways*, 17; Skeat, W. W. *Etymological Dictionary*, 667 under 'triumph'; Rodd, C. S. 'Salvation Proclaimed: XI. Colossians 2:8–15,' *ET*. Vol. 94, (1982), 39, 40, with some valuable remarks on the purpose and impact of metaphors, and a warning not to 'demetaphorize' them; Yates, R. 'Colossians 2:15: Christ Triumphant,' *NTStud*. Vol. 37 (1991), 573–591; Findlay, G. F. 'St. Paul's Use of Thriambeuō,' *Expositor*, 1st Series, Vol. 10, (1879), 403–421, Vol. 11, (1880), 78/79.

38. This is stressing the rejoicing of the victor rather than the shame of the vanquished. NEB, REB and other translations intrude 'captives' without warrant, placing Paul and early Christians on the wrong side, and confusing the metaphor in 2 Corinthians. See also Trench, R. C. *On the A. V. of the N. T.* 1859, 2nd ed. rev. J. W. Parker, 160/1, but especially J. B. McClellan, 'The Revised Version of the N. T.' *Expositor*, 6th Series, Vol. 10, (1904) 192–194, which very clearly emphasizes the causative form of the verb here; Rienecker, F et al. *Linguistic Key*, 457/8 and the other literature given there; Marshall, P 'A Metaphor of Social Shame: thriambeuein in 2 Cor. 2:14,' *NovTest*. Vol. 25 (1983), 302–317; Breytenbach, C. 'Paul's Proclamation and God's 'thriambos' (Notes on 2 Cor. 2:14–16b.' *NeoTest*. Vol. 24 (1990), 257–271; Williamson, L, 'Led in Triumph: Paul's Use of thriambeuō,' *Interpretation*, Vol. 22 (1968), 317–323.

39. Robertson, A. T. *Word Pictures*, Vol. 4, 291; Smith, D, *Life & Letters*, 203; Waugh, R. M. L. *Greek Testament*, 35; Burck, V, 'To Placard the Crucified (Gal. 3:1),' *ET*. Vol. 30 (1918/19), 232, 233.

40. Arndt, W. F. et al. *Greek-English Lexicon*, 353; Bruce, F. F. *The Ep. to the Hebrews*, (New London Commentary on the N. T), 1965, Marshall, Morgan & Scott, 265–270 & Gerasa inscription.

Chapter 6

The Human Body and Clothing

1. Head and Body—Christ and the Congregation.

The apostle Paul's illustration of the human body is briefly introduced to us in his letter to the Romans, allowing us to gather its principal purpose before looking at his more detailed discussion in the first letter to the Corinthians.

'For just as you have many members in one physical body and those members differ in their functions, so we, though many in number, compose one body in Christ and are all members to one another.' (Romans 12:4, 5 Phillips Rev.) Whatever our gifts or abilities, these we should use to the utmost, so contributing to the welfare spiritually of the whole body of Christ, his congregation.

In his first letter to the Corinthians (12:14–26), Paul analyses his illustration, and makes the following points:

1. The body comprises many parts all serving different purposes.
2. No one part has a monopoly, so as to consider the other parts unnecessary or useless.
3. Even the least important, weakest parts are needed, and contribute to the whole.
4. Parts serving a very menial function are yet much appreciated for the work they perform.
5. The pleasing parts supply their own recommendation.
6. God intended the human body to work as a harmonious whole, all parts feeling the hurt or suffering of any one part, and all rejoicing in a general feeling of well-being.

In verses 12, 13, 27–31, Paul applies the illustration. The congregation of Christ is united through holy spirit despite being composed of Jews, Greeks, slaves and free men. Each one brings and receives different gifts. No one person has them all, and whilst all should strive to improve their spiritual gifts, it is love that counts most and surpasses all others, and this leads naturally into Paul's famous thirteenth chapter on love.[1]

Obviously Paul does not apply the whole of his illustration, so we can draw further conclusions in harmony with that development. Some members of the congregation may appear frail and insignificant, contributing very little because of their age or infirmity. They may even feel that they are useless and a burden on others. But look at their faith in adversity, their steadfast patience and noble spirit! Is that not a fine example and tonic to everyone that knows them? Do younger Christians pause in their bubbling enthusiasm to reflect on the quiet, calm spirit that burns with a steady flame, that stays the course long after that first rush of zeal and energy has vaporized like steam? So even the most lowly and poor ones contribute something to the body, and they are needed and wanted. That is the spirit of true, harmonious Christianity.

Yet another facet of his illustration is the growth of the human body, and the importance of the head. 'It is from the head alone that the body, through the joints and ligaments, is nourished and built up and grows as God meant it to grow.' (Col. 2:19 Phillips Rev. Eph. 4:15, 16.) How true this is. The nerve centre is in the brain, directing all parts of the body. We use our head to see and to hear for spiritual growth, and our mouth to take in food for physical growth.[2]

The head of the congregation is Jesus Christ, and he has been set in that position by God himself. (Eph. 1:22, 23.) He communicates everything needed spiritually to the body, seeing and hearing on its behalf, and nourishing it as it grows. He superintends the feeding programme through his faithful slave or servant, so that everyone receives their food at the proper time. (Matt. 24:45–47.)

This illustration is more than a mere comparison. It reflects a picture of the healthy, strong and growing spirit-anointed congregation of God. This is not a picture of a disunited and ailing church organization, feeding on mere husks and experiencing a famine for God's Word, lacking real faith, with its very fabric crumbling to pieces. (Amos 8:11, Luke 15:14–19.)

The challenge is very apparent. Have we found the true Christian congregation of God that truly fulfils all the requirements of this metaphor? Is there really that quality of faith, hope, love and unity present that is implicit in this Biblical body under Christ's personal direction?

2. The Eye—Single Vision.

Since spiritual vision is so important in the teaching of Christianity, it would be unlikely that the eye would escape being used in an illustrative way. In his Sermon on the Mount Jesus drew the metaphor very clearly, saying, 'The lamp of the body is your eye. If, then, your eye should be single, [Greek 'haplous'], your whole body will be luminous. Yet if your eye should be wicked, your whole body will be dark.' (Matt. 6:22, 23a Concordant.)

What did Jesus mean by his use of the Greek term 'haplous'? Other translations render it by 'liberal' (McClellan), 'in single focus' (Wuest), 'generous' (Moffatt), 'healthy' (Adams), 'unclouded' (TCNT), 'sound' (Rieu, NEB, Goodspeed). It has been defined as 'that which is spread out, and thus without folds and wrinkles . . . singleness, simplicity, absence of folds.'But the idea of 'one-fold' linked with the Latin *simplex* (same ply), does not contradict 'without fold' and contrasts well with the idea of *duplex* (double fold) or duplicity.[3]

One whose eye is single or simple has vision that is clear and unobscured, in focus, a wide vision that gives rise to the idea of a generous or liberal eye. His vision is not imperfect due to an unsound, diseased eye, nor is he cross-eyed, cock-eyed, or one-eyed, with one eye on earthly treasures, while the other seems to be on spiritual things. Such double vision was the idea behind Jesus' very next comment, that one cannot serve two masters, God and Riches. (Matt. 6:24.) The eye can also be definitely evil, perhaps envious. (Matt. 20:15.) It can be grudging or niggardly, reflecting the attitude of mind and heart that lies behind it.[4]

A little later in that same discourse, Jesus applied his illustration of the eye to a specific problem that faces everyone, our ability to see other people's shortcomings and not our own. 'Why do you note the little splinter in your brother's eye, and take no notice of the beam in yours?' (Matt. 7:3 Rieu.) His use of hyperbole here emphasized the distortion of the mind as well as the eye, and again, translations have sought to heighten the contrast by a range of opposites: 'speck/plank' (NAB, NEB, RAV, TNT), 'speck/log' (Adams, NASB, RSV, TEV), 'straw/beam' (TCNT). Before we criticize our brothers and sisters, we need to work on our own faults, to improve our own vision.[5]

It is infinitely worse to be spiritually blind, and this condition is referred to several times by the apostle Paul. Speaking of his own people, the Jews, he said, 'Their minds became impenetrably insensitive. To this very day their eyes are covered by the same veil, when they hear the lesson from the old covenant being read in the synagogue.' (2 Cor. 3:14 Barclay.) Some translations use the word 'hardened' for the Greek 'pōrōsis' here (RV, ASV, RSV, NASB, NRSV), as if a film had dropped over the eyes, hardening them and bringing blindness. But this condition is one of moral and intellectual blindness rather than a hardness of heart, a mental blockage or obstinacy, resisting the holy spirit. (John 12:37–40, Acts 28: 25–28, Rom. 11:25.) The Gentile nations showed the same spiritual blindness, and because of their closed minds and insensible natures, their heart was also affected. (Eph. 4:18.)[6]

In encouraging Christians to improve their spiritual insight, Peter warned against those who failed to build up godly qualities and understanding. 'The man who has not got these virtues is short-sighted and cannot see. He has forgotten that his past sins have been washed away.' (2 Pet. 1:9 TNT.) The Greek verb 'muōpazō' is the origin of our word 'myopia' applied to those whose eyesight is such that they are 'seeing only what is near'. (RV, ASV.) They have to screw up their eyes to see and their field of vision is impaired, especially for distant objects. That is a real danger for Christians, who should not be narrow-minded, but single-minded with a single wide vision eye, always seeking first God's kingdom and his righteousness. (Matt. 6:33.)[7]

Paul well sums it up, 'Therefore, let there be no blur in your moral vision: take heed how you go on your way, not as unwise, but as wise.' (Eph. 5:15 Ward, p.144.) Because of the prevailing state of the world in general, a Christian needs to train his spiritual eye so that he can walk wisely, without stumbling or falling by the wayside.

3. The Ear—Listen and Act.

Because hearing the word of God is a principal theme of the Bible, there are many references to the ear used in the form of an illustration.

Jesus stressed the importance of listening attentively when he told his disciples, 'You . . . should have these words ringing in your ears, "The Son of Man is going to be delivered into the hands of men." But they failed to understand this saying.' (Luke 9:44, 45a Rieu.) Robertson's translation adds the note, 'Let them sink into your ears and beyond.' They needed to store them away carefully in their minds ready for use when the rest of the pattern was revealed. Then they would know immediately how to act in response.[8]

So hearing is really a process of taking words and ideas in through the ears, allowing them to sink down, applying them, and acting in obedience to what is called for. Paul suggested, 'Let him who is instructed in the word go shares with him who instructs him in all good things.' (Gal. 6:6 Sadler.) The footnote to the word 'instructed' mentions that the Greek word 'katēcheō' means 'to sound down to'. From this word comes our English catechumen, – 'to instruct, to impress upon, to din into one's ears'.[9] Paul stressed that five words that really reached his hearers, or were sounded down to them, were worth ten thousand spoken in a language not understood. (1 Cor. 14:19 Sadler footnote.)

The final result is often spoken of in close connection with the initial process of hearing with the ear; obedience or disobedience, the acceptance or rejection of the message. Both ideas come through clearly in one translation that contrasts Adam and Christ Jesus. 'For as through the deafness of the one man the many were set down as sinners, so also through the keen hearing of the one the many shall be set down as righteous.' (Rom. 5:19 Sadler.) The two contrasting words are 'parakoē' and 'hupakoē'. The first is to hear something amiss, to half hear it, due to inattention and careless hearing. The second is to hear precisely, carefully, placing oneself in the right position to hear. We might liken it to the loudspeaker on a railway station, where there are many distracting noises that could easily cause us to miss the train announcements. If we place ourselves directly under the speaker we are able to hear what is said, but if we are well to one side, we will likely miss the announcement or hear it incorrectly.[10]

Jesus was always obedient to his Father, so much so that it was prophetically said of him, 'You, who wanted no sacrifice or oblation, opened my ear [lit. ears you have digged for me – Hebrew Interlinear Psalms, Bagster] . . . then I said, "Here I am; I am coming!"' (Ps. 40:7 JB. Heb. 10:5–7.) But many of his contemporaries refused to hear, shutting up their ears in defiance. (Acts 7:57.) Others only wanted to have their ears tickled, listening to what pleased and flattered them, but not wishing to listen to the truth. (2 Tim. 4:3, 4, Acts 17:21, Ezek. 33:31–33.)

Another variation is suggested in the idea of an echo. An echo in a cave can ring true or it can be distorted, and it may also reverberate a number of times, giving the sense of repetition. When Paul went up to Jerusalem, he was told that some Jews had 'heard it rumoured' that he was teaching an apostasy, and the older men there wanted to know if there was any truth in these rumours. (Acts 21:21 Rotherham.) That rumour had been echoed from one person to another, being distorted in the process.

But in the case of Apollos, the context suggests the other idea associated with 'echoing down'. 'He had been well instructed ['katēcheō'] in the Cause of the Lord, and with burning zeal he spoke of, and taught carefully, the facts about Jesus, though he knew of no baptism but John's.' (Acts 18:25 TCNT.) Through good instruction and repetition he had accurately understood all that he had been taught, but because he was a new disciple, he did not have a complete rounded-out knowledge. So it was necessary for Aquila and Priscilla to give him some further instruction, and then he could give successfully all the needed answers to the Jews. (Acts 18: 26–28.)[11]

For us today to sound down the truth of God's Word, echoing it until we really understand it accurately, is to show our obedience to God's will, bringing our lives into harmony with the fine example set by his son Jesus Christ, and his clear admonition, 'If you have ears, use them'. (Matt. 13:9 TNT.)

4. The Word in Your Mouth—
The Message that is Very Near.

To travel into space or across a deep and mighty ocean may not seem so difficult for us today, but over 3, 000 years ago it represented something quite impossible or extremely unlikely. This is the illustration Moses used to the Israelites when he told them that the commandments he was giving were not too difficult for them to follow, nor beyond their reach. They did not need to climb into heaven or cross the sea, for 'the word is very near to you, it is in your mouth and in your heart for you to put into practice.' (Deut. 30: 11–14 NJB.)

The apostle Paul took this illustration and gave it a fresh application to Christ Jesus. Would anyone try to go up into heaven to bring Christ back to earth, or down into the depths of the earth, as it were, to try to bring him back from the dead? How unnecessary that would be, for 'The word is very near to you; it is in your mouth and in your heart, that is, the word of faith, the faith which we preach, that if you declare with your mouth that Jesus is Lord, and if you believe with your heart that God raised him from the dead, then you will be saved.' (Rom. 10:5–9 NJB.)

Some scholars have accused Paul of lifting a quotation from its context and twisting it to suit his own ideas. But these words of Moses had become almost proverbial by Jesus' time, so it was simply the illustration that Paul borrowed, and since the old Law covenant had ceased to be of importance to Christians, he was right to apply it to that which had replaced it, the teachings of Christ, which were still patterned on the Law in principle.[12]

The faith that a Christian could share was therefore not something inaccessible and obscure, but it could 'fit close to you' and be in a person's mouth and heart.[13] His heart could meditate upon it and his thoughts could be turned into conversation with others, and words could be readily framed in the mouth to teach the exciting and comforting message, the good news of God's Kingdom. The King Christ Jesus had been among them, close at hand. (Matt. 4:17 Weymouth, Phillips.)

Paul was quite conscious of the need to show how close God was to people. He was no 'Unknown God,' remote and hidden from mankind, who in all nations and races everywhere were his creation. His very purpose in putting them on the earth had that reason, 'And he did this so that they might seek the Deity and, by feeling their way towards him, succeed in finding him; and indeed he is not far from any of us, since it is in him that we live, and move, and exist.' (Acts 17:27, 28a NJB.) The Moffatt translation uses the phrase, 'on the chance of finding him as they grope for him,' but this is not really in context with Paul's argument. One commentator explains it like this: 'Instead of consciously realizing his presence, as by touch of hand, they had groped about, like men in the dark, without success; and yet there was no excuse for their failure, because God was close to man, even to every single individual, whether Greek or Barbarian.'[14]

Because God is invisible, faith in him is essential, and so that superb chapter on faith gives us the final clue; 'the man who draws near to God must believe that he exists and that he does reward those who seek him.' (Heb. 11:6 Moffatt.) Our search would be very half-hearted if from the start we had doubts that it would be successful. But the testimony of creation should erase such an idea from our minds, and one of the rewards that God gives is that he does not play 'hide and seek' with men, but will reveal himself to those who really seek him with an honest heart and open mind. To them the preaching of the good news brings an immediate response. They do not turn it away or pass it by. As their faith continues to build, so they come to feel a real relationship with God, and he becomes close to them, like a father, just as he did to the early apostles and disciples.

So we have to ask ourselves some questions as we think about this illustration. Are we really certain that God does exist? Are we using the means he has given to us to find him, his Word the Bible and the message being preached by word of mouth, things that are close by us, in most homes, waiting to identify the God who cares? We need not fear that others will force us out if we draw near to God, as might be the case with a human who is popular and sought after. We can all get close to God, and no one will ever be pushed out.

5. Hanging on the Lips—The Listener's Reaction.

The figurative expression 'to hang on' is a cliche of our modern society, but it is not new. The Greek expression has many similarities in its idea of 'hanging from,' clinging to something. It denotes rapt attention, as if suspended in mid-air in admiration and amazement. This picturesque speech serves to underline how powerful a speaker Jesus must have been, not just in the words he used, but also in the content of his message. 'All the People hung upon His lips [Greek 'ekkremamai'] listening to Him.' (Luke 19:48 Wade.)[15]

On an earlier occasion, at the end of his Sermon on the Mount, there was a similar reaction, expressed in slightly different words. 'The crowds were astonished and overwhelmed with bewildered wonder at his teaching.' (Matt. 7:28 Amplified.) Most translations fail to bring out the intensity of the reaction described in the Greek verb 'ekplēssō', usually contenting themselves with 'astonished', 'astounded' or 'filled with amazement'. A very few try to get at the emotion and feeling conveyed with 'dumbfounded' (C. B. Williams), 'struck with awe' (Alex Campbell), 'lost in admiration' (Kleist and Lilly), and 'stunned' (Lamsa). When we take into account other reactions, such as those men sent to arrest him, who said, 'No man ever spoke like that,' (John 7:46 Rieu) and that this was the first hearing of one of the world's most outstanding discourses, we expect to find a most unusual response. A. T. Robertson gets nearest to the idea when he says, 'the verb means literally, "were struck out of themselves".'[16] It calls for a double epithet, such as 'stunned astonishment' or 'swept off their feet with amazement.'

But what was the feeling amongst those who did not like the common people's enthusiasm, and who rejected Jesus as the Messiah, finding fault with all he said. When the disciples were accused of filling Jerusalem with the teaching of Christ, and Peter made a bold defence before the Sanhedrin, its members were deeply wounded, or some translations say, 'cut to the heart'. (Acts 5:33 AV, Darby, Rotherham.) The expression paints a more vivid picture than that; 'their hearts were, as it were, sawn in two with vexation and rage.' (Wuest, Weymouth 3rd ed. ftn.) It was just as if a sharp saw had cut them asunder (Greek 'diapriō', used literally at 1 Chron. 20:3 LXX).

The plain truth spoken boldly can bring some strong reactions. Our emotional response could make us antagonistic, like those Jews. But our clear perception of the ring of truth could bring us great joy, as it did to those early disciples of Jesus.

6. Craning the Neck—Expectation.

When we are anxious to catch the first glimpse of someone in the distance, we often stretch our neck to assist in seeing better, or we may act similarly to place our ear nearer to a quiet speaker so as not to miss anything that is said. The Greek word 'apokaradokia' means, 'to watch with the head stretched out, to keep an eager look-out'. It includes the ideas of both abstraction and absorption, 'abstraction from anything else that might engage the attention, and absorption in the object expected "till the fulfillment is realised".'[17]

This word is found twice in the Greek Scriptures, as when Paul expresses his 'eager expectation and hope' for the future. (Phil. 1:20 Adams.) One particular prospect that stirred the apostle was the thought of seeing the groaning creation set free at last from the burden of sin and corruption. 'The creation anxiously waits, eagerly anticipating the revelation of God's sons.' (Rom. 8:19 Adams.)

But there were those who took the opposite view. They did not want to share the good news, and refused to listen, or show eager expectation, despite their supposed interest in looking for the Messiah to come to the earth. It was Stephen who so upset such Jews by his outspoken discourse that they put him to death. Near the end of that wide ranging summary, he told them, 'Stiffnecked, stubborn, headstrong, obstinate, and uncircumcised in heart and ears, as for you, incessantly do you strive against the Holy Spirit. As your fathers did, so also do you.' (Acts 7:51 Wuest.)[18]

This expression 'stiffnecked' had its origin in the horse, ox or ass that refused to answer to the reins, and Israel had gained that reputation in the past. 'I knew that you were stubborn, your neck stiff as iron, your brow like bronze.' (Isa. 48:4 NEB, Jer. 17:23.)

Far better, then, to have a pliable neck, straining to watch in eager and confident expectation for all that God tells his servants to do, listening to his word and ready to obey his commands. In fact, many early Christians were willing to risk their necks, to stretch them, so to speak, on the block, in their desire to serve God and one another. (Rom. 16:4.)[19]

7. Bent of Mind—A Lack of Faith.

Our mind can become physically confused if for a period of time we do not breathe sufficient oxygen, or too much carbon dioxide.[20] In a spiritual sense the mind can be affected by how we feed it, or fail to feed it.

Because a doubter lacks faith his bent of mind is going to throw him off balance, and his conduct will reflect this – he may even become a 'Jekyll and Hyde'. James warned about this type of man, 'But let him ask in faith and have no doubts, for he who doubts is . . . a man of two minds [Greek 'dipsuchos'], undecided in every step he takes.' (James 1:6–8 Weymouth.) 'Cleanse your hearts, you double-minded men.' (James 4:8 TNT.)[21]

Does that mean that a Christian can never have any doubts without seeming to be a 'double-minded man'? No, but he does something to resolve those doubts. He reasons on God's Word, talks to others about the matter, and comes to a decision on it. All the time his faith is being built up, and his heart is being properly motivated, cleansed or renewed.

But what of the man whose interests are divided? He may selfishly wish to cling to material pleasures of the world, loving them more than he loves God, or he may 'observe the forms of religion, but . . . rejects its real power'. (2 Tim. 3:4, 5 TNT.) Loyalty is the quality where the bent of mind is all one way – Godward, but hypocrisy partakes of the double mind, resulting in an inconsistent, unstable attitude in all a person thinks and feels. Decisions may be changed without any basis or reason, because he is 'in two minds'. He can be easily swayed, side-tracked and misled. He may deliberately deceive others by his own lack of heart, quite a different thing from being 'half-hearted' as Weymouth would render James 4:8.

A lack of faith in another form may show a temporary wrong bent of mind, as was evident in Peter's case. Not realizing all that was involved in Jesus' destiny, he took the human viewpoint, urging Jesus to be kind to himself. Jesus replied in a way that must have shocked Peter, 'Out of my way, Satan! . . . you stand right in my path, Peter, when you think the thoughts of man and not those of God.' (Matt. 16:23 Phillips.)

It was as if Peter was temporarily possessed by the Devil, tempting Jesus through the inclinations of the flesh just as Satan might try to do. It has been well said that Jesus 'rebuked not his impulsiveness but his "bent of mind"' (Greek 'phronēma').[22] Why had Peter allowed his mind to be directed or set in this way, taking that side of the matter? At that time it was undoubtedly partly through ignorance, not understanding fully God's purpose with regard to Christ, something all the disciples shared, but which Peter, as usual, was the first to express. But when we see Peter after Pentecost, enlightened by the Spirit, what a difference! He had not only a clearer understanding, but his whole attitude of mind was changed, his mind was fully made over, and no longer subject to that previous 'bent of mind'. (Rom. 12:2 Phillips, NWT.)

Paul's advice to the Colossians can help Christians today from being subject to that wrong 'bent of mind' or 'double-mindedness'. 'And set your minds and keep them set on what is above – the higher things – not on the things that are on the earth.' (Col. 3:2 Amplified.)

8. Mending Joints and Nets— Readjustment and Restoration.

What do a fisherman mending his nets, a surgeon setting a dislocated knee, and a Christian helping a fellow who has stumbled in his faith have in common?

They are all trying to restore or repair something or someone that has experienced a break, a problem that no longer allows them to operate in a normal fashion. They all have in common the Greek word 'katartizō'.

This word was used about the sons of Zebedee who were mending their nets when Jesus called them. (Matt. 4:21, Mark 1:19.) Holes or breaks in their nets had to be repaired if they were going to continue as effective fishermen, and now Jesus was adding another little illustration – they were going to become fishers of men. (Matt. 4:19, Mark 1:17.)[23]

A division or break between brothers could cause the Christian congregation to founder, and the Corinthians were in that very danger. So Paul wrote to them, 'I exhort you . . . shun disputes, and have no divisions among you, but to be knit together ('katartizō') in the same mind, and the same judgment.' (1 Cor. 1:10 Conybeare, 2 Cor. 13:9–11.)

The other aspect of this illustration comes out well here, for the word was used in connection with setting or adjusting bones. The surgeon might need to set a dislocated or broken knee or arm, taking care to see that the joints are fitted back together in the right manner, so that they will properly knit together and can again function normally when full healing has taken place. That was how Paul wanted the Corinthians to come together, 'to be knit together in the same mind'.

As well as the surgeon, the work of an osteopath emphasizes other angles of the metaphor. One authority thus describes it, 'The object of an osteopathic treatment is to *readjust* the deranged parts or conditions so that the natural state of health may be regained . . . The matter of prime importance is the ability to locate the maladjusted part and to interpret its effects. To do this requires the most comprehensive knowledge of all parts of the body, and their respective uses.' Then describing the osteopath's deft hands it adds, 'His sense of touch must be delicately educated so that no variation from the normal in position or consistence of tissues can escape his notice.'[24]

Now consider these principles in applying the illustration when Paul wrote, 'Brothers, even though a man takes some false step before he is aware of it, you who have spiritual qualifications try to readjust ('katartizō') such a man in a spirit of mildness, as you each keep an eye on yourself, for fear you also may be tempted.' (Gal. 6:1 NWT.)

Those spiritual qualifications would include a thorough knowledge of God's Word and the problems that can test and try a person's faith. There would have to be a correct and delicate diagnosis of the reason for the false step, so that it could be readjusted with gentleness, tact and consideration. Then that person's spiritual health can be restored to normal.

We can appreciate why Jesus used this word when he said, 'every disciple, when he has been fully trained ['katartizō'] will be like his teacher.' (Luke 6:40 TNT.) Having finished thoroughly his training with full spiritual qualifications, the disciple has himself been set right, readjusted by his teacher, so that he can now go out and help to readjust others in the spirit of Galatians 6:1.

So 'katartizō' includes the ideas of restoring, reconciling, readjusting, supplying with a view to finishing thoroughly, putting into order, and is translated in a passage in Herodotus to 'restore all things there to their former condition'. Paul, writing to the Thessalonians expressed the hope that he might see them again, 'and repair the defects of your faith'. (1 Thess. 3:10 Smith.)[25]

Whether it is a false step we might have taken, or some hole or defect in our faith that has appeared, or even a dispute or schism in the congregation affecting a number of persons, are we all willing to accept readjustment from those who can render assistance, so that we can be restored to full spiritual health and harmony?

9. Burning Coals on the Head—Softening an Enemy.

One of the most vivid metaphors in the Greek Scriptures has divided commentators in their interpretations. Speaking of vengeance belonging only to God, Paul wrote, 'Never try to get revenge; leave that, my friends, to God's anger. As scripture says . . . if your enemy is hungry, you should give him food, and if he is thirsty, let him drink. Thus you heap red-hot coals on his head.' (Rom. 12:20 JB.) Paul took this quotation from Proverbs 25: 21, 22.

From the reading of Psalm 140:9, 10, one might conclude that dropping burning coals on an enemy was intended as a punishment. But the context of Paul's words is very different. Augustine was an early writer who said this about the verse, 'one would think a deed of malevolence was enjoined . . . let charity on the contrary call you back to benevolence, and interpret the coals of fire as the burning groans of penitence by which a man's pride is cured who bewails that he has been the enemy of one who came to his assistance in distress.'[26]

The literal happening that gave rise to the metaphor may have been the smelting of metal. Red-hot charcoal was heaped up all around and above the crushed ore, which as it melted ran out into a collecting pit or pot. But there was also an Egyptian rite where a person carried the glowing embers in a bowl on the head, or in another case, carried a tray of burning coals to indicate repentance.[27] Certainly, when applied to a person's head, even in a figurative sense, the idea of pain has to be associated with the action. What was the pain meant to do?

'It must refer to the burning pain of shame and remorse which the man feels whose hostility is repaid by love. This is the only kind of vengeance the Christian is at liberty to contemplate.'[28] Reasons for this conclusion rather than the idea of punishment are: 1). Paul has already said that any punishment is to be left to God; 2). you would not give food and drink to an enemy as a form of punishment; 3). Christians are to keep conquering evil with good, so this is an act of kindness and love.

Some translations transfer the metaphor, involving some of these ideas: 'a burning sense of shame' (Moffatt), 'you will make him feel the burning pangs of shame' (Barclay), 'induce him to repent' (Blackwelder).

However, nothing is said about the repentance of an enemy. That might be the result in certain cases, but at least the kind action might cause the opposer to feel ashamed. It might trouble his conscience, soften his attitude, so that at least his enmity might be reduced and his hatred become less implacable. If it does nothing to change him, then it will make certain that when God's wrath does fall upon him, it will have been fully justified.

10. A Capacious Bosom—Generosity.

When Jesus recommended generosity he used an interesting illustration. 'Give, and others will give to you; into the fold of your garment they will pour out for you good measure, pressing it down and shaking it together until it runs over; for the measure you use for others will be used for you in return.' (Luke 6:38 TNT.) Most translations fail to give the idea behind this illustration, using 'laps' (the modern equivalent to our thinking), for the Greek word 'kolpos', which literally means 'bosom'.

Cunningham Geikie explains how the Eastern dress was arranged to form this 'bosom' or great pocket. The long robe or shirt falling to the ankles was fastened around the waist by a belt or girdle. Above this it was open at the man's chest or bosom, forming a pocket for carrying things. 'As, moreover, the dress is very loose, he can easily pull it far enough through the girdle to make an overhanging bag in which to carry grain or anything else he chooses.' He then describes the official measure for grain called a 'timneh', and how a skilful merchant sitting cross-legged before it fills it to the brim. Then he shakes it and twists it around, presses down the contents, and then piles it on top until it forms a cone, and the grain runs over the sides. By this method he makes the timneh hold twelve pounds more than if he only once filled it normally.[29]

So imagine the generous giver telling you to pull out more of your robe so that he can cram more grain into your bosom pocket, until you finally head for home almost staggering under the weight, desperately holding the folds of your garment so that the overflowing grain does not run out. Your own earlier generosity might well have caused your friend to give you all you could possibly carry. Even lambs are described as being carried in the bosom. (Isa. 40:11.)

When Paul urged the Corinthians to give in a similar generous way, he referred to God loving the man who gives cheerfully, from the heart. On every count, this is the way God has given to mankind, 'more than you can ever need', and with enough left over for all other requirements. Seed is always plentiful, resulting in fine harvests if sown liberally. 'The more you are enriched the more scope will there be for generous giving,' and if this attitude is always shown by Christians, then it results in 'an overflowing tide of thanksgiving to God.' (2 Cor. 9:5–12 Phillips.) How well Jesus mirrored the fine principles of generosity demonstrated by his Father. May we always follow such a fine example.

11. A Miscarriage—Paul's Sudden Conversion.

The apostle Paul listed an impressive testimony to the resurrection of Jesus Christ when he wrote his first letter to the Corinthians. (1 Cor. 15:3–7.) His own experience of seeing Jesus was very different, 'it was like a sudden, abnormal birth.' (1 Cor. 15:8 REB.) The variety in translation here shows the problem in understanding just what Paul meant by this illustration. 'My birth into the family of Christ was as violent and unexpected as an abortion.' (Barclay.) 'The one whose birth was an abnormality.' (Adams.) 'He appeared also to me, an unperfected, stillborn embryo.' (Wuest.)

The last, quite distinctive translation follows the idea that the Greek word used, 'ektrōma', was an insulting and offensive word, possibly used by his erstwhile Jewish associates to suggest that his conversion was 'a miscarriage' which resulted in his death so far as Judaism was concerned. Paul himself said that he had become as one dead to the Law of Moses. (Gal. 2:19.)

But the context also suggests a contrast with the rest of the apostles and disciples referred to in the previous verses. They had been with Jesus and had been taught by him, and had come to spiritual birth and maturity in a natural gradual way. But Paul experienced a sudden, forceful conversion, for which he was quite unprepared, and so by comparison, he was like an unperfected foetus. (cp. Job, 3:16 LXX.) He could pick up his taunter's own term, and alter it triumphantly to show how this seemingly dead and stunted result (with a hint at his possible small stature) of a 'miscarriage' could become a leader, a foremost apostle, not a whit behind any of the others in the fullness of time. (1 Cor. 15:9–11, Acts 22:6–11, 2 Cor. 11:5, 23, 12:11, Gal. 2:6–9.)[30]

Paul was also able to rejoice that his death to the Mosaic Law and to sin meant a new life through Christ Jesus and by means of the spirit of God. (Rom. 7:4–6, 13, 24, 25. 8:2.) It might be a continual battle whilst still in a fleshly body, but he could triumph in feeling that his unusual and painful conversion made him as much a sharer in the revelation of Christ's glory as was experienced by those very privileged apostles at Jesus' transfiguration. (1 Peter 5:1, Matt. 16:28–17:9.)

12. Changing our Garments—
A Genuine Personality Change.

The idea behind this metaphor is that the garments a person wears identify his condition within, and not just his appearance. So those approved by God are shown arrayed in white outer garments, clean and undefiled. (Rev. 3:4, 5, 7:14.) The defiled inner garment is something to be avoided; in other words, while efforts would continue to save a person, his bad course of action would not be approved or allowed to affect Christians. (Jude 23.)

The change of garments has to be a complete one. 'You have stripped off [Greek 'apekduōmai'] the old self with its doings, and have clothed [Greek 'enduō'] yourselves with the new self which is being remoulded into full knowledge so as to become like Him who created it.' (Col. 3:9, 10, Weymouth 3rd.) R. A. Ward suggests that it would be better to render the first part, 'fling off from yourselves . . .' Once we come to realize how soiled we are, we need to get rid of those bad ways as we would swiftly dispose of a heap of filthy rags, not wishing to be identified with them. Then we can put on the new, clean and spotless clothes and qualities. (Col. 3:8, 12–14. Eph. 4:22–24.)[31]

But such a change of garments has to be permanent. So if someone should show that he has again turned back to his previous wrong actions and is causing division in the congregation, after due warning he is to be rejected and avoided. 'Such a person has utterly changed [Greek 'ekstrephō'] – is perverted and corrupted; he goes on sinning [though] he is convicted of guilt and self-condemned.' (Titus 3:11 Amplified.) The word here is literally 'turned inside out' (K. Int), as a garment might be, and so twisted, perverted.[32] Again, this emphasizes how the alteration to the garment is represented as a change in the entire person, right through.

When Paul writes to the Corinthians, 'we have all to appear without disguise [Greek 'phaneroō'] before the tribunal of Christ, each to be requited for what he has done with his body, well or ill,' (2 Cor. 5:10 Moffatt) it is clear that the garments a person is clothed in represent the real person. There can be no hypocrisy or disguise, putting on garments that are false or deceptive. So the power of the illustration is in the principle that the garments *are* representative of the true person.[33]

13. No Spot or Wrinkle—Pure and Holy.

Even today we tend to associate the spot and the wrinkle. Perhaps that relationship is linked with the apostle Paul's interesting metaphor.

Paul draws a parallel between the relationship of a husband and wife and that of Jesus Christ and his bride, the composite congregation of anointed Christians. After speaking of cleansing and sanctifying the congregation (not a church building as some have thought), he continues, 'that he [Christ] might present the congregation to himself in its splendour, not having a spot or a wrinkle or any of such things, but that it should be holy and without blemish.' (Eph. 5:27 NWT.)

The illustration centres around a Middle Eastern wedding with its practice of purification before marriage. (Esther 2:12, 13.) In one of the most descriptive Messianic Psalms, the bride is shown to be ready for the king. 'The king's daughter is all glorious within [the house]; Her clothing is with settings of gold. In woven apparel she will be brought to the king.' (Ps. 45:13, 14a NWT.) But not only is her clothing spotless, or as we might put it, carefully washed and ironed and without a stain, but she is morally clean and pure, and without any disfigurement or wrinkle of age. The Greek word 'spilos' (spot) originates in 'spilas', with the idea of a rock, and could refer to the agate, which is sprinkled with spots, which are therefore irremovable.[34]

So it is not just the beautiful and spotless appearance of the bride that Paul is highlighting, but her purity and continued holiness, as emphasized by his final phrase in Ephesians 5:27. Writing to Timothy, Paul mentioned that he should, as a member of the congregation, 'observe the commandment in a spotless and irreprehensible way.' (1 Tim. 6:14 NWT.) Peter, after identifying in 2 Peter 2:13, the loose conduct and worldly living which he describes as 'spots and blemishes', in the next chapter puts the contrasting admonition for all Christians, 'Since all these things are thus to be dissolved, what sort of persons ought you to be in holy acts of conduct and deeds of godly devotion . . . . Hence, beloved ones, since you are awaiting these things, do your utmost to be found finally by him spotless and unblemished and in peace.' (2 Peter 3:11, 14, NWT.)

James also urges Christians, 'to keep oneself without spot from the world' if their worship is to remain 'clean and undefiled from the standpoint of our God and Father.' He goes on to distinguish between the bad fruits resulting from worldly wisdom and those coming from 'the wisdom from above' which is 'first of all chaste'. (James 1:27, 3:13–18, NWT.)

Peter also gives the reason for being without spot or blemish or wrinkle, in the context of the illustration. Explaining how the congregation is delivered from the reprehensible course of the world, he shows that it is not by a ransom paid, with silver or gold, 'But it was with precious blood, like that of an unblemished and spotless lamb, even Christ's.' (1 Peter 1:18, 19 NWT.) The King Christ Jesus is without spot or blemish, and so his bride, the congregation, must be also. It matches beautifully the description of the king in that famous Psalm, 'You have loved righteousness and you hate wickedness, [anything spotted up and stained] . . . All your garments are myrrh and aloeswood [and] cassia . . . the queenly consort has taken her stand at your right hand in gold of Ophir.' (Ps. 45:7–9 NWT.)

As J. B. Rotherham has pointed out in his excellent *Studies in the Psalms*, Paul uses the same Greek word (taken her stand), that is found in the Septuagint of Psalm 45:9, presenting ('paristēmi') the congregation in all its splendour 'to himself' or placing her alongside himself, both entirely pure and holy. What a superb illustration of the true relationship between a Christian husband and wife.[35]

14. Tied with Knots—Keep Tight Hold.

Eastern robes are frequently loose and free-flowing, but on certain occasions they would be gathered up with a girdle, tied with a knot, or clasped with a fibula. Often a slave did this so that he could work more easily, and Jesus himself set the example in a lesson that demonstrated to his disciples his great humility. In the words of one translation of the Greek preposition with the sense of 'completely' or 'fully', 'he gave them the perfect love-token' by his action. (John 13:1.)[36]

The gospel record says that Jesus took off his outer garments and 'picked up a towel and fastened it round his waist.' Then he washed the feet of his disciples, using the tied towel to dry them off. But Peter protested that he would not submit to what he felt could only be a humiliation. Jesus' reply quickly altered Peter's mind, for he was told that unless he permitted Jesus to do so 'you cannot be my true partner'. (John 13:2–10 Phillips.)

The idea of tying on a garment with knots is associated with humility at 1 Peter 5:5. 'All of you tie on the apron of humility toward one another, because "God opposes the proud, but helps the humble".' (Adams; 'as with the apron of one who waits on others.' – Weymouth 3rd ftn.) This godly quality is often despised as indicating a sign of weakness, so the Christian is urged to tie it on in such a way that it cannot lightly be removed, or as Bengel puts it, it 'cannot be stripped from you by force easily'.[37] Other tender qualities such as compassion, kindness, gentleness, and long-suffering also need firmly tying on. (Col. 3:12.) Otherwise, the Christian may be provoked into losing those valuable traits by the spirit of the world in general.

The idea is also used in suggesting strength for its own sake. Job was urged to 'gird up his loins' like a man, to summon up all his strength. (Job 38:3.) In the case of the Israelites leaving Egypt, having their loins girded also included being dressed suitably for a long walk, where the long flowing robe might impede them. (Ex. 12:11.)[38] It is once again Peter who uses this as an illustration to keep tight hold on our senses, to be alert, all our spiritual strength mustered ready, 'buckling the belts of your minds for action'. (1 Pet. 1:13 Adams.)

What an illustration of contrast! On the one hand holding tight to the gentle qualities that identify a Christian, yet not becoming soft or weak when temptation arises, but with strength gathered, and garments tied securely for action, being ready to meet any challenge.

15. To Untie Knots—
God Unties His Word Better than Man.

When Jesus used a parable or illustration it often was not understood by those who had no spiritual perception. Later, when alone with his disciples, Jesus would explain it, or untie, release or disclose its meaning. (Mark 4:34.)

This is the idea behind an interesting verse that has caused some problems in its understanding too. One meaning of 2 Peter 1:20 is given by translations similar to Moffatt's rendering, and suggested the end result, 'no prophetic scripture allows a man to interpret it by himself'. Quite the opposite, suggesting origin, is found in those translations that are similar to Weymouth's third edition, 'no prophecy in Scripture will be found to have come from the prophet's own prompting.'

The Greek noun used here for 'interpretation' or 'prompting' is 'epilusis' – 'to loosen upon'. Although the noun is only used in this one verse, the verb is used twice, both referring to untying a problem, in Mark 4:34 above, and Acts 19:39, where it carries the thought of receiving or settling a difficult question in the assembly. So does this verse in Peter speak of (1), not untying or unfolding the hard knots of Scripture by our own personal interpretations, or (2), that no prophecy gives its own explanation, but requires the event to disclose or untie it, or (3), does it have reference to the source of the prophetic impulse, that it does not spring or rise from a prophet's own ideas or disclosure?

The context from verse 16 of Second Peter chapter 1 favours the third alternative; it talks of the transfiguration scene making the prophetic word more certain, so that we should give heed to what it says. Verses 20 and 21 then strengthen our faith by pointing out the origin and source of those prophecies, not springing or arising from the individual's own thinking, or from the personal will or desire of any person, but through the holy spirit carrying them along, so that it could truly be said that they spoke from God.[39] So the prophecy is not unloosed or unfolded, untied, on its own, but it is God who unties or releases it. How different from the false prophets, who spoke visions prompted by their own minds and hearts, rather than what was released or untied by God. Here the idea comes full circle, for if it did apply to untying or unfolding the meaning, this too would be of God, for in the famous words of Joseph in Genesis 40:8, 'Do not interpretations belong to God?' (AV, Moffatt.)

16. New Cloth on an Old Garment— The Old Law Replaced.

Along with the metaphor of the new wine and the wineskins, (see chapter one number 11) Jesus gave what seemed to be a parallel illustration, but which has subtle differences when examined in more detail. This was his comment, 'Now nobody puts a patch of unshrunk cloth on an old garment because the patch will pull away from the garment and the hole will be larger.' (Matt. 9:16 Adams.)

So it would not be the course of wisdom to cut a patch from either a new garment, or a section of new cloth that could be made up into one, to patch a garment that is already old and worn, and shortly to be thrown out. When it is wetted, the new cloth will shrink, and it will only tear the old weak area of cloth, leaving a hole that is worse than before. In addition, the piece cut from the new garment or length of cloth has spoiled that too.[40]

Jesus did not try to patch up the old garment of Judaism, for he knew that would never succeed. It would only result in a schism, the very Greek word he used ('schisma'), for the hole or tear becoming larger. Instead he introduced an entirely new garment, which was later very well put in these words, 'On the one hand, a former commandment is set aside because of its weakness and uselessness . . . By speaking about a new covenant, He has made the first obsolete, and whatever is becoming obsolete and ageing is ready to disappear.' (Heb. 7:18, 8:13 Adams.)

The old Law covenant had served its purpose in bringing Israel to the Messiah, and now it had to change into the new garment, and throw away the old one. Otherwise the new garment might be endangered by trying to keep the old one in use alongside. How could kingly love really work if the rules and prescriptions of the old covenant were still being automatically carried out? So in the account in Luke a slightly different ending is given, 'the patch wouldn't match the old clothing.' (Luke 5:36 Adams.) One might be tempted to keep the old garment because of liking its colour or feel, however old and worn out it might be. That was true of Judaism, for its adherents liked its 'feel' and its outward appearance, which suited their comfort, but gave little heed as to whether it really kept them warm and contributed to their lasting welfare. When their great Temple was destroyed in 70 C.E., they found they had lost much of their old garment, and they didn't then have a new one to replace it.[41]

So as well as having differences in detail, this illustration places the emphasis on the old and what happens to it, and the following one on the wineskins stresses the new and its careful preservation.

17. Sleeping and Waking—Death and Resurrection.

The family of Lazarus and his sisters Mary and Martha were friends for whom Jesus had much affection. But he did not hurry to visit them when he received a message that Lazarus was ill. So on the journey Jesus said to his disciples, 'Lazarus our friend has fallen asleep, but I intend to go and wake him.' (John 11:11 Rieu.) The disciples seemed to feel this was a little unkind – far better to let him sleep on to aid him in his recovery. So Jesus had to say more plainly that Lazarus had died. He then went to the tomb, had the stone at the doorway removed, and brought Lazarus back to life. (John 11: 12–44.)

This description of death as a sleep is repeated in a number of other cases. Stephen 'fell asleep', so did David, and Jesus' patriarchal forefathers. (Acts 7:60, 13:36, 2 Peter 3:4.) Some translations add the explanatory words 'in death'. The apostle Paul also uses the same Greek word 'koimaō' when he says a wife is free to remarry if her husband 'falls asleep in death'. (1 Cor. 7:39 Bruce.) In the famous resurrection chapter he speaks in the same way about many of the 500 brothers who witnessed Jesus' appearances, and says Christ was the firstfruits of those 'who have fallen asleep'. In concluding his discussion about the hope of the resurrection he adds about those raised instantaneously at the time of the second presence, that they will 'not all sleep the sleep of death'. (1 Cor 15: 6, 51, Bruce, cp. 1 Thess. 4:14, 15.)

Many scholars merely dismiss the term 'sleeping' as a euphemism. This is defined as 'a figure by which a less distasteful word or expression is substituted for one more exactly descriptive of what is intended.'[42] Was this true of these examples above, or is there a real purpose in the use of 'sleeping', an illustration valuable in showing us something about the death state, especially of Christians?

The question arises, why is this word 'koimaō' used in certain contexts instead of the more usual words for death and dying? This is especially true in 1 Corinthians 15 where verses 20 and 22 contrast the words 'koimaō' (sleep) and 'apothneskō' (death/dead). It has been suggested that 'koimaō' was used deliberately by both Jesus and Paul to indicate the hope of a resurrection, and that it is therefore only used in connection with persons faithful to God to the death. Although it is not so restricted in the Septuagint, it was only from the time of Christ that teaching of the resurrection was fully introduced.[43]

In looking again at the case of Lazarus, we note Jesus' initial comment on hearing that his friend was ill. 'Beyond the illness of this man I see, not death, but the glory of God and glory coming to the Son of God.' (John 11: 4 Rieu.) He was aware from that moment that he would be able to demonstrate the power of resurrection, and this clearly seems to have influenced his use of the word 'sleep'. Only when his disciples became so confused did he use the word 'died' ('apothneskō').

Then he also spoke of going to awaken Lazarus. (John 11:11.) It is clear that the idea of 'waking up' is central to the Greek word 'egeirō' 'to raise up,' used in many of the resurrection narratives. When Jesus made his notable comment on the resurrection hope, he spoke of those coming out of 'memorial tombs' (Greek 'mnēmeion'), and the Greek word 'koimētērion' means 'sleeping place' from which comes the Latin *cemeterion* and our English word 'cemetery'.[44] The apostle Paul used the same idea when he wrote, 'For he died for us so that we, whether awake or asleep, should live together with him.' (1 Thess. 5:10 Bruce, cp. 4:15–17.) Those asleep in death at Christ's second presence would need to be awoken or resurrected, whilst those awake would still be alive into that time.[45]

When Jesus died, his last words according to Luke were a quotation from Psalm 31:5, 'Father, to thy hands I entrust my spirit.' (Luke 23:46 Rieu.) He then expired, or gave up the spirit of life. Professor J. Duncan Derrett makes an interesting study of this statement from Psalms. He points out that this was a prayer before going to sleep at night, and that the word 'entrust' was used in the sense of deposit. So each night the life of a person was, as it were, placed on deposit with Yahweh (Jehovah) for safe keeping. Then upon waking, 'Yahweh restores new every morning the spirit which the individual has left in his hands the night before.'

What better words could be the last that Jesus uttered, to show his supreme confidence in his Father! He knew in the metaphor of that Psalm that he could place his life *as a deposit* in God's hands, and it would be restored to him in a short time in all its fullness. (John 10:17, 18.)

In the same way those faithful ones who fall asleep in death know that they too can entrust their spirit to God. As Derrett so well sums it up, 'If he restores the spirit of man which was his own gift, each morning in life, how much more will he restore it afresh, bright and new, in the world to come, at the general resurrection.' (cp. 1 Pet. 4:19.)[46]

The idea of sleeping in death, and awakening anew in the resurrection is not just a euphemism, but a clear illustration to show that just as one expects to awaken next morning after a good night's sleep, so one going into the deeper sleep of death, can expect a reawakening by God if he has been faithful, as was Jesus and Stephen and David and the 500. Their lives were entrusted to God, on deposit, as it were, and there is no danger that such a deposit will ever be stolen, or mislaid and lost.

Notes and References:

1. Daines, B. 'Paul's Use of the Analogy of the Body of Christ – With Special Reference to 1 Corinthians 12,' *EvangQuart*, Vol. 50 (1978), 71–78; Field, B, 'The Discourses Behind the Metaphor 'The Church is the Body of Christ' as used by St. Paul and the 'Post-Paulines'', *AsiaJournTheol*. Vol. 6 (1992), 88–107.

2. Howard, G. 'The Head/Body Metaphors of Ephesians,' *NT Stud* Vol

20 (1974), 350–356, Jesus is 'head' over all things under his 'feet,' and 'body' is seen as secondary.

3. Trench, R. C. *Synonyms*, 197 for the quotation; Trench, R. C. *Study of Words*, 72; Cadbury, H. J. 'The Single Eye,' *HTR*, Vol. 47 (1954), 69–74.

4. Hatch, E. *Essays in Biblical Greek*, 1970rp, Amsterdam, Philo Press, 81/2; Roberts, R. L. 'An Evil Eye (Matthew 6:23),' *RestorQuart*. Vol. 7 (1963), 143–147; Elliott, J. H. 'The Fear of the Leer. The Evil Eye from the Bible to Li'l Abner,' *Forum* Vol. 4, (4/1988) 42–71; Savage, H. E. *The Gospel*, 199–202; Morgan, G. C. *Parables*, 16.

5. King, G. B, 'The Mote and the Beam,' *HTR* Vol. 17 (1924), 393–404; King, G. B. 'A Further Note on the Moat and the Beam,' *HTR*, Vol. 26 (1933), 73–76; There are a number of Rabbinic parallels – see Lightfoot, J, *Horae Hebraicae* Vol. 2, 157 and a convenient grouping of them in Dalman, G. H. *Jesus-Jeshua*, 229, also see Lachs, S. T. *Rabbinic Commentary*, 137; Bishop, E. F. F. *Jesus of Palestine*, 81, mentions Al Ya'qubi's meaning of the beam as 'the trunk of a palm tree,' and Ward, R. A. *Royal Sacrament*, 131 sees the modern equivalent as a telegraph pole; on how foreign bodies were removed from the eye, see, Crocker, P. T, 'Nets, Styli and Ophthalmology – a Mystery Solved,' in *Buried History*, (Melbourne), Vol. 27, (1991), 59–63.

6. Turner, N, *Christian Words*, 50; Robinson, J. A. *Ephesians*, 264–274; McClellan, J. B. *The N. T. . . . A New Translation*, Vol. 1, The Four Gospels, 1875, Macmillan, 108, 673; Robertson, A. T. *Word Pictures*, Vol. 4, 539.

7. Pittman, R. T. *Words and Their Ways*, 15; Moulton, J. H. *Grammar* Vol. 2, 290; Weymouth footnote to 2 Pet. 1:9.

8. Vine. W. E. *Expository Dictionary* 189, 'take them into your mind and keep them there.' Rienecker, F. & Rogers, C, *Linguistic Key* 167.

9. Skeat, W. W. *Etymological Dictionary*, 96/7.

10. Trench, R. C. *Synonyms*, 234; Bengel, J. A. *Gnomon*, Vol. 3, 75 'Adam was seduced through carelessness and indolence of mind.' See also Sadler translation footnote.

11. Jackson, F. J. F & K. Lake, *Beginnings* Vol. 2, 508; Zerwick, M. *Biblical Greek*, 1963, Rome, Pontifical Biblical Inst. 81, re Luke 6:47, 49; Moulton, H. K. *Challenge*, 168.

12. Sanday W, & A. C. Headlam, *A Critical & Exegetical Commentary on . . . Romans*, (ICC Series), 1905, 5th ed. Edin. Clark, 288/9.

13. Guillemard, W. H. *Hebraisms*, 60.

14. Rackham, R. B. *The Acts of the Apostles*, (West. Comm). 1939, 12th ed. Methuen, 316.

15. Robertson, A. T. *Word Pictures*, Vol. 2, 247/8; McClellan, J. B. *N. T. Translation* op. cit. note 6, Margin notes to Luke 19:48.

16. Robertson, A. T. *Word Pictures*, Vol. 1, 63; Yahuda, J. *Hebrew is Greek*, 196, who renders it, 'drive out of one's senses by a sudden shock,' cp. Isa. 29:14, NEB.

17. Perschbacher, W. J. Ed. *Analytical Greek Lexicon*, 43 for the first quotation; Vine, W. E. *Expository Dictionary*, 218 line 8, for the second quotation; Marshall, A. *Gleanings*, 46; Pittman, R. T. *Words and Their Ways*, 22; Trench, R. C. *Study of Words* 241; Wuest, K. *Word Studies*, Vol. 3. 1973, Grand Rapids, MN, Eerdmans, *Golden Nuggets*, 46/7; Robertson, A. T. *Word Pictures*, Vol. 4, 375; Denton, D. R.

'Apokaradokia,' *ZeitNTWiss*. Vol. 73 (1982), 138–140; Pope, R. M. *Studies*, 55–60.

18. Turner, N. *Christian Words*, 431; Robertson, A. T. *Word Pictures*, Vol. 3, 95.

19. Robertson, A. T. *Word Pictures*, Vol. 4, 426.

20. Ridley, G. N. *Your Brain and You*, 1952, Watts, 156/7.

21. This Greek word dipsuchos literally means 'two-souled,' two persons, or a division through the person so that they act in that way. Turner, N. *Christian Words*, 117; Seitz, O. J. 'Afterthoughts on the Term 'Dipsuchos',' *NTStud*. Vol. 4 (1958), 327–334, perhaps linked to the Hebrew "double heart" i. e. with thought and purpose divided.'

22. McNeile, A. H. *The Gospel According to Matthew, The Greek Text with Notes*, 1928, Macmillan, 245.

23. Wuellner, W. H. *The Meaning of 'Fishers of Men'*, 1967, Philadelphia, Westminster Press, 256pp.

24. Woodall, P. H. *Osteopathy, The Science of Healing by Adjustment*, 6th ed. n. d. Orange, N. J. American Osteopathic Assoc. 22, 23, 70.

25. *Herodotus*, Book 5, 106, Henry Cary's translation. Smith, D. *Life & Letters*, 161 ftn, referring to Galen, Opera XIX, 461, (Kuhn); Cremer, H, *Biblico-Theological Lexicon of N. T. Greek*, 1962rp, Edin. Clark, 652; Eadie, J. *A Commentary on the Greek Text of . . . Thessalonians*, 1877, Macmillan, 115; Earle, R. *Word Meanings*, 215; Wuest, K. op. cit. (17), *Golden Nuggets*, 23–25; Waugh, R. M. L. *Greek Testament*, 69, 70; Barclay, W. *N. T. Words*, 168–170.

26. Augustine, Works, 1873, Edin. Clark, *On Christian Doctrine*, ch. 16, Vol. 9, 95.

27. Neuberger, A. *Technical Arts*, 13–27; Conybeare, W. J. *The Epistles of Paul*, (see Translation Abbrev), 127 ftn; Cotterell, P & Turner, M, *Linguistics*, 302–305; Kittel, G. Ed. *TDNT*, Vol. 6. 945; Klassen, W. 'Coals of Fire: Sign of Repentance or Revenge?' *NTStud*. Vol. 9 (1963), 337–350, re the Egyptian rite; Yonge, J. E. 'Heaping Coals of Fire on the Head,' *Expositor*, 3rd Series, Vol. 2 (1885), 158/9; Hanson, A. T. *Studies in Pauline Technique & Theology*, 1974, SPCK, 131–134.

28. Nicoll, W. R. Ed. *Expositor's Greek Testament*, Vol. 2, 694.

29. Geikie, C. *The Holy Land*, 257/8; Jebb, J. *Sacred Literature*, 1831, new ed. Duncan & Cochrane, 331–334, for the terms used by Luke; Jeremias, J, *Parables*, 222ftn; Bishop, E. F. F. *Jesus of Palestine*, 80/1; Couroyer, B, 'De la mesure dont vous mesurez il vous sera mesure,' *RevBib*, Vol. 77, (1970), 366–370, re Matt. 7:2 which emphasizes just repayment, and not the generosity of Luke 6:38; For another description, see Rihbany, A. M. *Syrian Christ*, 188–190.

30. Alford, H. *Greek Testament*, Vol. 2, 604; Nicoll, W. R. Ed. *Expositor's Greek Testament*, Vol. 2, 921; Earle, R. *Word Meanings* 242; Arndt, W. F. & Gingrich, F. W. *Greek-English Lexicon*, 246; Ward, R. A. *Hidden Meaning*, 118; Robertson, A & Plummer, A, *A Critical & Exegetical Commentary on the First Epistle . . . to the Corinthians*, 1914, 2nd ed. Edin. Clark, 339; *Translator's N. T.* note 482; Huxtable, P, 'The Sense in Which St. Paul Calls Himself an Ectroma – 1 Corinthians 15:8.' *Expositor*, 2nd Series, Vol. 3 (1882), 268–280, 364–380.

31. Ward, R. A. *Hidden Meaning*, 62; Robertson, A. T. *Word Pictures* Vol. 4, 501/2; *Josephus*, Ant. Book 6. ch.

14, (2) 330, where King Saul strips off his royal robes before going to see the witch of Endor, so that she might not recognize him, using the same Greek word, but note a variant in the text.

32. Humphry, W. G. *Commentary on the Revised Version of the N. T.* 1888, new ed. rev. SPCK, 401; Robertson, A. T. *Word Pictures*, Vol. 4, 608.

33. Arndt, W. F & Gingrich, F. W. *Greek-English Lexicon*, 853, shown or revealed for what a person really is.

34. Arndt & Gingrich op. cit. 762, but note the alternative idea of a rock hidden beneath the sea, and its link with Jude 12. See also Moulton, J. H. *Grammar*, Vol. 2. 360/1; Robinson, J. A. *Ephesians*, 207; on possible variant see Whallon, W. 'Should we Keep, Omit, or Alter the oi in Jude 12?' *NTStud.* Vol. 34(1988) 156–159.

35. Rotherham, J. B. *Studies in the Psalms*, 1911, Allenson, 214.

36. Blass, F. & Debrunner, A. *A Greek Grammar of the N. T.* . . . Rev. by R. W. Funk, 1961, Camb. U. P. 112, section 207 (3).

37. Bengel, J. A. *Gnomon*, Vol. 5, 81; Daddow, W. B. *Buried Pictures*, 98–104; Levine, E. 'On the Symbolism of the Pedilavium,' *AmBenRev*, Vol. 33, (1982), 21–29, suggesting that the girded towel replaced the ancient wrestling belt as a symbol.

38. Keil, C. F. & Delitzsch, F. *Commentary on the O. T.* 1978rp, Grand Rapids, MN, Eerdmans, Vol. 2, Exodus, 16; Vallauri, E, '"Succincti lumbos mentis vestrae" (1 Piet 1:13) nota per una traduzione,' *BibOr* Vol. 24(1982), 19–22, argues for retaining the image of girding the spiritual loins rather than translating it, 'Prepare your mind for action.' Adams'

translation makes a neat compromise.

39. Bullinger, E. W. *Enjoy the Bible*, 186–188; Alford, H, *Greek Testament*, Vol. 4, 400/1; Robertson, A. T. *Word Pictures*, Vol. 6, 158/9; Barnes, A. *Notes . . . on the N. T.* Glasgow, Blackie, 1848, Vol. 10, 231–233; Green, M, 2 *Peter and Jude, Intro. & Commentary*, 1968, Tyndale Press, 89–91.

40. Pallis, A, *Notes on St. Mark and St. Matthew*, 1932, Oxford U. P. 76; Robertson, A. T. *Word Pictures*, Vol. 1, 73.

41. Jeremias, J. *Parables*, 118; Trench, R. C. *Studies in the Gospels*, 1867, Macmillan, 173–177; Hahn, F. 'Die Bildworte vom neuen Flicken und vom Jungen Wein (Mk 2:21 f parr),' *EvangTheol.* Vol. 31 (1971), 357–375, compares the Synoptic accounts of the double metaphor; Good, R. S. 'Jesus, Protagonist of the Old, in Lk 5:33–39,' *NovTest.* Vol. 25(1983), 19–36.

42. *Shorter Oxford English Dictionary*, Vol. 1, 687.

43. Bowmer, J. C. 'A Note on Apothnēskō and Koimaō in 1 Corinthians 15:20, 22,' *ET*, Vol. 53 (1941/2), 355; Milligan, G, *St. Paul's Epistles to the Thessalonians, Greek Text with Notes*, 1908, Macmillan, 55/6; Waugh, R. M. L. *Greek Testament*, 80/1.

44. Evans, C. F. *Resurrection and the N. T.*, (Studies in Biblical Theology – 2nd series 12), 1970, SCM, 22–24; Skeat, W. W. *Etymological Dictionary*, 99; Marshall, A, Ed. *GSM*, 1932, May, 275; Thomson, J. G. S. 'Sleep: An Aspect of Jewish Anthropology,' *VT*, Vol. 5 (1955), 421–433. The Hebrews originally had no belief in a dualism of soul and body, but rather complete unity

of personality. Sleep is linked with the deposit at night, and with death.

45. Marshall, A. Ed. *GSM*, 1933, April, 357, argues for taking v. 1 & 10 as spiritual sleep, but Howard, T. L. 'The Meaning of 'Sleep' in 1 Thessalonians 5:10 – A Reappraisal,' *Grace TheolJourn*. Vol. 6, (1985), 337–348. shows all the evidence favours taking this as a metaphor for death, 46.

46. Derrett, J. D. M. *Jesus's Audience*, 195–200; Ward, R. A. *Royal Sacrament*, 56/7.

Chapter 7

Human Relationships
and Emotions

1. The Ambassador—Reconciling People to God.

The ambassador is a familiar figure in the political world. He is usually a minister of high rank sent by the sovereign or government of one country on a mission or service to another country. Their purpose included advancing 'their country's policies, to conduct personal negotiations, and to maintain their ruler's dignity and prestige abroad.' Ambassadors were known in the ancient Greek world, and are referred to by Jesus. (Luke 14:32, 19:14.)[1]

It is not surprising that the apostle Paul, who so treasured his valuable ministry, should pick up this idea to illustrate the course of one representing the great kings, God and Christ. 'A Jew, born in a Greek city, and possessed of the Roman franchise, he was in his own person the meeting-point of three civilizations.' [2] 'It is, then, on Christ's behalf that we are acting as ambassadors [Greek 'presbeuō'], God, as it were, appealing to you through us. We implore you, on Christ's behalf – Be reconciled to God.' (2 Cor. 5:20 TCNT.) Everything is here, the appeal, the imploring emdeavour to reconcile those who are not at peace with God, to heal the rift, to bring the two together in a new personal relationship.

The whole testimony about Paul suggests that he was an able and successful ambassador, but there were those who questioned his actions at times, perhaps because he was always so zealous and forthright, never compromising in his ministry. So it was necessary for him to show clearly his marks as an apostle, his credentials as an ambassador. (2 Cor. 12:12 Sadler footnote.)

In his own hired house, yet as a prisoner in Rome, Paul could pray that he might continue to have free speech, 'that when I begin to speak, words may be given me, so that I may fearlessly make known the inmost truth of the Good News, on behalf of which I am an Ambassador – in chains!' (Eph. 6:19, 20a TCNT.)

In a personal letter to Philemon, Paul also draws on his role of intercession on behalf of the slave Onesimus. His tactful entreaty did not fall on deaf ears. 'And so, though my union with Christ enables me, with all confidence, to dictate the course that you should adopt, yet the claims of love make me prefer to plead with you – yes, even me, Paul, though I am an ambassador for Christ Jesus, and now, a prisoner for him as well. I plead with you for this Child of mine, Onesimus, to whom, in my prison, I have become a Father.' (Philemon 8–10a TCNT.)[3]

Perhaps a Christian today may not be in such a foremost position as were those anointed followers of Jesus, spearheading the preaching work, and then in its formative years. They may merely be assisting, in the role of an *envoy* yet in principle this makes no difference to the attitude they display. (Prov. 25:13, Phil. 2:25.) By remembering all that is best in the office of an ambassador, a Christian can make his ministry one that upholds God's majesty and purpose at all times, recommending it with gracious and delightful words of truth. (Col. 4:6, Eccl. 12:10.)

2. Burden and Load—Helping Ourselves and Others.

Jesus showed much concern over the burdens put upon the ordinary people. In his scathing denunciation of the scribes and Pharisees he said they not only put heavy loads on people's shoulders, but 'don't want to lift a finger to budge them'. (Matt. 23:4 Adams.) Later in the same chapter (verse 23), his reference to their neglect of the 'weightier matters of the law: justice and mercy and faith', may have been an intentional link with his earlier remark. They didn't hesitate to put weighty burdens on others, but wouldn't touch the weighty matters they should have been shouldering themselves.

On another occasion an interesting contrast was made. Jesus invited his listeners, 'Come to Me, all who labor and are heavily burdened, and I will refresh you.' Then after explaining about his yoke (for which see chapter one) he added, 'My yoke is easy to wear and My burden is light.' (Matt. 11:28, 30 Adams.) The spiritual and mental refreshment they would receive would bring them joy and happiness with peace and contentment, making the load seem light and easy.

When the apostle Paul takes up the same illustration, some have thought he contradicted himself within a few verses. After saying, 'Carry one another's burdens [Greek 'baros'],' he continues by urging everyone to "test his own work", for '"each man", as the saying is, "will shoulder his own pack [Greek 'phortion']."' (Gal. 6:2–5 Bruce.)

We may naturally think of the soldier with his pack on his back. Josephus describes what the Roman soldier carried in addition to his weapons. 'The equipment of the latter further includes a saw, a basket, a pick and an axe, not to mention a strap, a bill-hook, a chain and three days' rations.' This pack was extra large because the Roman soldier was an engineer as well, used to building his own fortifications, hence the wicker basket for moving earth.[4]

So each man in the Roman army was expected to shoulder his own pack, and received his proper pay for his service. The next man had his own to carry, and could not be expected to help another man as fit and strong as himself. But as an organized army they had ample provision (for those times) to care for the wounded, with field dressing stations and hospitals. They could thus carry the burden of the sick and wounded with a view to restoring such highly trained men to health.[5]

The mountaineer also needs to carry his own pack, one scaled down to the absolute necessities. But what happens when one of them falls into a crevasse and gets injured? Not only is he helped by the others with him, but his pack will be divided among the others, or certain items may be disposed of to lighten the total load.

Paul's thought is not therefore a contradictory one. Each Christian has his own responsibility before God, and he shoulders that, and properly accepted with joy and willingness, it is an easy yoke and a light burden. But in Galatians 6:1, Paul had spoken about restoring a man who had taken a false step. He had become spiritually sick, and this was the occasion for bearing the burden of another and taking off the heavy weight. The whole Christian association of brothers would see to it that all help was given toward restoring the ailing one to full health and strength again.

Interestingly, Paul draws the same sort of contrast as did Jesus, but in a different setting, that of persecution by opposers and affliction from imperfect fleshly bodies. Yet the deliberate use of antonyms points up the illustration very vividly. 'This temporary light affliction is producing for us an eternal weight of glory that is beyond all comparison.' (2 Cor. 4:17 Adams.) There is, however, one vital difference. The soldier earns his pay for his service; the Christian receives everlasting life as a gift from God. (Rom. 6:23.)

3. Go Two Miles—Willing Service.

The famous Sermon on the Mount is filled with more illustrations considering its length, than any other comparable section in the Bible. In this one, Jesus uses the figure of speech known as hyperbole (hy-per-boly), to drive home the point he wishes to make, that of willing service and unstinting sacrifice for love of neighbour, and even love of one's enemy. (Matt. 5:42–48.)

Jesus told his listeners not to resist a wicked man, but to turn the other cheek, and then he reinforced this attitude by a pair of linked illustrations. 'If anyone wishes to go to law with you and to deprive you of your under garment, let him take your outer one also.' (Matt. 5: 40 Weymouth 3rd ed.) It was not too difficult to put up with being deprived of one's undergarment, a kind of long cotton or sometimes woollen shirt or tunic. But the outer garment was a very different matter, for this long cloak or robe was especially valuable on a journey. At night the traveller could wrap himself in this cloak and keep himself snug and warm. The Mosaic Law actually prescribed that if for any reason the cloak was seized as a pledge, it had to be returned before sunset, so that its owner could lie down in it during the night as his only covering. (Exodus 22: 26, 27.) To give up willingly that outer garment was therefore a supreme sacrifice, so this stood for anything very much prized.

The second illustration has quite a different setting. 'And whoever shall compel you to convey his goods one mile, go with him two.' (Matt. 5:41 Weymouth 3rd ed.) The Greek word for 'compel' is 'angareuō', and meant to 'requisition' or 'impress into service'. (cp. Matt. 27:32.) It had its origins in ancient Persia, when a courier system enabled messages to be transmitted swiftly across the many provinces, and post-station agents could be asked to give these couriers fresh horses.[6]

In Roman times a similar situation existed in those countries brought into the Empire. A Roman column of soldiers could impress into service some of the local population to assist in carrying their baggage. This may be hinted at in Jesus' advice to those in the army, for it was certainly viewed as part of the harassment which had to be borne by the people. (Luke 3:14.)[7]

But Jesus' illustration turned that viewpoint right around. If a duty had to be performed, or a service carried out, however onerous it might be, the true Christian was to do it willingly; if necessary, going far beyond what was required to demonstrate the Christian spirit of self-sacrifice and love of even one's enemy. So Paul gives the example of food which we may like and wish to eat, but if it might stumble our brother to do so, we would abstain from eating it, so as not to depart from 'walking along the road of love'. (Rom. 14:15, Ward p. 80.) We may not be a very good walker, and going two miles instead of one may cost us much, but it would bring its own rewards. What a contrast there is between this Christian course and the selfish spirit of the world, where people will often do as little as they can to help another person in need.

4. To Run Ahead, Step Over—To Overreach, Defraud.

When John the Baptist was preaching repentance, he was asked by many how they should alter their previous course of action, in line with their new baptism. To the soldiers he replied, 'No one you should harass nor should you take by fig-showing.' Later, Zacchaeus, a chief tax-collector, told Jesus, 'anything I took by fig-showing I am giving back fourfold.' (Luke 3:14, 19:8. K. Int.)[8]

The Greek word for 'fig-showing' ('sukophanteō') is behind our English word 'sycophant' – an informer or false adviser. Its etymology is lost in earlier Greek times, but was related to informing against persons who exported figs from Attica, contrary to the law.

As a reward was paid to those who so informed, innocent people were often accused, and so the word came gradually to mean 'to accuse falsely'.[9] It was often used in the Greek Septuagint Version with this meaning. (Gen. 43:18, Lev. 19:11, Ps. 71:4 LXX), and also with the thought of one who oppressed others. (Prov. 14:31, 22:16, 28:3, 16, Eccl. 4:1 LXX.)

Zacchaeus realised that Jesus' teaching recognized the equality and rights of all men, and that they should love one another as much as they loved themselves. (Matt. 22:39.) So he quickly promised to make restitution to those he had wronged or oppressed, or from whom he had extorted money by false means.

The apostle Paul took a similar position, not wanting to encroach on others, or defraud them in any way; 'invade his rights' or 'step over' his brothers, as an oppressor would do so often. (1 Thess. 4:6 NEB.) He could honestly say, 'We have wronged no one, ruined no one, taken advantage of no one.' (2 Cor. 7:2 NEB.)

The Epistles of John also lay great emphasis upon love as the touchstone of Christianity, but that was not really something new that only appeared with Jesus, although he placed it in an entirely new light. It was rooted in God's love for mankind, so deceivers and 'fig-showers' out for selfish advantage were to be avoided. In fact, 'Anyone who runs ahead too far, and does not stand by the doctrine of the Christ is without God.' (2 John 5–9 NEB.) One could even defraud others in a spiritual sense, over-reaching the understanding of faithful persons with superior worldly knowledge not in harmony with true doctrine. Paul urged Timothy, 'Turn a deaf ear to empty and worldly chatter, and the contradictions of so-called "knowledge", for many who lay claim to it have shot far wide of the faith.' (1 Tim. 6:3–5, 20, 21 NEB.)

Zacchaeus didn't want to miss Jesus, so he literally 'ran ahead' to climb a sycamore or fig-mulberry tree (with a leaf like a mulberry tree, and allied to the banyan tree, not to our English sycamore or plane tree), to see him clearly, which Jesus did – and called him as a result. From that time Zacchaeus ceased to run ahead of others metaphorically, and tried to live by his new-found faith that treated all men in the honest straight-forward way that is still the mark of true Christianity.

5. A Breath of Fresh Air—Temporary Relief and Rest.

When the apostle Paul was in prison, how much he looked forward to visits from his friends and brothers. Writing to Timothy he commended Onesiphorus because, 'His visits have always been like a breath of fresh air to me. He was not ashamed to visit me in gaol.' (2 Tim. 1:16 Barclay.) The word Paul used for a 'breath of fresh air' (Greek 'anapsuchō'), means to cool or refresh, reminding us of the proverb, 'Like a draught of snow-cooled water in the time of harvest is a faithful messenger to those who send him; he refreshes the spirit of his master.' (Prov. 25:13 Goodspeed.)[10]

On several other occasions Paul used this sort of phrase to suggest a temporary relief, to relax and rest for a short time. 'I want to come joyfully to you and so to be rested and refreshed in your company.' (Rom. 15:32 Barclay.) To Philemon he wrote, 'You have been the means by which the hearts of God's people have been refreshed.' (Philemon 7, Barclay.) He commended the Corinthians for making Titus happy, 'by the way in which you have made it possible for him to rest and relax in your company.' (2 Cor. 7:13 Barclay.) He was glad such men were leading the Christian congregations; 'they have set my mind at rest – and yours too.' (1 Cor. 16:18 Barclay.)[11]

Not only can God's servants be a breath of fresh air to us, cheering us up with their encouragement, putting fresh heart into us, but the message of the good news is also refreshing and upbuilding. No wonder Jesus urged, 'Come to me, all you who are tired and bent beneath your burdens, and I will give you rest . . . for my yoke is kindly and my load is light.' (Matt. 11:28–30 Barclay.) Judaism had become a burden with all its detailed requirements and tradition, but the Christian message was at once simple and peaceful, bringing confidence and hope to worried and bemused minds.

One day in the Temple soon after the day of Pentecost when the spirit was poured out upon the disciples, Peter told his listeners, 'Repent, therefore, and reform your lives, so that the record of your sins may be cancelled, and that there may come seasons of refreshment from the Lord, and that he may send the Christ appointed beforehand for you – even Jesus.' (Acts 3:19, 20 Weymouth 5th ed. cp. Isa. 28:12.) What a contrast to the metaphorically polluted air spoken of in Paul's letter to the Ephesians! 'You followed the ways of this present world order, obeying the commander of the spiritual powers of the air, the spirit now at work among God's rebel subjects.' (Eph. 2:2 REB.) Jesus identified that commander as Satan the devil. (Matt. 4:8–10, John 12:31, 14:30)

From a human point of view, we may welcome a temporary relief or breath of fresh air, especially on a hot day, but how much better to have *seasons* of it, providing a continuous flow of fresh, cooling air – only the message of God through Christ can give that in this overheated polluted world today.

6. A Stirring Up—Provoking to Love.

When Paul and Barnabas were discussing who should be taken with them on one of their journeys, 'there arose a sharp altercation between them'. (Acts 15:36–40 Weymouth 5th ed.) The Greek word used for 'sharp altercation' is 'paroxusmos', from which comes our English word 'paroxysm'. The word 'oxus' means sharp or acid, and is used in 'oxygen' – 'generator of acids'.[12]

In his famous chapter on love, Paul says that one of its facets is that it does not become provoked, and here the same word is used (the verb 'paroxunō'). (1 Cor. 13:5.) Yet this word is found in the opposite sense in Hebrews 10:24, where the Christian is urged to 'provoke to love and to good works'. How can this apparent contradiction be explained?

We sometimes use the expression 'he rubbed me up the wrong way', and that is just what happened between Paul and Barnabas. But that phrase also suggests it is possible to rub people up *the right way*. That is the exact thought in Hebrews; 'to stir a response in love' (JB), 'to stimulate one another to love' (C. B. Williams), 'to incite to love' (ABUV, NWT). A sharp taste need not always be bitter, but can also refresh us. 'As iron sharpens iron, so one person sharpens the wits of another.' (Prov. 27:17 REB.) If this is done in love and kindness, it can be most encouraging.

Writing to the Corinthians, Paul referred to their exemplary attitude, and how he had been able to boast about it to the Macedonians; 'your enthusiasm has stirred most of them to action.' (2 Cor. 9:2, NIV.) Although this is a different word, linked with the idea of exciting, summoning or calling out, it also carries the same general thought of stirring up, arousing a person (to incite, urge forward). Barclay brings out both ideas in his translation, 'your enthusiasm has stimulated and challenged most of them'. Or we might say colloquially, their zeal had rubbed off on others.

Often the difference between rubbing a person up the wrong way or the right way is a very fine one. When dealing with the feelings of others, a Christian needs to show love and consideration, and then his encouraging words can build up others and fire their enthusiasm. He will guard against using the wrong words, or even the wrong tone, which might irritate rather than stimulate. He will, in other words, watch how he stirs.

7. Taking by the Hand—Personal Assistance.

When Peter tried to walk on the Sea of Galilee, he suddenly lost confidence and began to sink. He cried out to Jesus to save him, and, 'Instantly, Jesus stretched out his hand and caught hold of him [Greek 'epilambanō'].' (Matt. 14:31 Weymouth 3rd ed.) That literal idea of taking someone by the hand is also present when Jesus 'took a young child' and stood him in the centre of the group to reinforce his illustration of humility. (Luke 9:47 Weymouth.) Since the same word is used it is likely that he took the child by the hand to lead him to that position.

During Paul's visit to Athens the same word appears when the Athenians took him up to the Areopagus to listen to what he had to say. (Acts 17:19.) Weymouth, in a footnote, suggests that while this may have been by the hand, they more likely caught his wrist to draw him on, though with due courtesy. In a much rougher manner the crowds laid their hands on Paul when he was in the Temple in Jerusalem. They had listened to rumours that Paul had taken a gentile into the Temple beyond the permitted barriers, and they would have killed him if the Roman soldiers had not intervened. (Acts 21:30.)

On most other occasions where this form of the verb is used, a physical taking hold of a person is involved, a seizing of him, or a taking by the hand.[13] But this idea is the basis for an interesting illustration in the letter to the Hebrews. Looking back to the time of the Exodus, God made a covenant with the Israelites, 'On the day when I took them by the hand to lead them out from the land of Egypt'. (Hebrews 8:9 Weymouth, cp. Jer. 31:3, 8, 9, 32.) What a loving thought to express it in that way, that deliverance was effected as if God had personally taken them by the hand to guide them to freedom out from the land of slavery. The action can be compared with that of the angels who seized hold of the hands of Lot's family to rush them out of the doomed city of Sodom. That was because of 'the compassion of Jehovah upon him'. (Gen. 19:16 NWT.)

That brings us to the most moving example of all, for it concerns our salvation today. The death of Christ was to bring about the destruction of the Devil, and free mankind from the great enemy, death. Then the writer of Hebrews continues, 'For assuredly it is not to angels that He [Jesus Christ] is continually reaching a helping hand, but it is to the descendants of Abraham.' (Hebrews 2:14–16 Weymouth 3rd ed.) As the chapter concludes, Jesus' time on earth made him fully appreciate man's position, and so he became compassionate and sympathetic, and concerned to help those who are tempted and tried.

So just as God extended a helping hand at the Exodus, Jesus Christ does the same since his resurrection to heaven. It is God's desire that all kinds of men should be saved, and how well this is illustrated by the idea of personally taking by the hand, as it were, those who are seeking and demonstrating faith, that they might get salvation. (1 Tim. 2:4, Acts 17:26, 27.)

8. Beggars and Paupers—Asking for Spiritual Riches.

'You have the poor with you always,' said Jesus. (Matt. 26:11 Barclay.) But who were 'the poor' in his day? Two quite distinct Greek words come to our attention, the first used only once ('penēs'), and the second one frequently ('ptōchos').

The only place where the noun 'penēs' is used is when Paul says of God, 'He scattered, he gave to the needy'. (2 Cor. 9:9 Cunnington.)

The poor here earned their daily bread by labour, and so were paupers (Latin *penuria* – with nothing over or superfluous) but not beggars with nothing at all. Trench distinguishes these two words very clearly when he observes of the second group, 'he is the 'beggar' and lives not by his own labour or industry, but on other men's alms . . . a far deeper depth of destitution is implied.' Many translations fail to make this distinction.[14]

It is the beggar that is more often referred to in the Scriptures, for they were also an oppressed class, and Jesus felt pity for their condition, because 'they were skinned and thrown about like sheep without a shepherd.' (Matt. 9:36 NWT.) So when Christ became poor for our sakes he joined those oppressed ones and was stripped of everything. (2 Cor. 8:9, Isa. 53:3–5.)[15]

In his Sermon on the Mount, Jesus took this literal situation of the beggar, and used it as an illustration concerning spiritual things. 'Blessed are the beggars in spirit; for theirs is the kingdom of heaven.' (Matt. 5:3 Penn 1836, Weymouth 3rd ed. footnote.) The beggar or mendicant has to ask for help because he knows his 'destitute' condition (Rotherham). Later in this same sermon Jesus said that those who realised their need to ask God for help, would be given what they needed. If they were truly hungry or thirsty for what is right, they would be filled and satisfied and made happy. (Matt. 5:6.)

Essentially, there had to be that recognition of one's spiritual beggarly or destitute condition. As a literal beggar didn't know when he might next receive some crumbs or cast off titbits, he often looked to God simply to survive. So spiritually, one has to trust in God alone.[16] For many, their pride prevented that. Like those of Laodicea, they said, '"I am rich, and have acquired wealth and do not need a thing". But you do not realize that you are wretched, pitiful, poor, blind and naked.' (Rev. 3:17 NIV.)

But what was the result of taking the good news to the poor? (Matt. 11:5.) Paul showed it to be the exact opposite of those Laodiceans. 'To look at us you would think we are destitute, but we have brought God's wealth to many. On the face of it we have nothing, yet we possess everything.' (2 Cor. 6:10 Barclay.)

The point of the illustration turns on the contrast between spiritual and material riches. Having one usually means forfeiting the other

– we cannot serve two masters. (Matt. 6:24.) If we really are beggars for the spiritual things, God will indeed give us true riches. (Luke 16:9–13.)

9. Blot Out, Wipe Away—Forgive and Forget.

The strength of forgiveness lies more in the word 'forget'. Someone may say that he has 'buried the hatchet', but this is of no value if he remembers where he buried it. The forgiveness of God is complete, for the word often used denotes a blotting out, a wiping off.

Shortly after Pentecost, Peter urged his listeners to accept the resurrected Christ Jesus, saying, 'Repent then and turn to God, so that your sins may be wiped out [Greek 'exaleiphō'].' (Acts 3:19 NEB.) To remove something completely was to wipe it away so that it was impossible to read what had been written. Today, we may cancel a document by marking a large cross over it, and precisely the same thing happened in Jesus' day. The papyrus documents that have been unearthed reveal examples of bonds or certificates with the Greek letter 'chi' shaped as a cross written through them, and these might even be publicly exhibited or nailed up to let everyone know that the debt had been cancelled. But though cancelled the writing can still be read now. In other cases a manuscript was rubbed or scraped clean of the writing so that it could be used again, such a manuscript being called a palimpsest. Where this was imperfectly accomplished, the old writing still shows through underneath. But where ink was made just from soot and gum, with no acid in it, it was comparatively easy to wash it off, to wipe it away entirely.[17]

Writing to the Colossians, Paul spoke of the Mosaic Law particularly when he explained how Christ's death affected it; 'Having cancelled and blotted out and wiped away the handwriting of the note [bond] with its legal decrees and demands, which was in force and stood against us [hostile to us].' (Col. 2:14 Amplified.) Adams' translation uses the idea of the palimpsest manuscript, 'erasing the handwritten certificate . . .' It has been suggested that since this was written to mainly gentile Christians at Colossae the use of 'us' indicates a wider application than the Mosaic Law, to all forms of decree that might prevent a Christian from really turning his back on his past course of life, whether in writing or in conscience.[18]

It might be argued that since we still have the record of that Mosaic Law in the Bible it has not truly been wiped away. But it is completely blotted out so far as God sees his dealings with those whom he has forgiven. Jesus highlighted this in the Lord's prayer when he taught his disciples to say, 'Forgive us the wrong we have done . . .' (Matt. 6:12 NEB), that is, wipe it off, let it go off the record completely.

This double idea of forgive and forget is found throughout the Bible. Again it is God who says, 'I alone, I am He, who for his own sake wipes out your transgressions, who will remember your sins no more.' (Isa. 43:25 NEB.) The Psalmist pleaded, 'blot out my misdeeds, Wash away all my guilt and cleanse me from my sin.' (Ps. 51:1 NEB.) The washing away leaves no marks, no traces of what was there before. The record is completely clean.

But that forgiveness has to be genuine, based upon Christ's ransom sacrifice, and reflected in our attitude to others. The second part of the verse from the Lord's prayer continues, '. . . as we have forgiven those who wronged us.' (Matt. 6:12 NEB.) To draw the parallel correctly can mean only one thing, we must already have forgiven and forgotten, if we wish to have the true forgiveness of God.

10. A Well-glued and Tied Joint Bond— Unity of the Spirit through Love and Peace.

When the Pharisees asked Jesus about the matter of divorce, Jesus took the opportunity to emphasize the strength of the bond in a marriage by quoting from Genesis 2:24. 'For this reason a man shall leave his father and mother and be joined to his wife, and the two shall become one.' (Matt. 19:5 TNT.) The verb 'joined' here is the Greek 'kollaō', meaning literally 'shall be glued,' and how well this illustrates what God intended for human marriage, a true joint-bond, unbreakable and permanent.[19]

The same word is used in the Acts of the Apostles in connexion with those joining themselves to the early Christians. After Paul had spoken to a Greek audience on the Areopagus hill in Athens, it is recorded that 'Some men attached themselves to him [having been glued to him – K. Int] and became believers . . .' (Acts 17:33, 34 TNT.) This new found faith became an unbreakable attachment, as if joined by glue or cement.[20] Then, writing to the Corinthians, Paul links the two ideas together, but this time by referring to an illicit union with a harlot, he cleverly warns against immorality, for it still results in the two persons becoming one flesh. So a Christian could find himself glued into an unholy association displeasing to God. The contrast is swiftly set against this situation by a deliberate play on the metaphor, 'But he who joins [Greek 'kollaō'] himself to the Lord is one spirit with him.' (1 Cor. 6:16, 17 TNT.)[21]

How can this relationship come about? Writing to the Romans, Paul explains, 'Love must be sincere. Hate evil and cling to what is good [glueing selves to the good – K. Int].' (Rom. 12:9, 10 TNT.) True love for God and Christ will make this unbreakable attachment possible, as another Greek word carrying a very similar illustration serves to underline.

That word is 'sundesmos', with the root 'deo', a tie or bond.[22] It is well portrayed in Acts 8:23, where Peter described the mercenary Simon as a 'bundle ['sundesmos'] of iniquity.' (Goodspeed.) It was as if all his wicked ideas and ways were tied or bound together as in a bundle.

Paul used this word when recommending a course of love one toward another. 'Make every effort to maintain the unity of the Spirit through the tie ['sundesmos'] of peace.' (Eph. 4:3 Goodspeed.) So use peace in the congregation to strengthen the bond of unity, as it were, tieing it firmly and tightly so that nothing can break the bond.

But perhaps the most vivid passage to convey the illustration to us is Colossians 3:12–17. Paul here urges Christians to put on all the desirable qualities as if they were clothes to be worn. These include kindness, humility, gentleness and forbearance. We are to think of the typical Middle Eastern form of dress, loose, long and flowing. Then Paul adds his crowning climax, 'And over all these put on love, which completes them and fastens them all together.' (Col. 3:14 Goodspeed.) Like a girdle or belt tied around the middle, so love encircles and enfolds all these other qualities in a strong and perfect bond.

Add the two metaphors together, and the illustration is doubly strong. Through the unity brought about by submission to God's Spirit, and the promotion of love and peace by every individual Christian in the congregation, there is formed an attachment to God in personal relationship, and to one another, that is as strong as if it had been glued and cemented, and then bonded together with a strong and firmly tied girdle. It is apparent to all. 'By this they will all know that you are my disciples – by your love for one another.' (John 13:35 Goodspeed.)

11. A Cave of Robbers—The Temple a Refuge of Intrigue.

In the first century the activities of robbers and brigands were notorious throughout Palestine. Jesus acknowledged this by setting his parable of the good Samaritan on the road to Jericho, where the victim was attacked by robbers, beaten and left half-dead. (Luke 10:30.)

Just what did Jesus mean, then, by his remark in the Temple after he turned out those buying and selling, and upset the tables of the moneychangers. Quoting from two prophets, Isaiah and Jeremiah, he said, 'Scripture says, "My house shall be called a house of prayer;" but you are making it a robbers' cave.' (Matt. 21:13 NEB.)

It would at first seem that he was suggesting that the moneychangers were cheating and extorting excessive sums of commission for changing coinage so that the Temple tax could be paid as required in Phoenician half-shekels. But it has been argued that the commission rate was very reasonable, and that it was a useful service for Temple worshippers. Much of the buying and selling was conducted with the animals needed for the sacrifices, and was therefore considered legitimate.[23]

Much more lies behind the statement, however, for why should Jesus speak of a *'cave* of robbers'? These were not just ordinary thieves, relying on deception and sleight of hand which would usually go unnoticed at the time. Some translations use such words, but the Greek phrase refers to violent highway robbers or brigands.

Josephus refers to these robbers, and how they made caves their hideouts. Because of the hold they had over certain areas in Galilee,

Herod the Great in 38 B.C.E., finally had to flush them out with his troops, dropping them down in cribs or cradles from above into the cave entrances to fight them hand to hand. (Ant. Book 14, ch. 15, (4, 5), 415–430, War Book 1, ch. 16, (4), 304–313.)[24]

So when Jesus used the phrase 'cave of robbers' he was suggesting something much wider in scope than ordinary deception and theft. Those caves in the hills of both Galilee and Judea became places of planning and intrigue where fresh plots and schemes were hatched. They were safe hideouts to retire to until the hue and cry of pursuit had died down, but they also became scenes of heated disputes and wrangling when the robbers fell out.

All this background comes into the picture to show how apt and fitting was Jesus' illustration. Josephus himself tells us what went on in the Temple. In his possibly feigned appeal during the Roman siege to the defenders of Jerusalem, he refers to their hopes for divine intervention, but asks how they can expect this in view of their catalogue of crimes. 'How much more impious are you than those who have been defeated in the past . . . in rapine and murder you vie with each other in opening up new and unheard of paths of vice; aye, and the temple has become the receptacle for all, and native hands have polluted those divine precincts.' (War Book 5, ch. 9, (4),. 401/2.)

Whilst the war of 66–70 C.E., brought about a worse situation than ever before, yet the *attitude* towards the Temple had persisted for decades, and indeed, save for some intervals, was the same back in the time of the Israelites, which occasioned the original statement about the cave of robbers in Jeremiah chapter 7.[25]

There Jeremiah told them plainly that they shed innocent blood, oppressed the alien, and trusted in the lie. 'You steal, you murder, you commit adultery and perjury . . . then you come and stand before me in this house, which bears my name, and say, "We are safe"; safe, you think to indulge in all these abominations. Do you think that this house, this house which bears my name, is a robbers' cave?' (Jer. 7:9–11 NEB.)

So Jesus was not idly repeating a Scripture text. He meant what he said. The Jews then plotted and intrigued in the Temple as if it were a robbers' cave. Although it should have been a peaceful, holy place of prayer, they argued and wrangled with each other over their traditions and interpretations. They also thought that whatever might be their hypocritical stance and double standards, they were insured against the consequences of their sins, and were absolved from them if they dutifully came to the Temple. Sadly, some of this intrigue and plotting was against Jesus himself, and its purpose and aim was eventually realized, with his betrayal, arrest and death.[26]

12. Thief in the Night—Keep Awake and Watchful.

The illustration of the thief in the night is found in the comments of Jesus, the writings of Paul and Peter, and the vision of John. But we have to examine it and think about it before we can really see the power in the illustration.

Jesus had been answering the question of his disciples about the time of his presence (the distinctive Greek word 'parousia', Matt. 24:3, 27, 37, 39), and near the end of the sign given he said, 'Be sure of this; if the master of the house had known at what time of night the thief was coming, he would have kept watch, and not allowed his house to be broken open. And you too must stand ready; the Son of Man will come at an hour when you are not expecting him.' (Matt. 24: 43, 44 Knox.)

The phrase 'broken open' is translated by Rotherham as 'dug through'. The typical house in Jesus' day was constructed of clay bricks at the best, or more likely of wattle and daub, with a floor of beaten earth, and flat roofs in wattle and beaten earth, or rough tiles. A small stone roller was often used to keep it waterproof. From the story of the paralytic it can be seen how easily the roof could be 'broken open' or 'dug through' after perhaps in this case removing some tiles. (Mark 2:4, Luke 5:19.) Even the better class houses, often built around a central courtyard, and using stone, were still very susceptible to thieves, although they might take longer to break in.[27]

So the illustration especially highlights the ease with which the Palestinian house could be broken into, and the difficulty of any real form of security, even though locks and keys were known, albeit simple ones by comparison with today. The best remedy was to be ever watchful and alert – just the point Jesus stressed. It was the thief's purpose to catch out the householder or watchman, perhaps coming at dead of night and using great stealth. (Rev. 3:3, 16:15, 2 Peter 3:10.)

When the apostle Paul uses the simile, it has the same general application, to the final coming of Christ as a stealthy thief in the night. But rather than a warning to those who might be caught out, Paul takes into account the now quite well advanced spirituality and understanding of the Thessalonian Christians. So now he cleverly changes the illustration to the Day of the Lord itself, by highlighting the stealthy breaking of day by the dawn. This adds great cogency to his point; Christ comes as a thief, and so does the Day itself in which he comes to end wickedness. 'But you, brothers, are not in the darkness, and the Day should not steal on you like a thief. You all belong to the light, to the day.' (1 Thess. 5:4 TNT.)[28]

So although the world in general will be caught out at that final end, and just when they think the conditions are all leading to a situation when they will say, 'how peaceful and secure everything is,' then the 'Day of the Lord will come as a thief in the night comes'. Paul then emphasizes how watchful Christians need to be. 'So we must not sleep as everyone else does. We must be watchful and sober.' (1 Thess. 5:2, 3, 6 TNT.)

Notes and references:

1. Howat, G. M. D. & Taylor, A. J. P. Ed. *Dictionary of World History*, 1973, Nelson, 57 for quotation; Moulton & Milligan, *Vocabulary*, 534; Deissmann, G. A. *Light*, 374; Mitchell, M, M, 'New Testament Envoys in the Context of Greco-Roman Diplomatic and Epistolary Conventions: The Example of Timothy and Titus,' *JBL*, Vol. 111 (1992), 641–662.

2. Robinson, J. A. *Ephesians*, 5.

3. Westcott, B. F. & Hort, F. J. A. *The N. T. in the Original Greek*, 1882, Vol. 2. Appendix, Notes on Select Readings, 136, which favours the reading 'ambassador' rather than 'old man;' see also Lightfoot, J. B. *Colossians*, 335–337.

4. *Josephus War* Book 3, ch. 5 (5) 95, translated by H. St. J. Thackeray, 1967, Loeb Classical Library; Webster, G, *The Roman Army*, 1956, Chester, Grosvenor Museum, 29; Waugh, R. M. L. *Greek Testament*, 71; Hogg, C. F. & Vine, W. E. *The Epistle of Paul the Apostle to the Galatians, with Notes*, 1922, 318; *Translator's N.T.* note 491/2; Xenophon, *Memoirs of Socrates*, Book III, 13. 6.

5. Webster, G. op. cit (4) 14.

6. Deissmann, G. A. *Bible Studies*, 86, 87; Barclay, W. *N. T. Words*, 30–32;

Arndt, W. F. & Gingrich, F. W. *Greek-English Lexicon*, 6; Montefiore, C. G. *Synoptic Gospels*, Vol. 2, 74; Xenophon, *Institution of Cyrus*, Book VIII, 6. 17; Herodotus, Book VIII, Urania, 97, 98 'This mode of travelling by horses the Persians call angareion.' (H. Cary translation).

7. *Josephus Antiquities*, Book 13, ch. 2 (3) 52; Hatch, E. *Essays in Biblical Greek*, 1970 reprint, Amsterdam, 38; Bishop, E. F. F. *Jesus of Palestine*, 75.

8. Feldman, A, *Parables*, 150f.

9. Skeat, W. W. *Etymological Dictionary*, 624; Partridge, E, *Origins, A Short Etymological Dictionary of Modern English*, 1966, 4th ed. 688; Milligan, G. *Here and There Among the Papyri*, 1922, 103, 'to lay a false accusation'; Vincent, M. R. *Word Studies*, Vol. 1, 149; Robertson, A. T. *Word Pictures*, Vol. 2, 40, 41; Perschbacher, W. J. Ed. *Analytical Greek Lexicon*, 384.

10. Robinson, W. G. *N. T. Treasure*, 25; Earle, R, *Word Meanings*, 404 'In the stuffy dungeon, it was as if the air conditioning had been turned on!'

11. Moulton & Milligan, *Vocabulary*, 36, showing that this word was used as a technical term in agriculture, to rest the land by sowing light crops on it.

12. Skeat, W. W. *Etymological Dictionary*, 421, 430.

13. Lattey, C Ed. *The Westminster Version of the Sacred Scriptures, The N. T.* Vol. !V, 7, In a footnote, Prof. P. Boylan comments on Hebrews 2:16, 'the Greek may be used either of a friendly or hostile grip, according to the context.'

14. Trench, R. C. *Synonyms*, 124/5; Robertson, A. T. *Word Pictures*, Vol. 1, 40, Vol. 4, 249; Skeat, W.

W. *Etymological Dictionary*, 441; Of the translations, Schonfield uses 'oppressed,' Wuest reads, 'destitute and helpless,' Barclay has 'destitution,' and Berkeley 'spiritual poverty.' John Bowes *N. T. Translated from the Purest Greek*, 1870, Dundee, uses, 'mendicants in spirit,' with the footnote, 'Beggars in spirit.' The footnote to S. Zodhiates *Hebrew-Greek Key Study Bible*, 1984, Grand Rapids, MN, Baker 1141, distinguishes well the two Greek words. Ptōchos is the word used at Luke 16:20, 22 for the beggar Lazarus.

15. Bullinger, E. W. *Enjoy the Bible*, 255/6; Wordsworth, C. *Greek Testament*, Vol. 2, 168.

16. Barclay, W. *N. T. Words*, 248; Franzmann, M. H. 'Beggars before God. The First Beatitude,' *CTM*, Vol. 18 (1947), 889–899.

17. Vincent, M. R. *Word Studies*, Vol. 2, 907; Barclay, W. *N. T. Words*, 116–118.

18. Waugh, R. M. L. *Greek Testament*, 62/3, 'A Cancelled Bond'; Rodd, C. S. 'Salvation Proclaimed: XI, Colossians 2:8–15,' *ET*, Vol. 94 (1982) 36–41; Lightfoot, J. B. *Colossians*, 185; Yates, R, 'Colossians 2:14: Metaphor of Forgiveness,' *Biblica*, Vol. 71 (1990), 248–259.

19. Vincent, M. R. *Word Studies*, Vol. 1, 65; Earle, R. *Word Meanings*, 18. There is a variant reading for Matt. 19:5, proskollaō, which is a strengthened form of kollaō. see Nestle Aland, *N. T. Graece*, 1981, 26th ed. Stuttgart, 52.

20. 'They believed after close and intimate intercourse,' Guillemard, W. H. *Hebraisms*, 47, cp. Acts 5:13; King, E. *Morsels of Criticism tending to Illustrate Some few Passages in the Holy Scriptures . . .* 1788,

518, Latin *conglutino*, cement together, bind closely.

21. Miller, J. I. 'A Fresh Look at 1 Corinthians 6:16f. ' *NTStud*. Vol. 27 (1980) 125–127.

22. Robertson, A. T. *Word Pictures*, Vol. 4, 497/8, 504; Yahuda, J. *Hebrew is Greek*, 234/5, 282.

23. Abrahams, I, *Studies in Pharisaism*, 1st series 82–89.

24. Perowne, S. *The Life & Times of Herod the Great*, 1956, Hodder & S. 61.

25. Bishop, E. F. F. *Jesus of Palestine*, 218, refers to Mark 11: 16, where Jesus stopped the Temple being used as a short cut or 'right of way.'

26. Edersheim, A. *Life and Times*, Vol. 1, 367–373, Vol 2. 377–379.

27. Daniel-Rops, *Daily Life in Palestine at the Time of Christ* 1962, Weidenfeld & Nicolson, 223–226.

28. The Westcott & Hort text here substitutes kleptas for kleptēs, which may seem to be a small change, but it results in a total inversion of the metaphor, and the thief or thieves becomes the object instead of the cause. See Lightfoot, J. B. *Notes on Epistles*, 74, and Milligan, G, *St. Paul's Epistles to the Thessalonians*, 1908, Macmillan, 66. But the context is really against this, as well discussed by Findlay, G. G. CGT, for *Thessalonians*, 1925, 111. On the MS. evidence see Metzger, B. M. Ed. *A Textual Commentary on the Greek N. T.*, 1975, UBS, 633. Paul's play on words in which he frequently indulges, therefore moves from the idea of the thief as a person, to the day as the thief, *the* Day of the Lord.

Chapter 8

Legal

1. Calling in the Advocate—Help for the Accused.

Not long before his death, Jesus tried to allay the anxiety of his disciples by assuring them that they would not be left alone without help or guidance. He said, 'And I will ask the Father, and He will give you another Advocate, to be forever with you – the Spirit of truth.' (John 14:16 Weymouth 3rd ed.) In a footnote, 'Advocate' is explained as being 'one called to one's side to help'. The role of the holy spirit would be like that of someone who would 'stand by you'. (Phillips.) This Greek legal term ('paraklētos'), was used of a person called in to aid the accused, to speak for you or defend you, perhaps testifying to your character, or pleading on your behalf.[1]

How good it is to have someone we can call on in times of need to advise us which course to take over a problem. The Greek word 'paraclete' used here, then, is often much wider in meaning than the word found in many older Bible translations, namely 'Comforter'. That meaning is still embraced in the idea of a helper, for it depends on what the problem is as to whether it is comfort that is called for, counsel and advice, or moral support and pleading on our behalf. It is this last idea that comes through strongly in 1 John 2:1, 'If anyone ever sins, we have One who pleads our cause with the Father, Jesus Christ, One who is righteous.' (C. B. Williams.) The footnote in this translation adds, 'Grk. 'paraclete', advocate; our attorney to plead our case.' We could have no better helpers than Jesus Christ and God's holy spirit!

Although Paul does not use the same word, he conveys the identical idea when he says, 'In the same way the Spirit helps us in our weakness, for we do not know how to pray as we should, but the Spirit itself pleads for us with inexpressible yearnings, and he who searches our hearts knows what the Spirit means, for it pleads for God's people in accordance with his will.' (Rom. 8:26, 27 Good-speed.)

Adolf Deissmann clearly linked the idea of the paraclete or helper/advocate with the Pauline formula 'through Christ'. Not only is Jesus Christ the Father's helper, and the one through whom God works, but so much of the help we receive comes to us 'through Christ', through his agency, and his intercession on our behalf by means of the ransom sacrifice. So the illustration is one that has a very wide application, and it gives us assurance that between Jesus Christ and God's holy spirit, we will not be left alone without help and assistance when it is wanted.[2]

2. Case for the Defence—Giving an Answer.

When people today make an apology, it is usually an expression of regret for an offence or wrong of some sort. But the word also has a stronger meaning, very evident in early Christian times. An Apology is a speech in one's defence, 'to talk oneself off from a charge preferred against one.'[3] So it often referred to a pleading for the defence made in a court of law, and the apostle Paul used it when speaking before governors Felix and Festus, and King Agrippa. (Acts 24:10, 25:8, 26:1, 2.) So when he wrote his letter to the Philippians Paul could truly say that they had shared with him, 'both in my prison bonds and in the defending and legally establishing of the good news.' (Phil. 1:7 NWT.)

Luke also mentioned in his gospel that Christians would be brought before courts to give a defence or apology for the faith. But he said, 'do not give anxious thought to the wording and the lines of your defence; for when the moment comes, the Holy Spirit will teach you what you ought to say.' (Luke 12:11 Rieu.) Later he added, 'Prepare no speeches in your defence, for I will endow you with such eloquence and wisdom as all your enemies will not be able to withstand or to refute.' (Luke 21:14 Rieu.) A Christian would have nothing to fear so long as he had the truth of God's word and purpose in his heart. However awesome the occasion, he would be able to make a bold defence, finding winsome thoughts and words.

The apostle Peter takes this word and uses it to illustrate a wider context when he wrote, 'Be always ready with your defence whenever you are called to account for the hope that is in you, but make that defence with modesty and respect.' (1 Peter 3:15 NEB.) This could often be outside a court of law, in fact, it could be any occasion when someone asks us why we believe what we do as Christians. There are those who say they will never discuss their religion with others because it is something private, but a true Christian will always want to be able to explain his faith, and recommend it to others. The reason takes us back to Luke's comments. We will not need to prepare in advance the words we will use, but if the love of Christ is in our hearts, it will soon come out, yet in a way that shows modesty and respect for the other person's ideas and beliefs.

It is also true that our enemies will not be able to withstand that defence. It is no coincidence that the illustration can be extended here, for our chief adversary is the Devil, as Peter showed just two chapters further on. (1 Pet. 5:8.) Although the picture here is of the Devil as a roaring lion, the idea of him as the adversary at law lingers in the background. (Matt 5:25, Luke 18:3.) He was the original prosecutor of faithful servants of God like Job (Job 1:6–12, 2:1–6) and he has continued to question the integrity of Christians ever since, so that they are often called on to defend their faith. (Rev. 2:10.) That defence is never apologetic in the more usual sense of the word, but it is a strong Apology within the Biblical meaning brought out by this illustration.[4]

3. Legal Examination—The Beroean Spirit.

When Jesus came before Pontius Pilate following his betrayal and arrest, the governor examined his case, and gave this verdict, 'Now I have gone into the matter itself in your presence, and found no grounds in the man for any of the charges you bring against him.' (Luke 23:14 NJB.) The original word used for 'gone into the matter' was 'an Athenian law term for a preliminary investigation (distinct from the actual 'krisis' or trial), in which evidence was collected and the prisoner committed for trial, if a true bill was found against him.'[5]

This is very evident when we look at Paul's situation described in Acts chapter 25. He had appealed to have his case heard by Caesar himself. But because the provincial governor Festus didn't know what to write to Caesar, he had Paul brought before King Agrippa, so that he could undergo a judicial examination. (Acts 25:26.) In the next chapter Paul enlarges on the evidence, speaking eloquently in his own defence, and ending his appeal to Agrippa with the words, 'The king understands these matters, and to him I now speak fearlessly. I am confident that nothing of all this comes as a surprise to him; after all, these things were not done in a corner.' (Acts 26:26 NJB.) Yes, there was so much evidence, for the matter had not been kept secret, hidden in a corner, and Agrippa acknowledged that Paul could have been freed had he not already appealed to Caesar.

How is this type of legal examination used to illustrate what we can call 'the Beroean Spirit'? Because a Christian is called upon to exercise faith does not mean that he is a credulous man. He is expressly told to test the claims of those who say they speak from God. (1 John 4:1.) How can he do this? Paul uses this same legal term when he contrasts the natural man's lack of spirituality with the way a true Christian will seek for understanding. 'But the spiritual man tries [Greek 'anakrinō'] all things [he examines, investigates, inquires into, questions, and discerns all things],' (1 Cor. 2:15a Amplified.) This does not mean that he is critical, or a doubter, but that he gathers the evidence, he sifts it and probes every angle so that his living faith in action is built upon a rock that is firm enough to withstand every storm. (Matt. 7:24, 25.) 'I wish I had your faith', is a comment sometimes heard from people who do not have this spiritual fourth dimension in their lives.

The people who particularly used this sifting and testing process were the early Beroeans. Paul and Silas taught in the synagogue and their hearers' spirit comes in for special commendation. 'These Jews of Beroea were better disposed than those in Thessalonica, for they welcomed the Message with great readiness, and daily examined [Greek 'anakrinō'] the Scriptures to see if what was said was true.' (Acts 17:11 TCNT.) They used the Scriptures so far as they were then complete to make an examination to see if the evidence matched what Paul and Silas were saying.

There is good reason to think that it was the early Christians who made the codex or book form popular, gradually making the scroll form redundant.[6] We can readily see why. It would be difficult to check references in Scriptures written on scrolls, unrolling from one end whilst rolling onto the other end, then possibly right back again to near to the beginning. A codex would be easy to use by comparison. Perhaps this was one of the occasions when the problem of the scroll first dawned upon them, for it was not likely to be realized by those who did not possess the Beroean spirit, and rarely opened a scroll from one month to the next.

So we can learn from this illustration. We will show we have the Beroean spirit if we make good use of our Bibles to learn at first hand what God is speaking to us in this modern day. What is more, our printed Bibles, replete with chapter and verse numbers, are easier to use than an early papyrus codex, even if some of the chapter divisions are erroneous. So have you looked up the reference in John's first letter a couple of paragraphs back? Let's copy those early Beroean Christians!

4. Testimony in Court—The Witness of Conscience.

It is sometimes difficult to determine the role of the conscience, and the way in which it acts within us. But Paul used an illustration which helps to show the relationship that conscience has to reason and judgment, especially as it applies to Christians.

His picture is that of the court room, and its drama unfolds as he contrasts the position of those who have law to follow, with those who are without a law code. He explains it this way, 'when Gentiles who have no Law, do by natural instinct the Law's requirements, these men, though they have no Law, are a Law to themselves, since they display the Law's work written on their hearts, their conscience bearing witness with it and their reasonings debating in condemnation or defence.' (Rom. 2:14, 15 Smith.) In a footnote to the same translation in his book *The Life and Letters of St. Paul* (389), David Smith identifies the parties in the law court, 'The unwritten law is the statute, Conscience the witness, their reasonings prosecutor and advocate, God the judge.'

So the man without any law reasons on a matter, and his reasonings argue first one way and then another, as if the prosecutor sets forth his case, and is then answered by the defence lawyer. In the middle stands the witness, with both prosecutor and advocate appealing to him for support. But the witness must speak the truth, and prove whether the prosecutor is right or the case for the defence. A man will follow his conscience as witness, relying on its truthfulness and proper balance, but it is God who is the final judge in the case.

Then Paul puts some hard questions to the Jew who claims to 'pillow your head on the law'. (Rom. 2:17 Smith.) Yes, because he so rests on the Mosaic Law as a pillow for his head, he could go right off to sleep, so that his conscience fails to speak out. He could be worse than the man who has no law to follow, and so is found guilty before the judge of breaking the very law he claims to hold so devoutly.

But how reliable is the conscience as a witness? Just as it is possible for a witness to perjure himself by giving false testimony, so Paul speaks of 'the hypocrisy of men that speak lies, branded in their own consciences as with a hot iron.' (1 Tim. 4:2 ASV.) The heat of an iron has to be balanced; if it gets too hot it can accidentally make a permanent mark on the clothes. Paul is thinking particularly of those who quite deliberately seek to mislead, so that their conscience has been seared with a branding-iron, an implement designed to make an indelible mark.

How can the conscience be kept true? Like the mind and heart, it can be trained to always take a stand for truth, and God's Word is a guide to help in that training. Then motive has an important part to play, and if love of God and love of neighbour is the firm basis of our conduct, we can avoid acquiring a bad conscience, as Paul had shown earlier in that same letter to Timothy. (1 Tim. 1:5.) Then our conduct will reflect that, and our conscience will bear us favourable witness – we will receive approval for our course deep within ourselves. (2 Cor. 1:12.)

But the witness in court does not just stand on his own bearing witness to truth. The part that can be played by the advocate, the defence lawyer, is very important, for he can draw out the truth in a matter. Later in his letter to the Romans, Paul brings out this thought when he says, 'I am speaking the truth as a Christian, and my own conscience, enlightened by the Holy Spirit, assures me it is no lie.' (Rom. 9:1 NEB.)

Because the 'Spirit of God joins with our spirit' as advocate (Rom. 8:16 NEB), then we can be certain that God, who is the judge in court, is going to find in our favour. This united testimony of conscience and holy spirit gives a true Christian confidence to pursue his course, no matter how much the prosecuting council within our human flesh urges us to take the opposite way.

5. Lifting The Legal Burden—The End of Servitude.

Part of Paul's argument in his letter to the Romans is well illustrated by the way the Greek word 'katakrima' is used in early Christian times, in various papyrus documents that have been found in Egypt. Certain lands were sold free of all burdens of any kind, whether they were debts or taxes, or any burden which came about following a judicial pronouncement. Without such a release, the land might continue indefinitely under its legal burden ('katakrima'). How does this illustration help us with Paul's argument?[7]

This word occurs twice in the fifth chapter of Romans, and the gist of the argument is summed up concisely in verse 18, 'Again, as one man's fall brought condemnation ['katakrima'] upon everyone, so the good act of one man brings everyone life and makes them justified.' (JB.) Instead of simply 'condemnation' the fall of Adam brought a judicial sentence from God, and everyone descended from him came under that burden or servitude which resulted. Jesus Christ, by his death, removed out of the way the burden legally imposed, so that man could be freed from his servitude. Returning to verse 16 where the word 'katakrima' is first used, we can follow Paul's reasonings. 'The results of the gift also outweigh the results of one man's sin: for after one single fall came judgement with a verdict of condemnation, now after many falls comes grace with its verdict of acquittal.'(JB.)

We can now understand much better Paul's further argument in Romans chapter 8 which commences, 'Since deliverance is available then, there is no reason why those who are members of Christ Jesus should go on in a state of "penal servitude", ['katakrima'] for the

Spirit's law – the law of that life which is ours in Christ Jesus – has set you free from bondage to the law of sin and death.' (Rom. 8:1 Bruce.) Just as the land was declared free of all burden and encumbrance, so in Christ Jesus Christians are no longer under any legal burden or servitude.

So verse 33 rightly puts the question, 'Could anyone accuse those that God has chosen? When God acquits, could anyone condemn?' (JB.) The burden and servitude imposed upon humans through Adam is legally at an end, though the final results of that burden still linger until God has completely removed death from mankind. The chapter ends with Paul's note of rejoicing that nothing can again bring separation from God's love, so marvellously demonstrated by his son Christ Jesus in his action in freeing mankind.

6. The Guarantee—The Unfailing Promise.

We all feel a little more secure if we get a guarantee with goods that we purchase, although the integrity of men can still let us down. But the guarantee that God gives will never fail. The Greek word 'bebaiōsis' is used in the papyri with the thought of safeguarding a bargain, so that a seller had a definite obligation to the buyer, even involving the possible claims of a third party. So this fine illustration suggests real stability and firmness.[8]

If a person did not have full rights over his land, then no sale could take place that would be a legally guaranteed one. The Israelites were in this position, as the Greek Septuagint Version makes clear when it uses this word in Leviticus 25:23, 24, 'Now the land must not be sold forever ['bebaiōsis']; for the land is mine. Because you are strangers and sojourners before me, therefore in all the land of your possession, you shall grant a right of redeeming the land.' (LXX Thomson.)

Paul uses this illustration in speaking of God's promise to Abraham that 'by your descendants shall all the nations of the earth bless themselves'. (Gen. 22:18 RSV.) In Romans 4:16 he says of that promise, 'That is why it depends on faith, in order that the promise may rest on grace, and be guaranteed ['bebaios'] to all his descendants – not only to the adherents of the law but also to those who

share the faith of Abraham, for he is the father of us all.' (RSV.)
Then towards the end of his letter Paul adds, 'I would remind those
who are circumcised, that Christ came to relieve their needs; God's
fidelity demanded it; he must make good ['bebaioō'] his promises
to our fathers.' (Rom. 15:8 Knox.) It was through the work of Christ
in giving his life as a ransom that God would be able to guarantee
or 'make good' the word that he had previously given.

The interesting reasoning in the sixth chapter of Hebrews shows
just how dependable is God's promise, which in itself is a guarantee,
for there is no greater authority that could verify it. This is what
happens in a dispute between men, 'For men swear by the one
greater, and their oath is the end of every dispute, as it is a legal
guarantee to them.' (Heb. 6:16 NWT.) But when God so steps in
with an oath, we have '*two* irrevocable assurances, over which there
could be no question of God deceiving us, were to bring firm confidence to us poor wanderers, bidding us cling to the hope we have
in view.' (Heb. 6:18 Knox.) A second guarantee is added to the first
one, as if to give still greater evidence to those doubters who might
ask, will God really fulfil his promise after this long time? (Hebrews
6:13–20.)

This entire argument concerning the promise made to Abraham
provides a solid background against which to consider the words of
Peter when he refers to the nature of prophecy. He describes the
wonder of the Transfiguration scene in which he was both a partici-
pant and a witness. (Matt. 17:1–9.) Then he draws this conclusion,
'In this way we have been made more certain than ever ['bebaios']
of the fulfillment of prophecy. You had better give close attention
to the prophetic sayings. They are like a night-light shining till the
day dawns and the morning star rises in your hearts.' (2 Peter 1:19
Wand.)

The fulfillment of prophecy gives evidence that the guarantee
implicit in all utterances coming from God, has been fully backed
up by the performance. No greater testimony could be produced to
recommend the guarantor, in this case, the Almighty God himself.
Peter's final argument for the guarantee in God-given prophecy, is
that true servants of God were inspired or directed in what they said
by God's holy spirit. (2 Peter 1:21.)

The word of promise and the word of prophecy – both alike carry the best guarantee that any man could have, the seal and warranty of the great God of the universe.

7. Earnest Money—An Advance Instalment.

Originally an Eastern mercantile word, 'earnest' was introduced by the Phoenicians into Greece and Italy, and meant a pledge.[9] It is used in Genesis 38:17, 18, where Judah gives Tamar his seal ring and rod as an earnest or pledge that he will pay her a kid of the goats for having relations with her. That security was to be given back when the animal was duly delivered.

But the apostle Paul used the word in a different sense, which has been borne out by its meaning in the Greek papyri found in Egypt. This was not a security that was later to be reclaimed, but 'an instalment paid at once as a proof of the bona fides of the bargain. It is an actual portion of the whole which is hereafter to be paid in full.'[10] It was a pledge only in so far as it showed that a person was earnest or sincere, and would without fail pay the remaining balance. Today we would call this a deposit which shows the good intentions of the buyer.

Writing to the Corinthians, Paul dwells on the reliability of God's promises. They are not like those of men, who say 'yes' to something one minute, then change their minds and say 'no' instead. 'To all his promises God says 'Yes' in him [Jesus Christ]; that is why it is through him that we say the Amen to glorify God. It is God who strengthens [Greek 'bebaioō'] both us and you in Christ. It is God who has anointed us, put his seal of ownership on us, and given us the Spirit in our hearts as an instalment and pledge [Greek 'arrabōn'] of what is to come.' (2 Cor. 1:20–22 TNT.) That advance instalment of the holy spirit is 'the down payment' (NKJV Interlinear), 'the token payment guaranteeing the payment in full of our salvation (verse 22 Wuest).' (See also 2 Cor. 5:5. Eph. 1:14.)

That this first instalment gave a guarantee that the rest would be paid is shown by the frequent linking of the two Greek words, as Adolf Deissmann explains, 'in technical usage, 'arrabōn' and 'bebaioun' stand in an essential relation to each other. It is exactly in this way that Paul speaks – his indestructible faith representing the relation of God to believers under the image of a legally indisputable relation . . . the technical word makes the image still more effective.'[11]

But there is one important distinction from a deposit or pledge in a legal business transaction. God gives his holy spirit freely, and everlasting life is a gift from God, so that no one can say that God owes them salvation.

8. Shut up in Prison—In the Custody of Sin.

A picturesque word (Greek 'katakleiō') is used by Luke and Paul with the basic meaning of being shut up in prison, and it is found twice in this literal sense. (Luke 3:20, Acts 26: 10.) In another setting, a closely linked word ('sunkleiō'), is used for the great shoal of fish that was enclosed in the nets when Jesus urged his disciples to let them down again, despite a weary night's fishing with no results. (Luke 5:6.) The word 'enclosed' means 'shut together on all sides'.[12]

Paul enlists this word to describe the plight of mankind, in his letter to the Galatians. 'Scripture has described all mankind as shut up in a prison, ['sunkleiō'] with sin for their gaoler . . . Yes, before the advent of this faith even we Jews were as men imprisoned, with Moses' Law for our warder, in preparation for the faith which was destined to be unveiled.' (Gal. 3:22, 23 Way.) The Mosaic Law did nothing to free men from their imprisonment under sin, in fact it only showed up how dismal was that state of confinement. A. T. Robertson says it was 'as if the lid closed in on us over a massive chest that we could not move.'[13] Nothing that mankind could do was able to free them from this plight in which they found themselves all shut up together.

Only through faith in Christ Jesus could a chance for freedom present itself, and this because of the loving-kindness of God himself. 'God shut the door on them all when they passed into the prison cell of disobedience, only with the intention of having mercy on all.' (Rom. 11:32 Way.) Through his bringing in a new covenant, Christ Jesus could declare the Mosaic Law covenant old, moving the gaoler out of the way by His death, so that the prison could be opened, and all men showing faith could be freed from the custody of sin. (Luke 4:18, Isa. 61:1, 2.)

The particular value of this illustration is that it shows the helplessness of man in his predicament. Because they were inside the prison, they could not open the door by their own efforts. It required one who was always free from sin's prison to do that. The apostle had good reason to praise the great God who gave his Son, and made such freedom possible. (Rom. 11:33–36.)

9. Freeing a Slave by Purchase— The Christian's New Owner.

The Law of Moses made provision for the redemption or manumission of slaves before the Jubilee year, upon payment of a sum of money calculated in accordance with the number of years remaining up to the Jubilee. (Lev. 25:48–53.)[14] But when it came to redeeming a man in the eyes of God, so that he could continue to live and not see death as the penalty of sin, there was no means of doing so. Says the Psalmist, 'But man could never redeem himself or pay his ransom to God: it costs so much to redeem his life, it is beyond him.' (Ps. 49:7, 8 JB.) The price was beyond man's reach, however rich he might be.

There was only one way for man to gain salvation, and Peter gave it emphasis by contrasting it with the usual method of manumission. 'Remember that you were bought [Greek 'lutroō'] out of that purposeless life which your fathers handed down to you, bought not with things that decay like silver or gold, but with precious blood, like that of a lamb without fault or spot, the blood of Christ.' (1 Peter 1:18, 19 C. K. Williams.) As C. H. Dodd has pointed out, the metaphors of freedom and slavery are still fully alive, but the word 'redemption' is no longer suitable for expressing the idea. 'Release by ransom' is better, or 'purchasing with a price', because it includes both the idea of the payment of a ransom, and the deliverance which is effected as a result.[15] Deliverance alone only expresses part of the thought, and does not convey the metaphor, although some translations use this word. (Eph. 1:7, C. K. Williams, Weymouth, Concordant, Montgomery.)

The apostle Paul gives the same illustration as Peter when he writes to the Corinthians, but he uses a word related to the market or agora where slaves were often sold. 'You are not your own property; you have been bought [Greek 'agorazō'] and paid for. That is why you should use your body for the glory of God.' (1 Cor. 6:20 JB.) The purchase has been completed, and in the next chapter, Paul carries his argument further to explain what it really means for Christians to be free. 'A slave, when he is called in the Lord becomes Christ's slave. You have all been bought and paid for; do not be slaves of other men.' (1 Cor. 7:22, 23 JB.) The man who has always had worldly freedom is Christ's slave by purchase, and the man who was still a literal slave under Roman law was now the slave of Christ, but both alike are freedmen in Christ, for by his purchase of them he has set them free. (Rev. 5:9.)[16]

What superb use Paul makes of this illustration to drive home the superiority of Christ's release of men by means of his fully paid ransom price. Never will true Christians take a course that means they disown their new owner. That would make the purchase price abortive, and suggest that Christ should die a second time to save them, even though this would expose him to public ridicule. (2 Peter 2:1, Heb. 6:6.) Rather, a Christian will use his freedom to honour his owner, and show his appreciation for the cost paid out on his behalf.

10. The Slave's Mark—Belonging to Christ.

To stigmatize someone is to defame them publicly, or brand them with infamy, but originally the Greek word 'stigma' simply referred to a mark or brand burned with a red-hot iron. Slaves and animals would be marked with a stamp or tattoo denoting ownership, and this is the idea behind Paul's words at Galatians 6:17, 'From now on let no one make trouble for me, for I bear in my body the brandmarks of Jesus' ownership.' (Berkeley.)[17]

Since Paul was not literally a slave with brand marks burned onto his body, he was using this idea as an illustration. But this was no idle or imaginary metaphor, for it was undoubtedly prompted by the sufferings that Paul had undergone in his ministry, and which he later recounted in detail in his second letter to the Corinthians. They included natural difficulties met as he travelled from place to place, and many occasions when he was short of food or drink, cold and sleepless. He was robbed by highwaymen, deceived, considered to be an imposter, and defamed publicly (stigmatized in the modern sense). He was persecuted, imprisoned, beaten and left for dead. All these things he accepted as part of his ministry for God and Christ. (2 Cor. 6:4–10, 11:23–27.) Because he had suffered in this way for his love and adherence to Jesus Christ, they became as brand marks that proved to whom he belonged. He was not a slave of men, nor was he the Devil's slave.

This contrasting idea is also part of Paul's metaphor, for he refers to those who fall away from the faith as ones 'whose consciences are burnt black as with a hot iron'. (1 Tim. 4:2 C. K. Williams, 'a branding iron' – Berkeley.) A number of translations speak here of 'the devil's sign' (NEB), 'the devil's slaves' (Beck), or 'the devil's own mark' (TNT), but as this is not in the Greek text, it is clearly only an implication. (TNT note 515.)

Yet Christ's own thinking regarded those not on his side as being against him; there could really be no middle ground. (Matt. 12:30.) This is also the principle behind the mark of the beast in Revelation 13:15–17. No one could buy or sell unless he had that mark, a clear imprint in his life which showed that he was not one who had the ownership mark of Christ upon him.

This highlights the aspect of identification. The course of action of a Christian clearly identifies him, it marks him for Christ, and it sets him apart from a world that increasingly accepts the mark of violence, rebellion, greed and selfishness, and every other degrading trait possible. The line between those belonging to Christ (not just saying they are 'born again' or similar claims), and those belonging to this world becomes increasingly clearer. Any middle ground is fast disappearing. (Matt. 7:21–23.)

Notes and References:

1. Field, F. *Notes on the Translation of the N. T.* 1899, Camb. 102/103; Goodspeed, E. J. *Problems*, 110/111; Hastings, J. *Dictionary of the Bible*, Vol. 3. 665f; Brown, C. Ed. *NIDNTT*. Vol. 1. 88–92; Davies,

J. G. 'The Primary Meaning of Parakletos,' *JTS*, New Series, Vol. 4 (1953), 35–38.

2. Deissmann, A. *Light*, 336/337 for quotation; Turner, N. *Christian Words*, 73–78, who finds the idea of comfort or consolation predominates in the Christian setting, but recognizes its wider and earlier meaning in certain Scriptures, and especially in 1 John 2:1.

3. Wuest, K, *Word Studies*, Vol. 3, *Golden Nuggets*, 93.

4. Kittel, G. Ed. *TDNT*, Vol. 1. 374/375; Arndt, W. F. & Gingrich, F. W. *Greek-English Lexicon*, 73.

5. Lightfoot, J. B. *Notes on Epistles*, 182.

6. Roberts, C. H. *The Codex, Proceedings of the British Academy* Vol. XL, (1953), 185–189.

7. Deissmann, A. *Bible Studies*, 264/265; Moulton & Milligan, *Vocabulary*, 327/328.

8. Deissmann, A. *Bible Studies*, 104/105; Lyall, F. *Legal Metaphors*, 171–174.

9. Skeat, W. W. *Etymological Dictionary*, 187.

10. Robinson, J. A. *Ephesians*, 36, for the quotation; Yahuda, J, *Hebrew is Greek*, 97; Milligan, G. *The N. T. Documents*, 1913, Macmillan, 73 and ftn 2; Waugh, R. M. L. *Greek Testament*, 78; Barclay, W. *N. T. Words*, 58–60; Lyall, F. *Legal Metaphors*, 145/146; Ahern, B, 'The Indwelling Spirit, Pledge of our Inheritance. ' *CBQ*, Vol. 9. (1947), 179–189; Kerr, A. J. 'Arrabōn,' *JTS* Vol. 39, (1988), 92–97, he favours the translation 'a first instalment' rather than 'pledge. '

11. Deissmann, A. *Bible Studies*

108/109, Erlemann, K, 'Der Geist als arrabōn (2 Kor. 5, 5) im Kontext der paulinischen Eschatologie,' *ZeitNTWiss.* Vol. 83 (1992), 202–223.

12. Robertson, A. T. *A Translation of Luke's Gospel*, 1923, N. Y. 162 note; Yahuda, J, *Hebrew is Greek*, 233.

13. Robertson, A. T. *Word Pictures*, Vol. 4. 297; Moulton, H. K. *Challenge*, 182.

14. Vaux, R. De. *Ancient Israel, Its Life and Institutions*, Trans. by J. McHugh, 1961, Darton, Longman & Todd, 88.

15. Dodd, C. H. 'Problems,' *BT.* Vol. 13, (1962) 150; Waugh, R. M. L. *Greek Testament*, 60/61; Rienecker, F, & Rogers, C. *Linguistic Key, 522; Lightfoot, J. B. Notes on Epistles, 271, 316.*

16. Deissmann, A. *Light* 325/326; Lyall, F, *Legal Metaphors*, 39–43, which shows how the situation Paul describes would not apply to Greek or Jewish Law, but fits Roman Law, and Corinth was a Roman colony; Brown, C. Ed. *NIDNTT*, Vol. 1, 267/268; *NKJV Interlinear*, note to Rev. 5:9.

17. Skeat, W. W. *Etymological Dictionary*, 603; Meacham, H. G. *Light from Ancient Letters*, 1923, Allen & Unwin, 132; Waugh, R. M. L. *Greek Testament*, 87; Daddow, W. B. *Buried Pictures*, 30–35; Moulton, J. H. 'The Marks of Jesus,' *ET*, Vol. 21 (1909/10), 283f; Jones, C. P. 'Stigma: Tattooing and Branding in Graeco-Roman Antiquity. ' *JournRomStud.* Vol. 77, (1987), 139–155, for the full background.

Chapter 9

Military

1. Serving as a Soldier—Hardship.

The apostle Paul was well aware of the activities and reputation of the Roman army. There were several occasions when he had good reason to be thankful for their intervention. The Jerusalem garrison rescued him from a mob in the Temple precincts (Acts 21:30–40), and then sent him to Caesarea under strong guard to avoid a suspected ambush. (Acts 23: 12–35.) He appears to have established a good relationship with members of the Praetorian Guard in Rome. (Acts 23:35, 28:16, 30, 31, Phil. 1:13.)

So it is not surprising to find a number of military metaphors in his writings, sometimes carried through an entire section to sustain an argument by illustration, sometimes in very mixed metaphors, drawing a similar argument from several sources of illustration.

Our first example is the picture of the soldier himself, with particular emphasis on the hardship he has to put up with. 'Join the ranks of those who bear suffering like a loyal soldier of Christ Jesus. No soldier gets entangled in civil pursuits: his aim is to satisfy his commander.' (2 Tim. 2:3, 4 Moffatt.) He stresses here loyalty and singleness of purpose in serving the commander, Jesus Christ. But they could also look to the example of the prophets, 'that inspired by them you may wage the good warfare'. (1 Tim. 1:18 RSV.) They frequently had to do that against kings and princes, against men who sought to break down their faith and loyalty to God.

Because of that hardship suffered, and at the risk of his life, the soldier's loyalty and devotion has its rewards. He is fed and cared for, and in addition to his rations, a Roman soldier also received a small payment in money so that he might be able to buy his favourite relish to put on his bread. The Greek word for this was 'opsōnion', and this is the very word Paul used when he states that 'the wages paid ['opsōnion'] by Sin are death'. (Rom. 6:23 Weymouth 3rd ed, Luke 3:14.)[1]

So Paul argues, 'Does a soldier provide ['opsōnion'] his own supplies?' (1 Cor. 9:7 Moffatt.) Should it be considered wrong for Paul to have some material help for the spiritual help he is rendering in return as a soldier of Jesus Christ?

2. Armour—A Christian's Defence.

This is probably the most well-known of all Paul's metaphors – his description of the spiritual armour a Christian should put on if he is to be successful in defending himself. 'Put on all the armour which God provides . . . then you will be able to stand your ground when things are at their worst, to complete every task and still to stand.' (Eph. 6:11–13 NEB.) It is of no value to only use part of the armour, for the opposing forces will immediately go for the places we have left defenceless. Paul then itemizes the various parts of the armour, and these will be compared with the equipment used by the Roman soldier, as discussed by Graham Webster, in his booklet *The Roman Army*: [2]

1. 'Fasten on the belt of truth' (verse 14a NEB). 'The lower part of the body was protected by a wide belt with a sporran-like attachment . . . both heavily studded with metal.' (p.28 cp. Isa. 11:5.) A Christian must always be exemplary in standing fast in the truth and for the truth of God's Word.
2. 'For coat of mail put on integrity' (verse 14b NEB). 'The most common form consisted of two parts, a flexible system of overlapping metal strips and two pairs of plates over the chest and back. The body portion of strips hinged at the back and fastened at the front with studs and slots.' (p.27.) In a briefer mention of the armour in his first letter to the Thessalonians Paul says Christians should be 'armed with faith and love for coat of mail'. (1 Thess. 5:8 NEB.) Both these qualities are needed, if we are to show integrity, a standing firm for what is right or righteous, protecting the heart. (Prov. 4:23.)

3. 'Let the shoes on your feet be the gospel of peace, to give you firm footing' (verse 15 NEB) 'the legionaries had a heavy thick-soled sandal (caliga) . . . heavily studded with hollow-headed hob nails', tied on by thongs. It is interesting to notice the result, 'The effect must have been one of flexibility, coolness, comfort, and durability.' (p.28.) We are reminded of the words quoted from Isaiah 52:7, 'How lovely on the mountains, are the feet of the herald who comes to proclaim prosperity and bring good news, the news of deliverance.' (Rom. 10:15 NEB.) Those feet are fleet and nimble, equipped to deal with difficult terrain without giving up or tiring out. (cp. Ps. 18:32–36.) Their owners show such endurance and persistence because of the good news they carry; it impels them on as heralds in God's cause, and to those who welcome that good news, its bearers are indeed lovely and blessed. (Acts 10:36.)

4. 'With all these, take up the great shield of faith, with which you will be able to quench all the flaming arrows of the evil one.' (verse 16 NEB.) This was not the small light round shield or buckler, but the large or great rectangular shield, about 4' × 2½', 'curved to fit the body . . . made of leather or plywood bound at the edges with metal strips'. (p.28.) It was held by a handgrip inside, and also had a leather strip for the forearm. The origin of the Greek word here, 'thureos', is interesting. It referred to a door stone used to keep a door shut, and then later to a shield shaped like a door.[3] Is our faith like that, large enough to protect and cover every part of our body, and resistant to the most dangerous flaming arrows used in Roman times, putting out all the attacks by opposers? (1 John 5:4.)

5. Last, 'Take salvation for helmet' (verse 17 NEB) or 'the hope of salvation for helmet.' (1 Thess. 5:8 NEB, Isa. 59: 17.) The bronze helmet had a lined iron skull cap fitted inside, a brow ridge to protect nose and eyes, two hinged cheek pieces at the sides, and a swept back-guard for the back of the neck. (p.26/27.) Most important for gaining salvation is the protection of the head or mind, safeguarding thinking ability and balance, and keeping that hope bright and strong at all times. To this end Paul goes on to recommend prayer, which is compared to vigilance and alertness displayed by the well-protected soldier. (Eph. 6:18, 19.)

How complete is Paul's picture? The Christian can be entirely protected by this spiritual armour, but he needs all of it – a love for truth and righteousness, faith and hope, and a desire to share that good news with others, because of the joy it brings him, which is itself a protection.

3. Effective Weapons—Weapons of Righteousness.

What sort of weapons does a Christian use? Certainly not literal ones, for history testifies that the early Christians took a stand of neutrality to the wars around them. But these are used in illustration because they help us to picture how powerful and effective spiritual weapons can be, and that Christian activity is just as much a war against wicked forces. Paul lists ways by which his ministry is recommended to others, and amongst these mentions, 'the weapons of righteousness, for attack or for defense'. (2 Cor. 6:7 Montgomery.)

In his letter to the Romans, Paul explains what some of these weapons of righteousness are. 'Do not continue to present any part of your body to sin to be used as a weapon of unrighteousness. On the contrary, be presenting yourselves to God, as alive from the dead (spiritually), and the various parts of your bodies to be used as weapons of righteousness.' (Rom. 6:13 Montgomery.)

If we allow any part of our body to control our actions so that we sin, we may actually be turning a weapon upon ourselves, and making the battle more difficult to win.[4] Instead, we want to so use our physical bodies that they can help us in the daily fight, and so its various parts become weapons of righteousness – our minds, hearts and tongues to praise God, our feet to carry us in His ministry, just as Paul did.

These weapons are then seen in action in Paul's second letter to the Corinthians. 'I do not make war as the flesh does; the weapons of my warfare are not weapons of the flesh, but divinely strong to demolish fortresses – I demolish theories and any rampart [Greek 'hupsōma'] thrown up to resist the knowledge of God. I take every project prisoner to make it obey Christ.' (2 Cor. 10:3–5 Moffatt.)[5]

The principal weapon here, of course, is 'the sword of the Spirit, which is the Word of God.' (Eph. 6:17 Montgomery.) The letter to

the Hebrews explains that the Word of God is 'sharper than any
two-edged sword', (Hebrews 4:12 Montgomery) playing both a de-
fensive and an offensive role, and able when wielded effectively to
cut down false theories, and ramparts set up to defend those
ideas.[6]

The Roman soldier's weapon was very effective. 'The sword,
which was used in close-quarter fighting, had a short, broad blade,
two feet long, with a double edge. The quillons [the hilt's cross-
guard], were short and thick and the pommel [handle end] weighted
to give effective balance . . . They did not waste their energies in
any heroic swinging and hacking with this weapon.' [7]

The Christian really needs to get to know his Bible well so that
he can handle it effectively, not with any heroics, but in a fine and
balanced manner, showing that it does not contradict itself, but has
a truly powerful, harmonious message. At close quarters, or in personal conversation with people of all kinds, it will be shown to be
a book that has the answers able to overturn all reasonings that are
not of God.

4. Missing the Mark—Falling into Sin.

When a dispute broke out between the Israelites and the tribe of
Benjamin, it was said of the latter's left-handed slingmen of Gibeah,
'they could sling a stone, and not miss by a hair's breadth'. (Judges
20:16 REB.) In other words, they did not miss the mark or the target,
which is the idea behind some of the Greek words for 'sin' – 'to
miss the mark' of perfection of aim and accomplishment.[8]

Within the total idea of sin, trespass or transgression, the illustration of missing the mark can only be applied to certain aspects of
sinning. There is an endeavour to hit the target, but something
prevents its attainment. We can sub-divide these Greek words into
fairly precise groupings:

1. Missing the mark by failure, a falling short. The apostle Paul ex-
    plained the matter very simply when he said, 'All have missed the
    mark [Greek 'hamartanō] and have fallen short of God's glorious
    intention for them.' (Rom. 3:23 TNT.) God intended the human

race to remain perfect, but because of Adam and Eve's rebellion man fell into imperfection and fell short, or failed to reach the mark God had set.[9]

2. Missing the mark by a lapse or slip. In Romans 5:15 Paul refers to Adam's sin or trespass, and the Greek word here ('paraptōma') has the thought of a slip or a blunder, a falling to one side from the path, that causes the person to miss the mark, either due to carelessness or wilfulness. Similarly, the Israelites lapse opened the way for people of the nations to gain salvation too. (Rom. 11:11, 12.)[10]

3. Missing the mark by stumbling. We can stumble ourselves or others. 'We all of us make many mistakes [Greek 'ptaiō']. However, the man who never makes a mistake in what he says is perfect indeed.' (James 3:2 TNT.)

4. Missing the mark by a lack or shortcoming. Perhaps not taking an opportunity when it is presented. There is the other aspect of the Israelites' sin discussed in Hebrews chapter four. They missed the opportunity to enter into God's rest. 'The one thing we should fear is that any one of you should think he has missed [Greek 'hustereō'] his chance.' (Heb. 4:1 TNT.)

5. Missing the mark by ignorance of truth. One of the reasons for the existence of so many letters written by Paul is because he believed in the importance of communicating the truth, to make sure that his brothers knew about matters that seriously affected their spiritual welfare, and would prevent them from missing out, and so missing the mark and falling into some sin. So he begins a reference to a problem connected with the resurrection, 'And we would not have you miss the truth [Greek 'agnoeō'], brothers, regarding those who are falling asleep . . .' (1 Thess. 4:13 Smith.) Smith adds the footnote about such a situation, 'to be ignorant where one might and should have known'.[11] Similar expressions such as 'I do not wish you to ignore the fact, brothers . . .,' (Rom. 1:13 Smith) or 'Brothers, there is a hidden truth here, and I think you should know it . . .' (Rom. 11:25 TNT), often preface something Paul felt was a weighty truth they should not miss out on. (Rom. 6:3, 1 Cor. 10:1, 12:1, 2 Cor. 1:8.)

6. Missing the mark by swerving away, (Greek 'stochos', a mark, prefaced by 'a' to denote the negative, so 'astocheō'). Missing the

mark can be wilful. Rejecting truth for false knowledge, and deviating from the right, straight course, leads to the loss of a good conscience, and shows lack of love and faith. 'It is by missing [Greek 'astocheō'] these [lit. have missed the mark – Weymouth footnote] that some have swerved into futile talking.' (1 Tim. 1:6 Smith.) At the conclusion of that same letter, Paul added concerning false knowledge, 'It is by professing this that some have missed the mark in relation to the faith'. (1 Tim. 6: 21 Smith.) The Weymouth footnote says, 'Lit. have shot round about the target (of the true faith) but not hit it'.

In the second letter to Timothy, Paul names two of the apostates in his time, Hymenaeus and Philetus, and says of them, 'They have missed the mark in relation to the faith'. (2 Tim. 2:18 Smith.) Their bad example could also cause others to swerve away and fall into sin, or miss the mark of true faith.

Whilst the original missing of the mark related to failing to attain perfection, the Christian Greek Scriptures place the emphasis upon following the truth and having an unbreakable faith. But even in the Hebrew Scriptures it was finding God again that would save even an imperfect man. 'For whoever finds me finds life, and obtains the favour of Yahweh; but whoever misses me harms himself.' (Prov. 8:35, 36 NJB, cp. Acts 17:27.) Then the Psalmist brings us back to our illustration as he notes the failure of the Israelites as God's chosen people. 'But still they challenged the Most High God and defied him, refusing to keep his decrees; as perverse and treacherous as their ancesters, they gave way like a faulty bow.' (Ps. 78: 56, 57 NJB.) Our aim may be inaccurate as the arrow misses the mark, but if the bow itself is faulty, the very motive power deficient, then we cannot hope to hit the target.

Such was Israel's sad plight that they even came to reject the Messiah, so wide of the mark had they gone by the first century C.E. Their warning example should cause all professing Christians to examine their 'bow and arrows' or 'sling and stones', to review prayerfully and Scripturally whether they too might be missing the mark of truth and faith. Are we content with any kind of so-called Christian worship, or are we really searching for the full truth revealed in God's Word, the Bible?

5. To Cut Up the Road—A Hindrance.

Have you sometimes been driving your car quite happily along a clear road, and then had another car pass you, and cut in sharply in front of you? The natural reaction is to apply the brakes as your composure is suddenly shattered, and you perhaps utter imprecations under your breath.

Writing to the Galatians, Paul raised an interesting question and illustration. 'You were running well. Who cut in on you and thus hindered you from obeying the truth? This persuasion is not from the One who calls you.' (Gal. 5:7, 8 Wuest.) A. T. Robertson likens it to someone cutting in on our telephone conversation, and then notes the singular 'Who' (Greek 'tis'); 'There was some ringleader in the business'.[12]

That ringleader could be a human person, but Paul very likely identifies him when he writes to the Thessalonians, 'we set our heart on coming to you, indeed, I, Paul, not only once but twice, but Satan cut in on us and by that means thwarted us.' (1 Thess. 2:18 Wuest.)

The word 'cut in on' (Greek 'enkoptō'), was originally a military metaphor meaning, 'to break up a road by destroying bridges etc.,' and Fritz Rienecker adds, 'used of breaking up a road to render it impassable and later it was used in a military sense of making a break through the enemy's line. It was also used in the athletic sense of cutting in on someone during a race.'[13]

Satan is certainly intent on placing obstacles in our path, or breaking up our road ahead so that the going is no longer smooth and easy. Quite often he uses other people to cut in on us, and how easy it is for us to be offended by what someone says. We feel jangled, and our spiritual composure is threatened, we are thrown off our smooth forward course. Is that, though, going to hinder our progress in the truth, so that we fail to act in obedience of what we know to be right? Paul does not hesitate to tell us that such persuasion is not emanating from God or Jesus Christ.

So Paul's comments serve as a warning to us. By watching for any obstacles or hindrances on our road we can continue to make steady progress in the way of truth, not allowing anyone cutting in on us to upset our faith or spiritual balance. After explaining how he was pursuing the goal despite all hindrances, Paul concluded, 'At any rate, to what extent we have made progress, let us go on walking orderly in this same routine'. (Phil. 3:16 NWT.)

6. The Battle—The Fight to Uphold Truth.

The start of a battle is often the warning call to arms, and the apostle Paul uses this to introduce an interesting parallel: 'Unless the bugle notes are clear, who will be called to arms.' (1 Cor. 14:8 Phillips.) With a Christian's speech, it has to be clear and intelligible, so that everyone knows what he is talking about, otherwise, 'you might just as well be addressing an empty room'. (1 Cor. 14:9b Phillips.)

This is especially true where our hearers are firmly entrenched in wrong beliefs and ideas. Then the situation can truly be as Paul describes, 'Our battle is to break down every deceptive argument and every imposing defence that men erect against the true knowledge of God. We fight to capture every thought until it acknowledges the authority of Christ.' (2 Cor. 10:5 Phillips.)

Often the preaching of the good news may not be an easy task, so Paul admonished young Timothy to follow the pattern of a soldier, 'Proclaim the word, stick to your task, whether the conditions appear suitable or unsuitable.' (2 Tim. 4:2 Blackwelder.) The second phrase here is a word that 'was also used in a military sense; i.e. "to stay at one's post",' and not be side-tracked however bad the conditions might be.[14]

But that was no reason to simply waste ammunition by a pointless exchange of fire to no purpose, and this was why Paul also urged Timothy not to engage in 'word-battles' (Greek 'logomachia' – 1 Tim. 6:4 Blackwelder, Rotherham), with those who simply enjoy controversy and do not wish to arrive at the truth or sound doctrine. (1 Tim. 6: 3–5.)[15]

Paul had been involved in quite a number of controversies with opposers, so he could speak from experience when he counselled Timothy to tell his listeners, 'Charge them before God not to engage in battles about words, for such discussions yield nothing useful but only upset the hearers.' (2 Tim. 2:14 Blackwelder.) When emotions are involved, reason takes flight, but the truth of God's Word is based on reason and good logic, and that can flourish through constructive discussion and meditation.

7. Special Treasure, Top of the Heap— God's Own Possession.

When Abraham returned in triumph after defeating Chedorlaomer and his three associate kings, he was met by Melchizedek, King of Salem (later Jerusalem), who blessed him in the name of the Most High God, through whom he had gained the victory. In appreciation, Abraham gave him a tenth of the spoils he had taken. Why he did this is explained for us in Hebrews 7:4 (Amplified Bible), 'Now observe and consider how great [a personage] this was to whom even Abraham gave a tenth [the topmost or the pick of the heap] of the spoils.' What did this expression mean, 'the top of the heap'?

When an ancient city was captured its spoils were brought out and put into heaps. When something fine or valuable was discovered it was placed on top of a heap, so as to be displayed prominently to add to the rejoicing due to the capture of the city. It is rather like the greengrocer today who displays his fruit, often placing the best ones on top so as to advertise how fine are his wares. So to give as a tithe or tenth, 'the top of the heap', meant to part with the very best items, the most valuable, the 'first fruits', so to speak.[16] That alone was good enough for the Most High God, and Abraham (then still called Abram), was thus acknowledging God's part in the battle. Then he gave away all the remainder of the spoils so that no one could say Abraham had been made rich by the event. (Gen. 14:17–24.)

So the 'top of the heaps' came to express something special, a particularly fine portion of treasure, and here we can link it with another similar illustration. To the Ephesians the apostle Paul wrote, 'He [God] has let us know the mystery of his purpose . . . that he would bring everything together under Christ, as head . . . which brings freedom for those whom God has *taken for his own*, to make his glory praised.' (Eph. 1:9–14 JB.) Peter uses the same Greek word 'peripoiēsis' when he calls spiritual Israel 'a holy nation, a people to be *a personal possession* to sing the praises of God who called you out of the darkness into his wonderful light.' (1 Peter 2:9 NJB.)

Not only do we need to link in the Hebrew word for which the Septuagint translators chose the Greek equivalent, but also another closely related Greek word 'periousios', used in Titus 2:14, where Paul points out the importance of Christ's ransom in the arrangement. 'He offered himself for us in order to ransom us from all our faults and to purify a people to be *his very own* and eager to do good.' (NJB.) In the last two passages, the AV., uses the well-known term 'peculiar people', which originally occurs at Deuteronomy 14:2 and 16:18. In Exodus 19:5 and Psalm 135:4, Israel is called a 'peculiar treasure', and it is Peter who quotes the Exodus verse to apply it to spiritual Israel. The Hebrew word means 'to surround on all sides,' and thus 'to reserve, set apart, and appropriate'.[17]

Our English word 'peculiar' here owes its use to the Latin Vulgate's *peculium*. Until the seventeenth century it did not mean 'odd' or 'strange,' but rather 'belonging to a particular person or thing'. It referred to the private purse of a member of a family, even that of a slave who was allowed at times to gather something that belonged exclusively to him. For a king who had care of the public revenues it was even more important, it was the privy purse as distinct from the public treasury – his own special possession. (1 Chron. 29:3.) This is the 'peculiar treasure of kings' referred to in Ecclesiastes 2:8 AV. It was often the portion set aside as the share of the king before the rest of the spoils were distributed by lot or otherwise to the victorious army. Indeed it was 'the top of the heap'![18]

The nation of Israel was therefore the 'personal treasure', the 'special treasure' of Almighty God, but for a special purpose, to sing forth his praise, just as a notable person might have a special choir to sing for him, and to go before him to announce his coming. Spiritual Israel took on that privilege when they became 'God's own possession', to let their light shine to all nations.

So although God could truly say that 'all forest creatures are mine already, the animals on the mountains in their thousands, . . . the world and all it holds is mine.' (Ps. 50:10–12 NJB), and 'How countless are your works, Yahweh . . . the earth is full of your creatures' (Ps. 104: 24 NJB), yet he also has his own personal treasure, those who are 'the apple of my eye'. (Zech. 2:8 NJB, Deut. 32:9–14.)

Before all nations he publicly declares how much his own servants mean to him, those who have kept faith, and who are as precious as jewels in his sight. So he assures those who have been the 'light of the world' and sung forth his praise and glory, 'And they shall be Mine, says the Lord of hosts, in that day when I publicly recognize and openly declare them to be My jewels [My special possession, My peculiar treasure]. And I will spare them, as a man spares his own son who serves him.' (Mal. 3:17 Amplified.)

That intimate and personal relationship with God and his son Christ Jesus means their salvation. He surrounds them on all sides with his protection, for they are set aside, reserved for him personally as 'the top of the heap'. (Ps. 5:12, 32:7.)

Notes and References:

1. Lightfoot, J. B. *Notes on Epistles*, 299; Smith, D. *Life and Letters*, 413 and footnote; Pittman, R. T. *Words and Their Ways*, 17; Waugh, R. M. L. *Greek Testament*, 48, 49; Caragounis, C. C. 'Opsōnion: A Reconsideration of its Meaning.' *NovTest*. Vol. 16 (1974) 35–57. He considers that 'provisions' is a better translation than 'wages;' Ayers, D. M. *English Words*, 216, 217, traces our word 'salary' from this custom. Salt was included, for both seasoning and for promotion of good health, so this money came to be called 'salarium' (salt as in saline).

2. Webster, G. *The Roman Army, An Illustrated Study*, 1956, Chester, Grosvenor Museum; see also Howson, J. S. *Metaphors*, 22, 23; Cornfeld, G. Ed. *Josephus, The Jewish War Newly Translated* with extensive commentary and archaeological background illustrations, 1982, Grand Rapids, MN, Zondervan, 220; Brown, C. Ed. *NIDNTT*, Vol. 3, 965/6.

3. Cornfeld, G. op. cit (2) 220; Robinson, W. G. *N. T. Treasure*, 108; Howson, J. S. *Metaphors*, 27–29; Thayer, J. H. *Greek-English Lexicon*, 294; Arndt, W. F & Gingrich, F. W. *Greek-English Lexicon*, 365, 366 under thura and thureos.

4. Lightfoot, J. B. *Notes on Epistles*, 297, 'Sin is regarded as a sovereign who demands the military service of subjects, levies their quota of arms, and gives them their soldier's pay of death.'

5. Ward, R. A. *Hidden Meaning*, 79; Lightfoot, J. B. *On a Fresh Revision of the English N. T.*, 1872, 2nd ed. Macmillan, 143, 'our translators . . . appear not to have seen that this expression continues the metaphor of the campaign and the fortresses in the context, and that the reference is to the siege works thrown up for the purpose of attacking the faith.'

6. The context here might suggest that the Word of God is the personal Logos, but Westcott, B. F. *The Ep. to the Hebrews*, 1889, Macmillan, 101–103, considers that 'he cannot properly be likened to the sword' itself; Bruce, F. F. *Commentary on The Ep., to the Hebrews*, 1965, Marshall, Morgan & Scott, 80, 81, considers any personification to be 'slight.' But it is just possible that the writer intended a double meaning by a play on words. Howson, J. S. *Metaphors* 30, notes the interesting point that the Christian is only authorised to use one offensive weapon, the spiritual sword. There is no mention in Ephesians 6 of the Roman pike, or great pilum.

7. Webster, G. *The Roman Army*, (op. cit. 2) 25.

8. Trench, R. C. *Synonyms*, 231–240, still an important discussion; Turner, N, *Christian Words*, 412–415, bringing Trench up to date; Waugh, R. M. L. *Greek Testament*, 47–50.

9. Barclay, W. *N. T. Words*, 118f; Yahuda, J. *Hebrew is Greek*, 270, 271, 476.

10. Earle, R, *Word Meanings*, 163 for a very good analysis; Robertson, A. T. *Word Pictures*, Vol. 4, 359.

11. Smith, D. *Life and Letters*, 163 for footnote; Yahuda, J. *Hebrew is Greek*, 98, 451; Moulton & Milligan, *Vocabulary*, 4.

12. Robertson, A. T. *Word Pictures*, Vol. 4. 310.

13. Rienecker, F. & Rogers, C. *Linguistic Key*, 593; Pittman, R. T. *Words and Their Ways*, 19; Smith, D. *Life and Letters*, 213 ftn; Robertson, A. T. *Word Pictures*, Vol. 4. 23, 24.

14. Rienecker, F & Rogers, C, *Linguistic Key,*, 647; Pope, R. M, *Studies*, 102–109, appropriately entitled, 'The Perpetual Opportunity.'

15. Trench, R. C. *Study of Words*, 211; Howson, J. S. *Metaphors*, 31–36.

16. Humphry, W. G. *A Commentary on the Revised Version of the N. T.* 1888, new ed. SPCK, 413; Wordsworth, C. *Greek Testament*, Vol. 2. 401, 'from the prime spoils'; Perschbacher, W. J. *Analytical Greek Lexicon*, 13.

17. Lightfoot, J. B. *On a Fresh Revision* . . . (op. cit. 5), 236, 237, 241, 'the private treasure which a person acquires by himself alone, as distinguished from that which he shares with others.'

18. Room, A. *Dictionary of Changes in Meaning*, 1986, Guild Publishing, 202 for quotation; Ayers, D. M. *English Words*, 225; Lightfoot, J. B. *On a Fresh Revision* . . . (op. cit. 5), 234–242.

Chapter 10

Nature and Creation

1. Sun-Tested—Pure and Flawless.

When we speak of a person displaying sincerity, we usually mean that what they say is stated honestly and without any intention to deceive. Yet we may still think that they are mistaken in their belief. So the term is applied to the way a person expresses himself rather than to the correctness of what he has said. But this is not the meaning that attaches to the word for 'sincerity' as it was used in the time of the early Christians.

Writing to the Philippians the apostle Paul said, 'This is my prayer: may your love grow deeper and deeper; may it overflow in knowledge and sensitiveness! Then you will approve only what is right, and when the Day of Christ comes you will be pure and flawless.' (Phil. 1:9, 10 TNT.) The word for 'pure' or 'sincere' (Greek 'eilikrinēs'), literally means 'sun-tested', examined by the light of the sun, as when a glass of wine is held up to the light, and its searching rays fail to discover any impurities in its texture or quality.

Or we can think of the Middle Eastern bazaars, with a multitude of tiny shops cluttered and hung about with so many wares that little light penetrates to the interiors. To see fully some cloth or garment it is necessary to bring it out for inspection by the light of the sun, checking for flaws in the material by holding it up to the light. Yet a third aspect will bring out the full thought of the illustration, to sift or sieve out all foreign matter until what is left is completely purged and pure.[1]

The idea conveyed by the Greek word is that of complete purity, as we might say – through and through, without alloy, not false in any respect, flawless, transparently genuine and faultless, without stain, blemish or taint. So Paul's comment to the Philippians meant that their faith and the truths they held would have been refined with the aid of holy spirit and flawless, and so they would only approve what was really right in God's eyes. Writing of God's Word, which Paul said they had not adulterated, he added, 'No, it is in its purity, it is just as God gave it, that we speak it . . .' (2 Cor. 2:17b Smith, Knox.) This conveys a much clearer sense than the many translations that simply refer to speaking sincerely, or out of sincerity.

The idea of complete purity comes through very prominently when Paul talks about removing the leaven of wickedness in keeping the Lord's supper. 'So let us keep festival, not with the old leaven, not with the leaven of wickedness and evil, but with the unleavened bread of purity and truth.' (1 Cor. 5:8 TNT.)

We are now in a position through this illustration to look at a verse in Peter's second epistle that translators have found extraordinarily difficult to make plain. Many speak of just 'sincere mind/minds' (Adams, Weymouth, NASB), others of 'unsullied mind/minds' (Goodspeed, Berkeley, C. B. Williams and Wuest), still others simply of 'honest thought' (NEB) or 'better feelings' (TCNT); a few are closer with 'pure minds' (Lamsa, Beck). The translation that captures the entire thought which we have seen embraced in this illustration of the meaning of the word is Ronald Knox's version, 'I write such letters as a reminder, to awaken in you your clear sense of the truth'. (2 Peter 3:1 Knox.)

If a Christian has really absorbed what God has spoken through his Word the Bible, he can arrive at a position where he has mentally come to have a 'clear sense of the truth'. His mind is not just 'unsullied', that is, clean of wrong ideas, but it is also filled with the positive, right and pure ones. So it is not just 'clear thinking' or an 'unclouded understanding' but it needs to be qualified that it is true as well as clear. The word 'sense' which Knox adds also suggests something beyond mere knowledge. It gives the thought of the total internal harmony of that truth, a reasoning on it which makes sense.[2]

To look again at the illustration, it is as if the material of truth is carefully woven together, and the interlaced warp and weft is without fault, so that when it is held up to the light of God's truth from his Word, what is in the mind fully stands the test. There has been a successful transference of that truth into the individual person's own mind, and he is brought into complete harmony with his Creator – he is of the same mind and thought. (1 Cor. 1:10, Phil. 2:2.)

2. Moon and Stars, Meteors and Planets— Don't Be Misled.

The result of observing the heavens is evident in the formation of a number of Greek words. But when most of these are used in the Bible, the metaphor is dead. Nevertheless, the illustration is sometimes still latent in the thought pattern, and by bringing it out the meaning of the idea is heightened.

Matthew twice uses the word 'moonstruck' in relation to a particular case, and of several persons brought for Jesus to cure. (Matt. 4:24, 17:15.) Many translations render the word as 'epileptic' since the symptoms for this are similar. But other translations, taking a variant reading, associate the idea with a mental derangement or supernatural influence, similar to our modern word 'lunatic'. Though the metaphor is dead, it seems to take a long time lying down![3]

There is just one case where the word occurs from which we derive the name meteor, with the basic meaning of something suspended in mid air. Jesus told his listeners, 'cease seeking what to eat and what to drink and cease living in suspense [Greek 'meteōrizō'].' (Luke 12:29 Robertson.) When someone is worried or anxious over something they sometimes say, 'I feel all uncertain and up in the air'. [4] The picture in the word warns us not to let ourselves be tossed about so that we no longer have a balanced judgment, to keep our 'feet on the ground'.

Paul often told his hearers not to be misled or led astray, and Jesus and James used the same Greek word 'planētēs' from which we derive our word 'planet'. (1 Cor. 15:33, Gal. 6:7, Matt. 24:4, Mk 12:27, James 1: 16, 17.) Sadler renders this literally in a footnote 'Be not planet-struck'. What was the picture behind the statement? It had been observed by early astronomers that certain bodies wandered or roamed about the sky, appearing in different positions, whereas stars were generally fixed in position. A planet, then, was a wanderer, and by extension someone who could deceive or mislead.

If you were metaphorically struck by such a person you would be misled too.[5]

This word is also used in Jude 13, in a genuine live simile, but referring to stars rather than planets. Those that have followed the course of Cain, Balaam and Korah are 'like shooting stars [Greek 'aster planētēs'] bound for an eternity of black darkness'. (JB.) This was toned down to 'wandering stars' in the more accurate *New Jerusalem Bible*. But the conclusion about going into darkness does lend support to the idea of a shooting star.[6] What a graphic warning to help us to avoid following ones who mislead and deceive!

3. The Daystar—Bringing Light to Mankind.

The association of a star with the coming Messiah commenced early in the Bible writings, for Numbers 24:17 prophesied, 'I see him – but not in the present, I perceive him – but not close at hand: a star is emerging from Jacob, a sceptre is rising from Israel . . .' (NJB) Although applicable to David in the literal kingdom of Israel, the Aramaic Targum used the word 'Messiah' for sceptre, and so pointed forward still further.

Mention of the dawn and the dayspring are found linked with the illustration of the star. John the Baptist, as the forerunner of Jesus, was to make the way ready, as foretold by his father Zechariah. He was to give knowledge of salvation to the Jews, 'when the day shall dawn upon us from on high, to give light to those who sit in darkness and in the shadow of death.' (Luke 1:78b, 79a RSV.) The word here for dawn (Greek 'anatolē') means 'dayspring' or 'daybreak', the first streak of daylight seen in the night sky, springing up as it were.[7] That Jesus Christ realized such hopes was made clear by noting the fulfilment of the prophecy of Isaiah 9:1, 2, in Matthew 4:13–17.

The final book of the Bible draws these ideas together in these words, 'I Jesus . . . I am Myself both the Root and the Offspring of David, the brilliant Morning Star.' (Rev. 22:16 Berkeley; 'the bright star of Dawn' – NEB; 'the bright star that brings in the day' – Knox.)

The illustration is a very vivid one. It was first explained to me by an old soldier from the days of the British presence in India. Frank Marshall told me how he loved to have the last sentry duty of the night, for then he could see the bright daystar rise up, and the first streaks of day follow, gradually breaking into full light with the sunrise.

The ancient astronomers did not realize that the morning and evening stars were the same planet Venus at different elongations, so they gave it two names, Phosphorus and Hesperus. So bright is the reflection of the star-like planet that at times it can be seen with the naked eye in broad daylight, and against a dark sky it can cast a distinct shadow on any white surface.[8]

The illustration in the Greek Scriptures identifies Christ Jesus as the bright daystar or morning star, an object that could be picked out from a very early time for those informed in Bible prophecy. But he is also the dayspring or light of dawn, and even the 'sun of righteousness' bringing healing to mankind. (Malachi 4:2.) So John could well describe Jesus as the 'true light,' and when the true light is shining the darkness is already passing away. (John 1:4–9, 1 John 2:8. – see chapter 4, # 1.)

Writing to the Ephesians, the apostle Paul refers to everything being made open and manifest by the light, and then adds, 'Wake up, sleeper, Get up from the Dead, and Christ will make day dawn on you.' (Eph. 5:14 C. B. Williams.) Then in the words addressed to those who conquer in the Congregation of Thyatira is the promise, 'and I will give him the morning star.' (Rev. 2:28 RSV.)

The illustration receives its finest application in the apostle Peter's words, where he first talks about the value of the prophetic word. 'And so, we have the prophetic word more firm, to which you do well to take heed, in your hearts (as to a lamp shining in a dark place, till the day dawn, and the day star may arise).' (2 Peter 1:19 Estes, *The Better Version*, also the *Companion Bible*) Notice the contrast; the word of ancient prophecy is like a lamp, but Christ finally brings the full light of millennial day by fulfilling many of those prophecies as the Messiah ruling as king.

Many translations attach the words 'in your hearts' to the rising of the daystar, but this would suggest that the lamp of prophecy had no effect on the hearts of early Christians, and that they would have to wait until the 'day dawns'. But we know they had every confidence in the fulfilment of prophecy, and they held aloft that shining lamp to all those in darkness around them. As the *Companion Bible* says, the daystar arising was 'not a spiritual experience'.

This is further confirmed by the link with the transfiguration scene, which pointed to the glorious appearing of Christ in the second advent as a confirmation of that prophetic word, and this is also the subject of the third chapter of Second Peter. This was not merely to be an individual experience at different times in the hearts of Christians, but would happen when that day dawned, and the Messiah King took his sceptre of power to reign.[9]

4. Light and Darkness—The Christian's Fight.

The contest between light and darkness is an oft-repeated illustration in the Scriptures, especially in connection with Jesus, for he identified himself in this way, 'I am the light of the world. Whoever follows me shall by no means be walking in darkness. No, he shall have the life-giving light guiding him.' (John 8:12 Cassirer.)

At other times in his discourses, Jesus introduces this illustration, sometimes without any warning switching into it in the middle of quite normal conversation. 'I have come into the world as light, so that no one believing in me should remain in darkness.' (John 12:46 Cassirer.) That suggested the victory described by John in the very first chapter; 'the light which shines on in the darkness, and the darkness failing to gain mastery over it.' (John 1:5 Cassirer.)

So there is a battle between light and darkness, and men that love one usually hate the other. 'Men preferred darkness to the light because their doings were evil.' Jesus explained that this was because they were fearful that their secret and hidden actions would be exposed to view. (John 3:19–21 Cassirer.)

Paul takes up the same illustration and extends it to the time of Christ's second coming or presence. Then Christ would 'bring to light what is hidden in darkness and will lay bare the springs of action by which the minds of men have been guided.' (1 Cor. 4:5 Cassirer.) At the same time there can be a beneficial result for those with a receptive heart, 'It is the God who said, "Let light shine out of darkness", who has shone into our hearts for the spreading abroad of the light sent forth by the revelation of God's glory, even as it is seen upon the face of Christ.' (2 Cor. 4:6 Cassirer.)

The result is that 'while there was a time when you were all darkness, you are all light now that you are in union with the Lord. Rule your lives, then, as men native to the light.' (Eph. 5:8 Cassirer.) Writing to the Thessalonians, he ties in the sleep associated with night and darkness. 'No, you are, one and all, an offspring of the light, an offspring of the day. We do not belong to either night or darkness. Well then, let us not sleep like the rest of mankind, but let us keep watchful, let us keep sober.' (1 Thess. 5:5, 6 Cassirer.)

There remains an aspect that has puzzled many readers. The man without a wedding garment, and the worthless servant who did not use his talent are cast out 'into a place far away in which darkness reigns, where there shall be weeping and gnashing of teeth'. (Matt. 22:13, 25:30, 8:12 Cassirer.) Is this just literal darkness outside the bright lights of the wedding feast, or is it an 'outer darkness' as many translations have traditionally rendered it? Turner does not think that Jesus meant to distinguish between an inner and an outer darkness, but suggests that the comparative sense of the adjective is often intended to stand for the superlative sense. 'More likely that he [Jesus] envisaged an ever-increasing intensity of it as the sinner moves further from God's presence, and that he was warning the Jews of the danger facing them.' (Matt. 8:12.) So he would translate this, 'out into darkest darkness'. (cp. Jude 13.)[10]

5. Casting a Shadow—The Certainty of the Reality.

The illustration of the shadow usually appears in the Greek Scriptures when there is a reference back to the Mosaic Law covenant. So the Levite priests are described as 'men who devote their service to the type and the shadow of what has its true being in heaven'. (Heb. 8:5a Knox.) The type introduces a separate illustration with subtle differences which will be discussed under our next heading 'Type or Model'.

A shadow necessarily suggests an object which casts that shadow. Further, we know that the object has to first exist before it can cast a shadow, so how do we understand the Mosaic Law as being a shadow of something future, not yet present? It may best be likened to a person entering a shadow so huge that he cannot at first see or comprehend what it is that is throwing the shadow. He has to walk through the area of shadow, examining its outline and form, before he finds the object itself. So it was with the nation of Israel. They had to walk through a period of history, and their experience and appreciation of the form and nature of the shadow should have enabled them to immediately recognize the reality when they came to it. The apostle Paul clearly identified the reality when he said, 'all these [festivals, sabbaths etc.,] were but shadows cast by future events, the reality is found in Christ.' (Col. 2: 17 Knox.)

The Law was given to Israel to lead them to the Messiah, to bridge over the period that came between in the outworking of God's purpose for mankind. As a nation they failed to see the reality, except for a remnant, although the shadow in which they had walked gave them a much better opportunity than other nations enjoyed. They became too much engrossed with the shadow itself, and actually mistook it for the reality, so that they still continue to this day performing its rites and rules. It is the reality that counts, as the Epistle to the Hebrews so well expresses it, 'what the law contains is only the shadow of those blessings which were still to come, not the full expression of their reality.' (Heb. 10:1a Knox.) The reality brings with it the true and full blessings from God.

The word for shadow here (Greek 'skia'), has been much discussed as to its meaning. Some scholars have preferred the idea of a sketch or outline, something preparatory to the finished work, just as when an artist works up a rough sketch, or a sculptor makes a cast of wax or wood which he throws away when the real work is finished.[11]

But when we look at matters from God's own viewpoint we know that the finished work, the reality of the blessings of God's Kingdom and everything connected with his purpose, has been clearly there from the beginning. (Gen. 3:15.) So there is a danger that we might think in terms of man's limitations, first needing a rough sketch or outline before we can produce the reality in a suitable form. Similarly, we tend to talk about 'God's plan' as if he first needed to make one before being able to produce the reality. So 'shadow' does adequately convey the point of the illustration, and after all, what is a shadow but a mere outline, a silhouette, giving a general shape in flat form, unclear and indistinct. But its essential counterpart is the actual existence of the body or object throwing the shadow, and this fulfils all that Scripture suggests. But it required the faith of men such as Abraham to see that the reality did already exist, though they only saw it in shadowy outline. (Heb. 11:9, 10, 13–16.)

The most powerful aspect of this illustration is given by the disciple James in a verse that has caused many problems for translators. The last phrase incorporates a compound form of our word 'shadow' (Greek 'aposkiasma'). 'All God's gifts are good, and every perfect gift comes from above, from God the Father who created the heavenly lights. He never varies, nor turns away from us and leaves us in the shadow.' (James 1:17 TNT, Barclay.)[12]

That promise only confirms what the light of Christianity has brought about. God's purpose is clearly delineated today through the full canon of God's Word the Bible, and we are no longer dependant on the shadows of the past, but can walk in the full light that comes from that Word, and that proves to be a sure guide for those who trust in it and have the faith of Abraham.

6. Type or Model—A Pattern to Follow.

When a fashion show takes the floor, all eyes watch the models as they appear. Whatever the clothes may be, it is seeing them on the various types of individual that enables us to sum up the whole effect, and make a judgment upon them.

This is the idea behind the Biblical word for model or type (Greek 'tupos'). Its basic idea is brought out in John 20:25, where Thomas said he would not believe in Jesus' resurrection unless he saw the prints ('tupos') of the nails in his hands. Those marks were made by the blows that fixed the nails, and so by extension a figure, seal or model carved out by a tool can be embedded in wax, and leave a faithful impression there.[13]

Just as in the fashion show, it is the individual servants of God who so often form our types or models to follow today. Each one is different in make-up or personal form, and he appears before us clothed in a different set of circumstances. Different aspects of his course of faithfulness may be drawn to our attention as especially recommending him, but it is his entire life course that sets a pattern for us to follow, for us to model ourselves upon.

So Paul urged those in the congregations he had helped to establish, 'Agree together, my friends, to follow my example. You have us for a model; watch those whose way of life conforms to it.' (Phil. 3:17 NEB.) In the same way he counselled Timothy and Titus to be fine models or examples, and Peter recommended the same course to all elders or overseers of the flock of God. (1 Tim. 4:12, Titus 2:7, 1 Peter 5:3.) Even the fine example of the Thessalonian congregation had become such a model to follow. (1 Thess. 1:7.) But Christ Jesus was the perfect model to imitate. (1 Cor. 11:1.)

But individual persons or even groups do not exhaust the idea of Biblical types or models. Paul looked at certain events in Israelite history and stated this significant principle, 'Now these things which happened to our ancestors are illustrations of the way in which God works, and they were written down to be a warning to us who are living in the final days of the present order.' (1 Cor. 10:11 Phillips rev. ed.) So the Hebrew Scriptures contain a vast number of types or illustrations which can benefit Christians who look to those events and situations as models. (cp. also 2 Peter 2:6, and James 5:10, 11 using a related word 'hupodeigma'.)

Sometimes this typology involves contrasts as well as similarities, and the case of Adam is one that Paul draws particular attention to. 'Now the first man is a "type" of the Man who is to come, but his "typical" character is limited, for God's gift of grace is not on all fours with the original fall.' (Rom . 5:14b, 15a Bruce.) In the remainder of the chapter Paul draws out the contrasts between Adam and Christ in a set of interesting parallels that nicely illustrate the application of type and antitype.[14]

A final variation of this illustration is found in Paul's words to Timothy, 'Follow the pattern of the sound words which you have heard from me, in the faith and love which are in Christ Jesus; guard the truth that has been entrusted to you by the Holy Spirit . . .' (2 Tim. 1:13, 14 RSV.) The word 'pattern' is literally 'under-type' (Greek 'hupotupōsis'). This has been likened to the weaving of a carpet, where the motif and theme are worked out in a consistent and methodical outline throughout, with well-balanced design and harmonious colourings. So Paul's counsel to Timothy had in mind 'to show how the parts of the pattern were related, and how they converged on the centre – to bring to light the evidence of God's consistent purpose in history.'[15]

The whole superb illustration comes together in the idea of the blacksmith at work on his anvil. With his hammer he strikes blows on the metal he is shaping and forming, using the anvil as the base or type which plays a vital part in the process. This is shown by this description of an actual ancient smithy in Lynton, North Devon, now a museum; 'The hammer weighs about two pounds, and the blacksmith relies on a good anvil (about 3 cwt.), with spring so that every blow gives a rebound helping towards the next strike of the hammer. To help this spring the anvil is mounted on a tree stump.' All the productions of the blacksmith reflect a pattern as his skills are applied, and the clang of the blows rings true and marks the quality of his work. So the types and pictures in the Hebrew Scriptures form the anvil or springboard upon which the Christian pattern is formed. With the type and the antitype the message is formed by God, the Master Blacksmith, using holy spirit, and it takes shape, confirmed by the ring of truth. So Paul's counsel is sound for Christians today – 'Follow the pattern, . . . guard the truth'.[16]

7. Character and Image—The Perfect Copy.

When Paul talks about Christ being 'in the image of God' what does he really mean? (2 Cor. 4:4, Col. 1:15.) The word 'image' (Greek 'eikōn'), does not in itself carry the idea of perfection, but suggests a likeness or resemblance. Man is therefore in the image of Adam in that he bears a likeness to him. (1 Cor. 15:49.) Adam was in the image of God in his essential qualities. (Gen. 1:26, 27.)

For a more precise description of Christ we can turn to the opening of the Epistle to the Hebrews. There Christ is described in these words, 'He is the exact impression of his being, just as the mark is the exact impression of the seal.' (Heb. 1:3, Barclay.) The 'exact impression' is the Greek word 'charaktēr', and the mark which Barclay draws out as a paraphrastic parallel is the related word 'charagma', which is used in Revelation 14:9, 11, 15:2, 16:2, 19:20, 20:4 as the mark of the beast.

Thanks to discoveries amongst the ancient papyri, this word has been found used in connection with remains of stamps or seals, one of which Adolf Deissmann reproduced, and which reads, '35th year of Caesar'. The uncial lettering is set in a circle, and this was the imperial seal of Augustus, attached, often in red, to bills of sale and other official or autograph documents, to make them legal. The mark or charagma of the beast therefore, identified those stamped with it as belonging officially to him.[17]

From this the word 'charaktēr' came to mean a distinctive and individual impression or reproduction which is precise in every respect, a perfect and exact replica or facsimile, as made by a seal impressed on clay or wax.[18] So the Son of God was a perfect representation of his Father, knowing and understanding him fully, and able to speak for him as if God himself was making the pronouncement, and so he is also called the Logos, the spokesman for God, always perfectly expressing his Father's will and purpose.

The one single use of this word in Hebrews is designed to set apart the Son of God from all other impressions or reproductions, but by contrast we often find the word 'image' (Greek 'eikōn'), used in the Scriptures. In the well known discussion with Jesus when he requested that a coin be shown, and asked whose image it displayed, he was referring to the impression of Caesar's head in the metal. (Matt. 22:20.) Whether the image on the coin was accurate or not, flattering or derogatory, it showed the likeness sufficient for the purpose.

The apostle Paul used the idea in Genesis 1:26 to suggest the remoulding of the fallen image of man, so as to raise it up and begin to bring it back again to what God originally intended. To do this the Christian has to put on the new personality, altering his mind and qualities, and cultivating the fruitage of the Spirit. 'You have put on a new self which will progress towards true knowledge the more it is renewed in the image of its Creator.' (Col. 3:10 NJB, Eph. 4:23, 24.)[19] That means rejecting the mark of the beast, but being willing to have God make his mark or impression on us.

But it is when he writes to the Corinthians that Paul most successfully uses the illustration, combining it with another, that of the mirror. This is because he draws on the events where Moses came down from the mountain and his face reflected God's glory so much that he had to veil it until it gradually faded. Yet that veil was really upon the Israelite's hearts and linked with the Mosaic Law covenant now fulfilled and replaced, so Christ lifted the veil out of the way, and brought in true freedom. Then Paul is ready to make his grand conclusion. 'But all of us who are Christians have no veils on our faces, but reflect like mirrors the glory of the Lord. We are transformed in ever-increasing splendour into his own image, and this is the work of the Lord who is the Spirit.' (2 Cor. 3:18 Phillips.) That reflection does not fade, but is an inner permanent transformation that brings a person's entire character (used in our modern sense) into line with God's intended image, one of true glory like the rest of God's creation. (1 Cor. 11:7.)

8. Multi-Coloured—
The All-Embracing Wisdom of God.

One of the archaic expressions in the King James' Authorised Version that is remembered with some amusement by most people is that of 'divers diseases'. It has no reference to 'the bends'! Modern translations use such expressions as 'different diseases' or 'various diseases', but the Greek word used for 'divers' ('poikilos') hides a striking illustration far more colourful than is conjured up by 'different' or 'various'.

The full breadth of meaning gradually dawns upon us as we examine its use in the ancient Septuagint Version. There is Joseph's coat of many colours, ('variegated robe' – Thomson LXX), and the speckled and variegated animals in Jacob's flock. For the gorgeously coloured gold, blue, purple and scarlet embroidery in the furnishings of the Tabernacle the term is also used, as well as for the richly variegated stones that David collected for the decoration of the Temple. (Gen. 30:37, 39, 40, 31:8, 10, 12, 37:3, 23, 32, Ex. 26:36, 28:6, 15, 39, 35:35 etc. 1 Chron. 29:2, Job 38:36 LXX.)

From the papyri come other uses of the word, such as many-coloured house decorations, and tattoo-markings. By definition the word can include all the colours of the rainbow, the prism, the plaid and tartan, the veined, mottled and marbled, the spotted, speckled and striped, and inlaid and tessellated mosaic. Such a richly woven pattern also implies intricacy and complexity, yet always in nature with wonderful harmony of colour.[20]

When we come to the one occasion in the Bible where the word 'polupoikilos' is used, how can it be described if already the word 'poikilos' implies such a splendid tapestry of variegated colour? It is found in Ephesians 3:10, where the apostle Paul, in the latter part of the verse, says that 'there might be made known through the congregation the greatly diversified ['polupoikilos'] wisdom of God'. (NWT.) Other translations try to catch the tremendous scope of meaning in the word by using 'many-splendoured' (Bruce), 'all-embracing' (TCNT), 'intricate pattern' (Wand), 'infinite variety' (REB), 'much-variegated' (Wuest), or 'many-sided' (Adams, Beck, NJB, TNT).

How well the rich, dazzling display of many-coloured embroidery, or in nature the variegated plumage of exotic birds, conveys to our senses a little of the Creator's glory and wisdom. This is displayed through the Christian congregation as it expounds and makes known all that God has revealed of that splendour in his Word, of God's marvellous purpose for heaven and earth, and the unveiling of his sacred secret previously hidden from mankind. Even the angels observe this outstanding declaration of God's infinite wisdom. Just two verses earlier a reflection of it is caught in the reference to the 'boundless riches of Christ'. (TNT.)

That Christians have the opportunity of displaying something of all this word conveys is shown by Peter's statement, 'Serve one another with the particular gifts God has given each of you, as faithful dispensers of the wonderfully varied ['poikilos'] grace of God'. (1 Peter 4:10 Phillips.) Often in the weakness and humility of men that unmerited kindness of God can be seen to have its greatest power and variety, and through the application of the fruits of the Spirit, as Paul himself demonstrated. (2 Cor. 12:9, 1 Cor. 12: 28–31, Gal. 5:22, 23.) As we recognize the true source of such varied gifts, we give God all the praise for whatever benefits flow from our right use of them.

9. Hot or Cold—The Need for Zeal.

Writing to the Laodicean congregation, John used a very forceful illustration. 'I know what you are doing, and that you are neither cold nor hot. I wish you were either cold or hot! As it is, since you are tepid and neither cold nor hot, I am going to spit you out of my mouth!' (Rev. 3:15, 16 Goodspeed.) Those who read John's words knew very well what he was talking about, for there were hot springs near Laodicea, and a Roman aqueduct which brought hot water for six miles from Hierapolis to Laodicea, but by then its temperature was only tepid.[21]

This congregation was just a typical one, not only for some in John's day, but pointing forward to our day also. Is your congregation one that is apathetic, lethargic, half-hearted, sluggish, and indifferent towards the action that Christianity calls for? Do its members sit on the fence when it comes to giving out the good news, or act positively for truths that are central to the stand of a Christian? Those truths should be used in such a way that others see them as refreshingly cool, or they are moved by our zeal.

The word 'hot' (Greek 'zestos'), is drawn from the verb 'zeō', meaning 'to boil' and so to be zealous. But there can be a misplaced zeal, as was demonstrated by that hot-headed group in Jesus' time known as The Zealots.[22] So we have to let God's Word promote our motivation and spiritual growth in the right direction, and Jesus set the example in being able to do this. On the road to Emmaus the disciples said to each other, 'Did not our hearts glow when he was talking to us on the road, and was explaining the Scriptures to us?' (Luke 24:32 Goodspeed.)[23] Apollos was one such disciple of whom it is recorded, 'He had been well-instructed in the cause of the Lord, and with burning zeal he spoke of, and taught carefully, the facts about Jesus, though he knew of no baptism but John's.' (Acts 18:25 TCNT.) Notice that although he was still learning, what he had been taught he relayed with care and yet zealously. So his zeal did not mean he was not balanced, steady and reasonable. But he was bubbling inside, aglow with the Spirit, full of enthusiasm, yet not dogmatic or intolerant.

The apostle Paul also warned Christians, 'Do not put out the fire of the spirit.' (1 Thess. 5:19 NWT.) Then writing to Timothy about the faith he had developed through the devotion and training of his mother and grandmother, he added, 'For this very cause I remind you to stir up like a fire the gift of God which is in you . . .' (2 Tim. 1:6 NWT.) Those may seem to be almost contradictory thoughts, but think a little more about the illustration.

If you have an open fire in your home, have you sometimes taken the poker and given it a good stir? That sifts out the dead ash and causes the smouldering embers to burst once more into flame – it gives it a fresh initiative and life, and soon its brightness and heat will reward us for our action. As imperfect human creatures we can so easily begin to tail off spiritually as the ash of this present evil world surrounds us with its ways and attitudes. We need a spiritual poking or encouragement from time to time for the flames to burst out afresh to give light and warmth to others. (Heb. 10:23–25.)[24]

But sometimes we can pour cold water on the fire, which puts it right out. Or we may load it up with logs or coal without creating any draught to fan the dying embers, and the result is the same. The Spirit (or draught) has to have opportunity to work in us, but if we let ourselves be damped down by worldly and materialistic ways, we can become so overloaded that the Spirit is quenched altogether. No wonder Paul said, 'Don't slacken in diligence, be aglow in spirit, serving the Lord.' (Rom. 12:11 Adams.)[25]

So will we be like Jeremiah the prophet, whose spirit was brought low because of the persecution he received, the jeering and reproach which came upon him? He decided he would not speak out for God any more, 'but then there seemed to be a fire burning in my heart, imprisoned in my bones. The effort to restrain it wearied me, I could not do it.' (Jer. 20:9 NJB.) If we truly have God's spirit, we will not be silent or lukewarm, like the Laodicean congregation, but will zealously and enthusiastically tell out all the purpose of God.

10. Uncut Time, The Atom— An Instantaneous Change.

The temptations of Jesus by the Devil are recorded in both Matthew and Luke. One of these gave Jesus a view of all the kingdoms of the world, offering them to him if he would render just a single act of worship to the Devil. But only in Luke's record is a time element mentioned, 'Then the devil took Him up and showed Him all the kingdoms of the world in a split second [Greek 'stigmē'].' (Luke 4:5 Anderson.)

This Greek word has the idea of a prick or pinpoint, a dot of time, 'like our "second" of time or tick of the clock'. A. T. Robertson goes on to describe this panoramic view as 'mental, a great feat of the imagination (a mental satanic "movie" performance).'[26] In his translation he describes it as a 'second of time', yet even this may be too long to properly represent a tiny pinprick of time. The term is in any case merely illustrative in suggesting the briefest, speediest snapshot we could imagine. So the *New English Bible* uses 'in a flash'.

But when we turn to quite a different passage where Paul is describing the resurrection, it is somewhat disconcerting to find the *New English Bible* using the very same expression for a quite different Greek word. 'Listen! I will unfold a mystery: we shall not all die, but we shall all be changed in a flash [Greek 'atomos'], in the twinkling of an eye, at the last trumpet call.' (1 Cor. 15:51, 52, NEB.) Anderson also uses his same term 'in a split second, in the blink of an eye.'

Are the two terms used here meant to be synonymous? It would seem that they are not, for while the twinkling of an eye seems to have much in common with a flash, a dot or pinpoint of time, the first one is the Greek word 'atomos', from which we get our only too well-known word 'atom'. So for this word Wuest paraphrases 'in an instant of time so small that it cannot be divided into smaller units,' or 'uncut time', (*Kingdom Interlinear*). G. W. Cornish even takes it out of the realm of time with his 'a timeless instant'. (*St. Paul from the Trenches.*)

The measurement of time has continued to undergo amazing refinements, so that the term 'split-second' has time and again taken on new meaning. At first chronographs and chronoscopes were able to measure by fifths of a second, then tenths of a second, and finally thousandths of a second by means of a vibrating metal reed. By eliminating all mechanical movements, and using sparks, and later a beam of electrons, ten-thousandths of a second could be measured.[27]

Since then there has been the high precision quartz clock, the ammonia molecular clocks able to measure a frequency of 24 million cycles per second, maser clocks, and finally the atomic clock running on caesium atoms and ten times more accurate than the ammonia-maser. Now the 'second' seems antiquated, and is being replaced by the 'shake', a one hundred-millionth of a second, or one-hundredth of a microsecond.[28]

How does this affect what the apostle Paul wrote nearly two thousand years ago? It does not, but merely gives us perspective regarding the measurement of time. But we have to look at the view of the atom, or uncut time, as it was understood by Paul in his day.

Two Greek philosophers of the fifth century B. C. E., Leucippus and Democritus, developed the idea of the atom. They thought about finding the smallest piece of matter, cutting up materials until it was impossible to break them up any more – indivisible. The word for the result was 'atomos' – 'that which cannot be cut'. But no one could test the idea, and so it remained just a theory.[29]

This was Paul's meaning when he used the Greek word 'atomos'. He referred to the smallest uncut measurement of time then known, an instant of time, and he wanted his readers to think about the smallest particle of time possible. But then he added an illustration to make his meaning clearer; not exactly synonymous, but close enough for his purpose, to convey a very rapid and speedy event, far shorter than a second. So he described it as a 'blink of an eye'.

The Devil's snapshot of all the kingdoms of the world was very brief, the length of a flash. But the resurrection would be much quicker, an instantaneous one. And since God's power is greater than that of the Devil, it is reasonable to expect it would surpass all that anyone else might accomplish in cutting up time into the smallest particles or atoms.

11. Moving Mountains—Faith Removes Obstacles.

A mountain has often been viewed as a symbol of strength. Young David was well acquainted with the mountains of Judea, for they proved often to be a place of refuge for him when he fled from King Saul. So when he felt strong he came to associate the two ideas, and could say to God, 'You made me like a mighty mountain.' (Ps. 30: 7a Beck.)

To move something so strong and well-rooted therefore came to be proverbial. Among the Jews those teachers with profound learning were considered able to move mountains. 'They called Rabh Joseph Sinai, because he was very skilful in clearing of difficulties; and Rabbah Bar Nachmani, A rooter up of mountains, because he had a piercing judgment.'[30]

After Jesus had performed a miracle in driving out a demon from an epileptic boy, the disciples asked Jesus why they couldn't do that sort of thing. He said it was because their faith was not strong enough. If they had more faith, 'you will say to this mountain, "move from here to there," and it will move. Then you can do anything.' (Matt. 17:20 Beck.) When Jesus cursed the barren fig tree, they again wondered, and he repeated the illustration with the variation that this time the mountain could be thrown into the sea. (Matt. 21:21.)

Paul later picked up the same illustration, but gave it a new twist. 'Even if I have all the faith to move mountains, but don't have any love, I'm nothing.' (1 Cor. 13:2b Beck.) So moving mountains was not the most important thing. Nevertheless, faith with love as its foundation would be an excellent combination.

Of course, it might be literally possible for a man to move a mountain, and the rabbis had the answer. 'The wise man says, "I will carry off two loads by day and two loads by night and tomorrow I shall do likewise, till I shall have levelled the whole of it."' The comparison was then made with the person who wanted to master the law which was so voluminous and huge, like a mountain. The wise man would learn two laws a day until he had learned it all.[31]

But Jesus was clearly using an illustration, for there is a contrast with the amount of faith the size of a mustard grain. The mountain represented mighty obstacles that seemed to block a Christian's way, and these could only be moved by faith. Similarly, the preparation by John the Baptizer for the coming Messiah consisted of making a 'clear highway for him', including levelling every mountain and hill, metaphorically. (Luke 3:4, 5, Isa. 40:4.)

A further dimension can be added to the illustration by noting the situation when the Temple was being rebuilt in the time of Zerubbabel. He was told that the work could not be accomplished by human means. 'Not by might or by power, but by My Spirit, says the LORD of armies. What is a great mountain? Before Zerubbabel it shall be a plain.' (Zech. 4:6b, 7a, Beck.) Yes, it seemed that the opposition and the difficulties that Zerubbabel had to face were like a great mountain, but by God's spirit they would be overcome. Some scholars recall that the mountain in scripture often represents government or world powers, and that it was especially with political opposition that Zerubbabel had to contend. (Rev. 17: 9, 10.)[32]

In either case, it was the holy spirit of God that was all important to success. Jesus also relied heavily upon holy spirit and taught his disciples to do the same. That didn't reduce the importance of making their own faith stronger, for the spirit and its operation can be blocked by lack of faith. At the same time, it emphasizes that the real power that can move mountains both literal and metaphorical, is that of Almighty God himself, just as he through his spirit, brought into existence the literal mountains in the beginning. (Gen. 1:1, 2.)

12. Where Moths and Rust Prevail— Finding Lasting Treasure.

Among the many illustrations in Jesus' famous Sermon on the Mount is one about material wealth. 'Do not amass for yourselves treasures on earth where the moth eats them away, and the rust corrodes them, and thieves break in and steal.' (Matt. 6:19 Barclay.) Many people have been ruined by the sudden loss or theft of all their riches, and it has often broken or demoralized them, sometimes leading to suicide or an early death from mental breakdown.

Today there is great competition to provide the 'safe' method of investment, but banks and stocks and shares can vanish overnight, and companies can go into liquidation or prove fraudulent. Because some refuse to trust in banks they keep their money in a tin box under the bed, only to have their secret discovered, and their money disappear.

In Jesus' time it was popular to bury one's treasure, only to find it had become corroded with rust, or even that the hiding place had been forgotten. If a person died his heirs might not know where it had been hidden. A merchant in Bethlehem buried one of the Dead

Sea scrolls in his garden for safety while he tried to get a better price for it, but found it had just become a solid glutinous mass of no use to anyone.[33] A thief was often called by the Greeks a 'mud digger' because he would dig his way through the mud-brick wall of a house to break in and steal, or he would remove part of the roof to gain access.[34]

So Jesus advised his listeners to store their treasure in a heavenly place, as it were, where none of these problems could assail them, 'For your heart is found to be where your treasure is.' (Matt. 6:21 Barclay.) Ah, yes, that is the important root of the illustration. What have we set our heart upon? Is it material riches that can prove so transient, or spiritual ones that can win us God's approval, and which no one can take from us if we do not wish it?

The disciple James could have had Jesus' words in mind when he gave a similar warning, for he also mentions both moth and rust. Speaking to the rich men of the world he says, 'Your riches are destroyed and rotted, and your garments are motheaten. Your gold and silver are tarnished, and the rust of them will be a testimony against you, and will eat your flesh. The treasures which you have heaped together will be as fire to you for the last days.' (James 5:2, 3, Lamsa.)

The whole emphasis here is on the failure to use these riches to help the poor, or even for normal commercial purposes. This non-use for a long period has made them rot away, get moth-eaten, become tarnished and rusty, and that is the testimony of indictment against these rich men. That condemnation can be like something eating their very flesh, or burning them like fire. We recall Zacchaeus, who realized how he had extorted much of his wealth by unchristian principles, and only by making reparation could he avoid an adverse judgment, and prove his change of heart. But he did it happily, because he had suddenly realized where his heart should be, and which sort of treasure was really worth while. (Luke 19:1–10.)

But if we have no spiritual dimension, how can we come to appreciate that this is worth acquiring? Perhaps we need to sit down and meditate on which values are lasting and worthwhile. Which possessions give *true* happiness and satisfaction? Does not the possession of material things so often lead to a desire for more and more of them, far beyond what we may reasonably be able to use? Paul showed the excelling value of mental and spiritual contentment brought through Godly devotion, contrasted with the problems and worries of the love of money and the determination to be rich. (1 Tim. 6:6–10.)

Notes and References:

1. Barclay, W. *N. T. Words*, 66–68; Pope, R, M, *Studies*, 63–71; Kittel, G, Ed. *TDNT*, Vol. 2, 397, although Vol. 6, 486 rejects the idea; Smith, D. *Life & Letters*, 354 footnote which supports 'tested in the sunlight' etymology. Robertson, A. T. *Word Pictures*, Vol. 4, 437; Earle, R. *Word Meanings*, 331; Trench R. C. *Synonyms*, 306f; Trench R. C. *Study of Words*, 6; Daddow, W. B. *Buried Pictures*, 48–53, incl. p50, and the example of factories in the north of England which had 'south rooms' where the sun shone most brightly, and so materials could be held up to the light there to discover any defects; Simpson, E. K. *Words Worth Weighing* 29, 30.

2. Rienecker, F. & Rogers, C, *Linguistic Key*, 780.

3. J. M. Ross, 'Epileptic or Moonstruck?' *BT* Vol. 29 (1978), 126–128.

4. Skeat, W. W. *Etymological Dictionary*, 373; Robertson, A. T. *The Minister* 54, also 'tossed about in the air like a balloon. ' Pittman, R. T. *Words and Their Ways*, 36–38.

5. Skeat, W. W. *Etymological Dictionary*, 456.

6. Green, M, 2 *Peter & Jude*, 1968, Tyndale Press, 176.

7. Unger, M. F. *Unger's Bible Dictionary*, 1957, Chicago, Moody Press, 249; Robertson, A. T. *Word Pic-tures*, Vol. 2, 19. Yahuda, J, *Hebrew is Greek*, 178.

8. Brown, P. L. *Astronomy in Colour*, 1975, Blandford Press, 69; Davis, M. Ed. *Astronomy for Everyman*, 1954, Dent, 119.

9. Green, M. op. cit. (6), 87–89; Davidson, F, Ed. *New Bible Commentary*, 1954, 2nd ed, Inter-Varsity, 1146; Nicoll, W. R. Ed. *Expositor's Greek Testament*, Vol. 5, 131/2 discusses the grammatical alternatives, and favours the second advent understanding as giving most striking meaning to the metaphors.

10. Turner, N. *Grammatical Insights*, 58, 59.

11. Wordsworth, C. *Greek Testament*, Vol. 2, 410; Selwyn, E. G. *First Peter*, 298/9; Hurst, L. D, 'How 'Platonic' are Heb. 8:5 and 9:23f?' *JTS*, Vol. 34 (1983), 156–168, where hupodeigma is linked with skia to mean a sketchy outline.

12. Goodspeed, E. J. *Problems*, 189, 190; Adamson, J. B. *The Ep. of James*, (New Int. Comm. on N. T), 1976, Grand Rapids, Eerdmans, 75, 96/7, nothing can block God's light and put us 'in shadow. '

13. Moulton & Milligan, *Vocabulary*, 645; Kittel, G. Ed. *TDNT*, Vol. 8, 249–252; Turner, N, *Christian Words*, 168–171; Vincent, M. R. *Word Studies*, Vol. 1, 318; Bullinger, E. W. *Enjoy the Bible*, 241; Lee, E, K, 'Words denoting 'Pattern' in

the N. T.,' *NTStud.* Vol. 8 (1962), 169–171.

14. Antitype as used at 1 Peter 3:21, corresponding to the type, as set against it, so that the counterpart or parallel can be seen clearly. Kittel, G. Ed. *TDNT*, Vol. 8, 253–255. The word is used the other way round in Heb. 9:24, for here it was the tabernacle or temple arrangement that was set out to correspond with the already existing heavenly one. See also Selwyn, E. G. *First Peter*, 298/9; Lampe, G. W. H. & K. J. Woollcombe, *Essays on Typology*, 1957, SCM, 64.

15. Lampe, G. W. H. et al, op cit. 68; Turner N, *Christian Words*, 143/4; Lee, E, K, op. cit. (13), 171/2, 'a form outlined as the basis of further work.'

16. Kittel, G. Ed. *TDNT*, Vol. 8, 248.

17. Deissmann, G. A. *Bible Studies*, 240–247; Arndt & Gingrich, *Greek-English Lexicon*, 884; Ayers, D. M. *English Words*, 221/2, for the origin of the two different meanings associated with our English word 'character.'

18. Thayer, J. H. *Greek-English Lexicon*, 665; Pittman, R. T. *Words and Their Ways*, 54–55; NJB footnote 1975; Moulton & Milligan, *Vocabulary* 683; Kittel, G. Ed. *TDNT*, Vol. 9, 418–421.

19. Lightfoot, J. B. *Colossians*, 213/4.

20. Moulton & Milligan, *Vocabulary*, 523; Barclay, W, *N. T. Words*, 235–237, who ignored the Septuagint background, and missed completely the use of polupoikilos at Eph. 3:10; Yahuda, J, *Hebrew is Greek*, 96, Tabernacle coverings and ladies' shoes 'made of mottled, speckled and striped skins of gazelle, giraffe and zebra.'

21. Ramsay, W. M. *The Letters to the Seven Churches of Asia*, 1909,

Hodder, 413, 415; Swete, H. B. *The Apocalypse of St. John*, 1922, 3rd ed. Macmillan, 60; Pfeiffer, C. F. & H. F. Vos, *The Wycliffe Historical Geography of Bible Lands*, 1968, Oliphants, 378; Freedman, D. N. & E. F. Campbell Jr, *The Biblical Archaeologist Reader*, Vol. 2, 361–363; Porter, S. E. 'Why the Laodiceans Received Lukewarm Water, Rev. 3:15–18,' *TynBull*, Vol. 38, (1987), 143–149.

22. Marshall, A. *Gleanings*, 45; Brandon, S. G. F. *Jesus and the Zealots*, 1967, Manchester U. P. 36, 41/2, 46/7.

23. The word 'glow' here means 'set fire to and so glowing, burning.' Robertson, A. T. Luke, (see translation abbrev), 240.

24. Earle, R. *Word Meanings*, 402; Unnik, W. C. van. 'Den Geist loschet nicht aus, (1 Thess. 5:19).' *NovTest* Vol. 10, (1968) 255–269, on the fire and zeal of the spirit.

25. That the use of both draught and fire to describe the workings of the spirit is not a contradictory illustration, note the case of the spirit at Pentecost, Acts 2:2, 3.

26. Robertson, A. T. *Word Pictures*, Vol. 2, 50.

27. Ward, F. A. B. Time Measurement, Part 1, *Historical Review*, 1961, H.M.S.O. 47–51.

28. Livnnais, F. le. *Time*, 1960, Prentice-Hall, 68–78.

29. Larsen, E. *Atoms and Atomic Energy*, 1963, 8, 9; Boardman, J. J. Griffin & O. Murray, Ed. *The Oxford History of the Classical World*, 1988rp, 121, 837.

30. Lightfoot, J. *Horae Hebraicae et Talmudicae*, 1859, new ed. Oxf. Vol. 2. 283.

31. Feldman, A. *Parables*, 53; Hedrick, C. W. 'On Moving Mountains. Mark 11:22b–23, Matt. 21:21 and

Parallels,' *Forum*, Vol. 6 (1990), 219–237.

32. Keil, C. F. *Commentary on the O. T. Minor Prophets*, 1978rp, Grand Rapids, Eerdmans, Vol. 2. 271.

33. Trever, J. C. *The Untold Story of Qumran*, 1965, Pickering & Inglis, 146.

34. Bishop, E. F. F. *Jesus of Palestine*, 78; Savage, H. E. *The Gospel*, 197–199.

Chapter 11

Nautical

1. Fitted Out for Sea—Completely Equipped.

In the first century a sea voyage could be long and hazardous at the best of times, and delays and problems had to be expected and anticipated. So Paul urged Timothy to make full use of inspired Scripture as he sailed his ship of faith, because it could serve his needs in all circumstances. 'So that the man of God may be complete and proficient, well fitted and thoroughly equipped [Greek 'exartizo'] for every good work.' (2 Tim. 3:16, 17 Amplified.)

Commenting on this illustration, E. W. Bullinger said this word was 'used of fitting out a vessel for sea, which must take everything, on every voyage, which experience has shown may by any possibility be needed.'[1] This involved the feeding of the crew and passengers, their well-being during the voyage and basic comfort (including medical care); instruments of navigation with reasonable spares, and items for use in emergency – for undergirding the ship, for example. (Acts 27:17.) This required careful thought and planning, so that nothing was forgotten, for they would be away for many weeks, and possibly months.

God's Word is a storehouse of spiritual information complete in itself. It can provide everything that a Christian needs to build faith, and to be able to demonstrate that faith to others. Of course, he has to learn to draw on those treasures, and so he first needs instruction, 'but everyone when his training is complete (Greek 'katartizo'), will reach his teacher's level.' (Luke 6:40 NEB.) But really it is God who will 'personally equip, stabilize, strengthen, and firmly establish you.' (1 Peter 5:10 Berkeley.)

That is why the early Christian congregation received gifts in men, some as apostles, others as prophets or evangelizers, shepherds or

teachers, all 'in order fully to equip [Greek 'katartizō'] his people
for the work of serving – for the building up of Christ's body.'
(Eph. 4:12 Weymouth 3rd ed.)[2]

If a Christian's faith is to stand the test today he must be fully
equipped, and ready to make necessary adjustments in that equipment
as the voyage proceeds, to trim, as it were, his ship of faith. 'See
to it that you are being spiritually equipped and adjusted.' (2 Cor.
13:11 Wuest.) It should be the prayer of all for their fellow Christians, 'Now may the God of peace . . . fit you out with everything
good to do His will.' (Hebrews 13:20a, 21a, Berkeley.)

2. Putting on All Sail—Full Ahead in the Spirit.

This metaphor is illuminated by a very literal incident which gave
us one of the finest ancient descriptions of what could happen to a
storm-driven ship in mid-Mediterranean. The record of Acts chapter
27 is one of the most graphic and moving in that action-packed book.
The ship carrying Paul to Rome, coasting gently along the southern
shore of Crete, was suddenly hit by a tempestuous wind that came
down off the mountains, so that, with sails fully set, 'their ship was
caught by it, and could not face the wind, so we gave way and let
her run before it.' (Acts 27:15 Goodspeed; 'we let her go, and were
borne along.' Rotherham.) Finally, they were able to lower the yard
with the great sail attached, leaving only sufficient storm-sails set to
keep it on a starboard tack away from the dangerous Syrtis sandbanks
on the North African coast.[3]

To be 'borne along' (Greek 'pherō'), by a favourable wind in good
weather was much appreciated by Roman sailors, and could considerably shorten a long sea journey. With a north-west Etesian wind
the time to Egypt or Palestine in August might be only thirty days
from Rome. As a fisherman on the Sea of Galilee, Peter had frequently waited for a breeze to spring up to move his boat along, and
so he used this same word to describe the inspiration of writers of
prophecy by God's holy spirit when he said, 'For no prophecy ever
originated because some man willed it . . ., but men spoke from God
who were borne along (moved and impelled) by the Holy Spirit.' (2
Peter 1:21 Amplified.) Such was the force of inspiration that it

simply carried along those who were willing to be used by this invisible force. Just as a mighty ship would be borne along at full speed with its great sail fully set with a following wind.[4]

We can now turn to a passage where our illustration helps our understanding of what Paul is talking about. After distinguishing between baby food, and the solid food that helps children to grow to adulthood, he urges Christians to keep on growing spiritually. 'So let us get beyond the teaching of the elementary doctrines of Christ, and let us be borne along [Greek 'pherō'] toward what is mature.' (Heb. 6:1a Montgomery.) In a literal sense, the growth to maturity is something natural, inherent in the forces that work to change a child into an adult, a sapling into a fine fruit-bearing tree.

We may think that we can govern or control our becoming full grown in a spiritual sense, and some translations suggest this when they render it, 'let us press on unto perfection' (ASV), or 'let us try and advance towards that riper standard.' (Hayman.) This is to ignore that idea of letting the sails carry one along, or the part played by the holy spirit in this process. As Westcott so succinctly put it, 'The thought is not primarily of personal effort, 'let us go on', 'let us press . . . ' but of personal surrender to an active influence. The power is working (compare 1:3); we have only to yield ourselves to it. (Compare Acts 27:13, 17.) At the same time the influence and the surrender are continuous.'[5]

Our reaching physical maturity may be largely governed by our DNA characteristics, with some help from us by diet and exercise etc., but attaining spiritual maturity is by the direct influence of God's holy spirit in our lives. We have to allow it to work, not blocking or impeding it; then we can be 'borne along' to that maturity which it should be the goal of all Christians to reach. Does that mean that we can do little towards it? Not at all. We can put on all our sail, spreading our canvas to catch as much of the wind of the spirit as it is possible to do. This is how some grow more quickly than others. So give the holy spirit the fullest opportunity to act in your spiritual development, but give God himself the credit for supplying his active force.

3. Steering the Ship—Skilful Direction.

When the disciple James talks about the need to control the tongue, he draws on several illustrations in quick succession to drive home the great amount of damage that can be done by such a small part of the body. It is like a rudder, for 'Look too at the ships. Large as they are and driven along by stiff breezes, they are steered by a tiny rudder wherever the whim of the helmsman directs.' (James 3:4 Schonfield.)

The type of rudder of a Roman ship is shown by the Greek word used here, 'pēdalion', which comes from 'pēdon', meaning, 'the blade of an oar'. A large ship would have two long paddles, one on each side of the stern, passing through apertures in the ship's side. At the top was a horizontal handle or tiller. When the sea was calm one man could control both paddles, which acted independently of one another. In rough weather, two men would be required, both working in perfect unison.[6]

Well could the question be asked in ancient times, 'Why does the rudder, a small implement, and placed at the extremity of the vessel, possess such mighty force, that by a little helm, and by the strength of one man, and that scarcely put forth, the enormous bulk of ships is moved?'[7] It was the directing or control of that mighty force, the wind, that was all important for making the harbour safely. James attributes this to the 'whim' (Greek 'hormē') of the helmsman. Other translations use 'the mind' (Moffatt), 'the will' (Weymouth, RSV), 'the impulse' (ASV) or 'the inclination' (NWT) of the steersman.

So with the tongue. It is merely the tiny instrument that reveals the direction of the mind or impulse behind it. If a person lacks proper control, the tongue can indeed speak merely at the whim or impulse of that individual, doing great harm. But if the mind or will of that person is steady, trained and balanced, it can cause the tongue to speak upbuilding things which will benefit its hearers. So too, the trained helmsman, watching carefully where he is sending his ship, can avoid the rocks and reach the harbour safely. Of course, all persons are imperfect, as James points out, and so will say the wrong thing sometimes, but like the skilled pilot, those occasions when the ship goes off course will be reduced to the minimum.

A related illustration does not concern the rudder itself, but only the man at the helm. The word appears in the Septuagint Version, and again emphasizes the skill involved in his work; 'the person of understanding will acquire skill [Greek 'kubernēsis'] and attain to sound counsel (so that he may be able to steer his course rightly).' (Prov. 1:5b Amplified.)[8] Such skilful direction is especially required for rulers and those who govern, and 'When there is no skilful direction, the people fall.' (Prov. 11:14a NWT.) Just as the passengers and crew of a ship will suffer if the ship hits a rock for want of careful navigation, so too will nations suffer under incompetent rulers.

This can apply to the Christian congregation too, as Paul made clear on the only occasion when this word appears in the Greek Scriptures. He lists those who are 'gifts in men' set in their respective positions to advance the work of the congregation, and amongst the apostles, prophets, teachers etc., are those with 'gifts of guidance'. (1 Cor. 12:28b Sadler.)[9] They can steer the congregation on a spiritually successful course, so as to avoid 'the rocks hidden below water' and the threatening 'wild waves of the sea'. (Jude 12, 13 NWT.)

Whilst the early Christian congregation was in its infancy it needed those wise counsellors to guide it, but they did not do it in their own strength. For just as the helmsman is really making use of the wind, the mighty force that impels the ship on, so the Christian course is really guided by using the wind of God's holy spirit. (John 16:13.)

4. Drifting—The Gradual Slipping Away.

Picture a little boat on the Sea of Galilee, moored to a stake or jetty. The rope gradually works loose with the gentle ebb and flow of the slight current. Free of its restraint, the boat moves almost imperceptibly from the shore, not noticed by its dozing occupant. Before he realizes it he can be far out on the lake, in a dangerous situation.

That is the interesting illustration given in the book of Hebrews to show the need for Christians to hold on to their faith if they wish to gain salvation. 'We must pay more careful attention, therefore, to what we have heard, so that we do not drift away.' (Heb. 2:1 NIV.) The danger is well expressed by another Bible translator, J. B. Rotherham, 'Look at the danger: that of drifting away by slow and insensible degrees from the anchorage of our hope, until we are caught by the strong current of apostasy and become powerless to turn back even if we would.'[10]

The same Greek word 'pararrheō' is used in the Septuagint Version of Proverbs, and introduces the idea of the eyes and the mind guarding against taking the wrong course and letting faith slip away. (Prov. 3:21 LXX, 4:21 LXX Symmachus.)

However, the background of a small boat on the Sea of Galilee so familiar in the gospels, is not likely to lie behind this reference in the book of Hebrews. Whether Paul or someone else was its author, a large sea-going ship off a port in Asia Minor better fits the scene. So translators are divided in the way they render this verse, many of them preferring the idea of going past the anchorage, ' . . . lest at any time we should drift past them,' (Wuest) or freely rendered, 'Otherwise, we may well be like a ship which drifts past the harbour to shipwreck.' (Heb. 2:1a Barclay.)

Certainly Xenophon uses the word of a river flowing by, and so the action of the current is clearly involved. If the wind drops as a ship nears harbour, the current may well take over unless it is a warship where the crew could take to the oars. Westcott favoured this view, commenting, 'The idea is not that of simple forgetfulness, but of being swept along past the sure anchorage which is within reach . . . The image is singularly expressive. We are all continually exposed to the action of currents of opinion, habit, action, which tend to carry us away insensibly from the position which we ought to maintain.'[11]

The warning in this verse is underlined near to the end of the epistle. 'Do not be swept off your course [Greek 'parapherō'] by all sorts of outlandish teachings.' (Heb. 13:9 NEB.) Currents can be treacherous, and the pilot who wishes to gain the harbour safely has to be aware of the dangers if he is to negotiate them successfully. For the twentieth century Christian this is more true than ever. By taking to heart this fine admonition, he can keep the ship of faith skilfully directed so that he reaches the harbour of salvation.

Whether it is the almost imperceptible slow drifting away, or the danger of drifting past and away from our goal, by being caught in a current we did not suspect, it is the initial danger of being taken off guard that a Christian is warned about. In common with many other illustrations we have considered, it calls for an alert watch, and quick action to combat the problem before it gets out of control.

5. Furling the Sails—Drawing Back.

The ancient trading ships of Paul's day were different from modern times in one particular so far as the sails were concerned. They usually consisted of one very large sail set upon a single mast near the centre of the vessel, with just a small sail at the bow to aid them in 'putting about' to bring the ship's head round to the wind. To furl the great sail in stormy weather, ropes attached to the sail were pulled so as to brail it, or roll it up (somewhat like pulling up a window blind) towards the yard arms, from which the sail was suspended.[12]

This process provided Paul with a picturesque way of describing certain matters to his readers. In writing to the Corinthians he warned them that the time left was reduced, saying, 'All our futures are so foreshortened [Greek 'sustellō'] indeed, that those who have wives should live, so to speak, as though they had none.' (1 Cor. 7:29 Phillips.) It was as if time had been wrapped up or folded together, furled as a sail, so that it had become much less in length than it had formerly seemed.[13]

On another occasion Paul had to speak to Peter about his inconsistent course of action in Antioch. He had been eating quite openly with gentiles or non-Jews, but when some Jewish visitors from Jerusalem arrived, he was afraid of what they would say, so he withdrew from the gentiles, and friends of his followed his example. In the words of Paul's mixed metaphor, Peter 'began to trim his sails, [Greek 'hupostellō'], and fence himself off.' (Gal. 2:12 Ward p.94.)[14]

These examples merely serve to illustrate the idea which comes across most forcibly in two quite different contexts. The first is talking of the endurance of a Christian in the face of great opposition or stormy weather. (Heb. 10:32–37.) Then comes the bold conclusion, quoting from the Hebrew and Septuagint of Habakkuk 2:4, 'by faith my righteous one will live. If he shrinks back, I will not be pleased with him. Now, we're not those who shrink back, and so are lost, but we have faith and so are saved.' (Heb. 10:38, 39 Beck.)

The thought of 'shrinking back' (Greek 'hupostellō') is that of shortening sail to avoid danger.[15] But how can that apply here, since it was the action of furling sail that helped a ship to weather the storm and stay afloat? Perhaps once again it is a case of linking this idea with that famous saying of Jesus, 'If you want to save your soul, you will lose it. But if you will lose your soul for Me, you will find it.' (Matt. 16:25 Beck.) There is almost something in the way the passage in Hebrews is worded that reminds us of those words, and its author may have had them in mind. Certainly, the sentiments are the same, for the early Christians made no compromise against the storm by furling the sail, even at the cost of losing their lives. They firmly believed that if they lost their lives in the arena or anywhere else, their faith would be rewarded by a resurrection. So it is the context that explains why they sailed on regardless into the storm.

This situation helps us to understand Paul's thoughts when he saw the Ephesian elders for the last time. He had to brace himself against further persecution likely to cause his death, and he made clear that he had never held back from them anything that he should have said for their spiritual progress. 'I no way shortened sail ['hupostellō'] because of what befell me, but proclaimed to you and taught you, both in public and from house to house; testifying fully both to Jews and Greeks, the change of heart which God requires, and the faith we owe to Jesus our Lord.' (Acts 20:20, 21 Sadler.)[16] Boldly and without compromise he had told them the truth and counsel of God at all times, and so his conscience was quite clear, and he felt free of bloodguilt in every way. (Acts 20:26, 27.)

Does such a Christian course recommend itself today? It has to be said that few who call themselves Christian would show the staunch faith that Paul manifested, or would be prepared to speak out in proclaiming their faith. Instead, many persons take the attitude that their religion is their private business, not to be shared with anyone else at all. Can they really say they follow in the footsteps of Jesus or Paul when they so roll up or furl their sails?

6. Stormbound—Keeping Our Course.

In an earlier illustration, a little boat had drifted out into the Sea of Galilee without its occupant being aware of it. Why was he then in a dangerous situation? Because of the small size of the lake and its high mountains that close in around it, it is very susceptible to sudden storms that rush down on to a previously very calm sea. 'Then came a violent squall of wind which drove the waves aboard the boat until it was almost swamped.' (Mark 4:37 Phillips.) This was the occasion when Jesus rebuked the wind and calmed the sea, to the amazement of his disciples.

We can link with this idea a warning of Jesus, 'nor be of anxious [troubled] mind [unsettled, excited, worried, and in suspense].' (Luke 12:29b Amplified.) The word here (Greek 'meteōrizō'), from which comes our English word meteor – 'something suspended in the air', was used of a ship on the crest of a wave, tossed about in mid air, representing the state of mind of someone anxious or in doubt. The literal reaction of a storm-tossed boat gives rise to the feeling of the occupants, just as in the anxious fear of the disciples on the Sea of Galilee.[17]

James carried this illustration a little further when he said, 'The man who doubts is like the surging sea, driven ('anemizō') and tossed about by the wind. Such a man should not expect anything from the Lord.' (James 1: 6b, 7 TNT.) The doubter is unstable, first thinking this, and then that, changing from one opinion to another due to the slightest comment or suggestion. That is the very opposite of faith.[18]

But the vivid application of this storm-bound situation is within that of another illustration, the contrast between the mature Christian and the one who is a spiritual babe, never having grown up, and so unable to deal with the stormy complexity of thoughts opposed to truth. Paul counsels, 'cease to be infants raised aloft on successive waves and swung right round [Greek 'peripherō'] by every gust of teaching in the sea of trickery of men who stop at nothing in their schemes to mislead.' (Eph. 4:14 Ward p. 124.)[19]

The ship that is too small cannot withstand a storm at sea because it is unable to ride the giant waves and the buffeting wind. The vessel needs to be a large one, strongly built with a view to meeting those conditions, just like a full-grown man in a spiritual sense, a mature Christian. (Hebrews 5:12–14.) The strong winds of false teaching can whirl someone round and round, as in a tornado, and whip up the waves of the sea, causing many a life to be lost by spiritual drowning. (Compare 2 Peter 2:17 Phillips – 'like the changing shapes of whirling storm-clouds.')[20]

The ship of faith, however, can sail on 'in much certainty and assurance [Greek 'plērophoria']' (1 Thess. 1:5 Wuest), directed by the wind of the holy spirit, and able to cleave through the sea. It is not at the mercy of the wind and waves, and is thus able to reach its destination and harbour, having conquered the storms.[21]

7. Shipwreck—Losing Faith.

At least three times Paul suffered shipwreck, not including the instance related in Acts chapter 27. So it is not surprising that his experience should find its way into his vivid expression for one whose faith founders on the rocks. Speaking of two of his associates, Hymenaeus and Alexander, Paul said they had 'suffered shipwreck in relation to the Faith' (1 Tim. 1:19 Smith), and some would see in the previous phrase an extension of the metaphor, a 'pushing or thrusting aside' of a good conscience, as if the steersman had been thrown overboard, thus leading to disaster. Or it is like pushing off from land when conditions at sea do not make it advisable, leaving the refuge of a secure harbour. The land meant safety, avoiding the worst of a storm, but by an unsound course of action the inevitable result is shipwreck.[22]

More reasons for this shipwreck of faith appear further on in Paul's letter to Timothy. Temptations and snares for those who are rich can be disastrous, for 'they sink men in wreck and ruin'. (1 Tim. 6:9 Smith.) This expression means 'dragging to the bottom' and is used literally in Luke 5:7, when the huge catch of fish so weighed down the two boats that they 'began to sink'. Those who do not seek to control their materialistic desires, but give them full uninhibited reign can find that they completely overwhelm any faith or spirituality they might have had, and so they are 'dragged to the bottom' and drowned.

This can be worse than shipwreck, for then it is the ship that is broken to pieces, and individual men can still be saved from the water or the wreckage. To mix the metaphors, 'Others you should save by snatching them from the flames.' (Jude 23 REB, 1 Cor. 3:15.) Paul in First Timothy is talking of the loss of the individuals themselves.

Sad as is the shipwreck of faith or the drowning of individuals, it is not of God's doing. Paul raises the question concerning Israel, were they pushed or did they leave God themselves? 'God did not give His people a push away from Himself, did He?' (Rom. 11:1 Ward p. 169.) Never may that be, is Paul's vigorous argument, but they preferred to leave the safe harbour, to 'push off' from the shore, and so the whole nation suffered the shipwreck of its faith, with only a remnant 'picked up' as survivors. (Rom. 11:1–12.)

A striking simile adds strength to the warnings of shipwreck; 'the wicked are like a storm-tossed sea, a sea that cannot be still, whose waters cast up mud and dirt.' (Isa. 57:20, REB, see also Jude 13, Rev. 17:15.) The restless sea of mankind today is littered with the shipwrecks of faith that warn all Christians to make their determination strong. 'We have that hope as an anchor for our lives, safe and secure.' (Hebrews 6:19 REB.) Although often four anchors might be cast out to be sure a ship would hold fast, (Acts 27:29), here only one is needed, for it is 'firm and assured like a ship which is firmly anchored'.[23]

8. Sighting the Distant Shore—Hope Realised.

How often the ancient mariner searched the horizon for any sign of the distant shore for which he was heading. Sometimes familiar landmarks would confirm that the ship had not gone off course, and even if he had not visited a place before, a description of some of its hills and headlands would identify it for him. Speaking of the book of Hebrews, B. F. Westcott said, 'The imagery of the Epistle is drawn from many sources. Some of the figures which are touched more or less in detail are singularly vivid and expressive . . . a whole picture often lies in single words.' One of those in his list is 'the vision of the distant shore [Greek 'porrōthen']'.[24]

That famous chapter of Hebrews eleven tells of many faithful men of pre-Christian times who set out on a voyage for a distant shore. 'Controlled by faith all these went to their deaths without realizing the promises, but scanning and hailing them from a distance . . . Now, people who make such remarks make it plain that they are looking for a home country.' (Heb. 11:13a, 14 Berkeley.)

Prominent among such men of faith was Abraham, who had set out from Ur of the Chaldees to find a land promised to him by God, and which must have seemed a long distance away in those days of laborious travel. His faith then was not disappointed. (Gen. 12:1–5, Heb. 11:8, 9.) But at the end of his life he had a greater vision, for he was 'looking for the city with solid foundations, whose Architect and Builder is God'. (Heb. 11:10 Berkeley.) He had some idea of what that city looked like through his friendship with the architect, enough to recognize its outline, but not knowing all the grand features. Yet his faith in both its existence and its reality was such that it was just as if he had actually reached it. In his mind's eye he was there, a vision shared by many a mariner estranged from his beloved home for a long period.

Jesus was aware of Abraham's viewpoint, and so he was able to share it in what must have seemed a strange statement to his Jewish listeners, who prided themselves on knowing all about their forefather Abraham. 'Your father Abraham was delighted at the prospect of seeing My day; and he saw it and rejoiced.' (John 8:56 Adams.) Had Abraham actually been alive at that moment, he would have happily accepted the Messiah, for everything about him would have matched the features of the distant shore he had seen, as it were, in vision, unlike those faithless Jews, who had no such spiritual outlook.

Does our faith have the same realism about it as that of Abraham? He could see that the earth would receive God's blessing and be a beautiful home for man, and that the promise made to him would be fulfilled, 'And in your Seed [Christ] shall all the nations of the earth be blessed and [by Him] bless themselves, because you have heard and obeyed My voice.' (Gen. 22:18 Amplified.)

Notes and References:

1. Bullinger, E. W. *Enjoy the Bible*, 321.
2. Ward, R. A. *Hidden Meaning* 130, '"fitting"' . . . combines the repair of damage and taking aboard new stores;' The related word katartizō means 'to prepare, equip thoroughly, completely set up or put in a right position.' Cremer, H. *Biblico-Theological Lexicon of N. T. Greek*, 1962 rp, Edin. Clark, 651; Waugh, R. M. L. *Greek Testament* 70; Moule, H, C, G, *Ephesian Studies*, 1900, Hodder, 191, 'the equipment, the adjustment, the adaptation and furnishing.'
3. Smith, J. *The Voyage and Shipwreck of St. Paul*, 1880, 4th ed. rev. Longmans Green, 110–114.
4. Bouquet, A. C. *Everyday Life in N. T. Times*, 1953, Batsford, 100; Green, M. *2 Peter and Jude*, (Tyndale N. T. Commentaries), 1968, Tyndale Press, 91; Waugh, R. M. L. *Greek Testament*, 43.
5. Westcott, B. F. *Hebrews*, 143.
6. Smith, J. *The Voyage* . . . (op. cit. 3), 183–187; Neuburger, A, *Technical Arts*, 490; Robertson, A. T. *Word Pictures* Vol. 6, 41.
7. Jebb, J. *Sacred Literature* . . . 1831, Duncan & Cochran, 295, quoting Aristotle, Qu. Mach 6.
8. Marshall, A. Ed. *GSM* July 1929, 100, The Latin equivalent for this word is *gubernator* or 'governor,' used in the AV., of James 3:4, the man who steers by means of the *gubernaculum* the rudder.
9. *NKJV Interlinear* 613 footnote, 'originally meaning the steering, piloting performed by a ship's helmsman;' Kittel, G. Ed. *TDNT*, Vol. 3. 1035–1037.
10. Rotherham, J. B. *Studies in the Ep. to the Hebrews*, 1906, Allenson, 54; Waugh, R. M. L. *Greek Testament*, 43; Hilgert, E. *The Ship and Related Symbols in the N. T.* 1962, Assen, Van Gorcum, 133f.
11. Westcott, B. F. *Hebrews*, 37.
12. Smith, J. *The Voyage* . . . (op. cit. 3), 190–206; Neuburger, A. *Technical Arts*, 491–493.
13. Jones, H. S. Ed. Liddell & Scott *Greek-English Lexicon*, 1951 rp, 9th ed. Oxford, Vol. 2. 1735; Humphry, W. G. *A Commentary on the Revised Version of the N. T.* 1888, new ed. 304; Wordsworth, C. *Greek Testament*, Vol. 2. 107, 'wrapped up, or folded together (see Acts 5:6), or furled and reefed as a sail.'
14. Ward, R. A. *Hidden Meaning*, 94; Wordsworth, C. *Greek Testament*, Vol. 2, 50, applying the metaphor right through the incident.
15. Wordsworth, C. *Greek Testament*, Vol. 2, 414; Vine, W. E. *Expository Dictionary*, 184; Lewis, T, W, '. . . And if he shrinks back' (Heb. 10:38b),' *NTStud.* Vol. 22 (1975), 88–94. Withdrawal and concealment from the world as a mode of endurance would be displeasing to God, and 'would result in the Christian community drifting away.'
16. Humphry, W. G. *A Commentary* . . . (op. cit. 13), 237; Vincent, M. R. *Word Studies*, Vol. 1, 273, rejects this as a nautical metaphor, arguing that there are only three such in all of Paul's writings. This is not the view of most commentators however, e. g. Farrar, F. W. *Life and Work of St. Paul*, 1898, Cassell, 515

footnote, would render verse 20, 'reefed up.'

17. Pittman, R. T. *Words and Their Ways*, 36–38; Robertson, A. T. *Word Pictures*, Vol. 2. 177.

18. Turner, N. *Christian Words*, 119; Adamson, J. *The Ep. of James*, (New Int. Comm. on the N. T.), 1976, Grand Rapids, Eerdmans, 58, 59.

19. Simpson, E. K. *Words Worth Weighing*, 30.

20. Robertson, A. T. *Word Pictures*, Vol. 4. 538, Vol. 6. 168.

21. The metaphor here is less certain, due to the paucity of information on Greek plērophoria, which may carry the idea of a ship in full sail. Guillemard, W. H. *Hebraisms*, 90; Wordsworth, C. *Greek Testament*, Vol. 2. 7.

22. Humphry, W. G. *A Commentary* . . . (op. cit. 13), 383.

23. Brown, C, Ed. *NIDNTT*, Vol. 1, 660, for the quotation; Murray, J. J. 'The Anchor of Hope. Romans 8:24; Hebrews 6:19.' *Expositor*, 2nd series, Vol. 5 (1883), 435–442.

24. Westcott, B. F. *Hebrews*, xlviii, with an interesting list of metaphors and illustrations, including this one; Moulton, J. H. & Turner, N. *Grammar*, Vol. 4, 108; Wordsworth, C. *Greek Testament*, Vol. 2, 416; Nicoll, W. R. Ed. *Expositor's Greek Testament*, Vol. 4. 357 varies the image slightly by giving a closer view, of those on board ship seeing their friends on shore, and waving to them in recognition. This does not seem so appropriate as the distant shore, and recognition first of familiar hills and headlands, which is more in keeping with looking for a far off city and land.

Chapter 12

Religious Life and Education

1. Every Jot and Tittle—Complete Fulfillment.

In his intriguing Sermon on the Mount, Jesus made it clear how he viewed the Mosaic Law. In so doing he brought in an illustration that turns on the letters of the Hebrew alphabet. 'Do not think that I have come to abolish the Law or the Prophets; I have not come to abolish them but to fulfil them. I tell you the truth, until heaven and earth disappear, not the smallest letter, nor the least stroke of a pen, will by any means disappear from the Law until everything is accomplished.' (Matt. 5:17, 18 NIV.)

The variety in translation here reflects an endeavour to place the illustration in a modern setting (as with the NIV), or to give it a Hebrew or Greek background according to Jesus' actual words. Note some of the different wordings:

'one jot or one tittle' – AV.
'sooner than one jot, one flourish' – Knox.
'Not even a yoth or a dash' – Lamsa.
'not an iota, nor a dot' – RSV.
'not an iota, nor a comma' – Moffatt.
'not one dotting of an i, or crossing of a t' – Goodspeed.
'not a letter, not a stroke' – NEB.
'not one small letter, or a part of a letter' – TNT.
'not the least point nor the smallest detail' – TEV.

The first of these letters is 'iōta', the smallest Greek vowel, like our lower case 'i', but without the dot, and it reminds us of our English phrase, 'it makes not an iota of difference'. But the Hebrew letter behind this is the 'yodh', by then the smallest letter of the Hebrew alphabet, for a comparison of earlier scripts reveals how the

243

'yodh' shrank in size towards the first Christian century. Our English jot is familiar in 'I don't care a jot' and to 'jot down' something is to make a brief note.

The tittle is from the Latin *titulus*, a mark over a word in writing, but the Greek word 'keraia' refers to a little horn, a hook to a Hebrew letter that distinguishes one letter from another similar one. In Hebrew a careful distinction had to be made between 'Beth' (B), and 'Kaph' (K), between 'Resh' (R) and 'Daleth' (D). In English there is a similar small distinction between the capital letters C and G, and O and Q. It could also be applied to vowel points or Greek accents. Frank M. Cross, in an excellent comparison showing the development of the Hebrew scripts over several centuries, describes the tittle as 'an ornamentation of the Herodian book hand'.[1]

Jesus used this illustration to emphasize that he was only interested in the complete fulfilment of the Law, which he himself kept perfectly, the first man to do so. He also fulfilled the prophecies made by the prophets concerning the Messiah. (Luke 4:16–21.) He did not seek to make even the smallest alteration to the Law, for even a missing 'yodh', or the substitution of a different letter could alter the meaning of a verse. By this picturesque illustration he made his stand crystal clear.

2. Whitewashed Graves—
Beauty that is Only Skin-Deep.

During Jesus' strong denunciation of the scribes and Pharisees in Matthew chapter 23, he used some vivid speech to drive home the realism of his comments. One of these similes concerned their hypocritical course of action. 'You are like whitewashed tombs, which look beautiful on the outside, but on the inside are full of dead men's bones and everything unclean.' (Matt. 23:27 NIV.)

This referred to an annual event just before the Passover, when during the month Adar (corresponding to February/March), it was customary for graves and tombs to be whitewashed with lime (chalk tempered and infused in water), which the previous rainy season would have washed off. Some might be treated with a mixture of powdered marble and lime which filled in any cracks, and gave them a rich and lustrous appearance.[2]

But why such concern over rotting and decaying corpses? It was to prevent any pilgrims to the festival entering the Temple and being rendered ritually unclean by contact with a grave. (Num. 19:16.) Jesus was making the point that the Pharisees were too concerned with the outward appearance of things, while they neglected inward cleanliness and righteousness.

There is a further reference in Luke to this illustration, but it has often been dismissed as a mistake or a misunderstanding of the practice. Jesus tells the Pharisees, 'Woe to you, because you are like unmarked graves, which men walk over without knowing it.' (Luke 11:44 NIV.) But there need be no contradiction, for in the course of time many graves would be lost and forgotten, and grass would grow upon them, so that people would walk over them and not be aware that they were being rendered unclean. So too, the hypocrisy of the Pharisees could be so well covered over that many observers would be quite unaware of it.[3]

So from two different viewpoints, the Pharisees' hypocrisy was exposed and condemned. It has been argued that the Pharisees were themselves against hypocrisy and denounced it as much as Jesus. But it was the logicality of the Jewish system carried to its extreme that inevitably led to this web of contradiction which produced this hypocrisy. In particular, it fostered a repugnance for the 'am-ha-arets', the ordinary people who were viewed as unclean and ignorant, and this elevated the pride of the Pharisees, and induced a division of the classes. Jesus cut through this system to expose motives and principles which had become so twisted and warped.[4]

3. Forgive 77 Times—Unlimited Forgiveness.

When the apostle Peter asked how often he should forgive his brother who sinned against him, Jesus gave an interesting numerical illustration in answer. He replied, 'I do not say to you, seven times, but, Seventy-seven times.' (Matt. 18: 21, 22 TNT.)

Did that mean that a Christian should keep a notebook, checking carefully until someone had reached seventy-seven, and then telling him he had now exhausted the limit of Christian patience? Certainly not, for the equally important Christian principle of love says it 'does not keep an account (a record – note p. 481) of evil'. (1 Cor. 13:5 TNT.) The essence of Christian forgiveness is that it also includes forgetting about the matter. When the American Indians smoked the peace pipe commanded by the 'Great Spirit', then they agreed to 'bury the hatchet', but that would be of no benefit if, so to speak, they remembered where they had buried it!

On another occasion, Jesus showed that he did not literally mean seventy-seven times. Speaking of forgiving someone who shows repentance for the error or sin they had committed, he said, 'If he sins against you seven times in a day, and returns to you seven times and says that he is sorry, you must forgive him.' (Luke 17:4 TNT.)

Why did Jesus have to make such a point of this matter? It seems that the prevailing ideas of Judaism in the first century were exactly opposite, limiting forgiveness very severely. This was partly based upon a wrong understanding of Amos 1:3, where God was said not to forgive after three revolts by Damascus, and also on Job 33:29, where God would redeem a person up to three times. So Peter must have thought that he was stretching things by extending three times to seven![6]

Why then did Jesus pick on the number seventy-seven? Was it simply because it expressed a 'complete' number, the multiple of the heavenly seven and the earthly ten, plus Peter's original seven? It might have been. But it must also have been Jesus' purpose to reverse a wrong idea rooted in an early statement by Lamech in the book of Genesis. He had told his wives after he had killed a young man, 'If seven lives are taken to pay for killing Cain, Seventy-seven will be taken if anyone kills me.' (Gen. 4:24 TEV.) The numbers seven and seventy-seven had become linked in a sad note of hate and revenge. When Jesus came he taught the opposite, turning a vengeful seventy-seven into a forgiving seventy-seven. Peter saw the point, and so should we, that where true repentance is shown, unlimited forgiveness is the Christian way.

4. Keeping His Outer Garments—Keeping Watch.

The failure to appreciate a metaphor or illustration can cause a translator to convey quite the wrong idea, and this is certainly true here. This illustration is almost an aside, spoken in connection with the only occasion where the name Armageddon is mentioned, the great final battle of Almighty God with all opposing forces. 'I will surely come like a thief. Happy is he who is on the alert and retains his garments, lest he go about naked, and they see his shame.' (Rev. 16:15 Schonfield.)

Most translations speak of the person either keeping his clothes on or having them beside him in readiness. But the metaphor here is not that of an ordinary householder waiting for a thief breaking into his home, as in Luke 12:38. It is one connected with the Temple, as the context of the chapter shows, and it goes back to the practices employed in guarding that important centre of worship.

In the Jewish Mishnah the tractate Middoth (Measurements), begins by locating the places where the priests and Levites kept guard through the watches of the night. The captain of the Temple made periodic tours to check that all was well, and that the guards were awake and vigilant. He carried a flaming torch and made his rounds quietly, and if a guard did not greet him, 'and it was manifest that he was asleep, he would beat him with his staff, and he had the right to burn his raiment'. (Middoth 1. 2, Acts 4:1.)[7]

It has been said that this was a harsh punishment, but it seems likely that it was only on the second occasion that the offender's garments were set on fire, and a case is recorded of this happening. It must also be remembered that it was counted as a great privilege to serve and guard the Temple, and one conscious of this would not easily fall asleep.[8]

It is this position of a Christian as a guard that is emphasized by other Scriptures. After describing the conditions prevailing in the time of the End before Armageddon, Jesus added, 'So keep awake, pray constantly, that you may succeed in escaping all these things that are about to happen, and to stand in the presence of the Son of Man.' (Luke 21:36 Schonfield.) Here the one making the inspection as Captain of the Temple is the Son of Man Christ Jesus himself, and what shame it would mean to be found asleep by him! (cp. Matt. 26: 40–46.)

The guardian aspect again comes through in the final chapter of Hebrews. 'Obey your leaders and give way to them, for they keep watch over your souls as those who must render an account . . .' (Heb. 13:17 Schonfield.) This keeping watch by the elders or spiritual overseers is literally an 'abstaining from sleep' (K. Int), due to an appreciation of the privilege enjoyed. Yet above and beyond all that men can do there has to be the awareness that we do not guard or keep on the watch in our own strength but in God's, for 'unless the Lord watches over the city, the watchman keeps vigil in vain'. (Ps. 127:1 Tanakh.)

5. Fences that Divide—
Removing Division, Creating Separation.

In 1871 an inscription was discovered in Jerusalem which came from the first century Temple. It was a warning to non-Jews not to go beyond the Court of the Gentiles, and it read as follows:

No man of another nation to enter within the fence and enclosure round the Temple. Whoever is caught will have himself to blame that his death ensues.[9]

Josephus describes this fence or balustrade, in which these warning slabs were placed at regular intervals, some worded in Greek, others in Latin. The Romans assisted the Jews in maintaining its strict sanction, so it is little wonder that Titus referred to this barrier in his verbal outburst during the siege of Jerusalem in 70 C. E., when the Jews themselves desecrated the Temple with bloodshed. He offered to spare the Temple if they would continue the fight somewhere else, but they would not listen. (War, Book 5, ch. 5 (2), 193–195, Book 6, ch. 2 (4) 124–128.)

Some years before this there had been uproar in Jerusalem when it was rumoured that the apostle Paul had taken the gentile Trophimus into the Temple, so disregarding the fence and its warning inscriptions. (Acts 21:27–32.) Although Paul always showed respect for the Temple and its regulations, there lay behind this suspicion of the Jews the knowledge that Christians had removed all divisions between peoples, and that they no longer believed in a fence that separated Jews from other nationalities, so called aliens (the Greek word in the inscription) or gentiles. (War Book 2, ch. 17, (4) 417.)

That change went back to the conversion of Cornelius, and the direct command by God to Peter to stop calling defiled the things God had cleansed, and it was sealed when the holy spirit was poured out upon people of other nationalities. (Acts 10: 9–48.) So when Paul wrote his letter to the Ephesians, that experience in Jerusalem doubtless came to mind, and caused him to use that fence or barrier as an illustration. Speaking of the scope of Christ's sacrifice, he said, 'For he is our peace-maker, who has united both Jew and Gentile, having demolished the dividing partition-wall, and having in his person neutralized the cause of enmity, the Law of commandments set down in ordinances.' (Eph. 2:14, 15a, Schonfield.)

This removal of all divisions did not contradict the purpose of the fence or wall as much as may appear at first sight. Originally the barrier ('soreg') was erected as a protection rather than separation. In a metaphorical way Jewish tradition regarded the wisdom of Solomon as the sand on the seashore, acting as a fence against the encroachments of the sea. (1 Kings 4:29.) The 'fence' also acted to protect those books of the Hebrew Scriptures which were of divine origin, from those which emanated purely from human wisdom. Here, too, divisions have been removed, for today those Hebrew Scriptures are united with the Greek Scriptures, which by their application of the Hebrew section or Old Testament, have become part of the message available to people of all nationalities. In every way there is no longer a fence to divide true Christians.[10]

The Fence Separating Christians from the World

Whilst true Christianity has broken down so many barriers, yet there is one fence that has been strengthened in a very strange way. The apostle Paul makes an interesting play on one word (not unusual for him), which has been described as 'a metaphor for complete separation'. Concluding his letter to the Galatians, he writes, 'But as for me, Heaven forbid that I should boast about anything except the execution-stake of our Lord Yeshua the Messiah! Through him, as far as I am concerned, the world has been put to death on the stake; and through him, as far as the world is concerned, I have been put to death on the stake.' (Gal. 6: 14 Stern.)[11]

Professor Bruce mentions in a footnote to this verse, 'There seems to be a play on the two senses of Greek 'stauroō' here: (a) to erect a fence, (b) to crucify.' So he renders the first reference as 'a permanent barrier between the world and me'. (Gal. 6:14 Bruce.) Another translation has this footnote on 'stauroō', 'Originally it meant to fence by driving stakes; then, as the stauros, stake, became an instrument of execution, 'stauroō' described the action of executing by affixing a person to a stake, or cross.' Then on Mark 8:34, a further note adds, 'Whether the stauros included a horizontal cross-piece (either at the top or slightly lower) by the time of Jesus is debated.' (NKJV Interlinear.)

According to Stern's rendering, Paul is separated from the world and its godless ways just as much as the living are separated from the dead. But this is not precisely what Paul's play on the word is showing, which Bruce has brought out so well. This is where the play on the simple upright stake is so telling, for it is as if Christ's stake is multiplied many-fold so that it builds into a long line of stakes that altogether form a fence, just like those the Romans erected around the besieged Jerusalem before 70 C. E. That fence is a 'permanent barrier' between Christians and the world. Christ is their king and saviour, and so they repudiate the world and its leaders and ways.

This also follows on well from Paul's earlier argument of the two fields. 'Those who keep sowing in the field of their old nature, in order to meet its demands, will eventually reap ruin; but those who keep sowing in the field of the Spirit will reap from the Spirit everlasting life.' (Gal. 6:5 Stern.) That fence of stakes separates the two fields, the field of this perverted world, and the field of true Christianity, and it is the ransom sacrifice of Christ that has made that separation, by buying persons out of this world and death, into a new united Christian brotherhood that gives true life.

To complete the picture, this is why no true Christian can 'sit on the fence' between the two worlds, for he is then not fully accepting all that Christ's sacrifice means and entails. Paul expresses it forcibly when he wrote to the Corinthians, 'Wherefore go forth out of their midst and be distinguished from them [footnote – to mark off land by boundaries], saith the Lord, and do not cling to anything unclean; and I will admit you.' (2 Cor. 6:17 Sadler.)

6. Following in the Footsteps—Copying Closely.

A man is traced by his footsteps, and as the poet Longfellow well observed, many men have left behind them 'footprints on the sands of time'. (Resignation.)

One of those men was faithful Abraham, whose fine example outshines many other men of faith recorded in the Hebrew Scriptures. The apostle Paul reminded Roman Christians about Abraham, and called him the 'father' of uncircumcised persons having faith, as well as the father of circumcised ones who 'do not rely upon their circumcision alone, but also walk in the footprints [Greek 'ichnos'] of the faith which our father Abraham had while he was yet uncircumcised.' (Rom. 4:12 NEB.)

It is because we have the record of Abraham's faith that we can study his example, and try to place our feet in his footprints, as it were. Even if a man died a long time ago, literal prints or remains may tell us much about him, like the Ice Man discovered in 1991 in the Otztaler Alps, or a written record of the past can do the same. Through archaeology and excavation much that seemed forever buried and lost has been found, and can now speak to us. In the record of Abel's faith it could also be said, 'through faith he continued to speak after his death'. (Heb. 11:4 NEB.)

But to find those footprints means searching for them. In his autobiography, the Jewish historian Josephus tells how he was lured from Tiberias by the report of Roman horsemen having been seen some distance from the town. Sensing a plot, Josephus still felt he must check the matter, but 'when I was at the place, I found not the least footstep ['ichnos'] of an enemy', so he quickly returned to foil his colleagues' plans. There was 'no trace' (Thackeray Loeb translation) of horsemen, so the search proved unrewarding, but if it had been an accurate report, his search, if thorough, would have provided the evidence. (Life 55 (283) Whiston translation.)

Writing to the Corinthians, Paul countered the arguments of those who accused him of getting material benefits from them, or of sending other disciples to exploit them. Of one of those men he said, 'Titus did not take advantage of you in anything, did he? Did we not order our behaviour by means of the same Spirit, and in the same footsteps?' (2 Cor. 12:18 Wuest.)

Walking in the footsteps of those men of faith who have blazed the trail, may not be so difficult then. The holy spirit can help to place our feet where they should go, so we have that ready assistance both in searching for, and walking in those footsteps.

The one we wish to follow more than any other is, of course, Christ Jesus, and Peter drew a fine illustration to show how this could be done. 'Christ also suffered on your behalf, leaving behind for you a model to imitate, in order that by close application you might follow in His footprints.' (1 Peter 2:21 Wuest.)

The word 'model' here is Greek 'hupogrammos', which literally means 'to write under'. In early Christian times wax tablets were used in schools for training boys to write the alphabet and their first words. The teacher would inscribe an example with his stylus within parallel lines, and then perhaps guide the boy's hand in tracing over the letters and words. Then on the line below, the student would copy as closely as he could the words the teacher had written above. He literally followed in the lines and curves of each letter, in the footprints, as it were. The word could also be applied to an artist's sketch or outline, which required to be filled in or coloured by someone else, working carefully within that outline provided.[12]

The early Christians saw to it that a careful detailed record of many of Jesus' thoughts and actions was made, even to the extent that three synoptic gospels were written, presenting a like view, to which was added John's, which filled in many other details. In spite of those who talk about the difficulty of the quest of the historical Jesus, we really have quite enough evidence to show how different Jesus was from all other so-called great men of this world. Most of all, his teachings come through very clearly, and these are also elaborated in the rest of the Greek Scriptures, or New Testament, which makes a rounded-out inspired record to follow in great detail.

No greater teacher has left such a perfect example to follow.

Indeed, the most impressive footprints on the sands of time are those of the Messiah, Jesus Christ.

7. The Pedagogue—Growing to Full Faith.

The pedagogue is an interesting figure in Greek society that has been subject to a variety of interpretations in different Bible translations. Paul's illustration concerns the Mosaic Law and its purpose. 'And so the Law has been like a guardian [Greek 'paidagōgos'] escorting us to Christ, that we might be made right with God through faith: but now that faith has come we are no longer under a guardian.' (Gal. 3:24, 25 TNT).

Some translations have kept the 'schoolmaster' image which is present in the Authorised King James' Version. They have used 'master' (NCV), 'governess' (Phillips) and 'tutor' (Knox, Rotherham, Cassirer). But the teaching aspect is not the point of Paul's illustration. The pedagogue (literally 'boy leader'), was a trusted slave in a patrician household who was given the complete care of the son and heir. He superintended the boy's whole life *except* for his actual education, and so this included his moral behaviour, his manners and habits, his recreation and general training. He would administer discipline when necessary, and so act in most respects as we think a parent would. But Paul makes that important contrast, 'Though you may have thousands of guardians ['paidagōgos'] in Christ, you have not many fathers.' (1 Cor. 4:15 TNT.)[13]

One of the pedagogue's duties would be to take the boy to school, where he was handed over to the teacher, and this particular duty has been singled out by some scholars as the crux of Paul's comparison. 'The law was therefore the servant who brought us to the door of the school of Christ . . .' (Gal. 3: 24 Barclay.) But this is to lose the overall perspective of the illustration.[14]

Israel needed a guardian in all aspects of its national life through the centuries of what we might liken to its minority; its growing-up period. When it had reached the time for Christ to appear, the nation should have been ready to emerge into full freedom along with faith in Christ. In the same way the pedagogue or guardian would be able to relinquish his care and responsibility when his charge reached maturity, and could enter into his full position as a member of the household at the time set for him by his father.

So too, God had set the time for his Son to come to bring Israel to its full status as a spiritual nation having complete faith and freedom. When Israel failed to fulfil this promise, a new spiritual Israel took its place, which fully exercised the faith required. (Gal. 4:1–7.)[15]

Paul's illustration thus involves the entire training and care of the pedagogue up to the youngster's full maturity, and not just the single duty of taking him to the door of the school.

8. The Breadth and Length, Height and Depth— Grasping Understanding Fully.

One of Paul's illustrations has at first struck some readers as strange, for he seems to be talking about boxes! In his letter to the Ephesians he wrote, 'that you may be thoroughly able to grasp mentally with all the holy ones what is the breadth and length and height and depth, and to know the love of the Christ which surpasses knowledge, that you may be filled with all the fullness that God gives.' (Eph. 3:18, 19 NWT.) Some translations apply the four dimensions to Christ's love, but this is clearly something separate and additional to understanding. This is realised when we examine more closely the word for 'grasp mentally' (Greek 'katalambanō'), for this is talking about the acquisition of knowledge by the mental faculties of a person.[16]

Why did Paul use this illustration? He wanted to explain in a simple way the need for Christians to get as complete an understanding as was mentally possible. Already in his day, with the Hebrew Scriptures available, and the additional wealth of information opened up through Christ's teaching and ministry, there was a great deal to know about God as a person, his qualities and purpose. That is why Paul placed such emphasis upon the study of God's Word, the need to become mature and to grow to greater understanding and a closer relationship with God. Meditation and pondering upon all these things would give them a full grasp of all that God had made known, and they would be in a position to answer those who asked a reason for the hope within them. (1 Peter 3:15.)

Of course, Paul intended the four dimensions he gave to be viewed as a whole, and not in their separate parts. But we can arrive at a better appreciation of what he was getting at by looking at the separate parts through some other comments he made. Writing to the Corinthians he told them, 'we throw our hearts wide open to you', In turn, he urged them, 'open your hearts wide too'. (2 Cor. 6:11–13 Knox.) If their hearts were not really willing and receptive, with breadth of generosity, but perhaps restricted by selfishness or wrong motives, then that would also restrict their thinking and re-sponse to the message.

Height and depth might be thought to be the same measurement, but in our common description of things, they reveal a different viewpoint. As Gilpin expresses it in a footnote to his translation, 'the apostle measures the last, as it were, back again, so that discov-ering the depth of God's riches can lift us to the height of exaltation.' That reaction in our hearts and minds can be just as important for our spiritual development as the actual discovery made.[17]

How often the aspect of depth appears in the Bible. Jesus spoke of the man that 'dug deep' to lay secure foundations for his house, and the Christian needs to do the same with regard to building his faith. In another illustration Jesus said that the seed sown in rocky places had no depth of soil for the root to get firm hold, and the sun quickly withered the plant and it died. (Luke 6:48, Matt. 13:5, 6.)

In an eloquent doxology to the Romans, Paul recommended the knowledge of God in these words, 'How great are God's riches! How deep are his wisdom and knowledge! Who can explain his decisions? Who can understand his ways?' (Rom. 11:33 TEV.) Did that mean that we could not plumb those depths? No, it didn't, for on the same theme to the Corinthians, he added, 'But it was to us that God made known his secret by means of his Spirit. The Spirit searches everything, even the hidden depths of God's purposes.' (1 Cor. 2:10 TEV.) Naturally, this still relates to a relative knowledge and understanding appropriate to our requirements, not to infinity.

Although we think of most things on earth as three dimensional, yet here a fourth dimension is clearly added – the spirit of God. Acquiring the spiritual dimension is essential for Christians, for it is a way of looking at things that natural men of the world miss out on completely. It only comes by handling spiritual treasures regularly, so that seeming clods of earth are found to hide precious stones, as it were, through the activity of God's spirit upon us and in us. But there is a vital factor necessary to opening up these treasures. 'He [Christ Jesus] is the key that opens all the hidden treasures of God's wisdom and knowledge.' (Col. 2:3 TEV.) We need to have an appreciation of Christ's ransom and all he did for mankind if we are going to understand God's purposes.

Knowledge in itself is insufficient. It has to be used correctly, to gain a real understanding or mental grasp of all that true Christianity means and demands of us, and to be willing to respond whole-heartedly to that. But having tried to make known all that this entails by this fine illustration, Paul adds the clinching argument. If we wish to be filled with all the fullness that God gives, in addition we must come to know the unending love of Christ for us, and that is something which 'surpasses knowledge'. It cannot be encompassed in mere understanding, however broad and long and high or deep that is. So by all means get that full mental grasp that the Bible opens up to us, but let the love of Christ in our hearts be the wellspring of our faith. (Eph. 3:17.)

Notes and References:

1. Earle, R. *Word Meanings*, 3, 4; Bengel, J. A. *Gnomon*, Vol. 1, 170; Sutcliffe, E, F, 'One Jot or Tittle, Matt. 5:18,' *Biblica*, Vol. 9 (1928), 458–460; Bruce, F. F. *Hard Sayings*, 42; Lachs, S. T. *Rabbinic Commentary*, 88; Savage, H. E. *The Gospel*, 93–95; McNeile, A. H. *The Gospel According to St. Matthew, Greek Text & Notes*, 1928, Macmillan, 59; Cross, F. M. 'The Development of the Jewish Scripts,' in *The Bible and the Ancient Near East, Essays in honor of W. F. Albright*, 1961, Routledge & Kegan Paul, 176, 199.

2. Lightfoot, J, *Horae Hebraicae*, Vol. 2, 299, 300; Abrahams, I. *Studies in Pharisaism*, 2nd series, 'VI. Whited Sepulchres,' 29, 30; Morgan, G. C. *Parables*, 123; Lachs, S. T. 'On Matthew 23: 27–28,' *HTR*, Vol. 68 (1975), 385–388, who refers to the mixing of powdered marble and lime; Schwarz, G. 'Unkenntliche Graber? (Lukas 11:44),' *NT Studies*, Vol. 23 (1977), 345–346; Kaminker, S. F. *Footloose in Jerusalem*, 1981, N. Y. Crown Pub. Inc., 36; Often bones were transferred to ossuaries, and as these were frequently made of limestone, they would undergo a similar spring clean. A cave or purpose built tomb might contain many ossuaries of an entire family, and here too the walls might be whitened, recalling Paul's reference to the High Priest as a 'whitewashed wall'. – Acts 23:3.

3. Marshall, I. H. *The Gospel of Luke, A Commentary on the Greek Text,* (New Int. Greek Test. Comm), Exeter, 1978, Paternoster Press, 499; Bishop, E. F. F. *Jesus of Palestine,* 231, mentions the discovery of rows of early graves in Jerusalem over which people had walked for hundreds of years without knowing it; as long ago as 1699 J. Le Clerc made an enlightening reconciliation of these different gospel verses, see his *A Supplement to Dr. Hammond's Paraphrase & Annotations on the N. T.,* 1699, Buckley, 80.

4. Forster, W. *Palestinian Judaism in N. T. Times,* 1964, Oliver & Boyd, 170–174, 208–210; Lightley, J. W. *Jewish Sects & Parties in the Time of Christ,* 1925, Epworth Press, 138–143; Moore, G. F. *Judaism in the First Centuries of the Christian Era,* 1927, 1966rp, Camb. MS, Harvard U. P. Vol. 2. 157–161, 192, 193; Abrahams, I. *Studies in Pharisaism,* 2nd series, 30–32.

5. Goodspeed, E. J. *Problems,* 29–31 for an excellent history of how this number has been rendered through the centuries.

6. Lightfoot, J. *Horae Hebraicae,* Vol. 3, 178; Montefiore, C. G. *Rabbinic Literature and Gospel Teachings,* 1930, Macmillan, 267, 268, where the Scriptural proof following Rabbi Yose b. Chanina's statement, 'Let him who asks his fellow for forgiveness do so three times and not more" is described as 'fanciful'; Cripps, R. S. *A Critical & Exegetical Commentary on the Book of Amos,* 1960, SPCK, 118, on Amos 1:3 'Certainly no special significance attaches to the precise figures 'three', 'four', . . . the phrase here is intended to suggest a large, but indefinite, number . . . cp. Job 33:14, 29,' for consecutive numerals in pairs.

7. Danby, H. *The Mishnah Translated from the Hebrew* . . . 1933, Oxford U. P. 590; Hollis, F. J. *The Archaeology of Herod's Temple,* with a Commentary on the Tractate 'Middoth,' 1934, J. M. Dent. 235–241, gives plan of 21 Levite guard positions, cp. 1 Chron. 26: 17–19, and 3 priests, 24 in all.

8. Edersheim, A. *The Temple, Its Ministry and Services,* 1874, RTS, 119, 120; Ford, J. M. *Revelation, Introduction/Translation and Commentary,* (Anchor Bible), 1975, N. Y. Doubleday, 263; Rienecker, F & Rogers, C. *Linguistic Key,* 848.

9. Deissmann, G. A. *Light,* 79f; Robinson, J. A. *Ephesians,* 60.

10. Rienecker, F & Rogers, C. *Linguistic Key,* 526; Taylor, C. *Sayings of the Jewish Fathers,* Comprising Pirke Aboth . . . 1897, Camb. U. P. 134, 135; Feldman, A, *Parables,* 35–37.

11. Zerwick, M & Grosvenor, M. *A Grammatical Analysis of the Greek N. T.* 1979, Rome, Biblical Inst. Press, Vol. 2, 577.

12. Pittman, R. T. *Words and Their Ways,* 25; Barclay, W. *N. T. Words,* 138–140; Kittel, G. Ed. *TDNT,* Vol. 8, 250; Thayer, J. H. *Greek-English Lexicon,* 642; Daddow, W. B. *Buried Pictures* 130–133, who tells about a statue of a tidy, well-dressed Greek slave girl in an Italian city. A poor street Arab girl saw it and was captivated by it. She went away, washed her face and combed her hair, then went back and looked again. She then washed and mended her tattered clothes, then went back once more. Each time she made more small improvements until she was tranformed into a beautiful attractive girl. Her secret was to study every detail of her 'model'; Lee, E. K 'Words denoting 'Pattern' in

the N. T,' *NTStud*, Vol. 8 (1962), 172/173; Selwyn, E. G. *First Peter*, 179, using the example in Aeschylus of footprints in the sand, which because of the medium used, leaves a very clear impression of the foot.

13. Pittman, R. T. *Words and Their Ways*, 82–86; Daddow, W. B. *Buried Pictures*, 26–28; Smith, D, *Life and Letters*, 206, 207; Young, N. H. 'Paidagōgos: The Social Setting of a Pauline Metaphor,' *NovTest*. Vol. 29, (1987), 150–176; Young, N. H. 'The Figure of the Paidagōgos in Art and Literature,' *BA*, Vol. 53, (1990), 80–87.

14. Barclay, W. *N. T. Words*, 206–209, whilst Barclay outlines the historical background of the pedagogue, he fails to arrive at the final result in applying the illustration, and this is also evident in his translation.

15. Daddow, W. B. *Buried Pictures*, 28, 29; Longenecker, R. N. 'The Pedagogical Nature of the Law in Galatians 3:19 – 4:7,' *JnlEvang TheolSoc*. Vol. 25 (1982), 53–61; Lyall, F, *Legal Metaphors*, 112–114.

16. Moulton, J. H. *Grammar*, Vol. 1, 158; Abbott-Smith, G. *Greek Lexicon*, 235; Robinson, J. A. *Ephesians*, 176; Westcott, B. F. *St. Paul's Ep. to the Ephesians, Greek Text with Notes*, 1906, Macmillan, 52.

17. Gilpin, W. *An Exposition of the N. T.*, 1798, 3rd ed. Vol. 2, 245.

Chapter 13

Trades and Business Documents

1. Honest Tradesmen—
Standing by God's Word and Principles.

The course of dishonest tradesmen is not something peculiar to our day. Their tricks are commented on in Bible times, like using the bag of dishonest weights. (Deut. 25:13, Micah 6:11.)

So Paul urged Christians to 'see that they engage in honourable occupations . . . and our own people must be taught to engage in honest employment to produce the necessities of life.' (Titus 3: 8, 14 NEB.) The verb rendered 'engage in' (Greek 'proistēmi') carries the idea of a trader standing before his shop, and being diligent to attract customers in to inspect his wares. It gradually came to mean exercising a calling or profession. W. G. Robinson therefore paraphrases Titus this way, 'Christians should stand by their wares', for he both believes in what he is doing and gives honest endeavour at all times.[1]

When it comes to Christian teaching, that principle must be applied even more. Paul defended his ministry when he wrote to the Corinthians, 'Who is equal to the responsibility of such a calling? We are not like so many who adulterate the message of God and pass it off like so much second-rate merchandise; we proclaim His genuine word . . .' (2 Cor. 2:17 Bruce.) Or as Schonfield puts it, 'I am not like the majority who water down God's message . . .' What did he mean?

It was the custom in Roman times for the wine merchants and innkeepers to water down their wine. They would also mix with it new harsh wine, and yet pass the product off as first-rate old wine of quality, with the intention of making profit from the enterprise. So the word Paul used (Greek 'kapēleuō') has the double idea of adulterating and cheating, and the innkeeper ('cauponari') or peddler was one who sold it, often in short measure too.[2]

The Christian must be careful not to water down the truth of God's Word. That message may not at times be very pleasant to those who listen to it. It might involve discipline or correction, as did frequently the message of the ancient prophets. It might have to oppose the weaknesses of fallen mankind in sex and morals, or urge a course of action that might be difficult, even bringing with it persecution and perhaps ostracism. But Paul spoke out fearlessly the clear and entire word of God, never adulterating or mixing it to make it more palatable to his hearers, so that he might be viewed more favourably. Because of that he was thrown out from some cities, and finally brought to Rome to stand trial before Caesar. Can we as Christians today show the same uncompromising faithfulness to God's Word, the Bible?

Peter had the same message, and after Pentecost he became a strong and valiant speaker for truth. He urged Christians of his day, 'Laying aside, therefore, everything base and deceitful . . . be eager like newborn babes for the pure and wholesome milk . . . that you may grow to salvation by it.' (1 Peter 2:1, 2 Schonfield.) That which was 'pure and wholesome' (Greek 'adolos') was unadulterated, and our English word 'sincere' (AV), originally had this meaning of pure and unmixed. Milk could be adulterated by mixing it with gypsum, so Peter was warning Christians to make sure that they grew according to the true principles and word of God, lest they became counterfeit Christians not able to endure in the time of harvest.[3]

So in their secular occupations, and in their work of preaching the gospel, Christians have to be pure and unadulterated. They will be like Nathaniel, of whom Jesus, with his keen perception, could say, 'there is a true Israelite, a completely honest man'. (John 1:47 TNT.)

2. The Distinguishing Hall-mark—
Love Among Yourselves.

After setting forth his new command on love, Jesus made a most significant statement. 'The mark by which all men will know you for my disciples will be the love you bear one another.' (John 13:35 Knox.)

Another rendering is, 'If you bear love to one another, this shall be the token by which all will know that you are my disciples.' (Cassirer.) Kleist and Lilly's translation also uses the word 'token', and Gilpin calls it 'the great distinguishing mark'. Other commentators use such phrases as 'the badge of discipleship', 'a Sign to the world', and 'a distinctive mark'. So there is every reason for the illustration of the 'hall-mark', for that originally meant the standard by which the purity of gold or silver was judged. It came to be the word used from the hall where this assaying took place from the eighteenth century, the Goldsmith's Hall in London.[4]

Jesus gave this mark as the standard by which true Christians would be identified. Many would take up the name of Christ and call themselves 'Christian' but if they did not *act* as such, then they failed the test, and showed they did not have the 'hall-mark'. The example is given of the man who says he loves God, but he hates his own brother, and John without hesitation calls that man a liar. Then he adds, 'this is the divine command that has been given us: the man who loves God must be one who loves his brother as well.' (1 John 4:20, 21 Knox.)

The two great commands for Christians were, first to love God with our whole heart, soul, mind and strength, and then to love our neighbour as ourselves. (Matt. 22:36–40.) The second of these is called the 'royal' or 'kingly' law (James 2:8), because it is a superior law to so many others; it is the king of laws. So how appropriate that it should be the hall-mark of Christianity, which follows the King of Kings.

We might expect that faith would be the hall-mark, for faith is often extolled in the Scriptures, no less so than in the famous eleventh chapter of Hebrews. Or we might put forward hope, for the Christians' hope was more extensive and expansive, and it seemed to be more firmly established in the future than any of the competing philosophies. Yet Paul made this interesting comment at the end of his chapter in praise of love, 'So faith, hope and love endure. These are the great three, and the greatest of them is love.' (1 Cor. 13:13, Goodspeed.)

But we still need to discover why it is that love transcends all other qualities, and why it should be the special hall-mark for Christians that it would not be for other peoples. Paul explains that a

Christian has to really change to a new personality that conforms to all the things he lists in Colossians 3:5–13. Only Christians are 'God-taught [Greek 'theodidaktos'] to love one another.' (1 Thess. 4:9 Young.) This was a word which appears to be specially coined by Paul, perhaps with Isaiah 54:13 in mind. It teaches them to overcome even such things as racial prejudice and family ostracism.

Then Paul again shows how love is the crowning evidence that the person is now really a Christian. 'And over all these things put on love, which completes them and fastens them all together.' (Col. 3:14 Goodspeed.) The very communication of the good news was an extension of that love to others. When they became Christians, people were like human 'letters of recommendation' for the ministry (2 Cor. 3:2, 3), and that bound the Christian community still closer together. Without doubt, love is certainly the special 'hall-mark' of a true Christian.

3. The Deposit—A Trust to Guard.

The apostle Paul concluded his first letter to Timothy with this warning, 'O Timothy, guard the deposit, shunning the profane babblings and incongruities of the "knowledge" so falsely named.' (1 Tim. 6:20 Smith.)

What was 'the deposit' to which Paul here referred? The Greek word is 'parathēkē', a bankers' term which means, 'what is put down' or 'put beside', or entrusted for safekeeping. Looking at the contrast Paul draws with the false knowledge of Gnostics and other groups, 'the deposit' referred to the body of truth handed down through the apostles from Christ Jesus, with its associated teachings and doctrines, and the faith engendered from them. Paul urges Timothy to ensure that the truth was safeguarded, and nothing was either lost or changed. So an extra word is inserted when he later repeats the thought. 'The *genuine* Deposit guard through the Holy Spirit who dwells in us.' (2 Tim. 1:14 Smith.)[5]

This was not a deposit to be locked away, inaccessible and of little benefit to anyone. So Paul continued, 'You then, my child, find your power in the grace which Christ Jesus supplies; and what you heard from me with the corroboration of many witnesses, deposit in the keeping of faithful men, such as will be qualified in turn to teach others.' (2 Tim. 2:12 Smith.) This was a living faith, and a vital body of truth, and to use it correctly and pass it on faithfully was the best means of guarding it.[6]

An interesting addition to this illustration can be drawn from Jesus' words, where he uses the idea of a 'treasure store' as the deposit. 'When, therefore, a teacher of the law has become a learner in the kingdom of Heaven, he is like a householder who can produce from his store both the new and the old.' (Matt. 13:52 NEB.) The 'learner in the kingdom' has taken in the new teachings of Jesus Christ, and has been able to apply them to his previous knowledge of the Hebrew Scriptures as a teacher of the law. He is now well versed in both the old and the new, and has a fine 'store' of treasure with which to enrich his audience.

The word here is Greek 'thēsauros', meaning 'a treasury of knowledge', and from which we derive the word for a dictionary or encyclopaedia, a thesaurus. For the Christian, that thesaurus is especially the Bible, since it contains the 'deposit' as Paul understood it, now well refined for our generation through more accurate translations, so that we have his words and those of other Bible writers speaking more clearly to us than at any time since the first century. May we continue to 'guard the deposit' and go on teaching it to faithful men.[7]

4. Tested in the Fire—The Approved Condition.

Because a Christian lives in a selfish and alien world, he has to expect that his or her faith will come under test or trial, and Jesus himself warned that this would happen. But what is likely to be the result of such trials? An interesting illustration used by the apostles Peter and Paul gives us the answer.

Writing to the Corinthians, Paul put two questions to them. 'Examine yourselves: are you living the life of faith? Put yourselves to the test [Greek 'dokimazō']. Surely you recognize that Jesus Christ is among you? – unless of course you prove unequal to the test ['adokimos']. I hope you will come to see that we are not unequal to it.' (2 Cor. 13:5, 6 NEB.)

The type of test referred to here was a technical term used for assaying metal or coinage. The mined ore was put into the fire so that the dross mixed in could be drawn off, leaving the pure metal behind. The owner of the ore did not work through this process unless he hoped that a reasonable quantity of genuine metal would be found. So it is with the testing permitted by God – he is confident that those with genuine faith will pass the test. 'The melting pot is for silver and the crucible for gold, but it is the Lord who assays the hearts of men.' (Prov. 17:3 NEB.)[8]

Paul's confidence reflects this conviction when he writes to the Romans, 'More than this: let us even exult in our present sufferings, because we know that suffering trains us to endure, and endurance brings proof that we have stood the test ['dokimē'], and this proof is the ground of hope. Such a hope is no mockery, because God's love has flooded our inmost heart through the Holy Spirit he has given us.' (Rom. 5:3–5 NEB.)

Peter takes up the same illustration with the same sort of confidence, but he lifts it even higher by first introducing the most valuable metal of all, gold, and then drawing attention to its perishable nature when compared with tested faith. 'Even gold passes through the assayer's fire, and more precious than perishable gold is faith which has stood the test ['dokimion']. These trials come so that your faith may prove itself worthy of all praise, glory, and honour when Jesus Christ is revealed.' (1 Peter 1:7 NEB.)

R. C. Trench offers a final conclusion that is worth repeating. He compared 'dokimazō' with a similar Greek word 'peirazō', but found the latter had the flavour of putting to the proof 'with the intention and hope that the "proved" may not turn out "approved," but reprobate. [i.e. Matt. 4:1, 3, 1 Cor. 7:5, Rev. 2:10] But 'dokimazein' could not be used of Satan, seeing that he never proves that he may approve, nor tests that he may accept.'[9] Only God does that, and how precious to him – more than all the gold on earth – is the tested faith of his servants, ancient and modern.

5. Crediting the Account—Our Standing with God.

The apostle Paul draws an interesting contrast between sin and righteousness, as if these were debit and credit entries in a ledger – the 'ledger of life'. (Rom. 5:13 Rutherford.) As H. K. Moulton puts it, in discussing Paul's use of the Greek word 'logizomai', 'This is thinking in the sense of "reckoning it out", "calculating", getting all the implications clear. It implies putting it all down to the accounts so that they balance; not paying out something here, something there, without being sure how it has been spent.'[10]

Paul's thinking is clear in the case of the runaway slave Onesimus, who became a Christian, and now returns to Philemon as a brother. Paul recommends him to the extent that he says to Philemon, 'And if he was ever dishonest or is in your debt, debit me [Greek 'ellogeō'] with the amount. I, Paul write this with my own hand – I will pay you in full.' (Philemon 18, 19a. Weymouth 3rd ed.)[11]

But his greater application of the metaphor relates to how man stands with God. Since God is love, the principles that Paul sets out regarding love for mankind, find their source in him, and amongst these Paul includes, 'love keeps no score ['logizomai'] of the wrong'. (1 Cor. 13:5 NEB.) That love was climaxed by God sending his own son to the earth, as Paul explains in his second letter to the Corinthians, 'We are to tell how God was in Christ reconciling the world to Himself, not charging ['logizomai'] men's transgressions to their account.' (2 Cor. 5:19 Weymouth 3rd ed.)

In his letter to the Romans, Paul enlarges on the subjects of justification and righteousness, and he refers again to the account situation. As Moulton paraphrases his thought, 'Work it out ['logizē'] you critical man. Do you really calculate that you are likely to be free from condemnation yourself?'[12] The Mosaic Law only served to show up man's sinfulness by his failure to keep it, so man could never justify himself before God by what he did, or attain a righteous standing by his own efforts. The only acceptable way was by demonstrating faith in God and in his Son Jesus Christ, and his great sacrifice.

Such a faith was shown by Abraham, but as he lived long before Christ came to offer an atoning sacrifice, how could he attain the righteous standing which he had in God's eyes? Paul explains by first quoting from Genesis 15:6, 'Abraham believed God [put his faith in God – NEB] and this was placed to his credit [Greek 'logizomai'] as righteousness.' (Rom. 4:3 Weymouth 3rd ed.)

Paul then adds a further illustration about a man who works, and earns his money because of that, so that his employer is not paying him as a favour, but because it is a debt he owes to him. But as a man cannot work for or earn righteousness, he has to demonstrate his faith in God, and 'his faith is placed to his credit as righteousness'. (Rom. 4:5b Weymouth 3rd ed.) Such a man can be counted happy, for David had recorded in Psalm 32:2, 'Blessed is the man of whose sin the Lord will not take account ['logizomai']'. (Rom. 4:8 Weymouth 3rd ed.)

Yet in Abraham's case this credit was put to his account before he was circumcised, so this gives hope to many outside the nation of Israel, that their faith might also result in a credit to them as they walk in Abraham's footsteps. (Rom. 4:9–12.) And just as he was called 'God's friend' because he drew so close to God through his faith, so Christians today by their faith can also become friends of God. (James 2:23, Gen. 18:19 Rotherham, 2 Chron. 20:7, Isa. 41:8.)

6. Receipt in Full—How do we Wish to be Paid?

In concluding his letter to the Philippians, the apostle Paul commends them for assisting him in a financial and practical way, even after he had left them to go to Thessalonica. He tells them, 'I have been paid in full [Greek 'apechō'], I have been overpaid. I have more than enough, now that I have received from Epaphroditus the things sent . . .' (Phil. 4:18 C. K. Williams.)

That word 'apechō' has turned up hundreds of times in ancient papyrus receipts found in the dry sands of Egypt since the turn of the century. It is a technical term in business and means, 'receipted in full', 'fully paid'. In one case the receipt is scribbled on an ostracon, a broken piece of pottery, and the word 'apechōn' is clearly seen after the person's name.[13]

We can now note the contrast when Paul asks Philemon to welcome back Onesimus. 'If he has done you any injury, or owes you anything, put that down on my account. I, Paul, am writing this with my own hand, I will pay it back [Greek 'apotinō'] . . .' (Philemon 18, 19a, C. K. Williams.)

The metaphor of receiving and making payments now helps us considerably as we turn to Jesus' words about the scribes and Pharisees in the Sermon on the Mount. Three times Jesus refers to their course of action; first, when they give money to the poor, and let everyone know that they are doing so that they may win the praises of men. Then Jesus added, 'truly I tell you, they have been paid their wages in full ['apechō'].' Second, when they pray prominently, 'for men to see, truly I tell you, they have been paid their wages in full.' Third, when it comes to fasting, they make it obvious 'so that they may be seen to be fasting. Truly I tell you, they have been paid their wages in full.' (Matt. 6:2, 5, 16 C. K. Williams.)

After each of these three examples, Jesus tells his followers to do these same acts in secret, to give in secret, to pray in their inner room, and to fast without making it apparent, and then each time he adds, 'and your Father who sees in secret will pay you [Greek 'apodidōmi']'. (Matt. 6:4, 6, 18 C. K. Williams.)

Both 'apodidōmi' and 'apotinō' are words expressing the debtor's intention to repay what is owed. In the papyrus documents these 'promises to repay' are usually in the debtor's own handwriting, just as Paul had done.[14]

Those who do things that men may see them are fully paid by the praises of men; those who seek to please God know that, although done secretly, he is aware of their faithful course of action, and 'promises to repay' them, as Jesus confirmed.

7. The Potter's Prerogative—Serving as God Directs.

The potter (Greek 'kerameus', from which comes our English word 'ceramics'), was an important person in Biblical times. His products were widely used by everyone, from the highest in the land to the humblest peasant. The result of many years of archaeological research is a great variety of pottery of all kinds, which has become very valuable as a means for dating past civilizations, as pottery types have changed and advanced in style and sophistication. From the pot made entirely in the potter's two hands, the art progressed to the use of a 'slow wheel', a single wheel rotated slowly by the hand or foot. Finally there appeared the true potter's wheel, the 'kick wheel', where the lower flywheel was kicked into motion, and in turn rotated the upper throwing wheel.[15]

It is to this last type of dual wheel that Jeremiah refers when he says, 'Then I went down to the potter's house, according to the word of the Lord, and behold, he was doing work on the wheel [wheels – Rotherham, Goodspeed, NWT]. And the vessel which he was making of clay was spoiled in the hand of the potter; so he mixed the clay and made it into another vessel, as seemed good to him.' (Jer. 18:3, 4 Lamsa.) Then Jeremiah is told to apply the illustration. God can deal with the nation of Israel as the potter. If they repent and obey God he can preserve the national 'pot', but if they continue in a bad and wrong course he can destroy the pot – they are in his hand like a fragile vessel.

The prophet Isaiah showed God in the wider sense as the Great Potter, not just of the nation of Israel, but of all mankind, formed or created upon the earth that he had made for the purpose. (Isa. 29:16, 45:9–12, 18.)

The apostle Paul quotes from Isaiah in his letter to the Romans when he enlarges on this illustration. 'However, O man, who are you to question God? Shall the thing formed say to him who formed it, Why have you made me like this? Does not the potter ['kerameus'] have power over his clay, to make out of the same lump vessels, one for special occasions, and the other for daily service?' (Rom. 9:20, 21 Lamsa.)

Then like Jeremiah, he applies the illustration. God in his mercy saved a remnant from national Israel and added to them gentiles who showed faith. They became the favoured pottery vessels. (Rom. 9:23, 24.) But Paul also speaks of 'vessels of wrath which were ready for destruction'. (Rom. 9:22 Lamsa.) The nation of Israel had come into this position by their continual stiff-necked rebellion, just as Pharoah had displayed that attitude and become the original vessel of wrath in Paul's set of comparisons. (Rom. 9:17.)

As the Great Potter, God could have 'simply rubbed out' Pharoah (as John Robinson puts it), and so with unfaithful Israel, they could have been broken in pieces, so that there would not be a large enough fragment or sherd to carry fire from the hearth, or lap up a little water to drink. (Isa. 30:14.) But Pharoah remained so that God's name Yehowah or Jehovah might become known throughout the earth (Rom. 9:17), and Israel remained so that a remnant might be saved (verses 27–29). This very patience of God showed the true character of those vessels in time, rather than what they just seemed like externally.[16]

Paul also uses this metaphor in an individual sense in his second letter to the Corinthians. 'But we have this treasure in earthen [Greek 'ostrakinos'] vessels, that the excellency of power may be from God, and not from us.' (2 Cor. 4:7 Lamsa.) A rather plain and ordinary looking earthen vessel might not seem to be worth very much, but imagine its value when it has been found to preserve a treasure of inestimable worth, just as actually happened with some of the Dead Sea Scrolls, protected through some 2,000 years from damp and rodents.

Yes, that humble human creatures can be used to proclaim a message of such treasured good news is due to God's power through his active force – his holy spirit. Though 'harassed on all sides, we are not conquered', says Paul, 'Persecuted, but not forsaken; cast down, but not destroyed.' (2 Cor. 4:8b, 9 Lamsa.) If literal pots seem frail and fragile, easily broken in pieces, the Christian can rest assured that the Great Potter is quite capable of protecting the metaphorical pots, his faithful servants, who are willing to be used in his service in any way he directs, whether it be for special occasions, or menial service day in and day out.

8. Measure and Canon—The Straight Edge.

In ancient Egypt and Palestine the reed was much more common than it is today. From it all kinds of products were made, including paper from the papyrus plant. Many of these reeds grew extremely straight and tall, sometimes exceeding twelve feet, so when cut they were useful as measuring rods. The generic name for these reeds of various species is Hebrew 'qaneh' or 'kaneh', from which are derived the Greek 'kanna', the Latin *canna*, and the English word 'cane'.[17]

Such a reed (Greek 'kalamos') was given to the apostle John to measure the Temple and the city of New Jerusalem. (Rev. 11:1, 21:15, 16.) This reed or measuring rod might be marked off in units, just as a modern ruler is marked, and a series of these marks on a straight edge was called a canon (Greek 'kanōn'). Gradually this came to have a metaphorical application, as a rule of faith, a rule of truth or a standard to follow, a model, and finally, a list or series of books following such a rule of truth.[18]

This is how the apostle Paul uses the word when he speaks about those following Jesus Christ, and becoming 'a new creation' by the changes made in their lives. 'May all who rule ['kanōn'] their conduct by this principle find peace and mercy – they who are the Israel of God.' (Gal. 6:16 TCNT.)

A difficult passage in Paul's second letter to the Corinthians uses 'kanōn' three times in four verses, and raises the question, was Paul using the term literally in reference to an area of territory measured off, or with a boundary line, or was he using it as an illustration metaphorically? Some scholars have accused Paul of writing vaguely here, but could it be that he used both meanings in a deliberate play on words, of which he was so fond? Some evidence of this is that he introduces the term 'measure' (Greek 'metron') several times as well.

Paul first refers to his competitors who measure themselves by their own ideas, and see room for boasting in their achievements. (2 Cor. 10:12.) This verse clearly sets the metaphor rolling. Then he continues, 'By contrast we do not intend to boast beyond measure, but will measure ourselves by the standard ['kanōn'] which God laid down for us, namely that of having come all the way to you. . . . So we are not boasting beyond measure, about other men's work; in fact, we hope, as your faith increases, to grow greater and greater by this standard ['kanōn'] of ours, by preaching the gospel to regions beyond you, rather than boasting about work already done in someone else's province ['kanōn'].' (2 Cor. 10:13–16 NJB.)

So God's standard or canon was to seek to do his will, and Paul tried to use that as his straight-edge, and that motivated him to take the good news to Corinth in the first place, and to other regions not already covered by others. The increase in the Corinthians' faith would encourage him, and show his course was blessed by God. That in turn would stir his zeal for more new fields as God directed, rather than turning to territory already measured out to someone else.

So by a skilful mix of literal and metaphorical application of canon and measure Paul explains why he will not boast beyond what God has assigned to him. The ideas of literal measured territory assignments and spheres of spiritual influence, both theirs and his, are so cleverly integrated as to be almost inseparable.[19]

9. Cutting Straight Lines—
Accurate Handling of God's Word.

When Paul urged Timothy to be a good workman he visualized a scene then common in the Middle East, and applied it as a metaphor. 'Strive diligently to present thyself approved of God, a workman that has not to be ashamed, cutting in a straight line the word of truth.' (2 Tim. 2:15 Darby.)

That this was intended as a metaphor is clear from Paul's use of 'workman' (Greek 'ergatēs'), a labourer, rather than a teacher. But what does the word 'cutting' refer to? This is used in Proverbs 11:5 LXX, for cutting a straight path, and Weymouth's footnote (3rd ed) says, 'Lit. "cutting" or "laying out", like a new road'. The NKJV Interlinear footnote points out that 'the emphasis is on the idea of "straight" and not "cutting".' The principle of 'straight-cutting' can be applied to many things. So one translation reads, 'a labourer who needs not to blush for his work, but who drives the ploughshare of truth in a straight furrow.' (Way.) It might refer to Paul's cutting of his rough camel-hair cloth for his tent-making, and if that was not cut straight, the tent would have gaps and strains that would affect its efficiency. Conybeare thinks it applies to the carpenter, who needs to cut his wood accurately and straight.

But perhaps the most appropriate picture is that of the stonemason, who needs to cut his stones true and straight if he wishes them to fit well together, making a solid and strong building. The Egyptian pyramids provide a superb testimony to the skill of the ancient mason, for it is difficult to insert a knife blade between the outer casing stones, so finely were they trimmed. Paul was also familiar with the Roman Appian Way, called the 'queen of great roads' with exactly cut stones, fitting perfectly without cement or irons.[20]

But just how would the metaphor apply in Timothy's handling of God's Word? To straight-cut the word of truth is always to handle it skilfully and accurately, correctly analysing it without distortion. Some translations partly retain the metaphor: 'cutting a straight course by handling properly the word of truth' (Blackwelder), 'following a straight course in preaching the truth' (NAB), 'having kept to the straight line with the Message of Truth' (Schonfield), 'but rightly shapes the message of truth'. (Goodspeed.)

Many translations remove the metaphor altogether, and a selection of their renderings will be helpful here:

'correctly interpreting the message of the truth.' – NBV.
'skilfully handling the word of truth.' – Rotherham.
'accurate in delivering the Message of the Truth.' – TCNT.
'who properly presents the message of truth.' – C. B. Williams.
'expounding soundly the word of the truth.' – Wuest.

So such a Christian would allow the Bible to speak for itself, seeing to it that context is carefully observed, that its various stones are fitted together exactly, in a harmonious fashion so that it rings true to itself. Paul is also stressing the responsibility of one who speaks God's Word, for his carelessness or inaccuracy could sow seeds of doubt in the minds of his listeners.

Such a situation is described by Paul when he wrote to the Galatians. He recalls how Peter took a wrong course when in Antioch, and because of his prominence, other Jewish Christians followed him, and even Barnabas was misled. When Paul saw this he spoke to Peter to correct his thinking, because 'I saw they were not walking straight according to the truth of the good news'. (Or if you prefer the analogy of the stonemason, 'their conduct did not square with the truth'. – NEB; Gal. 2:14 NWT.)[21]

Paul backed up his rebuke to Peter by reasoning from the principles of God's Word, showing the importance of faith rather than works of law, and concluding by enforcing the consequences; if we build up again what has been finished with, then Christ would have died for nothing. (Gal. 2:15–21.)

How easily had Peter become side-tracked, and others soon followed his lead. So there was good reason for Paul to warn Timothy about straight-cutting the road that others would follow, so that all could reach the goal of life successfully.

10. Buying Out Time—
Using Well Every Opportunity.

The apostle Paul was very conscious of the importance of time to the Christian. He saw this from two points of view. First, as time was related to the purpose of God, and so limited by the cutting short of the days of wickedness upon the earth. (1 Cor. 7:29.) Second, from the individual's own shortened lifetime, and the need for him to do all he could while he had the opportunity to do so. (2 Cor. 6:1, 2.)

Regarding the purpose of God, Paul uses two illustrations. 'Make no mistake about the age we live in,' he says, 'already it is high time for us to awake out of sleep; our salvation is closer to us now than when we first learned to believe. The night is far on its course; day draws near.' (Rom. 13:11, 12a Knox.) This was an apt illustration, for Christ had brought life and light into the world, and opened up a great wealth of fresh understanding through the Christian message. It was as if men had been asleep during the night, and now needed to wake up because the dawn was here, and a new day was coming for mankind.

His second illustration was based on the metaphor of shortening sail, contracting it, and so not leaving as much sail exposed to the wind. (See Chapter 11, #5.) This is what was happening to time. 'But this, brothers, I do say, there is not much time left now . . .' ('the time left is reduced' – ASV), and so one's course of action should be governed by this principle. He then gives several examples for applying this view, one of which is, 'If people buy, they must do so on the understanding that they have no secure possession of anything.' Then he gives the reason for not getting engrossed in the pursuit of material things, 'for this world in its present changing form will not last much longer'. (1 Cor. 7:29–31 Barclay.)[22]

How much more can we endorse Paul's words today when we look at the world's fast changing form, so that even the most stable things on which people think they can depend prove to be insecure and can disappear overnight.

But it is concerning each person's own individual life span that

Paul really drives home his illustration. He is emphasizing the right and best use of time, even gaining time wherever we can ('playing for time' – Dan. 2:8). 'See to it, therefore, that you conduct yourselves ever so carefully; not as foolish but as wise people who make the best possible use of their time, because these are evil days.' (Eph. 5:15, 16 Berkeley cp. Col. 4:5.) The Greek word here ('exagorazō') has the thought of buying up a commodity on the open market, taking the best opportunities for buying and selling when they are available. So it can be translated, 'cornering the market in opportunity'. (Ward p63, see also Way.)

Howson paraphrases this thought as, 'Buy out of the market what you may never buy so cheap again; use the opportunity while you have it.' John Tillotson (1630–1694), felt very strongly on the subject of time: 'nothing is more wastefully spent and more prodigally squandered . . . we give away such large portions of our time to our ease and pleasure, to diversion and idleness, or trifling and unprofitable conversation.' The particular Greek word Paul used here was 'kairos', the youthful, keen, determined aggressor, contrasted with 'chronos', 'the slow-moving, silent, almost inert teacher'. 'Kairos is that immediate present which is what we make it: Time charged with opportunity, our own possession to be seized and vitalized by human energy, momentous, effectual, decisive: Time, the inert, transformed into purposeful activity.'[23]

It is not just a case of 'redeeming the time' (AV), in the sense of making up for lost time. But some scholars understand the thought as 'buying away from' those who misuse it. We should view time as being in the wrong hands, and that we want to purchase it from them and use it properly. Our life span represents a certain unspecified length of time – it is not endless in this present system – so how to use *all* that time is up to us. We can corner the market for all the time available to us, not wasting it, but utilizing it in the most profitable way.[24]

In the land of Israel there are many wilderness areas. There a flash flood may transform a desert overnight, and flowers in brilliant colour and lovely form seem to spring up before the eyes. But they must be seen and enjoyed then, gathered in while they flourish, for tomorrow the hot sun and east wind may burn them up and they will fade and be gone.[25] Both Jesus and James showed that man's life span is similarly brief and short; 'If God clothes like that the wild flowers which have one brief day . . . .' (Matt. 6:30 Barclay, James 1:9–11, 4:14.) Our moments are precious, and Paul urged us to use them to the full in the best service of all, that of the God who gave us life to enjoy.

Notes and References:

1. Robinson, W. G. *N. T. Treasure*, 222; Field, F, *Notes on the Translation of the N. T.* 1899, Camb. U. P. 223, 224; Zerwick, M & Grosvenor, M. *A Grammatical Analysis of the Greek N. T.* 1979, Rome, Biblical Inst. Press, Vol. 2. 650, 651.

2. Trench, R. C. *Synonyms*, 220–223; Robinson, W. G. *N. T. Treasure*, 222–224; Vincent, M. R. *Word Studies*, Vol. 2, 813; Smith, D. *Life & Letters*, 354 footnote; cp. Isa. 1:22, wheat beer diluted with water.

3. Trench, R. C. *Synonyms*, 201; *Irenaeus Against Heresies*, Book III, ch. 17, (4),'giving lime mixed with water for milk.' Translated by A. Roberts & J. Donaldson, 1979rp, Grand Rapids MN, Eerdmans.

4. Gilpin, W, *An Exposition of the N. T.*, 1798, 3rd ed. Vol. 1, 379; Bernard, J. H. *Gospel According to St. John*, (I. C. C. series), 1928, Edinburgh, Clark, Vol. 2, 528; Lindars, B, *The Gospel of John*, (New Century Bible), 1972, Oliphants, 464; MacRory, J, *The Gospel of St. John, with Notes*, 1923, 7th ed. Clonskeagh Brown & Nolan, 235; *Shorter Oxford English Dictionary*, Vol. 1. 917.

5. Smith, D. *The Days of His Flesh*, 1910, Hodder, XV, XVI; Smith, D. *Life & Letters*, 593f; Earle, R. *Word Meanings*, 403, 404; Marshall, A, Ed. *GSM*, Aug. 1934, 483.

6. Derrett, J. D. M. *Jesus's Audience*, 175–177, who suggests that Matt. 12:35, likely refers to coins, genuine or counterfeit, and the bad man tries to pass off his coins as genuine. This is why Paul urges us to 'prove everything, retain the genuine. ' – 1 Thess. 5:22 Smith; Daddow, W. B. *Buried Pictures*, 120.

7. Morgan, G. C. *Parables*, 76–78; Waard, J. De. 'The Treasure of Life,' *EcumRev*. Vol. 34 (1982), 258–262.

8. Trench, R. C. *Synonyms*, 267–270; Turner, N. *Christian Words*, 444–447; Daddow, W. B. *Buried Pictures*, 105–114; Earle, R. *Word Meanings* 160; Deissmann, G. A. *Bible Studies*, 259–262.

9. Trench, R. C. *Synonyms*, 270; Wuest, K. *Word Studies*, 1973, Grand Rapids, MN, Eerdmans, Vol. 3, 'Treasures,' 126–131.

10. Moulton, H. K. *Challenge*, 161; Earle, R. *Word Meanings*, 157, 168; Marshall, A, *Gleanings*, 40–43; Barclay, W. *N. T. Words*, 124; Waugh, R. M. L. *Living Words*, 55–59; Thomas, W. H. G, 'Apostolic Arithmetic; A Pauline Word-Study,' *ET*, Vol. 17 (1905/6), 211–214.

11. Earle, R. *Word Meanings*, 162; Pentecost, J. D. 'Studies in Philemon. Part IV: Charge That to My Account. ' *BiblSac*. Vol. 130, (1973), 50–57.

12. Moulton, H. K. *Challenge*, 161.

13. Deissmann, G. A. *Light*, 110, 111

& fig. 14; *Bible Studies*, 229; Robinson, W. G. *N. T. Treasure*, 31, 32; Barclay, W. *N. T. Words*, 51–53.

14. Deissmann, G. A. *Light*, 331, 332; Zerwick, M. *Biblical Greek*, Trans. by Smith, J. 1963, Rome, Scripta Pontificii Inst. Biblici, 94; Smith, D. *Life & Letters*, 575 footnote, noting that apotinō is the stronger word, perhaps carrying a sanction for any failure to repay; Robinson, W. G. *N. T. Treasure*, 30, 31; Wilson, C. A. *Gospels*, 75; Simpson, E. K. *Words Worth Weighing*, 15–17.

15. Johnston, R. H. 'The Biblical Potter,' *BA*. Vol. 37, (1974), 86–106; Miller, M. S & J. L. *Bible Life*, 110–116; Wright, G, E, 'The Last Thousand Years Before Christ,' *NatGeogM*, Vol. 118, (Dec. 1960), 832/3, shows one of the oldest pottery wheels found, where the potter turned the upper wheel with one hand, whilst shaping the pot with the other.

16. Robinson, J. A. T. *Wrestling with Romans*, 1979, SCM, 115–120, which also clearly shows why predestination is not involved in Paul's argument; Bullinger, E. W. *Enjoy the Bible*, 397–399, 'The Potter's House;' Plumptre, E, H, 'The Potter and the Clay,' *Expositor* 1st series, Vol. 4 (1876), 469–480.

17. Tristram, H. B. *Natural History*, 433–437; Buttrick, G. A. Ed. *The Interpreter's Dictionary of the Bible*, 1962, N. Y. Abingdon Press, Vol. 2, 290, 295, 296.

18. Trench, R. C. *Study of Words*, 230, 231; Bruce, F. F. *The Canon of Scripture*, 1988, Downers Grove, IL. Inter-Varsity Press, 17, 18; Robinson, J. A. *Ephesians*, 261; Skeat, W. W. *Etymological Dictionary*, 89, 'a straight rod, a rule in the sense of 'carpenter's rule;' also, a rule or model, a standard of right.'

19. Earle, R. *Word Meanings*, 261 sums it up well; Plummer, A Ed. *The Second Ep. . . . to the Corinthians*, (CGT), 1912, Camb. U. P. 154–156; Plummer, A, *Second Ep. of St. Paul to the Corinthians*, (ICC series), 1915, Edin. Clark, 286–290; Menzies, A. *The Second Ep . . . to the Corinthians*, 1912, Macmillan, 74, 75; Vincent, M. R. *Word Studies*, Vol. 2, 835. Horsley, G. H. R., *New Documents Illustrating Early Christianity*, 1981, North Ryde, NSW, Australia, Macquarie Univ. 44, 45, recording an edict using 'kanōn' in a geographically related sense.

20. Edwards, I. E. S. *The Pyramids of Egypt*, 1972, New ed. Ebury Press & M. Joseph, 207, 208, quoting F. Petrie, 'the mean variation of the cutting of the stone from the straight line and from a true square is but 0. 01 on a length of 75 inches up the face, an amount of accuracy equal to the most modern opticians' straight-edges of such a length . . . the mean opening of the joint was but 1/100th inch;' Daddow, W. B. *Buried Pictures*, 70–76; Dodd, C. H. 'Some Problems of N. T. Translation,' *BT*, Vol. 13, (1962), 149; Neuburger, A. *Technical Arts*, 457–460, on Roman roads; Robertson, A. T. *Word Pictures*, Vol. 4, 619.

21. Simpson, E. K. *Words Worth Weighing*, 31; *NKJV Interlinear*, 'they were not straightforward about the truth of the gospel'.

22. Humphry, W. G. *A Commentary on the R. V. of the N. T.* 1888, SPCK, 304.

23. Howson, J. S. *Metaphors*, 133; Moffatt, J, *The Golden Book of Tillotson*, 1926, Hodder, 182, 183; Pope, R. M. *Studies*, 43 for the quotation from Butcher, *Harvard Lectures on Greek Subjects* 117–120.

24. Alford, H, *The Greek Testament*, 1857, 2nd ed. Rivingtons, Vol. 3, 129; Robertson, A. T. *Word Pictures*, Vol. 4, 510; Westcott, B. F. *St. Paul's Ep. to the Ephesians*, 1906, Macmillan, 81; Robinson, J. A. *Ephesians*, 202, who argues for buying out or away from, rather than buying up, favoured by Westcott; Lightfoot, J. B. *Colossians*, 230; Pope, R. M. *Studies*, 41–46; Brown, C. Ed. *NIDNTT*, Vol. 1, 267, 268.

25. Alon, A. *The Natural History of the Land of the Bible*, 1978, N. Y. Doubleday, 169, 170.

Select Bibliography

Books or articles are included if they are central to the overall theme, or if they are referred to frequently. Citations in the Notes use the underlined part of the title. Books are published in London unless stated. Other works on specific illustrations are referenced in the Notes.

Abbott-Smith, G. A Manual Greek Lexicon of the N. T. 1937, 3rd ed. N. Y. Scribner's.

Abrahams, I. Studies in Pharisaism and the Gospels, 1917, 1st series, Cambridge U. P. 178pp. esp. Ch. XII, The Parables.

Abrahams, I. Studies in Pharisaism and the Gospels, 1924, 2nd series, Cambridge U. P. 226pp.

Alford, H. The Greek Testament . . . with Critical & Exegetical Commentary, 1857–1877, var. ed. Rivington's, 4 vols.

Arndt, W. F. & Gingrich, F. W. A Greek-English Lexicon of the N. T., & Other Early Christian Literature, based on W. Bauer's German work, 1979, 2nd ed. rev. with Danker, F. W. Chicago U. P. 900pp.

Ayers, D. M. English Words from Latin and Greek Elements, 1965, Tucson, U. of Arizona Press, 271pp.

Barclay, W. New Testament Words, 1964, SCM, 288pp. Includes discussion on some 18 metaphors, but at times places too much emphasis on the classical Greek background.

Barr, J. The Semantics of Biblical Language, 1961, O. U. P. 313pp.

Back, J. R. The Healing Words of Jesus, 1993, Grand Rapids, Baker, 173pp. Examines six metaphors. Too late for use in text.

Bengel, J. A. Gnomon of the N. T. 1858, Edin. Clark, 5 vols. Rev. & Ed. by A. R. Fausset.

Bishop, E. F. F. Jesus of Palestine, 1955, Lutterworth Press, 328pp.

Brown, C. Ed. The New International Dictionary of N. T. Theology, 1986, Grand Rapids, Zondervan 4 vols. cited <u>NIDNTT</u>.

Bruce, F. F. The <u>Hard Sayings</u> of Jesus, 1983, Downers Grove, IL. Inter-Varsity, 266pp.

Bullinger, E. W. Ed. The <u>Companion Bible</u>, n.d. Lamp Press rp, 1914+227pp.

Bullinger, E. W. How to <u>Enjoy the Bible</u>, 1907, Eyre & Spottiswoode, 436pp.

Carson, D. A. Exegetical <u>Fallacies</u>, 1984, Grand Rapids, MN, Baker, 153pp.

Corswant, W. A <u>Dictionary of Life</u> in Bible Times, 1960, Hodder, 309pp.

Cotterell, P & M. Turner, <u>Linguistics</u> and Biblical Interpretation, 1989, Downers Grove, IL, Inter-Varsity Press, 348pp.

Daddow, W. B. <u>Buried Pictures</u> in our English Version of the Bible, 1911, Stockwell, 8+133pp. Scarce but valuable.

Dalman, G. H. <u>Jesus-Jeshua</u>, Studies in the Gospels, 1929, SPCK, 14+256pp.

Danby, H. <u>The Mishnah</u>, Translated from the Hebrew, 1933, Oxf. O. U. P. 32+844pp.

Deissmann, G. A. Bible Studies, 1903, 2nd ed. Edin. Clark, 15+384pp.

Deissmann, G. A. <u>Light</u> from the Ancient East, 1927, rev. ed. Hodder, 32+535pp.

Deissmann, G. A. <u>St. Paul</u>, A Study in Social and Religious History, 1912, Hodder, 19+316pp.

Derrett, J. D. M. Law in the N. T., 1970, Darton Longman & Todd

Derrett, J. D. M. <u>Jesus's Audience</u>, The Social and Psychological Environment in which He Worked. 1973, Darton Longman & Todd, 240pp.

Dodd, C. H. 'Some <u>Problems</u> of N. T. Translation,' BT Vol. 13, (1962) 145–157.

Earle, R. <u>Word Meanings</u> in the N. T. 1986, Michigan, Baker, 487pp.

Edersheim, A. The <u>Life and Times</u> of Jesus the Messiah, n.d. (1980's) rp. of 1886 ed. Mclean, VA, MacDonald, 698+828pp.

Farmer, L. We Saw the <u>Holy City</u>, 1953 rev. ed. Epworth, 272pp.

Farrar., F. W. The <u>Rhetoric</u> of St. Paul, Expositor ser. I, (1879), 1–27.

Feldman, A. The Parables and Similes of the Rabbis, Agricultural and Pastoral, 1924, Cambridge U. P. 9+290pp.

Fields, W. W. 'The Translation of Biblical Live and Dead Metaphors and Similes and other Idioms,' GraceTheolJnl, Vol. 2 (1981), 191–204.

Gadsby, J. My Wanderings: Being Travels in the East in 1846–47, 1850–51, 1852–53, 1881, Gadsby, 2 vols. 621+548pp.

Geikie, C. The Holy Land and the Bible, n.d. Cassell, Quiver ed. 12+948pp.

Goodspeed, E. J. Problems of N. T. Translation, 1945, Chicago, U. of Chicago Press, 15+215pp.

Gower, R. The New Manners and Customs of Bible Times, 1987, Chicago, Moody. 393pp.

Guillemard, W. H. Hebraisms in the Greek Testament, 1879, Camb. Deighton, Bell, 13+120pp.

Howson, J. S. The Metaphors of St. Paul, 1869, Strahan, 176pp. 3rd ed. 1883. Though old, the best overall coverage.

Jackson, F. J. F. & Lake, K. The Beginnings of Christianity, Part, 1, The Acts of the Apostles, 1920–1933, Macmillan, 5 vols.

Jeremias, J. The Parables of Jesus, 1963 rev. ed. SCM, 248pp.

Kittel, G. Ed. Theological Dictionary of the N. T. trans. by G. W. Bromiley, 1964, Grand Rapids, MN, Eerdmans, 10 vols. Cited as TDNT.

Lachs, S. T. A Rabbinic Commentary on the N. T. (Matthew, Mark & Luke), 1987 Hoboken NJ. Ktav. 29+468pp.

Lightfoot, J. Horae Hebraicae et Talmudicae, (Hebrew and Talmudical Excercitations), 1859 new ed. Oxford U. P. 4 vols.

Lightfoot, J. B. Notes on Epistles of St. Paul from Unpublished Commentaries, 1895, Macmillan, 9+336pp.

Lightfoot, J. B. The Ep. of St. Paul, To the Colossians and to Philemon, 1897, 3rd ed. Macmillan, 428pp.

Lightfoot, J. B. --To the Galatians, 1905, 10th ed.Macmillan, 384pp.

Lightfoot, J. B. --To the Philippians, 1908, 4th ed.Macmillan, 350pp.

Lyall, F. Slaves, Citizens, Sons, Legal Metaphors in the Epistles, 1984, Grand Rapids, MN, Zondervan. 288pp.

Macky, P. W. The Centrality of Metaphors to Biblical Thought. A Method for Interpreting the Bible, 1990, Lewiston, NY, Mellen, 5+311p.

Marshall, A. Gleanings from the Greek, n.d. (1930s), Martin, 46pp. Includes brief discussion of a dozen metaphors.

Marshall, A. Ed. The Greek Student's Monthly, 1927–1934, Marshall, Kingston-Upon-Thames. (cited as GSM). A valuable periodical.

Martin, D. B. Slavery as Salvation: The Metaphor of Slavery in Pauline Christianity, 1990, New Haven, CT, Yale U. P. 23+245pp.

Miller, M. S & J. L. Encyclopedia of Bible Life, 1957, Black, 493pp.

Montefiore, C. G. The Synoptic Gospels, with Introduction and Commentary, 1927, 2nd ed. rev. Macmillan, 2 vols. 146+411+678pp.

Morgan, G. C. The Parables and Metaphors of Our Lord, 1953rp, Marshall, Morgan & Scott, 318pp.

Morton, H. V. In the Steps of the Master, 1943, 14th ed. Methuen, 388pp.

Morton, H. V. In the Steps of St. Paul, 1936. Rich & Cowan, 440pp.

Moulton H. K. The Challenge of the Concordance, 1977, Bagster, 288pp.

Moulton, J. H. From Egyptian Rubbish Heaps, 1916, Kelly, 143pp.

Moulton J. H. & Milligan, G. The Vocabulary of the Greek Testament, 1930, Hodder, 32+705pp

Moulton, J. H. & N. Turner, A Grammar of N. T. Greek, Edin. Clark, 1906–1976, 4 vols.

Neil, J. Strange Figures: or the Figurative Language of the Bible, 1892, Lang, Neil & Co., 96pp.

Neuburger, A. The Technical Arts & Sciences of the Ancients, 1969rp, Methuen, 32+518pp.

Nicoll, W. R. Ed. The Expositor's Greek Testament, 1988 rp. Grand Rapids, MN, Eerdmans, 5 vols.

Oesterley, W. O. E. The Gospel Parables in the Light of Their Jewish Background, 1936, SPCK, 8+245pp.

Park, D. M. 'Interpretative Value of Paul's Metaphors,' S. E. Asia Jnl of Theology, Manila, Vol. 18/2 (1977), 37–40.

Pershbacher, W. J. Ed. The New Analytical Greek Lexicon, 1990, Peabody, MS. Hendrickson, 449pp.

Pfitzner, V. C. Paul and the Agon Motif. Traditional Athletic Imagery in the Pauline Literature, 1967, Leiden, Brill, 10+222pp.

Pittman, R. T. Words and Their Ways in the Greek N. T. 1942, Marshall, Morgan & Scott, 142pp.

Pope, R, M. Studies in the Language of St. Paul, 1936, Epworth Press, 157pp.

Ramsay, W. M. Luke the Physician & Other Studies in the History of Religion, 1908, Hodder, 14+418pp. esp. Ch. X, 'St. Paul's Use of Metaphors Drawn from Greek & Roman Life.'

Rihbany, A. M. The Syrian Christ, 1920, 2nd ed. Melrose, 299pp. Excellent on Middle Eastern background.

Rienecker, F. & Rogers, C. Linguistic Key to the Greek N. T., 1982, Grand Rapids, MN, Zondervan, 864pp.

Robertson, A. T. The Minister and His Greek N. T. 1923, Hodder, 139pp. esp. Ch. IV, Pictures in Prepositions.

Robertson, A. T. Word Pictures in the N. T. 1930–33, rp. Nashville, TN, Broadman, 6 vols. a valuable aid, though comments on each word are brief.

Robinson, E. Biblical Researches in Palestine and the Adjacent Regions, 1856f, 2nd ed. 3 vols. Murray.

Robinson, J. A. St. Paul's Epistle to the Ephesians, 1907. 2nd ed. Macmillan, 9+314pp.

Robinson, W. G. New Testament Treasure, 1954, Independent Press, 238pp.

Rops, Daniel. Daily Life in Palestine at the Time of Christ, 1982, Weidenfeld & Nicolson, 500pp.

Savage, H. E. The Gospel of the Kingdom: Or The Sermon on the Mount . . . in the Light of Contemporary Jewish Thought and Ideals, 1910, Longmans Green, 18+274pp.

Selwyn, E. G. The First Epistle of St. Peter, 1946, Macmillan, 16+517pp.

Simpson, E. K. Words Worth Weighing in the Greek N. T. 1946, Tyndale Press, 32pp.

Skeat, W. W. An Etymological Dictionary of the English Language, 1953 rp, new ed. rev. Oxf. 44+780pp.

Smith, David, The Life and Letters of St. Paul, 1919, Hodder, 704pp. An excellent work.

Steinhauser, M. G. Doppelbildworte in den synoptischen Evangelien, Forschung zur Bibel 44, 1981, Wurzburg, Echter Verlag, 467pp. (on the double similitudes in the Synoptic Gospels).

Tangberg, K. A. 'Linguistics and Theology,' BT 24 (1973), 301–310.

Tenney, M. C. Galatians: The Charter of Christian Liberty, 1950 rev.

ed. Grand Rapids, MN, Eerdmans, 216pp. esp. Ch. VI, The Art of Expressing Truth: Rhetorical Method.

Thayer, J. H. A Greek-English Lexicon of the N. T. 1892, 2nd rev. & enl. ed. Edin. Clark.

Trench, R. C. Synonyms of the N. T. 1876, 8th ed. rev. Macmillan. 28+371pp.

Trench, R. C. On the Study of Words, Ed. by A. S. Palmer, 1904, Routledge, 12+258pp.

Tristram, H. B. The Natural History of the Bible, 1898, 9th ed. SPCK, 520pp.

Tristram, H. B. The Land of Israel, A Journal of Travels in Palestine, 1882, 4th ed. rev. SPCK. 651pp.

Turner, N. Christian Words, 1980, Edin. Clark, 513pp.

Turner, N. Grammatical Insights into the N. T,, 1965, Edin. Clark, 198pp.

Turner, N. 'Jewish and Christian Influence on N. T. Vocabulary,' NovTest. Vol. 16 (1974), 149–160.

Van-Lennep, H. J. Bible Lands: Their Modern Customs and Manners, 1875, Murray, 2 vols. 832pp.

Vincent, M. R. Word Studies in the N. T. n. d. (c. 1888), rp. of 2nd ed. Mclean, VA, MacDonald, 2 vols.

Vine, W. E, Unger, M. F. & White, W, Jr, Vine's Expository Diction-ary of Biblical Words, 1985, Nashville, TN, Nelson, 319+ 755pp.

Waard, J. de 'Biblical Metaphors and Their Translation,' BT. Vol. 25 (1974), 107–116.

Ward, R. A. Hidden Meaning in the N. T. 1969, Marshall, Morgan & Scott, 190pp. esp. ch 7, Sunken Treasure; an excellent work.

Ward, R. A. Royal Sacrament. The Preacher and His Message, 1960, 2nd ed. Marshall, Morgan & Scott, 192pp.

Waugh, R. M. L. Living Words, 1962, Epworth Press, 83pp.

Waugh, R. M. L. The Preacher and His Greek Testament, 1953, Epworth Press, 104pp.

Westcott, B. F. The Epistle to the Hebrews, the Greek Text with Notes & Essays, 1889, Macmillan, 84+504pp.

Wilson, C. A. New Light on the Gospels, 1970, Lakeland, 128pp.

Wilson, C. A. New Light on N. T. Letters, 1971, Lakeland, 125pp.

Wordsworth, C., Greek Testament with Introductions and Notes, 1877, new ed. Rivingtons, 2 vols.

Wuest, K. Word Studies from the Greek N. T. 1973, Grand Rapids, MN, Eerdmans, 3 vols.

Yahuda, J, Hebrew is Greek, 1982, Oxford, Beckett, 32+ 686pp. One does not have to accept the theory propounded to make use of this fine philological reservoir.

Index of Metaphors and Illustrations

Index of Greek Words

With coding to Strong's Exhaustive Concordance for those with little knowledge of Greek. Lexical forms generally shown in nominative singular, or for verbs, first person singular, active indicative.

adokimos (96). 80, 100, 263
adolos (97). 260
agnoeō (50). 197
agōnia (74). 113
agorazō (59). 189
akrogōniaios (204). 60
anakrinō (350). 180
anapsuchō (404). 163
anatolē (395). 208
anemizō (416). 237
anexichniastos (421). 13
angareuō (29). 161
anhupokritos (505). 118
antilutron (487). 94, 101
apaugasma (541). 79
apechō (568). 266, 267
apekduōmai (554). 144
aphanizō (853). 117
apodidōmi (591). 267
apokaradokia (603). 136, 154
aposkiasma (644) 213
apothnēskō (599). 151, 155
apotinō (661). 266, 267, 276
architektōn (753). 57
arrabōn (728). 186, 191
astēr (792). 208
astocheō (795). 197, 198
athleō (118). 110
atomos (823). 221, 222

baros (922). 159
bebaioō (950). 185, 186

bebaios (949). 184, 185
bebaiōsis (951). 184
bebaioun (– LXX). 186
belonē (956d). 44
brabeus (see katabrabeuō).

chalkos ēcheō (5475, 2278). 99
charagma (5480). 216
charaktēr (5481). 215, 216
chorēgeō (5524). 118
chronos (5550). 274

dianoigō (1272). 68
diapriō (1282). 136
dipsuchos (1374). 137, 154
dokimazō (1381). 263, 264
dokimē (1382). 264
dokimion (1383). 264

egeirō (1453). 151
eikōn (1504). 215, 216
eilikrinēs (1506). 205
ekkremamai (1582). 135
ekplēssō (1605). 135
ekstrephō (1612). 144
ektenōs (1619). 66
ektrōma (1626). 143
ellogeō (1677) 265
enduō (1746). 144
enkoptō (1465). 199
epichorēgeō (2023). 118
epieikēs (1933). 75

Index of Subjects

widens horizons, xxiv
millstones described, 23, 24
mind, bent of, 137, 138
ministry, Christian, 37, 68
mirrors: ancient, 77, 100, 217
  of Corinth, 100
  reflect back light, 79, 217
Mishnah cited, 45, 46, 81, 247, 257
misled, don't be, 207
Molech, fire of, 98
moments, all our, precious, 275
moor, lost on a, 88
Moorish soldier drinking, 53
moron, a, 34
Mosaic Law: a guardian, 181, 182, 253
  as pillow, 182
  cancelled, 120, 168
  could not justify man, 187, 265
  Jesus kept perfectly, 244
  old wine, 16
  our warder, gaoler, 187
  replaced, 133
  shadow only 211–213
  yoke of, 3, 31
Moses: choice to Israel, 88
  household, 56
  tells Israel word is near, 133
mountain: move two loads a day, 223
  symbol of strength, 222, 223
mountaineer's pack, 159
mud-diggers, thieves, 225
mustard tree, 9
myopia, 130

Nazarenes offended, 21
neck, keeping responsive, 136
needle, gate, 43
  sewing, 44
needles, ancient, 44
New English Bible's style, xxvi
New Jerusalem, 40
newly converted man, 10
new: order, 64, 70
  personality, 15, 144
  truths revealed, 16
news runners, Greek, 104
Nicodemus, 14
night, thief breaks in, 173, 174
nine fruits, 17
Noah walked with God, 92

oath and promise, God's, 185
obedience follows good hearing, 131, 132
obstacles: faith removes, 222–224
  in our path, 20, 22, 199
obstinacy, avoiding, 42
odour of life and death, 120
offence caused/taken, 21
  hinders our progress, 199
old wine tastes best, 16
Olympia, games of, see also games, 103
one day's beauty, 9
Onesimus, Paul pleads for, 158, 265, 266
Onesiphorus, refreshing visits, 163
opening up the Scriptures, 68
opportunities, grasping, 66, 67, 273–275
oppressed people, beggars, 167
orchard of trees, 18
orchestra, etymology of, 126
ossuaries, bones placed in, 256
osteopath, his knowledge & touch, 139
ostracon as receipt, 266
other sheep, 47
outcasts from world, 82
outer darkness, meaning, 211
outline, filling in an, 212, 252
  hazy, 77–79
  or sketch, shadow, 212
outside, cleaning the, 81, 82
overflowing love, 10, 66
overreach, defraud people, 161, 162
owner, Christ our new, 188, 189
oxen: in yoke, 2, 3
  on threshing floor, 27, 37
ox-goad, use of, 22, 42, 43
oxygen, sharp or acid, 164

paid, how to wish to be, 266, 267
  in full, 266, 267
palimpsest, writing erased, 168
Panathenaea relay race, 110
papyrus documents, xxii, 55, 168, 183,
  184, 186, 216, 266, 267
parables, xxi, 11, 46, 47
  explained, 148
parallel usage of words, xxiii
paroxysm, altercation, 164
paths to follow or avoid, 88
pattern to follow, 213–215
Paul: as persecutor, 87
  background as ambassador, 157
  before Felix, 88

Index of Bible References